Computer Vision Metrics

Survey, Taxonomy, and Analysis

Scott Krig

Selected For intel's Recommended Reading List

apress
open

Computer Vision Metrics: Survey, Taxonomy, and Analysis

Scott Krig

Copyright © 2014 by Apress Media, LLC, all rights reserved

ApressOpen Rights: You have the right to copy, use and distribute this Work in its entirety, electronically without modification, for non-commercial purposes only. However, you have the additional right to use or alter any source code in this Work for any commercial or non-commercial purpose which must be accompanied by the licenses in (2) and (3) below to distribute the source code for instances of greater than 5 lines of code. Licenses (1), (2) and (3) below and the intervening text must be provided in any use of the text of the Work and fully describes the license granted herein to the Work.

(1) **License for Distribution of the Work:** This Work is copyrighted by Apress Media, LLC, all rights reserved. Use of this Work other than as provided for in this license is prohibited. By exercising any of the rights herein, you are accepting the terms of this license. You have the non-exclusive right to copy, use and distribute this English language Work in its entirety, electronically without modification except for those modifications necessary for formatting on specific devices, for all non-commercial purposes, in all media and formats known now or hereafter. While the advice and information in this Work are believed to be true and accurate at the date of publication, neither the authors nor the editors nor the publisher can accept any legal responsibility for any errors or omissions that may be made. The publisher makes no warranty, express or implied, with respect to the material contained herein.

If your distribution is solely Apress source code or uses Apress source code intact, the following licenses (2) and (3) must accompany the source code. If your use is an adaptation of the source code provided by Apress in this Work, then you must use only license (3).

(2) **License for Direct Reproduction of Apress Source Code:** This source code, from *Computer Vision Metrics: Survey, Taxonomy, and Analysis, ISBN 978-1-4302-5929-9* is copyrighted by Apress Media, LLC, all rights reserved. Any direct reproduction of this Apress source code is permitted but must contain this license. The following license must be provided for any use of the source code from this product of greater than 5 lines wherein the code is adapted or altered from its original Apress form. This Apress code is presented AS IS and Apress makes no claims to, representations or warrantees as to the function, usability, accuracy or usefulness of this code.

(3) **License for Distribution of Adaptation of Apress Source Code:** Portions of the source code provided are used or adapted from *Computer Vision Metrics: Survey, Taxonomy, and Analysis, ISBN 978-1-4302-5929-9* copyright Apress Media LLC. Any use or reuse of this Apress source code must contain this License. This Apress code is made available at Apress.com/978143026136-0 as is and Apress makes no claims to, representations or warrantees as to the function, usability, accuracy or usefulness of this code.

ISBN-13 (pbk): 978-1-4302-5929-9

ISBN-13 (electronic): 978-1-4302-5930-5

Trademarked names, logos, and images may appear in this book. Rather than use a trademark symbol with every occurrence of a trademarked name, logo, or image we use the names, logos, and images only in an editorial fashion and to the benefit of the trademark owner, with no intention of infringement of the trademark.

The use in this publication of trade names, trademarks, service marks, and similar terms, even if they are not identified as such, is not to be taken as an expression of opinion as to whether or not they are subject to proprietary rights.

While the advice and information in this book are believed to be true and accurate at the date of publication, neither the authors nor the editors nor the publisher can accept any legal responsibility for any errors or omissions that may be made. The publisher makes no warranty, express or implied, with respect to the material contained herein.

President and Publisher: Paul Manning
Lead Editors: Steve Weiss (Apress); Stuart Douglas (Intel)
Technical Reviewers: Sanjay Addicam and Shahzad Malik
Coordinating Editor: Melissa Maldonado
Cover Designer: Anna Ishchenko

Distributed to the book trade worldwide by Springer Science+Business Media New York, 233 Spring Street, 6th Floor, New York, NY 10013. Phone 1-800-SPRINGER, fax (201) 348-4505, e-mail orders-ny@springer-sbm.com, or visit www.springeronline.com.

For information on translations, please e-mail rights@apress.com, or visit www.apress.com.

About ApressOpen

What Is ApressOpen?

- ApressOpen is an open-access book program that publishes high-quality technical and business information.

- ApressOpen eBooks are available for global, free, noncommercial use.

- ApressOpen eBooks are available in PDF, ePub, and Mobi formats.

- The user friendly ApressOpen free eBook license is presented on the copyright page of this book.

Thanks to my wife Janie, family, and parents for being part of my life.

Contents at a Glance

Contents

About the Author

 **Scott Krig** is a pioneer in computer imaging, computer vision, and graphics visualization. He founded Krig Research in 1988 (krigresearch.com), providing the world's first imaging and vision systems based on high-performance engineering workstations, super-computers, and dedicated imaging hardware, serving customers worldwide in 25 countries. Scott has provided imaging and vision solutions around the globe, and has worked closely with many industries, including aerospace, military, intelligence, law enforcement, government research, and academic organizations.

More recently, Scott has worked for major corporations and startups serving commercial markets, solving problems in the areas of computer vision, imaging, graphics, visualization, robotics, process control, industrial automation, computer security, cryptography, and consumer applications of imaging and machine vision to PCs, laptops, mobile phones, and tablets. Most recently, Scott provided direction for Intel Corporation in the area of depth-sensing and computer vision methods for embedded systems and mobile platforms.

Scott is the author of many patent applications worldwide in the areas of embedded systems, imaging, computer vision, DRM, and computer security, and studied at Stanford.

Scott also enjoys acoustic guitar design and lutherie work, particularly 12-string acoustic guitars, as well as acoustic guitar composition and performance.

Acknowledgments

This book would not be as well thought out without the early technical feedback, conversations, and observations on very rough materials by Vadim Pizarevsky of ITSEEZ, who also is a major force behind the OpenCV foundation. Vadim brings vast and quantitative expertise in computer vision across a wide range of application domains. Thanks, Vadim.

Special thanks also go to Stuart Douglas at Intel Press for the commission to write this book, and for introductions to people at Apress. Also, special thanks to the key editors at Apress, including Melissa Maldonado, Mark Powers, Jeffrey Pepper, Steve Weiss, Robert Hutchinson, James Markham, and Carole Berglie for making this book a reality, and for adding value through the editorial process.

Introduction

Dirt. This is a jar of dirt.

Yes.

... Is the jar of dirt going to help?

If you don't want it, give it back.

> —*Pirates Of The Carribean*, Jack Sparrow and Tia Dalma

This work focuses on a slice through the field - Computer Vision Metrics – from the view of feature description metrics, or how to describe, compute and design the macro-features and micro-features that make up larger objects in images. The focus is on the pixel-side of the vision pipeline, rather than the back-end training, classification, machine learning and matching stages. This book is suitable for reference, higher-level courses, and self-directed study in computer vision. The book is aimed at someone already familiar with computer vision and image processing; however, even those new to the field will find good introductions to the key concepts at a high level, via the ample illustrations and summary tables.

I view computer vision as a mathematical artform and its researchers and practitioners as artists. So, this book is more like a tour through an art gallery rather than a technical or scientific treatise. Observations are provided, interesting questions are raised, a vision taxonomy is suggested to draw a conceptual map of the field, and references are provided to dig deeper. This book is like an attempt to draw a map of the world centered around feature metrics, inaccurate and fuzzy as the map may be, with the hope that others will be inspired to expand the level of detail in their own way, better than what I, or even a few people, can accomplish alone. If I could have found a similar book covering this particular slice of subject matter, I would not have taken on the project to write this book.

What is not in the Book

Readers looking for computer vision "'how-to'" source code examples, tutorial discussions, performance analysis, and short-cuts will not find them here, and instead should consult the well-regarded http://opencv.org library resources, including many fine books, online resources, source code examples, and several blogs. There is nothing better than OpenCV for the hands-on practitioner. For this reason, this book steers a clear path around duplication of the "how-to" materials already provided by the OpenCV community and elsewhere, and instead provides a counterpoint discussion, including a comprehensive survey, analysis and taxonomy of methods. Also, do not expect all computer vision topics to be covered deeply with proofs and performance analysis, since the bibliography references cover these matters quite well: for example, machine learning, training and classification methods are only lightly introduced, since the focus here is on the feature metrics.

In summary, this book is about the feature metrics, showing "'what'" methods practitioners are using, with detailed observations and analysis of "'why'" those methods work, with a bias towards raising questions via observations rather than providing too many answers. I like the questions best because good questions lead to many good answers, and each answer is often pregnant with more good questions...

This book is aimed at a survey level, with a taxonomy and analysis, so no detailed examples of individual use-cases or horse races between methods are included. However, much detail is provided in over 540+ bibliographic references to dig deeper into practical matters. Additionally, some "'how-to'" and "'hands-on'" resources are provided in Appendix C. And a little 'perfunctory' source code accompanying parts of this book is available online, for Appendix A covering the interest point detector evaluations for the synthetic interest point alphabets introduced in Chapter 7; and in Appendix D for extended SDM metrics covered in Chapter 3.

What is in the Book

Specifically, Chapter 1 provides preamble on 2d image formation and 3d depth imaging, and Chapter 2 promotes intelligent image pre-processing to enhance feature description. Chapters 3 through 6 form the core discussion on feature description, with an emphasis on local features. Global and regional metrics are covered in Chapter 3, feature descriptor concepts in Chapter 4, a vision taxonomy is suggested in Chapter 5, and local feature description is covered in Chapter 6. Ground truth data is covered in Chapter 7, and Chapter 8 discusses hypothetical vision pipelines and hypothetical optimizations from an engineering perspective, as a set of exercises to tie vision concepts together into real systems (coursework assignments can be designed to implement and improve the hypothetical examples in Chapter 8). A set of synthetic interest point alphabets is developed in Chapter 7, and ten common detectors are run against those alphabets, with the results provided in Appendix A. It is difficult to cleanly partition all topics in image processing and computer vision, so there is some overlap in the chapters. Also, there are many hybrids used in practice, so there's inevitable overlap in the Chapter 5 vision taxonomy, and creativity always arrives on the horizon to find new and unexpected ways of using old methods. However, the taxonomy is a starting point and helped to guide the organization of the book.

Therefore, the main goal has been to survey and understand the range of methods used to describe features, without passing judgment on which methods are better. Some history is presented to describe why certain methods were developed, and what properties of invariance or performance were the goals, and we leave the claims to be proven by others, since "how" each method is implemented determines performance and accuracy, and "what" each method is tested against in terms of ground truth data really tells the rest of the story. If we can glean good ideas from the work of others, that is a measure of the success of their work.

Scope

For brevity's sake, I exclude a deep treatment of selected topics not directly related to the computer vision metrics themselves; this is an unusual approach, since computer vision discussions typically include a wider range of topics. Specifically, the topics not covered deeply here include statistical and machine learning, classification and training, feature database construction and optimization, and searching and sorting. Bibliography references are provided instead. Distance functions are discussed, since they are directly linked to the feature metric. (A future edition of this book may contain a deep dive into the statistical and machine learning side of computer vision, but not now.)

Terminology Caveat

Sometimes terminology in the literature does not agree when describing similar concepts. So in some cases, terminology is adopted in this work that is not standardized across independent research communities. In fact, some new and nonstandard terminology may be introduced here, possibly because the author is unaware of better existing terminology (perhaps some of the terminology introduced in this work will become standardized). Terminology divergence is most pronounced with regard to mathematical topics like clustering, regression, group distance, and error minimization, as well as for computer vision topics like keypoints, interest points, anchor points, and the like. The author recognizes that one is reluctant to change terminology, since so many concepts are learned based on the terminology. I recall a friend of mine, Homer Mead, chief engineer for the lunar rover and AWACS radar at Boeing, who sub-consciously refused to convert from using the older term condenser to use the newer term capacitor.

Inspiration comes from several sources, mostly the opportunity of pioneering: there is always some lack of clarity, structure and organization in any new field as the boundaries expand, so in this vast field the opportunity to explore is compelling: to map out structure and pathways of knowledge that others may follow to find new fields of study, create better markers along the way, and extend the pathways farther.

The inspiration for this book has come from conversations with a wide range of people over the years. Where did it all start? It began at Boeing in the early 1980s, while I was still in college. I was introduced to computer graphics in the Advanced Development Research labs where I worked, when the first computer-shaded 3D renderings of the space shuttle were made in raster form. At that time, mainly vector graphics machines were being used, like Evans & Sutherland Picture Systems, and eventually a BARCO frame buffer was added to the lab, and advanced raster computer renderings of shaded images from graphics models were pioneered by Jeff Lane and his group, as well as Loren Carpenter. Fractals, NURBS, and A-buffer techniques were a few of the methods developed in the labs, and the math of computer graphics, such as bi-cubic patches and bi-quintic patches, scared me away from graphics initially. But I was attracted to single pixels in the BARCO frame buffer, one pixel and line and frame at a time, since they seemed so intuitive and obvious. I initially pursued imaging and computer vision rather than all the computer graphics and associated math. However, it turned out that the computer vision and image processing math was far more diverse and equally complex anyway. Since then I have also spent considerable time in computer graphics. Back in the mid-1980s, Don Snow, my boss, who was co-founder and VP of research at Pacific

Western Systems and later at Applied Precision, asked me to analyze the View-PRB fixed-function hardware unit for pattern recognition to use for automatic wafer probing (in case we needed to build something like it ourselves) to locate patterns on wafers and align the machine for probing. Correlation was used for pattern matching, with a scale-space search method we termed "super-pixels." The matching rate was four 32x32 patches per second over NTSC with sub-pixel accuracy, and I computed position, rotation, and offsets to align the wafer prober stage to prepare for wafer probing; we called this auto-align. I designed a pattern recognition servo system to locate the patterns with rotational accuracy of a few micro-radians, and positional accuracy of a fraction of a micron. In the later 1980s, I went to work for Mentor Graphics, and after several years I left the corporate R&D group reporting to the president Gerry Langeler to start a company, Krig Research, to focus on computer vision and imaging for high-end military and research customers based on expensive and now extinct workstations (SGI, Apollo, Sun... gone, all gone now...), and I have stayed interested ever since. Many things have changed in our industry; the software seems to all be free, and the hardware or SOC is almost free as well, so I am not sure how anyone can make any money at this anymore.

More recently, others have also provided inspiration. Thanks to Paul Rosin for synthetic images and organizational ideas. Thanks to Yann LeCun for providing key references into deep learning and convolutional networks, and thanks to Shree Nayar for permission to use a few images, and continuing to provide the computer vision community with inspiration via the Cave Research projects. And thanks to Luciano Oviedo for vast coverage of industry activity and strategy about where it is all going, and lively discussions.

Others, too many to list, have also added to my journey. And even though the conversations have sometimes been brief, or even virtual via email or SKYPE in many cases, the influence of their work and thinking has remained, so special thanks are due to several people who have provided comments to the manuscript or book outline, contributed images, or just plain inspiration they may not realize. Thank you to Rahul Suthankar, Alexandre Alehi for use of images and discussions; Steve Seitz, Bryan Russel, Liefeng Bo, and Xiaofeng Ren for deep-dive discussions about RGB-D computer vision and other research topics; Gutemberg Guerra-filho, Harsha Viswana, Dale Hitt, Joshua Gleason, Noah Snavely, Daniel Scharstein, Thomas Salmon, Richard Baraniuk, Carl Vodrick, Hervé Jégou, and Andrew Richardson; and also thanks for many interesting discussions on computer vision topics with several folks at Intel including Ofri Weschler, Hong Jiang, Andy Kuzma, Michael Jeronimo, Eli Turiel, and many others whom I have failed to mention.

Summary

In summary, my goal is to survey the methods people are using for feature description—the key metrics generated—and make it easier for anyone to understand the methods in practice, and how to evaluate the methods using the vision taxonomy and robustness criteria to get the results they are looking for, and find areas for extending the state of the art. And after hearing all the feedback from the first version of this work, I hope to create a second version that is even better.

Scott Krig
Anno Domini 2014

CHAPTER 1

■ ■ ■

Image Capture
and Representation

"The changing of bodies into light, and light into bodies, is very
conformable to the course of Nature, which seems delighted with
transmutations."

—Isaac Newton

Computer vision starts with images. This chapter surveys a range of topics dealing with
capturing, processing, and representing images, including computational imaging,
2D imaging, and 3D depth imaging methods, sensor processing, depth-field processing
for stereo and monocular multi-view stereo, and surface reconstruction. A high-level
overview of selected topics is provided, with references for the interested reader to dig
deeper. Readers with a strong background in the area of 2D and 3D imaging may benefit
from a light reading of this chapter.

Image Sensor Technology

This section provides a basic overview of image sensor technology as a basis for
understanding how images are formed and for developing effective strategies for image
sensor processing to optimize the image quality for computer vision.

Typical image sensors are created from either CCD cells (charge-coupled device) or
standard CMOS cells (complementary metal-oxide semiconductor). The CCD and CMOS
sensors share similar characteristics and both are widely used in commercial cameras.
The majority of sensors today use CMOS cells, though, mostly due to manufacturing
considerations. Sensors and optics are often integrated to create *wafer-scale cameras* for
applications like biology or microscopy, as shown in Figure 1-1.

Figure 1-1. *Common integrated image sensor arrangement with optics and color filters*

Image sensors are designed to reach specific design goals with different applications in mind, providing varying levels of sensitivity and quality. Consult the manufacturer's information to get familiar with each sensor. For example, the size and material composition of each photo-diode sensor cell element is optimized for a given semiconductor manufacturing process so as to achieve the best tradeoff between silicon die area and dynamic response for light intensity and color detection.

For computer vision, the effects of sampling theory are relevant—for example, the Nyquist frequency applied to pixel coverage of the target scene. The sensor resolution and optics together must provide adequate resolution for each pixel to image the features of interest, so it follows that a feature of interest should be imaged or sampled at two times the minimum size of the smallest pixels of importance to the feature. Of course, 2x oversampling is just a minimum target for accuracy; in practice, single pixel wide features are not easily resolved.

For best results, the camera system should be calibrated for a given application to determine the sensor noise and dynamic range for pixel bit depth under different lighting and distance situations. Appropriate sensor processing methods should be developed to deal with the noise and nonlinear response of the sensor for any color channel, to detect and correct dead pixels, and to handle modeling of geometric distortion. If you devise a simple calibration method using a test pattern with fine and coarse gradations of gray scale, color, and pixel size of features, you can look at the results. In Chapter 2, we survey a range of image processing methods applicable to sensor processing. But let's begin by surveying the sensor materials.

Sensor Materials

Silicon-based image sensors are most common, although other materials such as gallium (Ga) are used in industrial and military applications to cover longer IR wavelengths than silicon can reach. Image sensors range in resolution, depending upon the camera used, from a single pixel phototransistor camera, through 1D line scan arrays for industrial applications, to 2D rectangular arrays for common cameras, all the way to spherical arrays for high-resolution imaging. (Sensor configurations and camera configurations are covered later in this chapter.)

Common imaging sensors are made using silicon as CCD, CMOS, BSI, and Foveon methods, as discussed a bit later in this chapter. Silicon image sensors have a nonlinear spectral response curve; the near infrared part of the spectrum is sensed well, while blue, violet, and near UV are sensed less well, as shown in Figure 1-2. Note that the silicon spectral response must be accounted for when reading the raw sensor data and quantizing the data into a digital pixel. Sensor manufacturers make design compensations in this area; however, sensor color response should also be considered when calibrating your camera system and devising the sensor processing methods for your application.

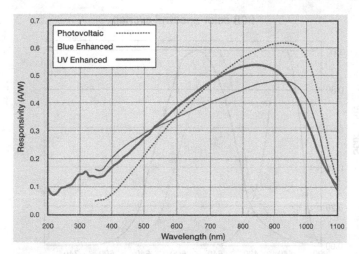

Figure 1-2. *Typical spectral response of a few types of silicon photo-diodes. Note the highest sensitivity in the near-infrared range around 900nm and nonlinear sensitivity across the visible spectrum of 400-700nm. Removing the IR filter from a camera increases the near-infrared sensitivity due to the normal silicon response. (Spectral data image © OSI Optoelectronics Inc. and used by permission)*

Sensor Photo-Diode Cells

One key consideration in image sensoring is the photo-diode size or cell size. A sensor cell using small photo-diodes will not be able to capture as many photons as a large photo-diode. If the cell size is below the wavelength of the visible light to be captured, such as blue light at 400nm, then additional problems must be overcome in the sensor design to correct the image color. Sensor manufacturers take great care to design cells at the optimal size to image all colors equally well (Figure 1-3). In the extreme, small sensors may be more sensitive to noise, owing to a lack of accumulated photons and sensor readout noise. If the photo-diode sensor cells are too large, there is no benefit either, and the die size and cost for silicon go up, providing no advantage. Common commercial sensor devices may have sensor cell sizes of around 1 square micron and larger; each manufacturer is different, however, and tradeoffs are made to reach specific requirements.

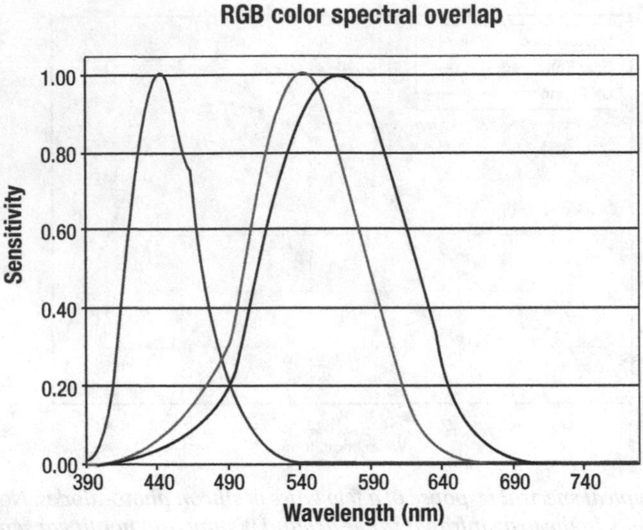

RGB color spectral overlap

Figure 1-3. Primary color assignment to wavelengths. Note that the primary color regions overlap, with green being a good monochrome proxy for all colors

Sensor Configurations: Mosaic, Foveon, BSI

There are various on-chip configurations for multi-spectral sensor design, including mosaics and stacked methods, as shown in Figure 1-4. In a *mosaic method*, the color filters are arranged in a mosaic pattern above each cell. The *Foveon*[1] *sensor stacking method* relies on the physics of depth penetration of the color wavelengths into the semiconductor material, where each color penetrates the silicon to a different depth, thereby imaging the separate colors. The overall cell size accommodates all colors, and so separate cells are not needed for each color.

---

[1]Foveon is a registered trademark of Foveon Inc.

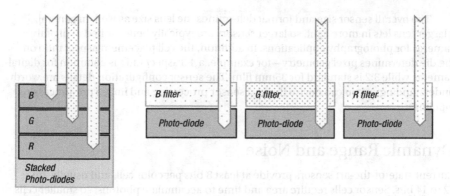

Figure 1-4. *(Left) The Foveon method of stacking RGB cells to absorb different wavelengths at different depths, with all RGB colors at each cell location. (Right) A standard mosaic cell placement with RGB filters above each photo-diode, with filters only allowing the specific wavelengths to pass into each photo-diode*

Back-side-illuminated (BSI) sensor configurations rearrange the sensor wiring on the die to allow for a larger cell area and more photons to be accumulated in each cell. See the Aptina [410] white paper for a comparison of front-side and back-side die circuit arrangement.

The arrangement of sensor cells also affects the color response. For example, Figure 1-5 shows various arrangements of primary color (R, G, B) sensors as well as white (W) sensors together, where W sensors have a clear or neutral color filter. The sensor cell arrangements allow for a range of pixel processing options—for example, combining selected pixels in various configurations of neighboring cells during sensor processing for a pixel formation that optimizes color response or spatial color resolution. In fact, some applications just use the raw sensor data and perform custom processing to increase the resolution or develop alternative color mixes.

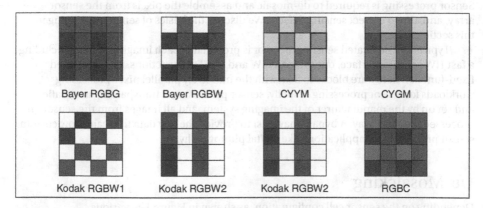

Figure 1-5. *Several different mosaic configurations of cell colors, including white, primary RGB colors, and secondary CYM cells. Each configuration provides different options for sensor processing to optimize for color or spatial resolution. (Image used by permission, © Intel Press, from Building Intelligent Systems)*

The overall sensor size and format determines the lens size as well. In general, a larger lens lets in more light, so larger sensors are typically better suited to digital cameras for photography applications. In addition, the cell placement aspect ratio on the die determines pixel geometry—for example, a 4:3 aspect ratio is common for digital cameras while 3:2 is standard for 35mm film. The sensor configuration details are worth understanding so you can devise the best sensor processing and image pre-processing pipelines.

Dynamic Range and Noise

Current state-of-the-art sensors provide at least 8 bits per color cell, and usually are 12 to 14 bits. Sensor cells require area and time to accumulate photons, so smaller cells must be designed carefully to avoid problems. Noise may come from optics, color filters, sensor cells, gain and A/D converters, post-processing, or the compression methods, if used. Sensor readout noise also affects effective resolution, as each pixel cell is read out of the sensor, sent to an A/D converter, and formed into digital lines and columns for conversion into pixels. Better sensors will provide less noise and higher effective bit resolution. A good survey of de-noising is found in the work by Ibenthal [409].

In addition, sensor photon absorption is different for each color, and may be problematic for blue, which can be the hardest color for smaller sensors to image. In some cases, the manufacturer may attempt to provide a simple gamma-curve correction method built into the sensor for each color, which is not recommended. For demanding color applications, consider colorimetric device models and color management (as will be discussed in Chapter 2), or even by characterizing the nonlinearity for each color channel of the sensor and developing a set of simple corrective LUT transforms. (Noise-filtering methods applicable to depth sensing are also covered in Chapter 2.)

Sensor Processing

Sensor processing is required to de-mosaic and assemble the pixels from the sensor array, and also to correct sensing defects. We discuss the basics of sensor processing in this section.

Typically, a dedicated sensor processor is provided in each imaging system, including a fast HW sensor interface, optimized VLIW and SIMD instructions, and dedicated fixed-function hardware blocks to deal with the massively parallel pixel-processing workloads for sensor processing. Usually, sensor processing is transparent, automatic, and set up by the manufacturer of the imaging system, and all images from the sensor are processed the same way. A bypass may exist to provide the raw data that can allow custom sensor processing for applications like digital photography.

De-Mosaicking

Depending on the sensor cell configuration, as shown in Figure 1-5, various de-mosaicking algorithms are employed to create a final *RGB* pixel from the raw sensor data. A good survey by Losson and Yang [406] and another by Li et al. [407] provide some background on the challenges involved and the various methods employed.

One of the central challenges of de-mosaicking is pixel interpolation to combine the color channels from nearby cells into a single pixel. Given the geometry of sensor cell placement and the aspect ratio of the cell layout, this is not a trivial problem. A related issue is color cell weighting—for example, how much of each color should be integrated into each *RGB* pixel. Since the spatial cell resolution in a mosaicked sensor is greater than the final combined *RGB* pixel resolution, some applications require the raw sensor data to take advantage of all the accuracy and resolution possible, or to perform special processing to either increase the effective pixel resolution or do a better job of spatially accurate color processing and de-mosaicking.

Dead Pixel Correction

A sensor, like an LCD display, may have dead pixels. A vendor may calibrate the sensor at the factory and provide a sensor defect map for the known defects, providing coordinates of those dead pixels for use in corrections in the camera module or driver software. In some cases, adaptive defect correction methods [408] are used on the sensor to monitor the adjacent pixels to actively look for defects and then to correct a range of defect types, such as single pixel defects, column or line defects, and defects such as 2x2 or 3x3 clusters. A camera driver can also provide adaptive defect analysis to look for flaws in real time, and perhaps provide special compensation controls in a camera setup menu.

Color and Lighting Corrections

Color corrections are required to balance the overall color accuracy as well as the white balance. As shown in Figure 1-2, color sensitivity is usually very good in silicon sensors for red and green, but less good for blue, so the opportunity for providing the most accurate color starts with understanding and calibrating the sensor.

Most image sensor processors contain a geometric processor for vignette correction, which manifests as darker illumination at the edges of the image, as shown in Chapter 7 (Figure 7-6). The corrections are based on a geometric warp function, which is calibrated at the factory to match the optics vignette pattern, allowing for a programmable illumination function to increase illumination toward the edges. For a discussion of image warping methods applicable to vignetting, see reference [490].

Geometric Corrections

A lens may have geometric aberrations or may warp toward the edges, producing images with radial distortion, a problem that is related to the vignetting discussed above and shown in Chapter 7 (Figure 7-6). To deal with lens distortion, most imaging systems have a dedicated sensor processor with a hardware-accelerated digital warp unit similar to the texture sampler in a GPU. The geometric corrections are calibrated and programmed in the factory for the optics. See reference [490] for a discussion of image warping methods.

Cameras and Computational Imaging

Many novel camera configurations are making their way into commercial applications using *computational imaging* methods to synthesize new images from raw sensor data—for example, depth cameras and high dynamic range cameras. As shown in Figure 1-6, a conventional camera system uses a single sensor, lens, and illuminator to create 2D images. However, a computational imaging camera may provide multiple optics, multiple programmable illumination patterns, and multiple sensors, enabling novel applications such as 3D depth sensing and image relighting, taking advantage of the depth information, mapping the image as a texture onto the depth map, and introducing new light sources and then re-rendering the image in a graphics pipeline. Since computational cameras are beginning to emerge in consumer devices and will become the front end of computer vision pipelines, we survey some of the methods used.

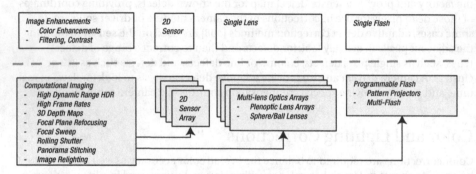

Figure 1-6. *Comparison of computational imaging systems with conventional cameras. (Top) Simple camera model with flash, lens, and imaging device followed by image enhancements like sharpening and color corrections. (Bottom) Computational imaging using programmable flash, optics arrays, and sensor arrays, followed by computational imaging applications*

Overview of Computational Imaging

Computational imaging [447,414] provides options for synthesizing new images from the raw image data. A computational camera may control a programmable flash pattern projector, a lens array, and multiple image sensors, as well as synthesize new images from the raw data, as illustrated in Figure 1-6. To dig deeper into computational imaging and explore the current research, see the CAVE Computer Vision Laboratory at Columbia University and the Rochester Institute of Technology Imaging Research. Here are some of the methods and applications in use.

Single-Pixel Computational Cameras

Single-pixel computational cameras can reconstruct images from a sequence of single photo detector pixel images of the same scene. The field of single-pixel cameras [103, 104] falls into the domain of compressed sensing research, which also has applications outside image processing extending into areas such as analog-to-digital conversion.

As shown in Figure 1-7, a *single-pixel camera* may use a *micro-mirror array* or a *digital mirror device* (DMD), similar to a diffraction grating. The gratings are arranged in a rectangular micro-mirror grid array, allowing the grid regions to be switched on or off to produce binary grid patterns. The binary patterns are designed as a pseudo-random binary basis set. The resolution of the grid patterns is adjusted by combining patterns from adjacent regions—for example, a grid of 2x2 or 3x3 micro-mirror regions.

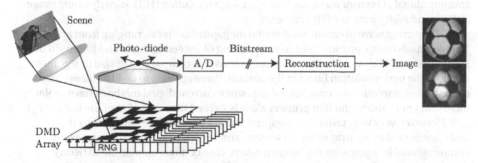

Figure 1-7. *A single-pixel imaging system where incoming light is reflected through a DMD array of micro-mirrors onto a single photo-diode. The grid locations within the micro-mirror array can be opened or closed to light, as shown here, to create binary patterns, where the white grid squares are reflective and open, and the black grid squares are closed. (Image used by permission, © R. G. Baraniuk, Compressive Sensing Lecture Notes)*

A sequence of single-pixel images is taken through a set of pseudo-random micro lens array patterns, then an image is reconstructed from the set. In fact, the number of pattern samples required to reconstruct the image is lower than the Nyquist frequency, since a sparse random sampling approach is used and the random sampling approach has been proven in the research to be mathematically sufficient [103, 104]. The grid basis-set sampling method is directly amenable to image compression, since only a relatively sparse set of patterns and samples are taken. Since the micro-mirror array us es rectangular shapes, the patterns are analogous to a set of HAAR basis functions. (For more information, see Figures 2-20 and 6-22.)

The DMD method is remarkable, in that an image can be reconstructed from a fairly small set of images taken from a single photo detector, rather than a 2D array of photo detectors as in a CMOS or CCD image sensor. Since only a single sensor is used, the method is promising for applications with wavelengths outside the near IR and visible spectrum imaged by CMOS and CCD sensors. The DMD method can be used, for example, to detect emissions from concealed weapons or substances at invisible wavelengths using non-silicon sensors sensitive to nonvisible wavelengths.

2D Computational Cameras

Novel configurations of programmable 2D sensor arrays, lenses, and illuminators are being developed into camera systems as *computational cameras* [424,425,426], with applications ranging from digital photography to military and industrial uses, employing computational imaging methods to enhance the images after the fact. Computational cameras borrow many computational imaging methods from confocal imaging [419] and confocal microscopy [421, 420]—for example, using multiple illumination patterns and multiple focal plane images. They also draw on research from synthetic aperture radar systems [422] developed after World War II to create high-resolution images and 3D depth maps using wide baseline data from a single moving-camera platform. Synthetic apertures using multiple image sensors and optics for overlapping fields of view using wafer-scale integration are also topics of research [419]. We survey here a few computational 2D sensor methods, including *high resolution* (HR), *high dynamic range* (HDR), and *high frame rate* (HF) cameras.

The current wave of commercial digital megapixel cameras, ranging from around 10 megapixels on up, provide resolution matching or exceeding high-end film used in a 35mm camera [412], so a pixel from an image sensor is comparable in size to a grain of silver on the best resolution film. On the surface, there appears to be little incentive to go for higher resolution for commercial use, since current digital methods have replaced most film applications and film printers already exceed the resolution of the human eye.

However, very high resolution gigapixel imaging devices are being devised and constructed as an array of image sensors and lenses, providing advantages for computational imaging after the image is taken. One configuration is the *2D array camera*, composed of an orthogonal 2D array of image sensors and corresponding optics; another configuration is the *spherical camera* as shown in Figure 1-8 [411, 415], developed as a DARPA research project at Columbia University CAVE.

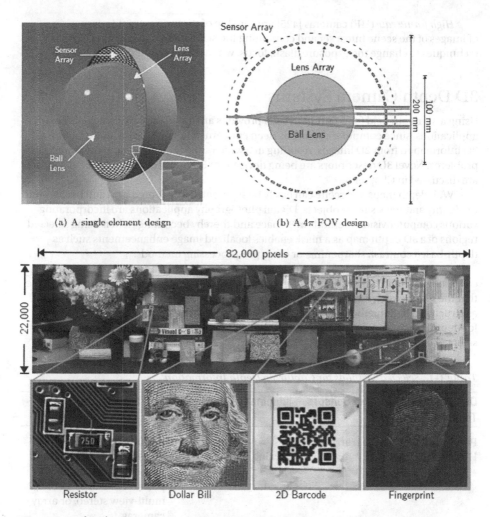

Figure 1-8. (Top) Components of a very high resolution gigapixel camera, using a novel spherical lens and sensor arrangement.(Bottom) The resulting high-resolution images shown at 82,000 x 22,000 = 1.7 gigapixels. (All figures and images used by permission © Shree Nayar Columbia University CAVE research projects)

High dynamic range (HDR) cameras [416,417,418] can produce deeper pixels with higher bit resolution and better color channel resolution by taking multiple images of the scene bracketed with different exposure settings and then combining the images. This combination uses a suitable weighting scheme to produce a new image with deeper pixels of a higher bit depth, such as 32 pixels per color channel, providing images that go beyond the capabilities of common commercial CMOS and CCD sensors. HDR methods allow faint light and strong light to be imaged equally well, and can combine faint light and bright light using adaptive local methods to eliminate glare and create more uniform and pleasing image contrast.

High frame rate (HF) cameras [425] are capable of capturing a rapid succession of images of the scene into a set and combining the set of images using bracketing techniques to change the exposure, flash, focus, white balance, and depth of field.

3D Depth Camera Systems

Using a 3D depth field for computer vision provides an understated advantage for many applications, since computer vision has been concerned in large part with extracting 3D information from 2D images, resulting in a wide range of accuracy and invariance problems. Novel 3D descriptors are being devised for 3D depth field computer vision, and are discussed in Chapter 6.

With depth maps, the scene can easily be segmented into foreground and background to identify and track simple objects. Digital photography applications are incorporating various computer vision methods in 3-space and thereby becoming richer. Using selected regions of a 3D depth map as a mask enables localized image enhancements such as depth-based contrast, sharpening, or other pre-processing methods.

As shown in Table 1-1, there are many ways to extract depth from images. In some cases, only a single camera lens and sensor are required, and software does the rest. Note that the *illumination method* is a key component of many depth-sensing methods, such as structured light methods. Combinations of sensors, lenses, and illumination are used for depth imaging and computational imaging, as shown in Figure 1-9. We survey a few selected depth-sensing methods in this section.

Table 1-1. *Selected Methods for Capturing Depth Information*

Depth Sensing Technique	# of Sensors	Illumination Method	Characteristics
Parallax and Hybrid Parallax	2/1/array	Passive – Normal lighting	Positional shift measurement in FOV between two camera positions, such as stereo, multi-view stereo, or array cameras
Size Mapping	1	Passive – Normal lighting	Utilizes color tags of specific size to determine range and position
Depth of Focus	1	Passive – Normal lighting	Multi-frame with scanned focus
Differential Magnification	1	Passive – Normal lighting	Two-frame image capture at different magnifications, creating a distance-based offset

(*continued*)

Table 1-1. (*continued*)

Depth Sensing Technique	# of Sensors	Illumination Method	Characteristics
Structured light	1	Active – Projected lighting	Multi-frame pattern projection
Time of Flight	1	Active – Pulsed lighting	High-speed light pulse with special pixels measuring return time of reflected light
Shading shift	1	Active – Alternating lighting	Two-frame shadow differential measurement between two light sources as different positions
Pattern spreading	1	Active – Multi-beam lighting	Projected 2D spot pattern expanding at different rate from camera lens field spread
Beam tracking	1	Active – Lighting on object(s)	Two-point light sources mounted on objects in FOV to be tracked
Spectral Focal Sweep	1	Passive – Normal Lighting	Focal length varies for each color wavelength, with focal sweep to focus on each color and compute depth [418]
Diffraction Gratings	1	Passive – Normal Lighting	Light passing through sets of gratings or light guides provides depth information [420]
Conical Radial Mirror	1	Passive – Normal Lighting	Light from a conical mirror is imaged at different depths as a toroid shape, depth is extracted from the toroid [413]

Source: Courtesy of Ken Salsmann Aptina [427], with a few other methods added by the author.

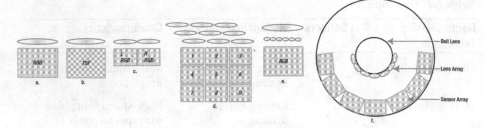

Figure 1-9. *A variety of lens and sensor configurations for common cameras: a. conventional, b. time-of-flight, c. stereo, d. array, e. plenoptic, f. spherical with ball lens*

Depth sensing is not a new field, and is covered very well in several related disciplines with huge industrial applications and financial resources, such as satellite imaging, remote sensing, photogrammetry, and medical imaging. However, the topics involving depth sensing are of growing interest in computer vision with the advent of commercial depth-sensing cameras such as Kinect, enabling graduate students on a budget to experiment with 3D depth maps and point clouds using a mobile phone or PC.

Multi-view stereo (MVS) depth sensing has been used for decades to compute digital elevation maps or DEMs, and digital terrain maps or DTMs, from satellite images using RADAR and LIDAR imaging, and from regional aerial surveys using specially equipped airplanes with high-resolution cameras and stable camera platforms, including digital terrain maps overlaid with photos of adjacent regions stitched together. *Photo mosaicking* is a related topic in computer vision that's gaining attention. The literature on *digital terrain mapping* is rich with information on proper geometry models and disparity computation methods. In addition, *3D medical imaging* via CAT and MRI modalities is backed by a rich research community, uses excellent depth-sensing methods, and offers depth-based rendering and visualization. However, it is always interesting to observe the "reinvention" in one field, such as computer vision, of well-known methods used in other fields. As Solomon said, "There is nothing new under the sun." In this section we approach depth sensing in the context of computer vision, citing relevant research, and leave the interesting journey into other related disciplines to the interested reader.

Binocular Stereo

Stereo [432, 433, 437] may be the most basic and familiar approach for capturing 3D depth maps, as many methods and algorithms are in use, so we provide a high-level overview here with selected standard references. The first step in stereo algorithms is to parameterize the projective transformation from world coordinate points to their corresponding image coordinates by determining the *stereo calibration* parameters of the camera system. Open-source software is available for stereo calibration.[2] Note that the L/R image pair is rectified prior to searching for features for disparity computation. Stereo depth *r* is computed, as shown in Figure 1-10.

---

[2]http://opencv.org, Camera Calibration and 3D Reconstruction

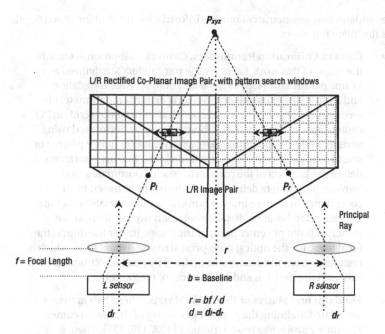

Figure 1-10. *Simplified schematic of basic binocular stereo principles*

An excellent survey of stereo algorithms and methods is found in the work of Scharstein and Szeliski [440] and also Lazaros [441]. The stereo geometry is a combination of *projective* and *Euclidean* [437]; we discuss some of the geometric problems affecting their accuracy later in this section. The standard online resource for comparing stereo algorithms is provided by Middlebury College,[3] where many new algorithms are benchmarked and comparative results provided, including the extensive ground truth datasets discussed in Appendix B.

The fundamental geometric calibration information needed for stereo depth includes the following basics.

- **Camera Calibration Parameters.** Camera calibration is outside the scope of this work, however the parameters are defined as 11 free parameters [435, 432]—3 for rotation, 3 for translation, and 5 intrinsic—plus one or more lens distortion parameters to reconstruct 3D points in world coordinates from the pixels in 2D camera space. The camera calibration may be performed using several methods, including a known calibration image pattern or one of many self-calibration methods [436]. *Extrinsic* parameters define the location of the camera in world coordinates, and *intrinsic* parameters define the relationships between pixel coordinates in camera image coordinates. Key variables include the calibrated baseline distance between two cameras at the principal point or center point of the image under the optics; the focal length of the optics; their pixel size and aspect ratio, which is computed from the sensor size divided by pixel resolution in each axis; and the position and orientation of the cameras.

- **Fundamental Matrix or Essential Matrix.** These two matrices are related, defining the popular geometry of the stereo camera system for projective reconstruction [438, 436, 437]. Their derivation is beyond the scope of this work. Either matrix may be used, depending on the algorithms employed. The *essential matrix* uses only the extrinsic camera parameters and camera coordinates, and the *fundamental matrix* depends on both the extrinsic and intrinsic parameters, and reveals pixel relationships between the stereo image pairs on epipolar lines.

In either case, we end up with projective transformations to reconstruct the 3D points from the 2D camera points in the stereo image pair.

Stereo processing steps are typically as follows:

1. **Capture:** Photograph the left/right image pair simultaneously.

2. **Rectification:** Rectify left/right image pair onto the same plane, so that pixel rows x coordinates and lines are aligned. Several projective warping methods may be used for rectification [437]. Rectification reduces the pattern match problem to a 1D search along the *x*-axis between images by aligning the images along the *x*-axis. Rectification may also include radial distortion corrections for the optics as a separate step; however, many cameras include a built-in factory-calibrated radial distortion correction.

3. **Feature Description:** For each pixel in the image pairs, isolate a small region surrounding each pixel as a *target feature descriptor*. Various methods are used for stereo feature description [215, 120].

4.   **Correspondence:** Search for each target feature in the opposite image pair. The search operation is typically done twice, first searching for left-pair target features in the right image and then right-pair target features in the left image. Subpixel accuracy is required for correspondence to increase depth field accuracy.

5.   **Triangulation:** Compute the disparity or distance between matched points using triangulation [439]. Sort all L/R target feature matches to find the best quality matches, using one of many methods [440].

6.   **Hole Filling:** For pixels and associated target features with no corresponding good match, there is a hole in the depth map at that location. Holes may be caused by occlusion of the feature in either of the L/R image pairs, or simply by poor features to begin with. Holes are filled using local region nearest-neighbor pixel interpolation methods.

Stereo depth-range resolution is an exponential function of distance from the viewpoint: in general, the wider the baseline, the better the long-range depth resolution. A shorter baseline is better for close-range depth (see Figures 1-10 and 1-20). Human-eye baseline or inter-pupillary distance has been measured as between 50 and75mm, averaging about 70mm for males and 65mm for females.

Multi-view stereo (MVS) is a related method to compute depth from several views using different baselines of the same subject, such as from a single or monocular camera, or an array of cameras. Monocular, MVS, and array camera depth sensing are covered later in this section.

Structured and Coded Light

Structured or coded light uses specific patterns projected into the scene and imaged back, then measured to determine depth; see Figure 1-11. We define the following approaches for using structured light for this discussion [445]:

- **Spatial single-pattern methods,** requiring only a single illumination pattern in a single image.

- **Timed multiplexing multi-pattern methods**, requiring a sequence of pattern illuminations and images, typically using binary or *n*-array codes, sometimes involving phase shifting or dithering the patterns in subsequent frames to increase resolution. Common pattern sequences include gray codes, binary codes, sinusoidal codes, and other unique codes.

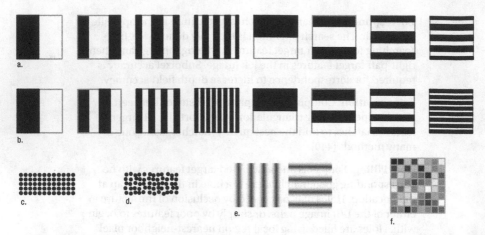

Figure 1-11. *Selected structured light patterns and methods: a. gray codes, b. binary codes, c. regular spot grid, d. randomized spot grid (as used in original Kinect), e. sinusoidal phase shift patters, f. randomized pattern for compressive structured light [446]*

For example, in the original Microsoft Kinect 3D depth camera, structured light consisting of several slightly different micro-grid patterns or pseudo-random points of infrared light are projected into the scene, then a single image is taken to capture the spots as they appear in the scene. Based on analysis of actual systems and patent applications, the original Kinect computes the depth using several methods, including (1) the size of the infrared spot—larger dots and low blurring mean the location is nearer, while smaller dots and more blurring mean the location is farther away; (2) the shape of the spot—a circle indicates a parallel surface, an ellipse indicates an oblique surface; and (3) by using small regions or a micro pattern of spots together so that the resolution is not very fine—however, noise sensitivity is good. Depth is computed from a *single image* using this method, rather than requiring several sequential patterns and images.

Multi-image methods are used for structured light, including projecting sets of time-sequential structured and coded patterns, as shown in Figure 1-11. In multi-image methods, each pattern is sent sequentially into the scene and imaged, then the combination of depth measurements from all the patterns is used to create the final depth map.

Industrial, scientific, and medical applications of depth measurements from structured light can reach high accuracy, imaging objects up to a few meters in size with precision that extends to micrometer range. Pattern projection methods are used, as well as laser-stripe pattern methods using multiple illumination beams to create wavelength interference; the interference is the measured to compute the distance. For example, common dental equipment uses small, hand-held laser range finders inserted into the mouth to create highly accurate depth images of tooth regions with missing pieces, and the images are then used to create new, practically perfectly fitting crowns or fillings using CAD/CAM micro-milling machines.

Of course, infrared light patterns do not work well outdoors in daylight; they become washed out by natural light. Also, the strength of the infrared emitters that can be used is limited by practicality and safety. The distance for effectively using structured light indoors is restricted by the amount of power that can be used for the IR emitters; perhaps

5 meters is a realistic limit for indoor infrared light. Kinect claims a range of about 4 meters for the current TOF (time of flight) method using uniform constant infrared illumination, while the first-generation Kinect sensor had similar depth range using structured light.

In addition to creating depth maps, structured or coded light is used for measurements employing optical encoders, as in robotics and process control systems. The encoders measure radial or linear position. They provide IR illumination patterns and measure the response on a scale or reticle, which is useful for single-axis positioning devices like linear motors and rotary lead screws. For example, patterns such as the binary position code and the reflected binary gray code [444] can be converted easily into binary numbers (see Figure 1-11). The gray code set elements each have a Hamming distance of 1 between successive elements.

Structured light methods suffer problems when handling high-specular reflections and shadows; however, these problems can be mitigated by using an optical diffuser between the pattern projector and the scene using the diffuse structured light methods [443] designed to preserve illumination coding. In addition, multiple-pattern structured light methods cannot deal with fast-moving scenes; however, the single-pattern methods can deal well with frame motion, since only one frame is required.

Optical Coding: Diffraction Gratings

Diffraction gratings are one of many methods of optical coding [447] to create a set of patterns for depth-field imaging, where a light structuring element, such as a mirror, grating, light guide, or special lens, is placed close to the detector or the lens. The original Kinect system is reported to use a diffraction grating method to create the randomized infrared spot illumination pattern. Diffraction gratings [430,431] above the sensor, as shown in Figure 1-12, can provide angle-sensitive pixel sensing. In this case, the light is refracted into surrounding cells at various angles, as determined by the placement of the diffraction gratings or other beam-forming elements, such as light guides. This allows the same sensor data to be processed in different ways with respect to a given angle of view, yielding different images.

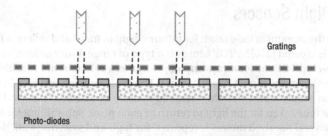

Figure 1-12. *Diffraction gratings above silicon used to create the Talbot Effect (first observed around 1836) for depth imaging. (For more information, see reference [430].) Diffraction gratings are a type of light-structuring element*

This method allows the detector size to be reduced while providing higher resolution images using a combined series of low-resolution images captured in parallel from narrow aperture diffraction gratings. Diffraction gratings make it possible to produce a wide range of information from the same sensor data, including depth information, increased pixel resolution, perspective displacements, and focus on multiple focal planes after the image is taken. A diffraction grating is a type of illumination coding device.

As shown in Figure 1-13, the light-structuring or coding element may be placed in several configurations, including [447]:

- Object side coding: close to the subjects

- Pupil plane coding: close to the lens on the object side

- Focal plane coding: close to the detector

- Illumination coding: close to the illuminator

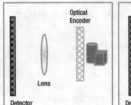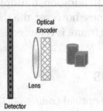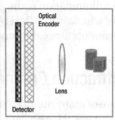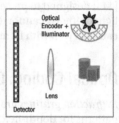

Figure 1-13. *Various methods for optical structuring and coding of patterns [447]: (Left to right): Object side coding, pupil plane coding, focal plane coding, illumination coding or structured light. The illumination patterns are determined in the optical encoder*

Note that illumination coding is shown as structured light patterns in Figure 1-11, while a variant of illumination coding is shown in Figure 1-7, using a set of mirrors that are opened or closed to create patterns.

Time-of-Flight Sensors

By measuring the amount of time taken for infrared light to travel and reflect, a *time-of-flight* (TOF) sensor is created [450]. A TOF sensor is a type of range finder or laser radar [449]. Several single-chip TOF sensor arrays and depth camera solutions are available, such as the second version of the Kinect depth camera. The basic concept involves broadcasting infrared light at a known time into the scene, such as by a pulsed IR laser, and then measuring the time taken for the light to return at each pixel. Sub-millimeter accuracy at ranges up to several hundred meters is reported for high-end systems [449], depending on the conditions under which the TOF sensor is used, the particular methods employed in the design, and the amount of power given to the IR laser.

Each pixel in the TOF sensor has several active components, as shown in Figure 1-14, including the IR sensor well, timing logic to measure the round-trip time from illumination to detection of IR light, and optical gates for synchronization of the electronic shutter and the pulsed IR laser. TOF sensors provide laser range-finding capabilities. For example, by gating the electronic shutter to eliminate short round-trip responses, environmental conditions such as fog or smoke reflections can be reduced. In addition, specific depth ranges, such as long ranges, can be measured by opening and closing the shutter at desired time intervals.

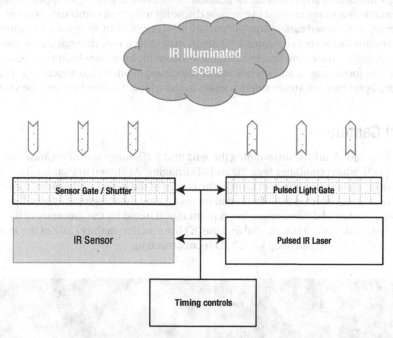

Figure 1-14. *A hypothetical TOF sensor configuration. Note that the light pulse length and sensor can be gated together to target specific distance ranges*

Illumination methods for TOF sensors may use very short IR laser pulses for a first image, acquire a second image with no laser pulse, and then take the difference between the images to eliminate ambient IR light contributions. By modulating the IR beam with an RF carrier signal using a photonic mixer device (PMD), the phase shift of the returning IR signal can be measured to increase accuracy—which is common among many laser range-finding methods [450]. Rapid optical gating combined with intensified CCD sensors can be used to increase accuracy to the sub-millimeter range in limited conditions, even at ranges above 100 meters. However, multiple IR reflections can contribute errors to the range image, since a single IR pulse is sent out over the entire scene and may reflect off of several surfaces before being imaged.

Since the depth-sensing method of a TOF sensor is integrated with the sensor electronics, there is very low processing overhead required compared to stereo and other methods. However, the limitations of IR light for outdoor situations still remain [448], which can affect the depth accuracy.

Array Cameras

As shown earlier in Figure 1-9, an *array camera* contains several cameras, typically arranged in a 2D array, such as a 3x3 array, providing several key options for computational imaging. Commercial array cameras for portable devices are beginning to appear. They may use the multi-view stereo method to compute disparity, utilizing a combination of sensors in the array, as discussed earlier. Some of the key advantages of an array camera include a wide baseline image set to compute a 3D depth map that can see through and around occlusions, higher-resolution images interpolated from the lower-resolution images of each sensor, all-in-focus images, and specific image refocusing at one or more locations. The maximum aperture of an array camera is equal to the widest baseline between the sensors.

Radial Cameras

A conical, or radial, mirror surrounding the lens and a 2D image sensor create a radial camera [413], which combines both 2D and 3D imaging. As shown in Figure 1-15, the radial mirror allows a 2D image to form in the center of the sensor and a radial toroidal image containing reflected 3D information forms around the sensor perimeter. By processing the toroidal information into a point cloud based on the geometry of the conical mirror, the depth is extracted and the 2D information in the center of the image can be overlaid as a texture map for full 3D reconstruction.

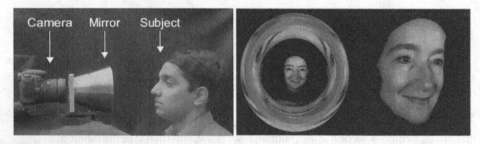

Figure 1-15. *(Left) Radial camera system with conical mirror to capture 3D reflections. (Center) Captured 3D reflections around the edges and 2D information of the face in the center. (Right) 3D image reconstructed from the radial image 3D information and the 2D face as a texture map. (Images used by permission © Shree Nayar Columbia University CAVE)*

Plenoptics: Light Field Cameras

Plenoptic methods create a 3D space defined as a *light field,* created by multiple optics. Plenoptic systems use a set of micro-optics and main optics to image a 4D light field and extract images from the light field during post-processing [451, 452, 423]. Plenoptic cameras require only a single image sensor, as shown in Figure 1-16. The 4D light field contains information on each point in the space, and can be represented as a volume dataset, treating each point as a *voxel,* or 3D pixel with a 3D oriented surface, with color and opacity. Volume data can be processed to yield different views and perspective displacements, allowing focus at multiple focal planes after the image is taken. Slices of the volume can be taken to isolate perspectives and render 2D images. Rendering a light field can be done by using ray tracing and volume rendering methods [453, 454].

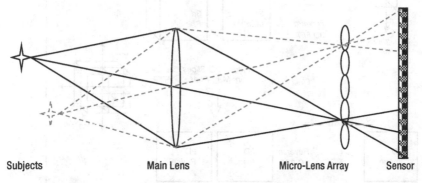

Subjects   Main Lens   Micro-Lens Array   Sensor

Figure 1-16. *A plenoptic camera illustration. Multiple independent subjects in the scene can be processed from the same sensor image. Depth of field and focus can be computed for each subject independently after the image is taken, yielding perspective and focal plane adjustments within the 3D light field*

In addition to volume and surface renderings of the light field, a 2D slice from the 3D field or volume can be processed in the frequency domain by way of the Fourier Projection Slice Theorem [455], as illustrated in Figure 1-17. This is the basis for medical imaging methods in processing 3D MRI and CAT scan data. Applications of the Fourier Projection Slice method to volumetric and 3D range data are described by Levoy [455, 452] and Krig [137]. The basic algorithm is described as follows:

1. The volume data is forward transformed, using a 3D FFT into magnitude and phase data.

2. To visualize, the resulting 3D FFT results in the frequency volume are rearranged by *octant shifting* each cube to align the frequency 0 data around the center of a 3D Cartesian coordinate system in the center of the volume, similar to the way 2D frequency spectrums are *quadrant shifted* for frequency spectrum display around the center of a 2D Cartesian coordinate system.

3. A planar 2D slice is extracted from the volume parallel to the FOV plane where the slice passes through the origin (center) of the volume. The angle of the slice taken from the frequency domain volume data determines the angle of the desired 2D view and the depth of field.

4. The 2D slice from the frequency domain is run through an inverse 2D FFT to yield a 2D spatial image corresponding to the chosen angle and depth of field.

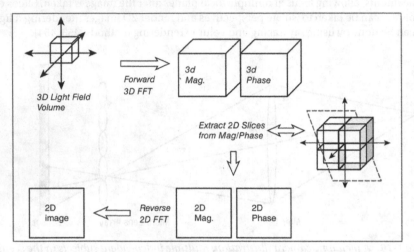

Figure 1-17. Graphic representation of the algorithm for the Fourier Projection Slice Theorem, which is one method of light field processing. The 3D Fourier space is used to filter the data to create 2D views and renderings [455, 452, 137]. (Image used by permission, © Intel Press, from Building Intelligent Systems)

3D Depth Processing

For historical reasons, several terms with their acronyms are used in discussions of depth sensing and related methods, so we cover some overlapping topics in this section. Table 1-1 earlier provided a summary at a high level of the underlying physical means for depth sensing. Regardless of the depth-sensing method, there are many similarities and common problems. Post-processing the depth information is critical, considering the calibration accuracy of the camera system, the geometric model of the depth field, the measured accuracy of the depth data, any noise present in the depth data, and the intended application.

We survey several interrelated depth-sensing topics here, including:

- Sparse depth-sensing methods
- Dense depth-sensing methods
- Optical flow

- Simultaneous localization and mapping (SLAM)

- Structure from motion (SFM)

- 3D surface reconstruction, 3D surface fusion

- Monocular depth sensing

- Stereo and multi-view stereo (MVS)

- Common problems in depth sensing

Human depth perception relies on a set of innate and learned visual cues, which are outside the scope of this work and overlap into several fields, including optics, ophthalmology, and psychology [464]; however, we provide an overview of the above selected topics in the context of depth processing.

Overview of Methods

For this discussion of depth-processing methods, depth sensing falls into two major categories based on the methods shown in Table 1-1:

- **Sparse depth methods**, using computer vision methods to extract local interest points and features. Only selected points are assembled into a sparse depth map or point cloud. The features are tracked from frame to frame as the camera or scene moves, and the sparse point cloud is updated. Usually only a single camera is needed.

- **Dense depth methods**, computing depth at every pixel. This creates a dense depth map, using methods such as stereo, TOF, or MVS. It may involve one or more cameras.

Many sparse depth methods use standard monocular cameras and computer vision feature tracking, such as optical flow and SLAM (which are covered later in this section), and the feature descriptors are tracked from frame to frame to compute disparity and sparse depth. Dense depth methods are usually based more on a specific depth camera technology, such as stereo or structured light. There are exceptions, as covered next.

Problems in Depth Sensing and Processing

The depth-sensing methods each have specific problems; however, there are some common problems we can address here. To begin, one common problem is *geometric modeling* of the depth field, which is complex, including perspective and projections. Most depth-sensing methods treat the entire field as a Cartesian coordinate system, and this introduces slight problems into the depth solutions. A camera sensor is a 2D Euclidean model, and discrete voxels are imaged in 3D Euclidean space; however, mapping between the camera and the real world using simple Cartesian models introduces geometric distortion. Other problems include those of *correspondence*, or failure to match features in separate frames, and *noise* and *occlusion*. We look at such problems in this next section.

The Geometric Field and Distortions

Field geometry is a complex area affecting both depth sensing and 2D imaging. For commercial applications, geometric field problems may not be significant, since locating faces, tracking simple objects, and augmenting reality are not demanding in terms of 3D accuracy. However, military and industrial applications often require high precision and accuracy, so careful geometry treatment is in order. To understand the geometric field problems common to depth-sensing methods, let's break down the major areas:

- Projective geometry problems, dealing with perspective

- Polar and spherical geometry problems, dealing with perspective as the viewing frustum spreads with distance from the viewer

- Radial distortion, due to lens aberrations

- Coordinate space problems, due to the Cartesian coordinates of the sensor and the voxels, and the polar coordinate nature of casting rays from the scene into the sensor

The goal of this discussion is to enumerate the problems in depth sensing, not to solve them, and to provide references where applicable. Since the topic of geometry is vast, we can only provide a few examples here of better methods for modeling the depth field. It is hoped that, by identifying the geometric problems involved in depth sensing, additional attention will be given to this important topic. The complete geometric model, including corrections, for any depth system is very complex. Usually, the topic of advanced geometry is ignored in popular commercial applications; however, we can be sure that advanced military applications such as particle beam weapons and missile systems do not ignore those complexities, given the precision required.

Several researchers have investigated more robust nonlinear methods of dealing with projective geometry problems [465,466] specifically by modeling epipolar geometry–related distortion as 3D *cylindrical distortion*, rather than as planar distortion, and by providing reasonable compute methods for correction. In addition, the work of Lovegrove and Davison [484] deals with the geometric field using a *spherical mosaicking* method to align whole images for depth fusion, increasing the accuracy due to the spherical modeling.

The Horopter Region, Panum's Area, and Depth Fusion

As shown in Figure 1-18, the *Horopter* region, first investigated by Ptolemy and others in the context of astronomy, is a curved surface containing 3D points that are the same distance from the observer and at the same focal plane. *Panum's area* is the region surrounding the Horopter where the human visual system fuses points in the retina into a single object at the same distance and focal plane. It is a small miracle that the human vision system can reconcile the distances between 3D points and synthesize a common depth field! The challenge with the Horopter region and Panum's area lies in the fact that a post-processing step to any depth algorithm must be in place to correctly fuse the points the way the human visual system does. The margin of error depends on the usual variables, including baseline and pixel resolution, and the error is most pronounced toward the boundaries of the depth field and less pronounced in the center. Some of the spherical distortion is due to lens aberrations toward the edges, and can be partially corrected as discussed earlier in this chapter regarding geometric corrections during early sensor processing.

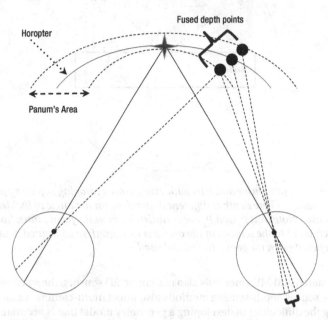

Figure 1-18. *Problems with stereo and multi-view stereo methods, showing the Horopter region and Panum's area, and three points in space that appear to be the same point from the left eye's perspective but different from the right eye's perspective. The three points surround the Horopter in Panum's area and are fused by humans to synthesize apparent depth*

Cartesian vs. Polar Coordinates: Spherical Projective Geometry

As illustrated in Figure 1-19, a 2D sensor as used in a TOF or monocular depth-sensing method has specific geometric problems as well; the problems increase toward the edges of the field of view. Note that the depth from a point in space to a pixel in the sensor is actually measured in a spherical coordinate system using polar coordinates, but the geometry of the sensor is purely Cartesian, so that geometry errors are *baked into the cake.*

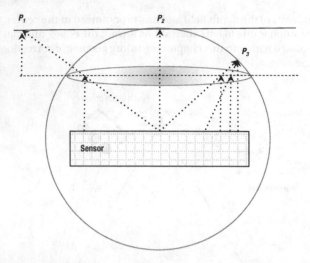

Figure 1-19. *A 2D depth sensor and lens with exaggerated imaging geometry problems dealing with distance, where depth is different depending on the angle of incidence on the lens and sensor. Note that P_1 and P_2 are equidistant from the focal plane; however, the distance of each point to the sensor via the optics is not equal, so computed depth will not be accurate depending on the geometric model used*

Because stereo and MVS methods also use single 2D sensors, the same problems as affect single sensor depth-sensing methods also affect multi-camera methods, compounding the difficulties in developing a geometry model that is accurate and computationally reasonable.

Depth Granularity

As shown in Figure 1-20, simple Cartesian depth computations cannot resolve the depth field into a linear uniform grain size; in fact, the depth field granularity increases exponentially with the distance from the sensor, while the ability to resolve depth at long ranges is much less accurate.

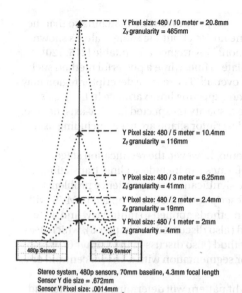

Y Pixel size: 480 / 10 meter = 20.8mm
Z_y granularity = 465mm

Y Pixel size: 480 / 5 meter = 10.4mm
Z_y granularity = 116mm

Y Pixel size: 480 / 3 meter = 6.25mm
Z_y granularity = 41mm

Y Pixel size: 480 / 2 meter = 2.4mm
Z_y granularity = 19mm

Y Pixel size: 480 / 1 meter = 2mm
Z_y granularity = 4mm

480p Sensor   480p Sensor

Stereo system, 480p sensors, 70mm baseline, 4.3mm focal length
Sensor Y die size = .672mm
Sensor Y Pixel size: .0014mm
Z_y Granularity = (.0014mm * Z^2mm) / (4.3mm * 70mm)

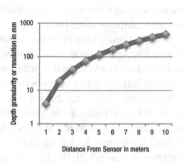

Figure 1-20. *Z depth granularity nonlinearity problems for a typical stereo camera system. Note that practical depth sensing using stereo and MVS methods has limitations in the depth field, mainly affected by pixel resolution, baseline, and focal length. At 10 meters, depth granularity is almost ½ meter, so an object must move at least + or- ½ meter in order for a change in measured stereo depth to be computed*

For example, in a hypothetical stereo vision system with a baseline of 70mm using 480p video resolution, as shown in Figure 1-20, depth resolution at 10 meters drops off to about ½ meter; in other words, at 10 meters away, objects may not appear to move in Z unless they move at least plus or minus ½ meter in Z. The depth resolution can be doubled simply by doubling the sensor resolution. As distance increases, humans increasingly use monocular depth *cues* to determine depth, such as for size of objects, rate of an object's motion, color intensity, and surface texture details.

Correspondence

Correspondence, or feature matching, is common to most depth-sensing methods. For a taxonomy of stereo feature matching algorithms, see Scharstein and Szeliski [440]. Here, we discuss correspondence along the lines of feature descriptor methods and triangulation as applied to stereo, multi-view stereo, and structured light.

Subpixel accuracy is a goal in most depth-sensing methods, so several algorithms exist [468]. It's popular to correlate two patches or intensity templates by fitting the surfaces to find the highest match; however, Fourier methods are also used to correlate phase [467, 469], similar to the intensity correlation methods.

For stereo systems, the image pairs are rectified prior to feature matching so that the features are expected to be found along the same line at about the same scale, as shown in Figure 1-11; descriptors with little or no rotational invariance are suitable [215, 120]. A feature descriptor such as a correlation template is fine, while a powerful method such as the SIFT feature description method [161] is overkill. The feature descriptor region may be a rectangle favoring disparity in the x-axis and expecting little variance in the y-axis, such as a rectangular 3x9 descriptor shape. The disparity is expected in the x-axis, not the y-axis. Several window sizing methods for the descriptor shape are used, including fixed size and adaptive size [440].

Multi-view stereo systems are similar to stereo; however, the rectification stage may not be as accurate, since motion between frames can include scaling, translation, and rotation. Since scale and rotation may have significant correspondence problems between frames, other approaches to feature description have been applied to MVS, with better results. A few notable feature descriptor methods applied to multi-view and wide baseline stereo include the MSER [194] method (also discussed in Chapter 6), which uses a blob-like patch, and the SUSAN [164, 165] method (also discussed in Chapter 6), which defines the feature based on an object region or segmentation with a known centroid or nucleus around which the feature exists.

For structured light systems, the type of light pattern will determine the feature, and correlation of the phase is a popular method [469]. For example, structured light methods that rely on phase-shift patterns using phase correlation [467] template matching claim to be accurate to $1/100^{th}$ of a pixel. Other methods are also used for structured light correspondence to achieve subpixel accuracy [467].

Holes and Occlusion

When a pattern cannot be matched between frames, a *hole* exists in the depth map. Holes can also be caused by occlusion. In either case, the depth map must be repaired, and several methods exist for doing that. A *hole map* should be provided, showing where the problems are. A simple approach, then, is to fill the hole uses use bi-linear interpolation within local depth map patches. Another simple approach is to use the last known-good depth value in the depth map from the current scan line.

More robust methods for handling occlusion exist [472, 471] using more computationally expensive but slightly more accurate methods, such as adaptive local windows to optimize the interpolation region. Yet another method of dealing with holes is *surface fusion* into a depth volume [473] (covered next), whereby multiple sequential depth maps are integrated into a depth volume as a cumulative surface, and then a depth map can be extracted from the depth volume.

Surface Reconstruction and Fusion

A general method of creating surfaces from depth map information is *surface reconstruction*. Computer graphics methods can be used for rendering and displaying the surfaces. The basic idea is to combine several depth maps to construct a better surface model, including the *RGB* 2D image of the surface rendered as a *texture map*. By creating an iterative model of the 3D surface that integrates several depth maps from different viewpoints, the depth accuracy can be increased, occlusion can be reduced or eliminated, and a wider 3D scene viewpoint is created.

The work of Curless and Levoy [473] presents a method of fusing multiple range images or depth maps into a 3D volume structure. The algorithm renders all range images as *iso-surfaces* into the volume by integrating several range images. Using a signed distance function and weighting factors stored in the volume data structure for the existing surfaces, the new surfaces are integrated into the volume for a cumulative best-guess at where the actual surfaces exist. Of course, the resulting surface has several desirable properties, including reduced noise, reduced holes, reduced occlusion, multiple viewpoints, and better accuracy (see Figure 1-21).

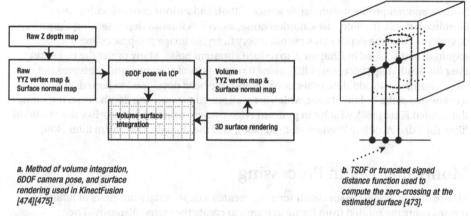

a. Method of volume integration, 6DOF camera pose, and surface rendering used in KinectFusion [474][475].

b. TSDF or truncated signed distance function used to compute the zero-crossing at the estimated surface [473].

Figure 1-21. *(Right) The Curless and Levoy [473] method for surface construction from range images, or depth maps. Shown here are three different weighted surface measurements projected into the volume using ray casting. (Left) Processing flow of Kinect Fusion method*

A derivative of the Curless and Levoy method applied to SLAM is the Kinect Fusion approach [474], as shown in Figure 1-22, using compute-intensive SIMD parallel real-time methods to provide not only surface reconstruction but also camera tracking and the 6DOF or *6-degrees-of-freedom* camera pose. Raytracing and texture mapping are used for surface renderings. There are yet other methods for surface reconstruction from multiple images [480, 551].

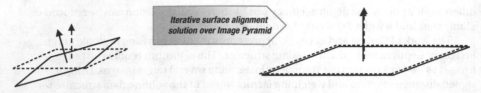

Figure 1-22. *Graphic representaion of the dense whole-image alignment solution to obtain the 6DOF camera pose using ESM [485]*

Noise

Noise is another problem with depth sensors [409], and various causes include low illumination and, in some cases, motion noise, as well as inferior depth sensing algorithms or systems. Also, the depth maps are often very fuzzy, so image pre-processing may be required, as discussed in Chapter 2, to reduce apparent noise. Many prefer the bi-lateral filter for depth map processing [302], since it respects local structure and preserves the edge transitions. In addition, other noise filters have been developed to remedy the weaknesses of the bi-lateral filter, which are well suited to removing depth noise, including the Guided Filter [486], which can perform edge-preserving noise filtering like the bi-lateral filter, the Edge-Avoiding Wavelet method [488], and the Domain Transform filter [489].

Monocular Depth Processing

Monocular, or single sensor depth sensing, creates a depth map from pairs of image frames using the motion from frame to frame to create the stereo disparity. The assumptions for stereo processing with a calibrated fixed geometry between stereo pairs do not hold for monocular methods, since each time the camera moves the *camera pose* must be recomputed. Camera pose is a *6 degrees-of-freedom* (6DOF) equation, including *x, y, and z* linear motion along each axis and roll, pitch, and yaw rotational motion about each axis. In monocular depth-sensing methods, the camera pose must be computed for each frame as the basis for comparing two frames and computing disparity.

Note that computation of the 6DOF matrix can be enhanced using *inertial sensors,* such as the accelerometer and MEMS gyroscope [483], as the coarse alignment step, followed by visual feature-based surface alignment methods discussed later in regard to optical flow. Since commodity inertial sensors are standard with mobile phones and tablets, inertial pose estimation will become more effective and commonplace as the sensors mature. While the accuracy of commodity accelerometers is not very good, monocular depth-sensing systems can save compute time by taking advantage of the inertial sensors for pose estimation.

Multi-View Stereo

The geometry model for most monocular multi-view stereo (MVS) depth algorithms is based on projective geometry and epipolar geometry; a good overview of both are found in the classic text by Hartley and Zisserman [437]. A taxonomy and accuracy comparison of six MVS algorithms is provided by Seitz et al. [478]. We look at a few representative approaches in this section.

Sparse Methods: PTAM

Sparse MVS methods create a sparse 3D point cloud, not a complete depth map. The basic goals for sparse depth are simple: track the features from frame to frame, compute feature disparity to create depth, and perform 6DOF alignment to localize the new frames and get the camera pose. Depending on the application, sparse depth may be ideal to use as part of a feature descriptor to add invariance to perspective viewpoint or to provide sufficient information for navigating that's based on a few key landmarks in the scene. Several sparse depth-sensing methods have been developed in the robotics community under the terms *SLAM*, *SFM*, and *optical flow* (discussed below).

However, we first illustrate sparse depth sensing in more detail by discussing a specific approach: *Parallel Tracking and Mapping* (PTAM)[456, 457], which can both track the 6DOF camera pose and generate a sparse depth map suitable for light-duty augmented reality applications, allowing avatars to be placed at known locations and orientations in the scene from frame to frame. The basic algorithm consists of two parts, which run in parallel threads: a tracking thread for updating the pose, and a mapping thread for updating the sparse 3D point cloud. We provide a quick overview of each next.

The *mapping thread* deals with a history buffer of the last N keyframes and an N-level image pyramid for each frame in a history buffer, from which the sparse 3D point cloud is continually refined using the latest incoming depth features via a bundle adjustment process (which simply means fitting new 3D coordinates against existing 3D coordinates by a chosen minimization method, such as the Levenberg-Marquardt [437]). The bundle adjustment process can perform either a local adjustment over a limited set of recent frames or global adjustment over all the frames during times of low scene motion when time permits.

The *tracking thread* scans the incoming image frames for expected features, based on projecting where known-good features last appeared, to guide the feature search, using the 6DOF camera pose as a basis for the projection. A FAST9 [138] corner detector is used to locate the corners, followed by a Shi-Tomasi [157] non-maximal suppression step to remove weak corner candidates (discussed in Chapter 6 in more detail). The feature matching stage follows a coarse-to-fine progression over the image pyramid to compute the 6DOF pose.

Target features are computed in new frames using an 8x8 patch surrounding each selected corner. *Reference features* are computed also as 8x8 patches from the original patch taken from the first-known image where they were found. To align the reference and target patches prior to feature matching, the surface normal of each reference patch is used for pre-warping the patch against the last-known 6DOF camera pose, and the aligned feature matching is performed using zero-mean SSD distance.

One weakness of monocular depth sensing shows up when there is a *failure to localize*; that is, if there is too much motion, or illumination changes too much, the system may fail to localize and the tracking stops. Another weakness is that the algorithm must be initialized entirely for a specific localized scene or workspace, such as a desktop. For initialization, PTAM follows a five-point stereo calibration method that takes a few seconds to perform with user cooperation. Yet another weakness is that the size of the 3D volume containing the point cloud is intended for a small, localized scene or workspace. However, on the positive side, the accuracy of the 3D point cloud is very good, close to the pixel size; the pose is accurate enough for AR or gaming applications; and it is possible to create a 360-degree perspective point cloud by walking around the scene. PTAM has been implemented on a mobile phone [456] using modest compute and memory resources, with tradeoffs for accuracy and frame rate.

Dense Methods: DTAM

Dense monocular depth sensing is quite compute-intensive compared to sparse methods, so the research and development are much more limited. The goals are about the same as for sparse monocular depth—namely, compute the 6DOF camera pose for image alignment, but create a dense every-pixel depth map instead of a sparse point cloud. For illustration, we highlight key concepts from a method for Dense Tracking and Mapping (DTAM), developed by Newcombe, Lovegrove and Davison [482].

While the DTAM goal is to compute dense depth at each pixel rather than sparse depth, DTAM shares some of the same requirements with PTAM [457], since both are monocular methods. Both DTAM and PTAM are required to compute the 6DOF pose for each new frame in order to align the new frames to compute disparity. DTAM also requires a user-assisted monocular calibration method for the scene, and it uses the PTAM calibration method. And DTAM is also intended for small, localized scenes or workspaces. DTAM shares several background concepts taken from the Spherical Mosaicking method of Lovegrove and Davison [484], including the concept of *whole image alignment,* based on the Efficient Second Order Minimization (ESM) method [485], which is reported to find a stable surface alignment using fewer iterations than LK methods [458] as part of the process to generate the 6DOF pose.

Apparently, both DTAM and Spherical Mosaicking use a spherical coordinate geometry model to mosaic the new frames into the dense 3D surface proceeding from coarse to fine alignment over the image pyramid to iterate toward the solution of the 6DOF camera pose. The idea of whole-image surface alignment is shown in Figure 1-22. The new and existing depth surfaces are integrated using a localized guided-filter method [486] into the cost volume. That is, the guided filter uses a guidance image to merge the incoming depth information into the cost volume.

DTAM also takes great advantage of SIMD instructions and highly thread-parallel SIMT GPGPU programming to gain the required performance necessary for real-time operation on commodity GPU hardware.

Optical Flow, SLAM, and SFM

Optical flow measures the motion of features and patterns from frame to frame in the form of a displacement *vector.* Optical flow is similar to sparse monocular depth-sensing methods, and it can be applied to wide baseline stereo matching problems [463]. Since the field of optical flow research and its applications is vast [459, 460, 461], we provide only an introduction here with an eye toward describing the methods used and features obtained.

Optical flow can be considered a sparse feature-tracking problem, where a feature can be considered a *particle* [462], so optical flow and particle flow analysis are similar. Particle flow analysis is applied to diverse particle field flow-analysis problems, including weather prediction, simulating combustion and explosives, hydro-flow dynamics, and robot navigation. Methods exist for both 2D and 3D optical flow. The various optical flow algorithms are concerned with tracking-feature descriptors or matrices, rather than with individual scalars or pixels, within consecutive fields of discrete scalar values. For computer vision, the input to the optical flow algorithms is a set of sequential 2D images and pixels, or 3D volumes and voxels, and the output is a set of vectors showing direction of movement of the tracked features.

Many derivations and alternatives to the early Lucas Kanade (LK) method [458, 459, 460, 461] are used for optical flow; however, this remains the most popular reference point, as it uses local features in the form of correlation templates (as discussed in Chapter 6). Good coverage of the state-of-the-art methods based on LK is found in *Lucas Kanade 20 years on,* by Baker and Matthews [480]. The Efficient Second Order Minimization (ESM) method [485] is related to the LK method. ESM is reported to be a stable solution using fewer iterations than LK. LK does not track individual pixels; rather, it relies on the pixel neighborhood, such as a 3x3 matrix or template region, and tries to guess which direction the features have moved, iteratively searching the local region and averaging the search results using a least-squares solution to find the best guess.

While there are many variations on the LK method [459, 460, 461], key assumptions of most LK-derived optical flow methods include small displacements of features from frame to frame, rigid features, and sufficient texture information in the form of localized gradients in order to identify features. Various methods are used to find the local gradients, such as Sobel and Laplacian (discussed in Chapter 2). Fields with large feature displacements from frame to frame and little texture information are not well suited to the LK method. That's because the LK algorithm ignores regions with little gradient information by examining the eigenvalues of each local matrix to optimize the iterative solution. However, more recent and robust research methods are moving beyond the limitations of LK [459,460], and include Deepflow [344], which is designed for deformable features and large displacement optical flow [394], using multi-layer feature scale hierarchies [404] similar to convolutional networks [339].

Applications of surface reconstruction to localization and mapping are used in *simultaneous localization and mapping* (SLAM) and *instructure from motion* (SFM) methods—for example, in robotics navigation. One goal of SLAM is to localize, or find the current position and the 6DOF camera pose. Another goal is to create a local region map, which includes depth. To dig deeper into SLAM and SFM methods, see the historical survey by Bailey and Hugh Durrant-Whyte [476, 477].

3D Representations: Voxels, Depth Maps, Meshes, and Point Clouds

Depth information is represented and stored in a variety of convertible formats, depending on the intended use. We summarize here some common formats; see also Figure 1-23.

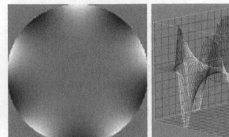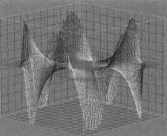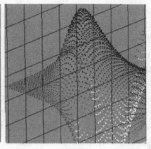

Figure 1-23. *Various 3D depth formats. Renderings of a Zernike polynomial. (Left to right): A depth map, a polygon mesh rendering using 3D quads, a point cloud rendering equivalent of voxels*

The ability to convert between depth formats is desirable for different algorithms and easy to do. Common 3D depth formats include:

- **2D Pixel Array, 3D Depth Map:** A 2D pixel array is the default format for 2D images in memory, and it is the natural storage format for many processing operations, such as convolution and neighborhood filtering. For depth map images, the pixel value is the Z, or depth value. Each point in the array may contain *{color, depth}*.

- **3D Voxel Volume:** A 3D volumetric data structure composed of a 3D array of voxels is ideal for several algorithms, including depth map integration for 3D surface reconstruction and raytracing of surfaces for graphical renderings. A voxel is a volume element, like a pixel is a picture element. Each voxel may contain *{color, normal}*; the depth coordinates are implicit from the volume structure.

- **3D Polygon Mesh:** Storing 3D points in a standard 3D polygon mesh provides a set of connected points or vertices, each having a surface normal, 3D coordinates, color, and texture. Mesh formats are ideal for rendering surfaces in a GPU pipeline, such as OpenGL or DirectX. Each point in the mesh may contain *{x, y, z, color, normal}*, and is associated with neighboring points in a standard pattern such as a quad or triangle describing the surface.

- **3D Point Cloud:** This is a sparse structure that is directly convertible to a standard 3D polygon mesh. The point cloud format is ideal for sparse monocular depth-sensing methods. Each point in the cloud may contain *{x, y, z, color, normal}*.

Summary

In this chapter, we surveyed image sensing methods and sensor image processing methods as the first step in the vision pipeline. We covered the image sensor technologies available, with an eye toward image pre-processing that may be useful for getting the most from the image data, since image sensoring methods often dictate the image pre-processing required. (More discussion on image pre-processing is provided in Chapter 2.) Sensor configurations used for both 2D and 3D imaging were discussed, as well as a wide range of camera configurations used for computational imaging to create new images after the data is captured, such as HDR images and image refocusing. Depth imaging approaches were covered here as well, and included stereo and time of flight, since mobile devices are increasingly offering 3D depth camera technology for consumer applications. Depth maps can be used in computer vision to solve many problems, such as 3D feature description and 3D image segmentation of foreground and background objects. The topic of 3D depth processing and 3D features is followed throughout this book; chapter 6 covers 3D feature descriptors, and chapter 7 and Appendix B cover 3D ground truth data.

CHAPTER 2

■ ■ ■

Image Pre-Processing

"I entered, and found Captain Nemo deep in algebraical calculations of x and other quantities."

—*Jules Verne*, 20,000 Leagues Under The Sea

This chapter describes the methods used to prepare images for further analysis, including interest point and feature extraction. Some of these methods are also useful for global and local feature description, particularly the metrics derived from transforms and basis spaces. The focus is on image pre-processing for computer vision, so we do not cover the entire range of image processing topics applied to areas such as computational photography and photo enhancements, so we refer the interested reader to various other standard resources in Digital Image Processing and Signal Processing as we go along [4,9,325,326], and we also point out interesting research papers that will enhance understanding of the topics.

■ **Note**   Readers with a strong background in image processing may benefit from a light reading of this chapter.

Perspectives on Image Processing

Image processing is a vast field that cannot be covered in a single chapter. So why do we discuss image pre-processing in a book about computer vision? The reason is to advance the science of local and global feature description, as image pre-processing is typically ignored in discussions of feature description. Some general image processing topics are covered here in light of feature description, intended to illustrate rather than to proscribe, as applications and image data will guide the image pre-processing stage.

Some will argue that image pre-processing is not a good idea, since it distorts or changes the true nature of the raw data. However, intelligent use of image pre-processing can provide benefits and solve problems that ultimately lead to better local and global feature detection. We survey common methods for image enhancements and corrections that will affect feature analysis downstream in the vision pipeline in both favorable and unfavorable ways, depending on how the methods are employed.

Image pre-processing may have dramatic positive effects on the quality of feature extraction and the results of image analysis. Image pre-processing is analogous to the mathematical normalization of a data set, which is a common step in many feature descriptor methods. Or to make a musical analogy, think of image pre-processing as a sound system with a range of controls, such as raw sound with no volume controls; volume control with a simple tone knob; volume control plus treble, bass, and mid; or volume control plus a full graphics equalizer, effects processing, and great speakers in an acoustically superior room. In that way, this chapter promotes image pre-processing by describing a combination of corrections and enhancements that are an essential part of a computer vision pipeline.

Problems to Solve During Image Pre-Processing

In this section we suggest opportunities for image pre-processing that are guided according to the feature descriptor method you've chosen. Raw image data direct from a camera may have a variety of problems, as discussed in Chapter 1, and therefore it is not likely to produce the best computer vision results. This is why careful consideration of image pre-processing is fundamental. For example, a local binary descriptor using gray scale data will require different pre-processing than will a color SIFT algorithm; additionally, some exploratory work is required to fine-tune the image pre-processing stage for best results. We explore image pre-processing by following the vision pipelines of four fundamental families of feature description methods, with some examples, as follows:

1. **Local Binary Descriptors** (LBP, ORB, FREAK, others)

2. **Spectra Descriptors** (SIFT, SURF, others)

3. **Basis Space Descriptors** (FFT, wavelets, others)

4. **Polygon Shape Descriptors** (blob object area, perimeter, centroid)

These families of feature description metrics are developed into a taxonomy in Chapter 5. Before that, though, Chapter 4 discusses the feature descriptor building concepts, while Chapter 3 covers global feature description and then Chapter 6 surveys local feature description. The image pre-processing methods and applications introduced here are samples, but a more developed set of examples, following various vision pipelines, is developed in Chapter 8, including application-specific discussions of the pre-processing stage.

Vision Pipelines and Image Pre-Processing

Table 2-1 lists common image pre-processing operations, with examples from each of the four descriptor families, illustrating both differences and commonality among these image pre-processing steps, which can be applied prior to feature description. Our intent here is to illustrate rather than proscribe or limit the methods chosen.

Table 2-1. *Possible Image Pre-Processing Enhancements and Corrections as Applied to Different Vision Pipelines*

Image Pre-Processing	Local Binary (LBP, ORB)	Spectra (SIFT, SURF)	Basis Space (FFT, Code books)	Polygon Shape (Blob Metrics)
Illumination corrections	x	x	x	x
Blur and focus corrections	x	x	x	x
Filtering and noise removal	x	x	x	x
Thresholding				x
Edge enhancements		x		x
Morphology				x
Segmentation				x
Region processing and filters		x		x
Point processing	x			x
Math and statistical processing	x			x
Color space conversions	x	x		x

Local binary features deal with the pixel intensity comparisons of *point-pairs*. This makes the comparisons relatively insensitive to illumination, brightness, and contrast, so there may not be much need for image pre-processing to achieve good results. Current local binary pattern methods as described in the literature do not typically call for much image pre-processing; they rely on a simple comparison threshold that can be adjusted to account for illumination or contrast.

Spectra descriptors, such as SIFT (which acts on local region gradients) and SURF (which uses HAAR-like features with integrated pixel values over local regions), offer diverse pre-processing opportunities. Methods that use image pyramids often perform some image pre-processing on the image pyramid to create a scale space representation of the data using Gaussian filtering to smooth the higher levels of the pyramid. Basic illumination corrections and filtering may be useful to enhance the image prior to computing gradients—for example, to enhance the contrast within a band of intensities that likely contain gradient-edge information for the features. But in general, the literature does not report good or bad results for any specific methods used to pre-process the image data prior to feature extraction, and therein resides the opportunity.

Basis space features are usually global or regional, spanning a regular shaped polygon—for example, a Fourier transform computed over the entire image or block. However, basis space features may be part of the local features, such as the Fourier spectrum of the LBP histogram, which can be computed over histogram bin values of a local descriptor to provide rotational invariance. Another example is the Fourier descriptor used to compute polygon factors for radial line segment lengths showing the roundness of a feature to provide rotational invariance. See Chapter 3, especially Figure 3-19.

The most complex descriptor family is the polygon shape based descriptors, which potentially require several image pre-processing steps to isolate the polygon structure and shapes in the image for measurement. Polygon shape description pipelines may involve everything from image enhancements to structural morphology and segmentation techniques. Setting up the pre-processing for polygon feature shape extraction typically involves more work than any other method, since thresholds and segmentation require fine-tuning to achieve good results. Also note that polygon shape descriptors are not local patterns but, rather, larger regional structures with features spanning many tens and even hundreds of pixels, so the processing can be more intensive as well.

In some cases, image pre-processing is required to correct problems that would otherwise adversely affect feature description; we look at this next.

Corrections

During image pre-processing, there may be artifacts in the images that should be corrected prior to feature measurement and analysis. Here are various candidates for correction.

- **Sensor corrections.** Discussed in Chapter 1, these include dead pixel correction, geometric lens distortion, and vignetting.

- **Lighting corrections.** Lighting can introduce deep shadows that obscure local texture and structure; also, uneven lighting across the scene might skew results. Candidate correction methods include rank filtering, histogram equalization, and LUT remap.

- **Noise.** This comes in many forms, and may need special image pre-processing. There are many methods to choose from, some of which are surveyed in this chapter.

- **Geometric corrections.** If the entire scene is rotated or taken from the wrong perspective, it may be valuable to correct the geometry prior to feature description. Some features are more robust to geometric variation than others, as discussed in Chapters 4, 5, and 6.

- **Color corrections.** It can be helpful to redistribute color saturation or correct for illumination artifacts in the intensity channel. Typically color hue is one of the more difficult attributes to correct, and it may not be possible to correct using simple gamma curves and the sRGB color space. We cover more accurate colorimetry methods later in this chapter.

Enhancements

Enhancements are used to optimize for specific feature measurement methods, rather than fix problems. Familiar image processing enhancements include sharpening and color balancing. Here some general examples of image enhancement with their potential benefits to feature description.

- **Scale-space pyramids.** When a pyramid is constructed using an octave scale and pixel decimation to sub-sample images to create the pyramid, sub-sampling artifacts and jagged pixel transitions are introduced. Part of the scale-space pyramid building process involves applying a Gaussian blur filter to the sub-sampled images, which removes the jagged artifacts.

- **Illumination.** In general, illumination can always be enhanced. Global illumination can be enhanced using simple LUT remapping and pixel point operations and histogram equalizations, and pixel remapping. Local illumination can be enhanced using gradient filters, local histogram equalization, and rank filters.

- **Blur and focus enhancements.** Many well-known filtering methods for sharpening and blurring may be employed at the pre-processing stage. For example, to compensate for pixel aliasing artifacts introduced by rotation that may manifest as blurred pixels which obscure fine detail, sharpen filters can be used to enhance the edge features prior to gradient computations. Or, conversely, the rotation artifacts may be too strong and can be removed by blurring.

In any case, the pre-processing enhancements or corrections are dependent on the descriptor using the images, and the application.

Preparing Images for Feature Extraction

Each family of feature description methods has different goals for the pre-processing stage of the pipeline. Let's look at a few examples from each family here, and examine possible image pre-processing methods for each.

Local Binary Family Pre-Processing

The local binary descriptor family is primarily concerned with point-pair intensity value comparisons, and several point-pair patterns are illustrated in Chapter 4 for common methods such as FREAK, BRISK, BRIEF, and ORB. As illustrated in Figure 2-4, the *comparative* difference (<, >, =) between points is all that matters, so hardly any image pre-processing seems needed. Based on this discussion, here are two approaches for image pre-processing:

1. **Preserve pixels as is.** Do nothing except use a pixel value-difference compare threshold, such as done in the Census transform and other methods, since the threshold takes care of filtering noise and other artifacts.

   if(|point1-point2|>threshold)

2. **Use filtering.** In addition to using the compare threshold, apply a suitable filter to remove local noise, such as a smoothing or rank filter. Or, take the opposite approach and use a sharpen filter to amplify small differences, perhaps followed by a smoothing filter. Either method may prove to work, depending on the data and application.

Figure 2-1 uses center-neighbor point-pair comparisons in a 3x3 local region to illustrate the difference between local threshold and a pre-processing operation for the local binary pattern LBP, as follows:

- Left image: Original unprocessed local 3x3 region data; compare threshold = 5, dark pixels > 5 from center pixel.

- Left center image: Compare threshold = 10; note pattern shape is different simply by changing the threshold.

- Right center image: After a Laplacian sharpening filter is applied to 3x3 region, note that the center pixel value is changed from 52 to 49, so with the compare threshold set to 5 the pattern is now different from original on the left.

- Right image: Threshold on Laplacian filtered data set to 10; note different resulting binary pattern.

35	53	59
38	52	47
48	60	51

35	53	59
38	52	47
48	60	51

35	53	59
38	49	47
48	60	51

35	53	59
38	49	47
48	60	51

Figure 2-1. *How the LBP can be affected by pre-processing, showing the compare threshold value effects. (Left) Compare threshold = 5. (Center left) Compare threshold = 10. (Center right) Original data after Laplacian fitler applied. (Right) Compare threshold = 5 on Laplacian filtered data*

Spectra Family Pre-Processing

Due to the wide range of methods in the spectra category, it is difficult to generalize the potential pre-processing methods that may be useful. For example, SIFT is concerned with gradient information computed at each pixel. SURF is concerned with combinations of HAAR wavelets or local rectangular regions of integrated pixel values, which reduces the significance of individual pixel values.

For the integral image-based methods using HAAR-like features such as SURF and Viola Jones, here are a few hypothetical pre-processing options.

1. **Do nothing.** HAAR features are computed from integral images simply by summing local region pixel values; no fine structure in the local pixels is preserved in the sum, so one option is to do nothing for image pre-processing.

2. **Noise removal.** This does not seem to be needed in the HAAR pre-processing stage, since the integral image summing in local regions has a tendency to filter out noise.

3. **Illumination problems.** This may require pre-processing;for example, contrast enhancement may be a good idea if the illumination of the training data is different from the current frame. One pre-processing approach in this situation is to compute a global contrast metric for the images in the training set, and then compute the same global contrast metric in each frame and adjust the image contrast if the contrast diverges beyond a threshold to get closer to the desired global contrast metric. Methods for contrast enhancement include LUT remapping, global histogram equalization, and local adaptive histogram equalization.

4. **Blur.** If blur is a problem in the current frame, it may manifest similar to a local contrast problem, so local contrast enhancement may be needed, such as a sharpen filter. Computing a global statistical metric such as an SDM as part of the ground truth data to measure local or global contrast may be useful; if the current image diverges too much in contrast, a suitable contrast enhancement may be applied as a pre-processing step.

Note in Figure 2-2 that increasing the local-region contrast results in larger gradients and more apparent edges. A feature descriptor that relies on local gradient information is affected by the local contrast.

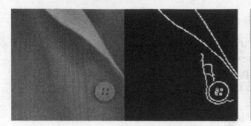

Figure 2-2. *The effects of local contrast on gradients and edge detection: (Left) Original image and Sobel edges. (Right) Contrasted adjusted image to amplify local region details and resulting Sobel edges*

For the SIFT-type descriptors that use local area gradients, pre-processing may be helpful to enhance the local gradients prior to computation, so as to affect certain features:

1. **Blur.** This will inhibit gradient magnitude computation and may make it difficult to determine gradient direction, so perhaps a local rank filter, high-pass filter, or sharpen filter should be employed.

2. **Noise.** This will exacerbate local gradient computations and make them unreliable, so perhaps applying one of several existing noise-removal algorithms can help.

3. **Contrast.** If local contrast is not high enough, gradient computations are difficult and unreliable. Perhaps a local histogram equalization, LUT remap, rank filter, or even a sharpen filter can be applied to improve results.

Basis Space Family Pre-Processing

It is not possible to generalize image pre-processing for basis space methods, since they are quite diverse, according to the taxonomy we are following in this work. As discussed in Chapters 4, 5, and 6, basis space methods include Fourier, wavelets, visual vocabularies, KTL, and others. However, here we provide a few general observations on pre-processing.

1. **Fourier Methods, wavelets, Slant transform, Walsh Hadamard, KLT.** These methods transform the data into another domain for analysis, and it is hard to suggest any pre-processing without knowing the intended application. For example, computing the Fourier spectrum produces magnitude and phase, and phase is shown to be useful in feature description to provide invariance to blur, as reported in the LPQ linear phase quantization method described in Chapter 6, so a blurry image may not be a problem in this case.

2. **Sparse coding and visual vocabularies.** These methods rely on local feature descriptors, which could be SURF, SIFT, LBP, or any other desired feature, derived from pixels in the spatial domain. Therefore, the method for feature description will determine the best approach for pre-processing. For example, methods that use correlation and raw pixel patches as sparse codes may not require any pre-processing. Or perhaps some minimal pre-processing can be used, such as illumination normalization to balance contrast, local histogram equalization or a LUT contrast remap.

In Figure 2-3, the contrast adjustment does not have much affect on Fourier methods, since there is no dominant structure in the image. Fourier spectrums typically reveal that the dominant structure and power is limited to lower frequencies that are in the center of the quadrant-shifted 2D plot. For images with dominant structures, such as lines and other shapes, the Fourier power spectrum will show the structure and perhaps pre-processing may be more valuable. Also, the Fourier power spectrum display is scaled to a logarithmic value and does not show all the details linearly, so a linear spectrum rendering might show the lower frequencies scaled and magnified better for erase of viewing.

Figure 2-3. *In this example, no benefit is gained from pre-processing as shown in the Fourier spectrum; (Left) Before. (Right) After contrast adjusting the input image*

Polygon Shape Family Pre-Processing

Polygon shapes are potentially the most demanding features when considering image pre-processing steps, since as shown in Table 2-1, the range of potential pre-processing methods is quite large and the choice of methods to employ is very data-dependent. Possibly because of the challenges and intended use-cases for polygon shape measurements, they are used only in various niche applications, such as cell biology.

One of the most common methods employed for image preparation prior to polygon shape measurements is to physically correct the lighting and select the subject background. For example, in automated microscopy applications, slides containing cells are prepared with florescent dye to highlight features in the cells, then the illumination angle and position are carefully adjusted under magnification to provide a uniform background under each cell feature to be measured; the resulting images are then much easier to segment.

As illustrated in Figures 2-4 and 2-5, if the pre-processing is wrong, the resulting shape feature descriptors are not very useful. Here are some of the more salient options for pre-processing prior to shape based feature extraction, then we'll survey a range of other methods later in this chapter.

Figure 2-4. *Use of thresholding to solve problems during image pre-processing to prepare images for polygon shape measurement: (Left) Original image. (Center) Thresholded red channel image. (Right) Perimeter tracing above a threshold*

Figure 2-5. *Another sequence of morphological pre-processing steps preceding polygon shape measurement: (Left) Original image. (Center) Range thresholded and dilated red color channel. (Right) Morphological perimeter shapes taken above a threshold*

1. **Illumination corrections.** Typically critical for defining the shape and outline of binary features. For example, if perimeter tracking or boundary segmentation is based on edges or thresholds, uneven illumination will cause problems, since the boundary definition becomes indistinct. If the illumination cannot be corrected, then other segmentation methods not based on thresholds are available, such as texture-based segmentation.

2. **Blur and focus corrections.** Perhaps not as critical as illumination for polygon shape detection, since the segmentation of object boundary and shape is less sensitive to blur.

3. **Filtering and noise removal.** Shape detection is somewhat tolerant of noise, depending on the type of noise. Shot noise or spot noise may not present a problem, and is easily removed using various noise-cleaning methods.

4. **Thresholding.** This is critical for polygon shape detection methods. Many thresholding methods are employed, ranging from the simple binary thresholding to local adaptive thresholding methods discussed later in this chapter. Thresholding is a problematic operation and requires algorithm parameter fine-tuning in addition to careful control of the light source position and direction to deal with shadows.

5. **Edge enhancements.** May be useful for perimeter contour definition.

6. **Morphology.** One of the most common methods employed to prepare polygon shapes for measurement, covered later in this chapter in some detail. Morphology is used to alter the shapes, presumably for the better, mostly by combinations or pipelines of erosion and dilation operations, as shown in Figure 2-5. Morphological examples include object area boundary cleanup, spur removal, and general line and perimeter cleanup and smoothing.

7. **Segmentation.** These methods use structure or texture in the image, rather than threshold, as a basis for dividing an image into connected regions or polygons. A few common segmentation methods are surveyed later in this chapter.

8. **Area/Region processing.** Convolution filter masks such as sharpen or blur, as well as statistical filters such as rank filters or media filters, are potentially useful prior to segmentation.

9. **Point processing.** Arithmetic scaling of image data point by point, such as multiplying each pixel by a given value followed by a clipping operation, as well as LUT processing, often is useful prior to segmentation.

10. **Color space conversions.** Critical for dealing accurately with color features, covered later in this chapter.

As shown In Figure 2-4, a range thresholding method uses the red color channel, since the table background has a lot of red color and can be thresholded easily in red to remove the table top. The image is thresholded by clipping values outside an intensity band; note that the bottom right USB stick is gone after thresholding, since it is red and below the threshold. Also note that the bottom center white USB stick is also mostly gone, since it is white (max RGB values) and above the threshold. The right image shows an attempt to trace a perimeter above a threshold; it's still not very good, as more pre-processing steps are needed.

The Taxonomy of Image Processing Methods

Before we survey image pre-processing methods, it is useful to have a simple taxonomy to frame the discussion. The taxonomy suggested is a set of operations, including point, line, area, algorithmic, and data conversions, as illustrated in Figure 2-6. The basic categories of image pre-processing operations introduced in Figure 2-1 fit into this simple taxonomy. Note that each stage of the vision pipeline, depending on intended use, may have predominant tasks and corresponding pre-processing operations.

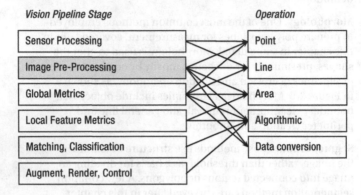

Figure 2-6. *Simplified, typical image processing taxonomy, as applied across the vision pipeline*

We provide a brief introduction to the taxonomy here, followed by a more detailed discussion in Chapter 5. Note that the taxonomy follows memory layout and memory access patterns for the image data. Memory layout particularly affects performance and power.

Point

Point operations deal with one pixel at a time, with no consideration of neighboring pixels. For example, point processing operations can be divided into math, Boolean, and pixel value compare substitution sections, as shown in Table 2-2 in the section later on "Point Filtering." Other point processing examples include color conversions and numeric data conversions.

Line

Line operations deal with discrete lines of pixels or data, with no regard to prior or subsequent lines. Examples include the FFT, which is a separable transform, where pixel lines and columns can be independently processed in parallel as 1D FFT line operations. If an algorithm requires lines of data, then optimizations for image pre-processing memory layout, pipelined read/write, and parallel processing can be made. Optimizations are covered in Chapter 8.

Area

Area operations typically require local blocks of pixels—for example, spatial filtering via kernel masks, convolution, morphology, and many other operations. Area operations generate specific types of memory traffic, and can be parallelized using fine-grained methods such as common shaders in graphics processors and coarse-grained thread methods.

Algorithmic

Some image pre-processing methods are purely serial or algorithmic code. It is difficult or even impossible to parallelize these blocks of code. In some cases, algorithmic blocks can be split into a few separate threads for coarse-grained parallelism or else pipelined, as discussed in Chapter 8.

Data Conversions

While the tasks are mundane and obvious, significant time can be spent doing simple data conversions. For example, integer sensor data may be converted to floating point for geometric computations or color space conversions. Data conversions are a significant part of image pre-processing in many cases. Example conversions include:

- Integer bit-depth conversions (8/16/32/64)

- Floating point conversions (single precision to double precision)

- Fixed point to integer or float

- Any combination of float to integer and vice versa

- Color conversions to and from various color spaces

- Conversion for basis space compute, such as integer to and from float for FFT

Design attention to data conversions and performance are in order and can provide a good return on investment, as discussed in Chapter 8.

Colorimetry

In this section, we provide a brief overview of color science to guide feature description, with attention to color accuracy, color spaces, and color conversions. If a feature descriptor is using color, then the color representation and processing should be carefully designed, accurate, and suited to the application. For example, in some applications it is possible to recognize an object using color alone, perhaps recognizing an automobile using its paint color, assuming that the vendor has chosen a unique paint color each year for each model. By combining color with another simple feature, such as shape, an effective descriptor can be devised.

Color Science is a well-understood field defined by international standards and amply described in the literature [249,250,251]. We list only a few resources here.

- The Rochester Institute of Technology's Munsel Color Science Laboratory is among the leading research institutions in the area or color science and imaging. It provides a wide range of resources and has strong ties to industry imaging giants such as Kodak, Xerox, and others.

- The International Commission on Illumination (CIE) provides standard illuminant data for a range of light sources as it pertains to color science, as well as standards for the well-known color spaces CIE XYZ, CIE Lab, and CIE Luv.

- The ICC International Color Consortium provides the ICC standard color profiles for imaging devices, as well as many other industry standards, including the sRGB color space for color displays.

- Proprietary color management systems, developed by industry leaders, include the Adobe CMM and Adobe RGB, Apple ColorSync, and HP ColorSmart; perhaps the most advanced is Microsoft's Windows Color System, which is based on Canon's earlier Kyuanos system using on CIECAM02.

Overview of Color Management Systems

A full-blown color management system may not be needed for a computer vision application, but the methods of color management are critical to understand when you are dealing with color. As illustrated in Figure 2-7, a color management system converts colors between the device color spaces, such as RGB or sRGB, to and from a *colorimetric color space,* such as CIE Luv, Lab, Jch, or Jab, so as to perform *color gamut mapping.* Since each device can reproduce color only within a specific gamut or color range, gamut mapping is required to convert the colors to the closest possible match, using the mathematical models of each color device.

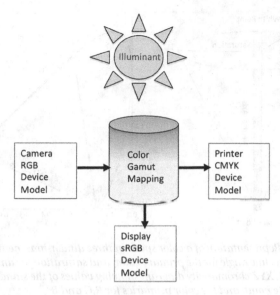

Figure 2-7. *Color management system with an RGB camera device model, sRGB display device model, CMYK printer device model, gamut mapping module, and an illuminant model*

Illuminants, White Point, Black Point, and Neutral Axis

An *illuminant* is a light source such as natural light or a fluorescent light, defined as the *white point* color by its spectral components and spectral power or color temperature. The white point color value in real systems is never perfectly white and is a measured quantity. The white point value and the oppositinal *black point* value together define the endpoints of the *neutral axis* (gray scale intensity) of the color space, which is not a perfectly straight color vector.

Color management relies on accurate information and measurements of the light source, or the illuminant. Color cannot be represented without accurate information about the light source under which the color is measured, since color appears different under florescent light versus natural light, and so on. The CIE standards define several values for standard illuminants, such as D65, shown in Figure 2-8.

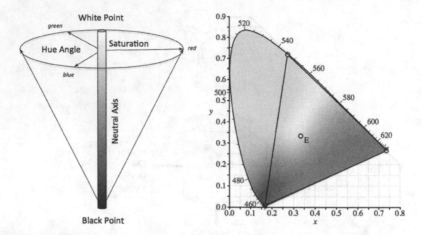

Figure 2-8. *(Left) Representation of a color space in three dimensions, neutral axis for the amount of white, hue angle for the primary color, and saturation for amount of color present. (Right) CIE XYZ chromaticity diagram showing values of the standard illuminant D65 OE as the white point, and the color primaries for R,G and B*

Device Color Models

Real devices like printers, displays, and cameras conventionally reproduce colors as compared against standard color patches that have been measured using calibrated light sources and spectrographic equipment—for example, the widely used Munsel color patches that define color in terms hue, value, and chroma (HVC) against standard illuminants. In order to effectively manage colors for a given device, a mathematical model or device color model must be created for each device, defining the anomalies in the device color gamut and its color gamut range.

For the color management system to be accurate, each real device must be spectrally characterized and modeled in a laboratory to create a mathematical device model, mapping the color gamut of each device against standard illumination models. The device model is used in the gamut transforms between color spaces.

Devices typically represent color using the primary and secondary colors RGB and CYMK. RGB is a primary, additive color space; starting with black, the RGB color primaries red, green, and blue are added to create colors. CYMK is a secondary color space, since the color components cyan, yellow, and magenta, are secondary combinations of the RGB primary colors; cyan = green plus blue, magenta = red plus blue, and yellow = red plus green. CYMK is also a subtractive color space, since the colors are subtracted from a white background to create specific colors.

Color Spaces and Color Perception

Colorimetric spaces represent color in abstract terms such as lightness, hue or color, and color saturation. Each color space is designed for a different reason, and each color space is useful for different types of analysis and processing. Example simple color spaces include HSV (hue, saturation, value) and HVC (hue, value, chroma). In the case of the CIE color spaces, the RGB color components are replaced by the standardized value CIE XYZ components as a basis for defining the CIE Luv and CIE Lab color spaces.

At the very high end of color science, we have the more recent CIECAM02 color models and color spaces such as Jch and Jab. CIECAM02 goes beyond just the colorimetry of the light source and the color patch itself to offer advanced color appearance modeling considerations that include the surroundings under which colors are measured [254,249].

While CIECAM02 may be overkill for most applications, it is worth some study. Color perception varies widely based on the surrounding against which the colors are viewed, the spectrum and angles of combined direct and ambient lighting, and the human visual system itself, since people do not all perceive color in the same way.

Gamut Mapping and Rendering Intent

Gamut mapping is the art and science of converting color between two color spaces and getting the best fit. Since the color gamuts of each device are different, gamut mapping is a challenge, and there are many different algorithms in use, with no clear winner. Depending on the intent of the rendering, different methods are useful—for example, gamut mapping from camera color space to a printer color space is different from mapping to an LCD display for viewing.

The CAM02 system provides a detailed model for guidance. For example, a color imaging device may capture the color blue very weakly, while a display may be able to display blue very well. Should the color gamut fitting method use color clipping or stretching? How should the difference between color gamuts be computed? Which color space? For an excellent survey of over 90 gamut mapping methods, see the work of Morovic [252].

In Figure 2-9 (left image), the sRGB color space is shown as fitting inside the Adobe RGB color space, illustrating that sRGB does not cover a gamut as wide as Adobe RGB. Each color gamut reproduces color differently, and each color space may be linear or warped internally. The right image in Figure 2-9 illustrates one gamut mapping method to determine the nearest color common to both color gamuts, using Euclidean distance and clipping; however, there are many other gamut mapping distance methods as well. Depending on the surrounding light and environment, color perception changes further complicating gamut mapping.

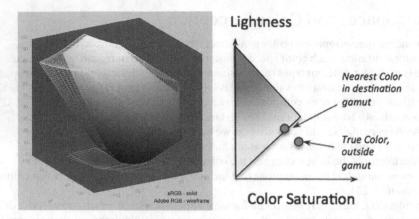

Figure 2-9. *The central problem of gamut mapping: (Left) Color sRGB and Adobe RGB color gamuts created using Gamutvision software. (Right) Gamut mapping details*

In gamut mapping there is a source gamut and a destination gamut. For example, the source could be a camera and the destination could be an LCD display. Depending on the rendering intent of the gamut conversion, different algorithms have been developed to convert color from source to destination gamuts. Using the *perceptual intent*, color saturation is mapped and kept within the boundaries of the destination gamut in an effort to preserve relative color strength; and out-of-gamut colors from the source are compressed into the destination gamut, which allows for a more reversible gamut map translation. Using the *colorimetric intent,* colors may be mapped straight across from source to destination gamut, and colors outside the destination gamut are simply clipped.

A common method of color correction is to rely on a simple gamma curve applied to the intensity channel to help the human eye better visualize the data, since the gamma curve brightens up the dark regions and compresses the light regions of the image, similar to the way the human visual system deals with light and dark regions. However, gamut correction bears no relationship to the true sensor data, so a calibrated, colorimetrically sound approach is recommended instead.

Practical Considerations for Color Enhancements

For image pre-processing, the color intensity is usually the only color information that should be enhanced, since the color intensity alone carries a lot of information and is commonly used. In addition, color processing cannot be easily done in RGB space while preserving relative color. For example, enhancing the RGB channels independently with a sharpen filter will lead to Moiré fringe artifacts when the RGB channels are recombined into a single rendering. So to sharpen the image, first *forward-convert* RGB to a color space such as HSV or YIQ, then sharpen the V or Y component, and then *inverse-convert* back to RGB. For example, to correct illumination in color, standard image processing methods such as LUT remap or histogram equalization will work, provided they are performed in the intensity space.

As a practical matter, for quick color conversions to gray scale from RGB, here are a few methods. (1) The G color channel is a good proxy for gray scale information, since as shown in the sensor discussion in Chapter 1, the RB wavelengths in the spectrum overlap heavily into the G wavelengths. (2) Simple conversion from RGB into gray scale intensity I can be done by taking I = R+G+B / 3. (3) The YIQ color space, used in the NTSC television broadcast standards, provides a simple forward/backward method of color conversion between RGB and a gray scale component Y, as follows:

$$\begin{bmatrix} R \\ G \\ B \end{bmatrix} = \begin{bmatrix} 1 & 0.9663 & 0.6210 \\ 1 & -0.2721 & -0.6474 \\ 1 & -1.1070 & 1.7046 \end{bmatrix} \begin{bmatrix} Y \\ I \\ Q \end{bmatrix}$$

$$\begin{bmatrix} Y \\ I \\ Q \end{bmatrix} = \begin{bmatrix} 0.299 & 0.587 & 0.114 \\ 0.595716 & -0.274453 & -0.321263 \\ 0.211456 & -0.522591 & 0.311135 \end{bmatrix} \begin{bmatrix} R \\ G \\ B \end{bmatrix}$$

Color Accuracy and Precision

If color accuracy is important, 8 bits per RGB color channel may not be enough. It is necessary to study the image sensor vendor's data sheets to understand how good the sensor really is. At the time of this writing, common image sensors are producing 10 to 14 bits of color information per RGB channel. Each color channel may have a different spectral response, as discussed in Chapter 1.

Typically, green is a good and fairly accurate color channel on most devices; red is usually good as well and may also have near infrared sensitivity if the IR filter is removed from the sensor; and blue is always a challenge since the blue wavelength can be hardest to capture in smaller silicon wells, which are close to the size of the blue wavelength, so the sensor vendor needs to pay special attention to blue ssnsing details.

Spatial Filtering

Filtering on discrete pixel arrays is considered *spatial filtering*, or time domain filtering, in contrast to filtering in the frequency domain using Fourier methods. Spatial filters are alternatives to frequency domain methods, and versatile processing methods are possible in the spatial domain.

Convolutional Filtering and Detection

Convolution is a fundamental signal processing operation easily computed as a discrete spatial processing operation, which is practical for 1D, 2D, and 3D processing. The basic idea is to combine, or convolve, two signals together, changing the source signal to be more like the filter signal. The source signal is the array of pixels in the image; the filter signal is a weighted kernel mask, such as a gradient peak shape and oriented edge shape or an otherwise weighted shape. For several examples of filter kernel mask shapes, see the section later in the chapter that discusses Sobel, Scharr, Prewitt, Roberts, Kirsch, Robinson, and Frei-Chen filter masks.

Convolution is typically used for filtering operations such as low-pass, band pass, and high-pass filters, but many filter shapes are possible to detect *features*, such as edge detection kernels tuned sensitive to edge orientation, or even point, corner, and contour detectors. Convolution is used as a detector in the method of convolution networks [85], as discussed in Chapter 4.

The sharpen kernel mask in Figure 2-10 (center image) is intended to amplify the center pixel in relation to the neighboring pixels. Each pixel is multiplied by its kernel position, and the result (right image) shows the center pixel as the sum of the convolution, which has been increased or amplified in relation to the neighboring pixels.

35	43	49
38	52	47
42	44	51

*

-1	-1	-1
-1	8	-1
-1	-1	-1

=

35	43	49
38	67	47
42	44	51

$-(35 + 43 + 49 + 47 + 51 + 44 + 42 + 38) + (52*8) = 67$

Figure 2-10. *Convolution, in this case a sharpen filter: (Left to right) Image data, sharpen filter, and resulting image data*

A convolution operation is typically followed up with a set of postprocessing point operations to clean up the data. Following are some useful postprocessing steps; many more are suggested in the "Point Filters" section that follows later in the chapter.

```
switch (post_processor)
{
case RESULT_ASIS:
        break;
case RESULT_PLUS_VALUE:
        sum += value;
        break;
```

```
case RESULT_MINUS_VALUE:
        sum -= value;
        break;
case RESULT_PLUS_ORIGINAL_TIMES_VALUE:
        sum = sum + (result * value);
        break;
case RESULT_MINUS_ORIGINAL_TIMES_VALUE:
        sum = sum - (result * value);
        break;
case ORIGINAL_PLUS_RESULT_TIMES_VALUE:
        sum = result + (sum * value);
        break;
case ORIGINAL_MINUS_RESULT_TIMES_VALUE:
        sum = result - (sum * value);
        break;
case ORIGINAL_LOW_CLIP:
        sum = (result < value ? value : result);
        break;
case ORIGINAL_HIGH_CLIP:
        sum = (result > value ? value : result);
        break;
}

switch (post_processing_sign)
{
case ABSOLUTE_VALUE:
        if (sum < 0) sum = -sum;
        if (sum > limit) sum = limit;
        break;
case POSITIVE_ONLY:
        if (sum < 0) sum = 0;
        if (sum > limit) sum = limit;
        break;
case NEGATIVE_ONLY:
        if (sum > 0) sum = 0;
        if (-sum > limit) sum = -limit;
        break;
case SIGNED:
        if (sum > limit) sum = limit;
        if (-sum > limit) sum = -limit;
        break;
}
```

Convolution is used to implement a variety of common filters including:

- **Gradient or sharpen filters,** which amplify and detect maxima and minima pixels. Examples include Laplacian.

- **Edge or line detectors,** where lines are connected gradients that reveal line segments or contours. Edge or line detectors can be steerable to a specific orientation, like vertical, diagonal, horizontal, or omni-directional; steerable filters as basis sets are discussed in Chapter 3.

- **Smoothing and blur filters,** which take neighborhood pixels.

Kernel Filtering and Shape Selection

Besides convolutional methods, kernels can be devised to capture regions of pixels generically for statistical filtering operations, where the pixels in the region are sorted into a list from low to high value. For example, assuming a 3x3 kernel region, we can devise the following statistical filters:

```
sort(&kernel, &image, &coordinates, &sorted_list);

switch (filter_type)
case RANK_FILTER:
        // Pick highest pixel in the list, rank = 8 for a 3x3 kernel 0..8
        // Could also pick the lowest, middle, or other rank
        image[center_pixel] = sorted_list[rank];
        break;
case MEDIAN_FILTER:
        // Median value is kernel size / 2, (3x3=9)/2=4 in this case
        image[center_pixel] = sorted_list[median];
        break;
case MAJORITY_FILTER:
        // Find the pixel value that occurs most often, count sorted pixel values
        count(&sorted_list, &counted_list);
        image[center_pixel] = counted_list[0];
        break;
}
```

The rank filter is a simple and powerful method that sorts each pixel in the region and substitutes a pixel of desired rank for the center pixel, such as substitution of the highest pixel in the region for the center pixel, or the median value or the majority value.

Shape Selection or Forming Kernels

Any regional operation can benefit from shape selection kernels to select pixels from the region and exclude others. Shape selection, or forming, can be applied as a pre-processing step to any image pre-processing algorithm or to any feature extraction method. Shape selection kernels can be binary truth kernels to select which pixels from the source image are used as a group, or to mark pixels that should receive individual processing. Shape selection kernels, as shown in Figure 2-11, can be applied to local feature descriptors and detectors also; similar but sometimes more complex local region pixel selection methods are often used with local binary descriptor methods, as discussed in Chapter 4.

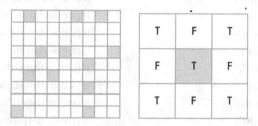

Figure 2-11. *Truth and shape kernels: (Left) A shape kernel gray kernel position indicating a pixel to process or use—for example, a pixel to convolve prior to a local binary pattern point-pair comparison detector.(Right) A truth shape kernel specifying pixels to use for region average, favoring diagonals—T means use this pixel, F means do not use*

Point Filtering

Individual pixel processing is typically overlooked when experimenting with image pre-processing. Point processing is amenable to many optimization methods, as will be discussed in Chapter 8. Convolution, as discussed above, is typically followed by point postprocessing steps. Table 2-2 illustrates several common pixel point processing methods in the areas of math operations, Boolean operations, and compare and substitution operations, which seem obvious but can be quite valuable for exploring image enhancement methods to enhance feature extraction.

Table 2-2. *Possible Point Operations*

// Math ops	// Compare & Substitution ops
NAMES math_ops[] = {	NAMES change_ops[] = {
"src + value -> dst",	"if (src = thresh) value -> dst",
"src - value -> dst",	"if (src = dst) value -> dst",
"src * value -> dst",	"if (src != thresh) value -> dst",
"src / value -> dst",	"if (src != thresh) src -> dst",
"(src + dst) * value -> dst",	"if (src != dst) value -> dst",
"(src - dst) * value -> dst",	"if (src != dst) src -> dst",
"(src * dst) * value -> dst",	"if (src >=thresh) value -> dst",
"(src / dst) * value -> dst",	"if (src >=thresh) src -> dst",
"sqroot(src) + value -> dst",	"if (src >=dst) value -> dst",
"src * src + value -> dst",	"if (src >=dst) src -> dst",
"exp(src) + value -> dst",	"if (src <= thresh) value -> dst",
"log(src) + value -> dst",	"if (src <= thresh) src -> dst",
"log10(src) + value -> dst",	"if (src <= dst) value -> dst",
"pow(src ^ value) -> dst",	"if (src <= dst) src -> dst",
"sin(src) + value -> dst",	"if (lo <= src <= hi) value -> dst",
"cos(src) + value -> dst",	"if (lo <= src <= hi) src -> dst",
"tan(src) + value -> dst",	};
"(value / max(all_src)) * src -> dst",	
"src - mean(all_src) -> dst",	
"absval(src) + value -> dst",	
};	
// **Boolean ops**	
NAMES bool_ops[] = {	
"src AND value -> dst",	
"src OR value -> dst",	
"src XOR value -> dst",	
"src AND dst -> dst",	
"src OR dst -> dst",	
"src XOR dst -> dst",	
"NOT(src) -> dst",	
"LO_CLIP(src, value) -> dst",	
"LO_CLIP(src, dst) -> dst",	
"HI_CLIP(src, value) -> dst",	
"HI_CLIP(src, dst) -> dst",	
};	

Noise and Artifact Filtering

Noise is usually an artifact of the image sensor, but not always. There are several additional artifacts that may be present in an image as well. The goal of noise removal is to remove the noise without distorting the underlying image, and the goal of removing artifacts is similar. Depending on the type of noise or artifact, different methods may be employed for pre-processing. The first step is to classify the noise or artifact, and then to devise the right image pre-processing strategy.

- **Speckle, random noise.** This type of noise is apparently random, and can be removed using a rank filter or median filter.

- **Transient frequency spike.** This can be determined using a Fourier spectrum and can be removed using a notch filter over the spike; the frequency spike will likely be in an outlier region of the spectrum, and may manifest as a bright spot in the image.

- **Jitter and judder line noise.** This is an artifact particular to video streams, usually due to telecine artifacts, motion of the camera or the image scene, and is complex to correct. It is primarily line oriented rather than just single-pixel oriented.

- **Motion blur.** This can be caused by uniform or nonuniform motion and is a complex problem; several methods exist for removal; see reference[305].

Standard approaches to noise removal are discussed by Gonzalez[4]. The most basic approach is to remove outliers, and various approaches are taken, including thresholding and local region based statistical filters such as the rank filter and median filter. Weighted image averaging is also sometime used for removing noise from video streams; assuming the camera and subjects are not moving, it can work well. Although deblurring or Gaussian smoothing convolution kernels are sometimes used to remove noise, such methods may cause smearing and may not be the best approach.

A survey of noise-removal methods and a performance comparison model are provided by Buades et al.[511]. This source includes a description of the author's NL-means method, which uses nonlocal pixel value statistics in addition to Euclidean distance metrics between similar weighted pixel values over larger image regions to identify and remove noise.

Integral Images and Box Filters

Integral images are used to quickly find the average value of a rectangular group of pixels. An integral image is also known as a *summed area table*, where each pixel in the integral image is the integral sum of all pixels to the left and above the current pixel. The integral image can be calculated quickly in a single pass over the image. Each value in the summed area table is calculated using the current pixel value from the image $i(n,m)$ combined with previous entries $s(n,m)$ made into the summed area table, as follows:

$$s(x,y) = i(x,y) + s(x-1,y) + s(x,y-1) - s(x-1,y-1)$$

63

As shown in Figure 2-12, to find a HAAR rectangle feature value from the integral image, only four points in the integral image table A,B,C,D are used, rather than tens or hundreds of points from the image. The integral image sum of a rectangle region can then be divided by the size of the rectangle region to yield the average value, which is also known as a *box filter*.

05	02	05	02
03	06	03	06
05	02	05	02
03	06	03	06

05	07	12	14
08	16	24	32
13	23	36	46
16	32	48	64

05$_A$	07	12$_B$	14
08	16	24	32
13$_D$	23	36$_C$	46
16	32	48	64

Figure 2-12. *(Left) Pixels in an image. (Center) Integral image. (Right) Region where a box filter value is computed from four points in the integral image: sum = s(A) + s(D) – s(B) – s(C)*

Integral images and box filters are used in many computer vision methods, such as HAAR filters and feature descriptors. Integral images are also used as a fast alternative to a Gaussian filter of a small region, as a way to lower compute costs. In fact, descriptors with a lot of overlapping region processing, such as BRISK [131], make effective use of integral images for descriptor building and use integral images as a proxy for a fast Gaussian blur or convolution.

Edge Detectors

The goal of an edge detector is to enhance the connected gradients in an image, which may take the form of an edge, contour, line, or some connected set of edges. Many edge detectors are simply implemented as kernel operations, or convolutions, and we survey the common methods here.

Kernel Sets: Sobel, Scharr, Prewitt, Roberts, Kirsch, Robinson, and Frei-Chen

The Sobel operator detects gradient magnitude and direction for edge detection. The basic method is shown here.

1. Perform two directional Sobel filters (x and y axis) using basic derivative kernel approximations such as 3x3 kernels, using values as follows:

2.
$$S_y = . \begin{bmatrix} -1 & -2 & -1 \\ 0 & 0 & 0 \\ 1 & 2 & 1 \end{bmatrix}$$

$$S_x = . \begin{bmatrix} -1 & 0 & 1 \\ -2 & 0 & 2 \\ -1 & 0 & 1 \end{bmatrix}$$

3. Calculate the total gradient as $G_v = |S_x| + |S_y|$

4. Calculate the gradient direction as $theta = ATAN(S_y/S_x)$

5. Calculate gradient magnitude $G_m = \sqrt{Sy^2 + Sx^2}$

Variations exist in the area size and shape of the kernels used for Sobel edge detection. In addition to the Sobel kernels shown above, other similar kernel sets are used in practice, so long as the kernel values cancel and add up to zero, such as those kernels proposed by Scharr, Prewitt, Roberts, Robinson, and Frei-Chen, as well as Laplacian approximation kernels. The Frei-Chen kernels are designed to be used together at a set, so the edge is the weighted sum of all the kernels. See reference[4] for more information on edge detection masks. Some kernels have compass orientations, such as those developed by Kirsch, Robinson, and others. See Figure 2-13.

$$\begin{pmatrix} 3 & 10 & 3 \\ 0 & 0 & 0 \\ -3 & -10 & -3 \end{pmatrix} \begin{pmatrix} 3 & 0 & -3 \\ 10 & 0 & -10 \\ 3 & 0 & -3 \end{pmatrix} \text{Scharr}$$

$$\begin{pmatrix} 1 & 0 \\ 0 & -1 \end{pmatrix} \begin{pmatrix} 0 & 1 \\ -1 & 0 \end{pmatrix} \text{Roberts}$$

$$\begin{pmatrix} 1 & 1 & 1 \\ 0 & 0 & 0 \\ -1 & -1 & -1 \end{pmatrix} \begin{pmatrix} 1 & 0 & -1 \\ 1 & 0 & -1 \\ 1 & 0 & -1 \end{pmatrix} \text{Prewitt}$$

$$\begin{pmatrix} 0 & 1 & 0 \\ 1 & -4 & 1 \\ 0 & 1 & 0 \end{pmatrix} \begin{pmatrix} .5 & 1 & .5 \\ 1 & -6 & 1 \\ .5 & 1 & .5 \end{pmatrix} \begin{pmatrix} 1 & 1 & 1 \\ 1 & -8 & 1 \\ 1 & 1 & 0 \end{pmatrix} \begin{pmatrix} 1 & -2 & 1 \\ -2 & 4 & -2 \\ 1 & -2 & 1 \end{pmatrix} \begin{pmatrix} -2 & 1 & -2 \\ 1 & 4 & 1 \\ -2 & 1 & -2 \end{pmatrix} \text{Laplacians}$$

$$\begin{pmatrix} 5 & 5 & 5 \\ -3 & 0 & -3 \\ -3 & -3 & -3 \end{pmatrix} \begin{pmatrix} 5 & 5 & -3 \\ 5 & 0 & -3 \\ -3 & -3 & -3 \end{pmatrix} \begin{pmatrix} 5 & -3 & 5 \\ 5 & 0 & -3 \\ 5 & -3 & -3 \end{pmatrix} \begin{pmatrix} -3 & -3 & -3 \\ 5 & 0 & -3 \\ 5 & 5 & -3 \end{pmatrix} \text{Kirsch Compass}$$

$$\begin{pmatrix} -3 & -3 & -3 \\ -3 & 0 & -3 \\ 5 & 5 & 5 \end{pmatrix} \begin{pmatrix} -3 & -3 & -3 \\ -3 & 0 & 5 \\ -3 & 5 & 5 \end{pmatrix} \begin{pmatrix} -3 & -3 & 5 \\ -3 & 0 & 5 \\ -3 & -3 & 5 \end{pmatrix} \begin{pmatrix} -3 & 5 & 5 \\ -3 & 0 & 5 \\ -3 & -3 & -3 \end{pmatrix} \text{Kirsch Compass}$$

$$\begin{pmatrix} -1 & 0 & 1 \\ -2 & 0 & 2 \\ -1 & 0 & 1 \end{pmatrix} \begin{pmatrix} 0 & 1 & 2 \\ -1 & 0 & 1 \\ -2 & -1 & 0 \end{pmatrix} \begin{pmatrix} 1 & 2 & 1 \\ 0 & 0 & 0 \\ -1 & -2 & -1 \end{pmatrix} \begin{pmatrix} 2 & 1 & 0 \\ 1 & 0 & -1 \\ 0 & -1 & -2 \end{pmatrix} \text{Robinson Compass}$$

$$\begin{pmatrix} 1 & 0 & -1 \\ 2 & 0 & -2 \\ 1 & 0 & -2 \end{pmatrix} \begin{pmatrix} 0 & -1 & -2 \\ 1 & 0 & -1 \\ 2 & 1 & 0 \end{pmatrix} \begin{pmatrix} -1 & -2 & -1 \\ 0 & 0 & 0 \\ 1 & 2 & 1 \end{pmatrix} \begin{pmatrix} -2 & -1 & 0 \\ -1 & 0 & 1 \\ 0 & 1 & 2 \end{pmatrix} \text{Robinson Compass}$$

$$\frac{1}{2\sqrt{2}} \begin{pmatrix} 1 & \sqrt{2} & 1 \\ 0 & 0 & 0 \\ -1 & -\sqrt{2} & -1 \end{pmatrix}, \frac{1}{2\sqrt{2}} \begin{pmatrix} -1 & 0 & 1 \\ -\sqrt{2} & 0 & \sqrt{2} \\ -1 & 0 & 1 \end{pmatrix}, \frac{1}{2\sqrt{2}} \begin{pmatrix} 0 & -1 & \sqrt{2} \\ 1 & 0 & -1 \\ -\sqrt{2} & 1 & 0 \end{pmatrix} \text{Fre - Chen}$$

$$\frac{1}{2\sqrt{2}} \begin{pmatrix} \sqrt{2} & -1 & 0 \\ 1 & 0 & -1 \\ 0 & 1 & -\sqrt{2} \end{pmatrix}, \frac{1}{2} \begin{pmatrix} 0 & -1 & 0 \\ -1 & 0 & -1 \\ 0 & -1 & 0 \end{pmatrix}, \frac{1}{2} \begin{pmatrix} -1 & 0 & 1 \\ 0 & 0 & 0 \\ 1 & 0 & -1 \end{pmatrix} \text{Frei - Chen}$$

$$\frac{1}{6} \begin{pmatrix} 1 & -2 & 1 \\ -2 & 4 & -2 \\ 1 & -2 & 1 \end{pmatrix}, \frac{1}{6} \begin{pmatrix} -2 & 1 & -2 \\ 1 & 4 & 1 \\ -2 & 1 & -2 \end{pmatrix}, \frac{1}{3} \begin{pmatrix} 1 & 1 & 1 \\ 1 & 1 & 1 \\ 1 & 1 & 1 \end{pmatrix} \text{Frei - CHen}$$

Figure 2-13. *Several edge detection kernel masks*

Canny Detector

The Canny method [154] is similar to the Sobel-style gradient magnitude and direction method, but it adds postprocessing to clean up the edges.

1. Perform a Gaussian blur over the image using a selected convolution kernel (7x7, 5,5, etc.), depending on the level of low-pass filtering desired.

2. Perform two directional Sobel filters (*x* & *y* axis).

3. Perform nonmaximal value suppression in the direction of the gradient to set to zero (0) pixels not on an edge (minima values).

4. Perform hysteresis thresholding within a band (high,low) of values along the gradient direction to eliminate edge aliasing and outlier artifacts and to create better connected edges.

Transform Filtering, Fourier, and Others

This section deals with basis spaces and image transforms in the context of image filtering, the most common and widely used being the Fourier transform. A more comprehensive treatment of basis spaces and transforms in the context of feature description is provided in Chapter 3. A good reference for transform filtering in the context of image processing is provided by Pratt [9].

Why use transforms to switch domains? To make image pre-processing easier or more effective, or to perform feature description and matching more efficiently. In some cases, there is no better way to enhance an image or describe a feature than by transforming it to another domain—for example, for removing noise and other structural artifacts as outlier frequency components of a Fourier spectrum, or to compact describe and encode image features using HAAR basis features.

Fourier Transform Family

The Fourier transform is very well known and covered in the standard reference by Bracewell [227], and it forms the basis for a family of related transforms. Several methods for performing fast Fourier transform (FFT) are common in image and signal processing libraries. Fourier analysis has touched nearly every area of world affairs, through science, finance, medicine, and industry, and has been hailed as "the most important numerical algorithm of our lifetime" [290]. Here, we discuss the fundamentals of Fourier analysis, and a few branches of the Fourier transform family with image pre-processing applications.

The Fourier transform can be computed using optics, at the speed of light [516]. However, we are interested in methods applicable to digital computers.

Fundamentals

The basic idea of Fourier analysis [227,4,9] is concerned with decomposing periodic functions into a series of sine and cosine waves (Figure 2-14). The Fourier transform is bi-directional, between a periodic wave and a corresponding series of harmonic basis functions in the frequency domain, where each basis function is a sine or cosine function, spaced at whole harmonic multiples from the base frequency. The result of the forward FFT is a complex number composed of magnitude and phase data for each sine and cosine component in the series, also referred to as *real data* and *imaginary data*.

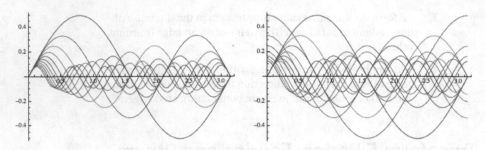

Figure 2-14. *(Left) Harmonic series of sine waves. (Right) Fourier harmonic series of sine and cosine waves*

Arbitrary periodic functions can be synthesized by summing the desired set of Fourier basis functions, and periodic functions can be decomposed using the Fourier transform into the basic functions as a Fourier series. The Fourier transform is invertible between the time domain of discrete pixels and the frequency domain, where both magnitude and phase of each basis function are available for filtering and analysis, magnitude being the most commonly used component.

How is the FFT implemented for 2D images or 3D volumes? The Fourier transform is a *separable transform* and so can be implemented as a set of parallel 1D FFT line transforms (Figure 2-15). So, for 2D images and 3D volumes, each dimension, such as the x, y, z dimension, can be computed in place, in parallel as independent x lines, then the next dimension or y columns can be computed in place as parallel lines, then the z dimension can be computed as parallel lines in place, and the final results are scaled according to the transform. Any good 1D FFT algorithm can be set up to process 2D images or 3D volumes using parallelization.

$$2\left(\theta\left(\frac{x}{L}\right)-\theta\left(\frac{x}{L}-1\right)\right)-1$$

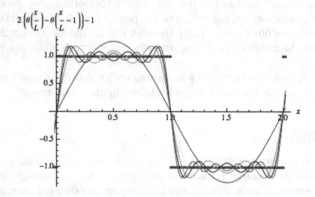

Figure 2-15. *Fourier series and Fourier transform concepts showing a square wave approximated from a series of Fourier harmonics*

For accuracy of the inverse transform to go from frequency space back to pixels, the FFT computations will require two double precision 64-bit floating point buffers to hold the magnitude and phase data, since transcendental functions such as sine and cosine require high floating point precision for accuracy; using 64-bit double precision floating point numbers for the image data allows a forward transform of an image to be computed, followed by an inverse transform, with no loss of precision compared to the original image—of course, very large images will need more than double precision.

Since 64-bit floating point is typically slower and of higher power, owing to the increased compute requirements and silicon real estate in the ALU, as well as the heavier memory bandwidth load, methods for FFT optimization have been developed using integer transforms, and in some cases fixed point, and these are good choices for many applications.

Note in Figure 2-16 that the low-pass filter (center right) is applied to preserve primarily low-frequency information toward the center of the plot and it reduces high-frequency components toward the edges, resulting in the filtered image at the far right.

Figure 2-16. *Basic Fourier filtering: (Left) Original. (Center left) Fourier spectrum. (Center right) Low-pass filter shape used to multiply against Fourier magnitude. (Right) Inverse transformed image with low-pass filter*

A key Fourier application is filtering, where the original image is forward-transformed into magnitude and phase; the magnitude component is shown as a Fourier power spectrum of the magnitude data, which reveals structure in the image as straight lines and blocks, or outlier structures or spots that are typically noise. The magnitude can be filtered by various filter shapes, such as high-pass, low-pass, band pass, and spot filters to remove spot noise, to affect any part of the spectrum.

In Figure 2-16, a circular symmetric low-pass filter shape is shown with a smooth distribution of filter coefficients from 1 to 0, with high multiplicands in the center at the low frequencies, ramping down to zero toward the high frequencies at the edge. The filter shape is multiplied in the frequency domain against the magnitude data to filter out the higher frequency components, which are toward the outside of the spectrum plot, followed by an inverse FFT to provide the filtered image. The low-frequency components are toward the center; typically these are most interesting and so most of the image power is contained in the low-frequency components. Any other filter shape can be used, such as a spot filter, to remove noise or any of the structure at a specific location of the spectrum.

Fourier Family of Transforms

The Fourier transform is the basis for a family of transforms [4], some of which are:

1.   **DFT, FFT.** The discrete version of the Fourier transform, often implemented as a fast version, or FFT, commonly used for image processing. There are many methods of implementing the FFT [227].

2.   **Sine transform.** Fourier formulation composed of only sine terms.

3.   **Cosine transform.** Fourier formulation composed of only cosine terms.

4.   **DCT, DST, MDCT.** The discrete Fourier transform is implemented in several formulations: discrete sine transform (DST), discrete cosine transform (DCT), and the modified discrete cosine transform (MDCT). These related methods operate on a macroblock, such as 16x16 or 8x8 pixel region, and can therefore be highly optimized for compute use with integers rather than floating point. Typically the DCT is implemented in hardware for video encode and decode applications for motion estimation of the macro blocks from frame to frame. The MDCT operates on overlapping macroblock regions for compute efficiency.

5.   **Fast Hartley transform, DHT.** This was developed as an alternative formulation of the Fourier transform for telephone transmission analysis about 1925, forgotten for many years, then rediscovered and promoted again by Bracewell[227] as an alternative to the Fourier transform. The Hartley transform is a symmetrical formulation of the Fourier transform, decomposing a signal into two sets of sinusoidal functions taken together as a *cosine-and-sine* or *cas( )* function, where $cas(vx) \equiv cos(vx) + sin(vx)$. This includes positive and negative frequency components and operates entirely on real numbers for input and output. The Hartley formulation avoids complex numbers as used in the Fourier complex exponential $exp\,(\,j\,w\,x\,)$. The Hartley tansform has been developed into optimized versions called the DHT, shown to be about equal in speed to an optimized FFT.

Other Transforms

Several other transforms may be used for image filtering, including wavelets, steerable filter banks, and others that will be described in Chapter 3, in the context of feature description. Note that transforms often have many common uses and applications that overlap, such as image description, image coding, image compression, and feature description.

Morphology and Segmentation

For simplicity, we define the goal of morphology as shape and boundary definition, and the goal of segmentation is to define regions with internal similarity, such as textural or statistical similarity. *Morphology* is used to identify features as polygon shaped regions that can be described with shape metrics, as will be discussed in Chapters 3 and 6, distinct from local interest point and feature descriptors using other methods. An image is *segmented into regions* to allow independent processing and analysis of each region according to some policy or processing goal. Regions cover an area smaller than the global image but usually larger than local interest point features, so an application might make use of global, regional, and small local interest point metrics together as an *object signature*.

An excellent review of several segmentation methods can be found in work by Haralick and Shapiro[321]. In practice, segmentation and morphology are not easy: results are often less useful than expected, trial and error is required, too many methods are available to provide any strict guidance, and each image is different. So here we only survey the various methods to introduce the topic and illustrate the complexity. An overview of region segmentation methods is shown in Table 2-3.

Table 2-3. *Segmentation Methods*

Method	Description
Morphological segmentation	The region is defined based on thresholding and morphology operators.
Texture-based segmentation	The texture of a region is used to group like textures into connected regions.
Transform-based segmentation	Basis space features are used to segment the image.
Edge boundary segmentation	Gradients or edges alone are used to define the boundaries of the region with edge linking in some cases to form boundaries.
Color segmentation	Color information is used to define regions.
Super-Pixel Segmentation	Kernels and distance transforms are used to group pixels and change their values to a common value.
Gray scale / luminance segmentation	Gray scale thresholds or bands are used to define the regions.
Depth segmentation	Depth maps and distance from viewer is used to segment the image into foreground, background, or other gradations of inter-scene features.

Binary Morphology

Binary morphology operates on binary images, which are created from other scalar intensity channel images. Morphology [9] is used to *morph* a feature shape into a new shape for analysis by removing shape noise or outliers, and by strengthening predominant feature characteristics. For example, isolated pixels may be removed using morphology, thin features can be fattened, and the predominant shape is still preserved. Note that morphology all by itself is quite a large field of study, with applications to general object recognition, cell biology, medicine, particle analysis, and automated microscopy. We introduce the fundamental concepts of morphology here for binary images, and then follow this section with applications to gray scale and color data.

Binary morphology starts with binarizing images, so typically thresholding is first done to create images with binary-valued pixels composed of 8-bit black and white values, 0-value = black and 255-value = white. Thresholding methods are surveyed later in this chapter, and thresholding is critical prior to morphology.

Binary morphology is a neighborhood operation, and can use a forming kernel with truth values, as shown in Figure 2-17. The forming kernel guides the morphology process by defining which surrounding pixels contribute to the morphology. Figure 2-17 shows two forming kernels: kernel a, where all pixels touching the current pixel are considered, and kernel b, where only orthogonally adjacent pixels are considered.

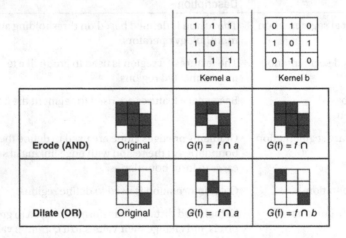

Figure 2-17. *3x3 forming kernels and binary erosion and dilation using the kernels; other kernel sizes and data values may be useful in a given application. (Image used by permission, © Intel Press, from Building Intelligent Systems)*

The basic operations of morphology include Boolean AND, OR, NOT. The notation used for the fundamental morphological operations is for *dilation* and for *erosion*. In binary morphology, dilation is a Boolean OR operator, while erosion is a Boolean AND operator. In the example provided in Figure 2-17, only kernel elements with a "1" are used in the morphology calculation, allowing for neighborhood contribution variations. For erosion, the pixels under all true forming kernel elements are AND'd together; the result is 1 if all are true and the pixel feature remains, otherwise the pixel feature is eroded or set to 0.

All pixels under the forming true kernel must be true for erosion of the center pixel. Erosion attempts to reduce sparse features until only strong features are left. Dilation attempts to inflate sparse features to make them fatter, only 1 pixel under the forming kernel elements must be true for dilation of the center pixel, corresponding to Boolean OR.

Based on simple erosion and dilation, a range of morphological operations are derived as shown here, where $\oplus$ = dilation and $\ominus$ = erosion.

Erode	$G(f) = f \ominus b$
Dilate	$G(f) = f \oplus b$
Opening	$G(f) = (f \oplus b) \ominus b$
Closing	$G(f) = (f \ominus b) \oplus b$
Morphological Gradient	$G(f) = f \ominus b$ or $G(f) = f \oplus b - f \ominus b$
Morphological Internal gradient	$G\ i(f) = f\ -\ f \ominus b$
Morphological External gradient	$G\ e(f) = f \oplus b - f$

Gray Scale and Color Morphology

Gray scale morphology is useful to synthesize and combine pixels into homogeneous intensity bands or regions with similar intensity values. Gray scale morphology can be used on individual color components to provide color morphology affecting hue, saturation, and color intensity in various color spaces.

For gray scale morphology or color morphology, the basic operations are MIN, MAX, and MINMAX, where pixels above the MIN are changed to the same value and pixels below the MAX are changed to the same value, while pixels within the MINMAX range are changed to the same value. MIN and MAX are a form of thresholding, while MINMAX allows bands of pixel values to be coalesced into equal values forming a homogenous region.

Morphology Optimizations and Refinements

Besides simple morphology [9], there are other methods of morphological segmentation using adaptive methods [254,255,256]. The simple morphology methods rely on using a fixed kernel across the entire image at each pixel and assume the threshold is already applied to the image; while the adaptive methods combine the morphology operations with variable kernels and variable thresholds based on the local pixel intensity statistics. This allows the morphology to adapt to the local region intensity and, in some cases, produce better results. Auto-thresholding and adaptive thresholding methods are discussed later in this chapter and are illustrated in Figures 2-24 and 2-26.

Euclidean Distance Maps

The distance map, or Euclidean distance map (EDM), converts each pixel in a binary image into the distance from each pixel to the nearest background pixel, so the EDM requires a binary image for input. The EDM is useful for segmentation, as shown in Figure 2-18, where the EDM image is thresholded based on the EDM values—in this case, similar to the ERODE operator.

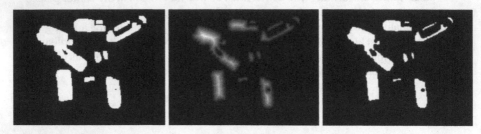

Figure 2-18. *Pre-processing sequence: (Left) Image after thresholding and erosion. (Center) EDM showing gray levels corresponding to distance of pixel to black background. (Right) Simple binary thresholded EDM image*

Super-Pixel Segmentation

A super-pixel segmentation method [257,258,259,260,261] attempts to collapse similar pixels in a local region into a larger super-pixel region of equal pixel value, so similar values are subsumed into the larger super-pixel. Super-pixel methods are commonly used for digital photography applications to create a scaled or watercolor special effect. Super-pixel methods treat each pixel as a node in a graph, and edges between regions are determined based on the similarity of neighboring pixels and graph distance. See Figure 2-19.

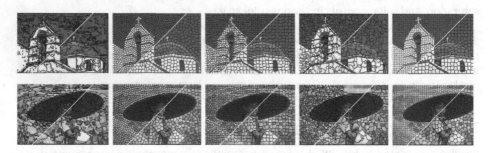

Figure 2-19. *Comparison of various super-pixel segmentation methods (Image © Dr. Radhakrishna Achanta, used by permission)*

Feature descriptors may be devised based on super-pixels, including super-pixel value histograms, shape factors of each polygon shaped super-pixel, and spatial relationships of neighboring super-pixel values. Apparently little work has been done on super-pixel based descriptors; however, the potential for several degrees of robustness and invariance seems good. We survey a range of super-pixel segmentation methods next.

Graph-based Super-Pixel Methods

Graph-based methods structure pixels into trees based on the distance of the pixel from a centroid feature or edge feature for a region of like-valued pixels. The compute complexity varies depending on the method.

- **SLIC Method** [258] Simple Linear Iterative Clusting (SLIC) creates super-pixels based on a 5D space, including the CIE Lab color primaries and the XY pixel coordinates. The SLIC algorithm takes as input the desired number of super-pixels to generate and adapt well to both gray scale and RGB color images. The clustering distance function is related to the size of the desired number of super-pixels and uses a Euclidean distance function for grouping pixels into super-pixels.

- **Normalized Cuts** [262,263] Uses a recursive region partitioning method based on local texture and region contours to create super-pixel regions.

- **GS-FH Method** [264] The graph-based Felzenszwalb and Huttenlocher method attempts to segment image regions using edges based on perceptual or psychological cues. This method uses the minimum length between pixels in the graph tree structure to create the super-pixel regions. The computational complexity is $O(n \, Log \, n)$, which is relatively fast.

- **SL Method** [265] The Super-Pixel Lattice (SL) method finds region boundaries within tiled image regions or strips of pixels using the graph cut method.

Gradient-Ascent-Based Super-Pixel Methods

Gradient ascent methods iteratively refine the super-pixel clusters to optimize the segmentation until convergence criteria are reached. These methods use a tree graph structure to associate pixels together according to some criteria, which in this case may be the RGB values or Cartesian coordinates of the pixels, and then a distance function or other function is applied to create regions. Since these are iterative methods, the performance can be slow.

- **Mean-Shift** [266] Works by registering off of the region centroid based on a kernel-based mean smoothing approach to create regions of like pixels.

- **Quick-Shift** [267] Similar to the mean-shift method but does not use a mean blur kernel and instead uses a distance function calculated from the graph structure based on RGB values and XY pixel coordinates.

- **Watershed** [268] Starts from local region pixel value minima points to find pixel value-based contour lines defining watersheds, or basin contours inside which similar pixel values can be substituted to create a homogeneous pixel value region.

- **Turbopixels** [269] Uses small circular seed points placed in a uniform grid across the image around which super-pixels are collected into assigned regions, and then the super-pixel boundaries are gradually expanded into the unassigned region, using a geometric flow method to expand the boundaries using controlled boundary value expansion criteria, so as to gather more pixels together into regions with fairly smooth and uniform geometric shape and size.

Depth Segmentation

Depth information, such as a depth map as shown in Figure 2-20, is ideal for segmenting objects based on distance. Depth maps can be computed from a wide variety of depth sensors and methods, including a single camera, as discussed in Chapter 1. Depth cameras, such as the Microsoft Kinect camera, are becoming more common. A depth map is a 2D image or array, where each pixel value is the distance or Z value.

Figure 2-20. *Depth images from Middlebury Data set: (Left) Original image. (Right) Corresponding depth image. Data courtesy of Daniel Scharstein and used by permission*

Many uncertainties in computer vision arise out of the problems in locating three-dimensional objects in a two-dimensional image array, so adding a depth map to the vision pipeline is a great asset. Using depth maps, images can be easily segmented into the foreground and background, as well as be able to segment specific features or objects—for example, segmenting by simple depth thresholding.

Depth maps are often very fuzzy and noisy, depending on the depth sensing method, so image pre-processing may be required. However, there is no perfect filtering method for depth map cleanup. Many practitioners prefer the bi-lateral filter [302] and variants, since it preserves local structure and does a better job of handling the edge transitions.

Color Segmentation

Sometime color alone can be used to segment and threshold. Using the right color component can easily filter out features from an image. For example, in Figure 2-6, we started from a red channel image from an RGB set, and the goal was to segment out the USB sticks from the table background. Since the table is brown and contains a lot of red, the red channel provides useful contrast with the USB sticks allowing segmentation via red. It may be necessary to color-correct the image to get the best results, such as gamut corrections or boosting the hue or saturation of each color to accentuate difference.

Thresholding

The goal of thresholding is to segment the image at certain intensity levels to reveal features such as foreground, background, and specific objects. A variety of methods exist for thresholding, ranging from global to locally adaptive. In practice, thresholding is very difficult and often not satisfactory by itself, and must be tuned for the dataset and combined with other pre-processing methods in the vision pipeline.

One of the key problems in thresholding is nonuniform illumination, so applications that require thresholding, like cell biology and microscopy, pay special attention to cell preparation, specimen spacing, and light placement. Since many images do not respond well to global thresholding involving simple methods, local methods are often required, which use the local pixel structure and statistical relationships to create effective thresholds. Both global and local adaptive methods for thresholding are discussed here. A threshold can take several forms:

- **Floor** Lowest pixel intensity allowed
- **Ceiling** Highest pixel intensity allowed
- **Ramp** Shape of the pixel ramp between floor and ceiling, such as linear or log
- **Point** May be a binary threshold point with no floor, ceiling, or ramp

Global Thresholding

Thresholding entire images at a globally determined thresholding level is sometimes a good place to start to explore the image data, but typically local features will suffer and be unintelligible as a result. Thresholding can be improved using statistical methods to determine the best threshold levels. Lookup tables (LUT) can be constructed, guided by statistical moments to create the floor, ceiling, and ramps and the functions to perform rapid LUT processing on images, or false-color the images for visualization.

Histogram Peaks and Valleys, and Hysteresis Thresholds

Again we turn to the old stand-by, the image histogram. Peaks and valleys in the histogram may indicate thresholds useful for segmentation and thresholding [319]. A hysteresis region marks pixels with similar values, and is easy to spot in the histogram, as shown in Figure 2-21. Also, many image processing programs have interactive sliders to allow the threshold point and even regions to be set with the pointer device.[1] Take some time and get to know the image data via the histogram and become familiar with using interactive thresholding methods.

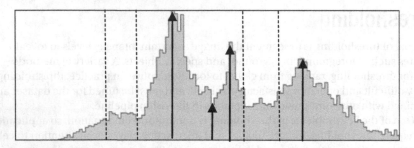

Figure 2-21. *Histogram annotated with arrows showing peaks and valleys, and dotted lines showing regions of similar intensities defined using hysteresis thresholds*

If there are no clear valleys between the histogram peaks, then establishing two thresholds, one on each side of the valley, is a way to define a region of hysteresis. Pixel values within the hysteresis region are considered inside the object. Further, the pixels can be classified together as a region using the hysteresis range and morphology to ensure region connectivity.

LUT Transforms, Contrast Remapping

Simple lookup tables (LUTs) are very effective for contrast remapping and global thresholding, and interactive tools can be used to create the LUTs. Once the interactive experimentation has been used to find the best floor, ceiling, and ramp function, the LUTs can be generated into table data structures and used to set the thresholds in fast code. False-coloring the image using pseudo-color LUTs is common and quite valuable for understanding the thresholds in the data. Various LUT shapes and ramps can be devised. See Figure 2-22 for an example using a linear ramp function.

---

[1] See the open-source package ImageJ2, and menu item Image ➤ Adjust-Brightness/Contrast for interactive thresholding.

Figure 2-22. *Contrast corrections: (Left) Original image shows palm frond detail compressed into a narrow intensity range obscuring details. (Center) Global histogram equalization restores some detail. (Right) LUT remap function spreads the intensity values to a narrower range to reveal details of the palm fronds. The section of the histogram under the diagonal line is stretched to cover the full intensity range in the right image; other intensity regions are clipped. The contrast corrected image will yield more gradient information when processed with a gradient operator such as Sobel*

Histogram Equalization and Specification

Histogram equalization spreads pixel values between a floor and ceiling using a contrast remapping function, with the goal of creating a histogram with approximately equal bin counts approaching a straight-line distribution. See Figure 2-23. While this method works well for gray scale images, color images should be equalized in the intensity channel of a chosen color space, such as HSV V. Equalizing each RGB component separately and rerendering will produce color moiré artifacts. Histogram equalization uses a fixed region and a fixed remapping for all pixels in the region; however, adaptive local histogram equalization methods are available [314].

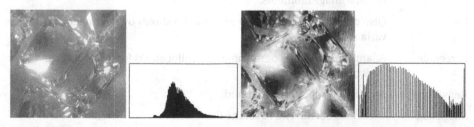

Figure 2-23. *(Left) Original image and histogram. (Right) Histogram equalized image and histogram*

It is possible to create a desired histogram shape or value distribution, referred to as *histogram specification*, and then remap all pixel values from the source image to conform to the specified histogram shape. The shape may be created directly, or else the histogram shape from a second image may be used to remap the source image to match the second image. With some image processing packages, the histogram specification may be interactive, and points on a curve may be placed and adjusted to create the desired histogram shape.

Global Auto Thresholding

Various methods have been devised to automatically find global thresholds based on statistical properties of the image histogram [320,513,514,515] and in most cases the results are not very good unless some image pre-processing precedes the auto thresholding. Table 2-4 provides a brief survey of auto thresholding methods, while Figure 2-24 displays renderings of each method.

Table 2-4. *Selected Few Global Auto-Thresholding Methods Derived from Basic Histogram Features [303]*

Method	Description
Default	A variation of the IsoData method, also knowm as iterative intermeans.
Huang	Huang's method of using fuzzy thresholding.
Intermodes	Iterative histogram smoothing.
IsoData	Iterative pixel averaging of values above and below a threshold to derive a new threshold above the composite average.
Li	Iterative cross-entropy thresholding.
MaxEntropy	Kapur-Sahoo-Wong (Maximum Entropy) algorithm.
Mean	Uses mean gray level as the threshold.
MinError	Iterative method from Kittler and Illingworth to converge on a minimum error threshold.
Minimum	Iterative histogram smoothing, assuming a bimodal histogram.
Moments	Tsai's thresholding algorithm intending to threshold and preserve the original image moments.
Otsu	Otsu clustering algorithms to set local thresholds by minimizing variance.
Percentile	Adapts the threshold based on pre-set allocations for foreground and background pixels.
RenyiEntropy	Another entropy-based method.
Shanbhag	Uses fuzzy set metrics to set the threshold.
Triangle	Uses image histogram peak, assumes peak is not centered, sets threshold in largest region on either side of peak.

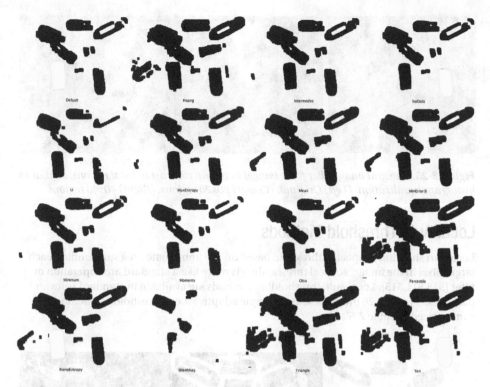

Figure 2-24. *Renderings of selected auto-thresholding methods (Images generated using ImageJ auto threshold plug-ins [303])*

Local Thresholding

Local thresholding methods take input from the local pixel region and threshold each pixel separately. Here are some common and useful methods.

Local Histogram Equalization

Local histogram equalization divides the image into small blocks, such as 32x32 pixels, and computes a histogram for each block, then rerenders each block using histogram equalization. However, the contrast results may contain block artifacts corresponding to the chosen histogram block size. There are several variations for local histogram equalization, including Contrast Limited Adaptive Local Histogram Equalization (CLAHE) [304].

Integral Image Contrast Filters

A histogram-related method uses integral images to compute local region statistics without the need to compute a histogram, then pixels are remapped accordingly, which is faster and achieves a similar effect (Figure 2-25).

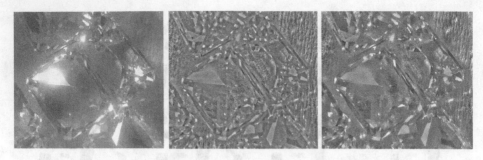

Figure 2-25. *Integral image filter from ImageJ to remap contrast in local regions, similar to histogram equalization: (Left) Original. (Center) 20x20 regions. (Right) 40x40 regions*

Local Auto Threshold Methods

Local thresholding adapts the threshold based on the immediate area surrounding each target pixel in the image, so local thresholding is more like a standard area operation or filter [513,514,515]. Local auto thresholding methods are available in standard software packages.[2] Figure 2-26 provides some example adaptive local thresholding methods, summarized in Table 2-5.

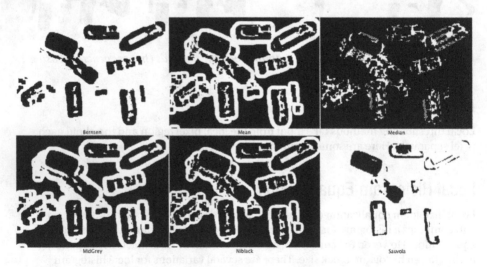

Figure 2-26. *Renderings of a selected few local auto and local thresholding methods using ImageJ plug-ins [303]*

---

[2]See the open-source package Imagej2, menu item Image ➤ Adjust ➤ Auto Local Threshold | Auto Threshold.

Table 2-5. Selected Few Local Auto-thresholding Methods [303]

Method	Description
Bernsen	Bernsen's algorithm using circular windows instead of rectangles and local midgray values
Mean	Uses the local gray level mean as the threshold
Median	Uses the local gray level mean as the threshold
MidGrey	Uses the local area gray level mean - C (where C is a constant)
Niblack	Niblack's algorithm is: p = (p > mean + k * standard_deviation - c) ? object : background
Sauvola	Sauvola's variation of Niblack: p = (p > mean * (1 + k *(standard_deviation / r - 1))) ? object : background

Summary

In this chapter, we surveyed image processing as a pre-processing step that can improve image analysis and feature extraction. We developed a taxonomy of image processing methods to frame the discussion, and applied the taxonomy to examples in the four fundamental vision pipelines, as will be developed in the taxonomy of Chapter 5, including (1) local binary descriptors such as LBP, ORB, FREAK; (2) spectra descriptors such as SIFT, SURF; (3) basis space descriptors such as FFT, wavelets; and (4) polygon shape descriptors such as blob object area, perimeter, and centroid. Common problems and opportunities for image pre-processing were discussed. Starting with illumination, noise, and artifact removal, we covered a range of topics including segmentation variations such as depth segmentation and super-pixel methods, binary, gray scale and color morphology, spatial filtering for convolutions and statistical area filters, and basis space filtering.

CHAPTER 3

■ ■ ■

Global and Regional Features

Measure twice, cut once.

—Carpenter's saying

This chapter covers the metrics of general feature description, often used for whole images and image regions, including textural, statistical, model based, and basis space methods. Texture, a key metric, is a well-known topic within image processing, and it is commonly divided into structural and statistical methods. Structural methods look for features such as edges and shapes, while statistical methods are concerned with pixel value relationships and statistical moments. Methods for modeling image texture also exist, primarily useful for image synthesis rather than for description. Basis spaces, such as the Fourier space, are also use for feature description.

It is difficult to develop clean partitions between the related topics in image processing and computer vision that pertain to global vs. regional vs. local feature metrics; there is considerable overlap in the applications of most metrics. However, for this chapter, we divide these topics along reasonable boundaries, though those borders may appear to be arbitrary. Similarly, there is some overlap between discussions here on global and regional features and topics that were covered in Chapter 2 on image processing and that will be discussed in Chapter 6 on local features. In short, many methods are used for local, regional, and global feature description, as well as image processing, such as the Fourier transform and the LBP.

But we begin with a brief survey of some key ideas in the field of texture analysis and general vision metrics.

Historical Survey of Features

To compare and contrast global, regional, and local feature metrics, it is useful to survey and trace the development of the key ideas, approaches, and methods used to describe features for machine vision. This survey includes image processing (textures and statistics) and machine vision (local, regional, and global features). Historically, the choice of feature metrics was limited to those that were computable at the time, given the limitations in compute performance, memory, and sensor technology. As time passed and technology developed, the metrics have become more complex to compute, consuming larger memory footprints. The images are becoming *multi-modal,* combining intensity, color, multiple spectrums, depth sensor information, multiple-exposure settings, high dynamic range imagery, faster frame rates, and more precision and accuracy in *x, y* and *Z* depth. Increases in memory bandwidth and compute performance, therefore, have given rise to new ways to describe feature metrics and perform analysis.

Many approaches to texture analysis have been tried; these fall into the following categories:

- **Structural**, describing texture via a set of micro-texture patterns known as texels. Examples include the numerical description of natural textures such as fabric, grass, and water. Edges, lines, and corners are also structural patterns, and the characteristics of edges within a region, such as edge direction, edge count, and edge gradient magnitude, are useful as texture metrics. Histograms of edge features can be made to define texture, similar to the methods used in local feature descriptors such as SIFT (described in Chapter 6).

- **Statistical**, based on gray level statistical moments describing point pixel area properties, and includes methods such as the co-occurrence matrix or SDM. For example, regions of an image with color intensity within a close range could be considered as having the same texture. Regions with the same histogram could be considered as having the same texture.

- **Model based**, including fractal models, stochastic models, and various semi-random fields. Typically, the models can be used to generate synthetic textures, but may not be effective in recognizing texture, and we do not cover texture generation.

- **Transform or basis based**, including methods such as Fourier, wavelets, Gabor filters, Zernike, and other basis spaces, which are treated here as a sub-class of the statistical methods (statistical moments); however, basis spaces are used in transforms for image processing and filtering as well.

Key Ideas: Global, Regional, and Local

Let's take a brief look at a few major trends and milestones in feature metrics research. While this brief outline is not intended to be a precise, inclusive look at all key events and research, it describes some general trends in mainstream industry thinking and academic activity.

1960s, 1970s, 1980s—Whole-Object Approaches

During this period, metrics describe mostly whole objects, larger regions, or images; pattern matching was performed on large targets via FFT spectral methods and correlation; recognition methods included object, shape, and texture metrics; and simple geometric primitives were used for object composition. Low-resolution images such as NTSC, PAL, and SECAM were common—primarily gray scale with some color when adequate memory was available. Some satellite images were available to the military with higher resolution, such as LANDSAT images from NASA and SPOT images from France.

Some early work on pattern recognition began to use local interest points and features: notably, Moravic[520] developed a local interest point detector in 1981, and in 1988 Harris & Stephens[156] developed local interest point detectors. Commercial systems began to appear, particularly the View PRB in the early 1980s, which used digital correlation and scale space super-pixels for coarse to fine matching, and real-time image processing and pattern recognition systems were introduced byImaging Technology. Rack-mounted imaging and machine vision systems began to be replaced by workstations and high-end PCs with add-on imaging hardware, array processors, and software libraries and applications by companies such as Krig Research.

Early 1990s—Partial-Object Approaches

Compute power and memory were increasing, enabling more attention to local feature methods, such as developments from Shi and Tomasi[157] improving the Harris detector methods, Kitchen and Rosenfeld[208] developing gray level corner detection methods, and methods by Wang and Brady[213]. Image moments over polygon shapes were computed using Zernike polynomials in 1990 by Khotanzad and Hong[276]. Scale space theory was applied to computer vision by Lindberg[520], and many other researchers followed this line of thinking into the future, such as Lowe [161] in 2004.

Metrics described smaller pieces of objects or object components and parts of images; there was increasing use of local features and interest points. Large sets of sub-patterns or basis vectors were used and corresponding metrics were developed. There was increased use of color information; more methods appeared to improve invariance for scale, rotational, or affine variations; and recognition methods were developed based on finding parts of an object with appropriate metrics. Higher image resolution, increased pixel depths, and color information were increasingly used in the public sector (especially in medical applications), along with of new affordable image sensors, such as the KODAK MEGA-PLUS, which provided a 1024x1024 image.

Mid-1990s—Local Feature Approaches

More focus was put on metrics that identify small local features surrounding interest points in images. Feature descriptors added more details from a window or patch surrounding each feature, and recognition was based on searching for sets of features and matching descriptors with more complex classifiers. Descriptor spectra included gradients, edges, and colors.

Late 1990s—Classified Invariant Local Feature Approaches

New feature descriptors were developed and refined to be invariant to changes in scale, lightness, rotation, and affine transformations. Work by Schmidt and Mohr[348] advanced and generalized the local feature description methods. Features acted as an alphabet for spelling out complex feature descriptors or vectors whereby the vectors were used for matching. The feature matching and classification stages were refined to increase speed and effectiveness using neural nets and other machine learning methods [142].

Early 2000s—Scene and Object Modeling Approaches

Scenes and objects were modeled as sets of feature components or patterns with well-formed descriptors; spatial relationships between features were measured and used for matching; and new complex classification and matching methods used boosting and related methods to combine strong and weak features for more effective recognition. The SIFT [161] algorithm from Lowe was published; SURF was also published by Bay et al.[160], taking a different approach using HAAR features rather than just gradients. The Viola-Jones method [504] was published, using HAAR features and a boosted learning approach to classification, accelerating matching. The OpenCV library for computer vision was developed by Bradski at INTEL™, and released as open source.

Mid-2000s—Finer-Grain Feature and Metric Composition Approaches

The number of researchers in this field began to mushroom; various combinations of features and metrics (bags of features) were developed by Czurka et al.[234] to describe scenes and objects using key points as described by Sivic [521]; new local feature descriptors were created and old ones refined; and there was increased interest in real-time feature extraction and matching methods for commercial applications. Better local metrics and feature descriptors were analyzed, measured, and used together for increased pattern match accuracy. Also, feature learning and sparse feature codebooks were developed to decrease pattern space, speed up search time, and increase accuracy.

Post-2010—Multi-Modal Feature Metrics Fusion

There has been increasing use of depth sensor information and depth maps to segment images and describe features and create VOXEL metrics by Rusu and Bradski et al.[398]; 2D texture metrics are expressed in 3-space; 3D depth sensing methods proliferate, increasing use of high-resolution images and high dynamic range (HDR) images to enhance feature accuracy; greater bit depth and accuracy of color images allows for valuable color-based metrics and computational imaging. Increased processing power and cheap, plentiful memory handle larger images on low-cost compute platforms. Faster and better feature descriptors using binary patterns have been developed and matched rapidly using Hamming distance, such as FREAK by Alehi et al.[131] and ORB by Rublee et al.[131]. Multi-modal and multivariate descriptors are composed of image features with other sensor information, such as accelerometers and positional sensors.

Future computing research may even come full circle, when sufficient compute and memory capacity exist to perform the older methods, like correlation across multiple scales and geometric perspectives in real-time using parallel and fixed-function hardware methods. This would obviate some of the current focus on small invariant sets of local features and allow several methods to be used together, synergistically. Therefore, the history of development in this field is worth knowing, since it might repeat itself in a different technological embodiment.

Since there is no single solution for obtaining the right set of feature metrics, all the methods developed over time have applications today and are still in use.

Textural Analysis

One of the most basic metrics is *texture*, which is the description of the surface of an image channel, such as color intensity, like an elevation map or terrain map. Texture can be expressed globally or within local regions. Texture can be expressed *locally* by statistical relationships among neighboring pixels in a region, and it can be expressed *globally* by summary relationships of pixel values within an image or region. For a sampling of the literature covering a wide range of texture methods, see references [13,59,60,310,16–20,312,313].

According to Gonzalez [4], there are three fundamental classes of texture in image analysis: statistical, structural, and spectral. *Statistical* measures include histograms, scatter plots, and SDMs. *Structural* techniques are more concerned with locating patterns or structural primitives in an image, such as parallel lines, regular patterns, and so on. These techniques are described in [11,1,5,8]. *Spectral* texture is derived from analysis of the frequency domain representation of the data. That is, a fast Fourier transform is used to create a frequency domain image of the data, which can then be analyzed using Fourier techniques.

Histograms reveal overall pixel value distributions but say nothing about spatial relationships. Scatter plots are essentially two-dimensional histograms, and do not reveal any spatial relationships. A good survey is found in reference[315].

Texture has been used to achieve several goals:

1. Texture-based segmentation (covered in Chapter 2).

2. Texture analysis of image regions (covered in this chapter).

3. Texture synthesis, creating images using synthetic textures (not covered in this book).

In computer vision, texture metrics are devised to describe the perceptual attributes of texture by using discrete methods. For instance, texture has been described *perceptually* with several properties, including:

- Contrast

- Color

- Coarseness

- Directionality

- Line-likeness

- Roughness

- Constancy

- Grouping

- Segmentation

If textures can be recognized, then image regions can be segmented based on texture and the corresponding regions can be measured using shape metrics such as area, perimeter, and centroid (as will be discussed in Chapter 6). Chapter 2 included a survey of segmentation methods, some of which are based on texture. Segmented texture regions can be recognized and compared for computer vision applications. Micro-textures of a local region, such as the LBP discussed in detail in Chapter 6, can be useful as a feature descriptor, and macro-textures can be used to describe a homogenous texture of a region such as a lake or field of grass, and therefore have natural applications to image segmentation. In summary, texture can be used to describe global image content, image region content, and local descriptor region content. The distinction between a feature descriptor and a texture metric may be small.

Sensor limitations combined with compute and memory capabilities of the past have limited the development of texture metrics to mainly 2D gray scale metrics. However, with the advances toward pervasive computational photography in every camera providing higher resolution images, higher frame rates, deeper pixels, depth imaging, more memory, and faster compute, we can expect that corresponding new advances in texture metrics will be made.

Here is a brief historical survey of texture metrics.

1950s thru 1970s—Global Uniform Texture Metrics

Auto-correlation or cross-correlation was developed by Kaiser[34] in 1955 as a method of looking for randomness and repeating pattern features in aerial photography, where auto-correlation is a statistical method of correlating a signal or image with a time-shifted version of itself, yielding a computationally simple method to analyze ground cover and structures.

Bajcsy[33] developed Fourier spectrum methods in 1973 using various types of filters in the frequency domain to isolate various types of repeating features as texture.

Gray level spatial dependency matrices, GLCMs, SDMs or co-occurrence matrices [6] were developed and used by Haralick in 1973, along with a set of summary statistical metrics from the SDMs to assist in numerical classification of texture. Some, but not all, of the summary metrics have proved useful; however, analysis of SDMs and development of new SDM metrics have continued, involving methods such as 2D visualization and filtering of the SDM data within spatial regions [26], as well as adding new SDM statistical metrics, some of which are discussed in this chapter.

1980s—Structural and Model-Based Approaches for Texture Classification

While early work focused on micro-textures describing statistical measures between small kernels of adjacent pixels, macro-textures developed to address the structure of textures within a larger region. K. Laws developed *texture energy-detection* methods in 1979 and 1980 [35–37], as well as *texture classifiers*, which may be considered the forerunners of some of the modern classifier concepts. The Laws method could be implemented as a texture classifier in a parallel pipeline with stages for taking gradients via of a set of convolution masks over Gaussian filtered images to isolate texture micro features, followed by a Gaussian smoothing stage to deal with noise, followed by the energy calculation from the combined gradients, followed by a classifier which matched texture descriptors.

Eigenfilters were developed by Ade[38] in 1983 as an alternative to the Laws gradient or energy methods and SDMs; eigenfilters are implemented using a covariance matrix representation of local 3x3 pixel region intensities, which allows texture analysis and aggregation into structure based on the variance within eigenvectors in the covariance matrix.

Structural approaches were developed by Davis[39] in 1979 to focus on gross structure of texture rather than primitives or micro-texture features. *Hough transforms* were invented in 1972 by Duda and Hart[228] as a method of finding lines and curves, and it was used by Eichmann and Kasparis[40] in 1988 to provide invariant texture description.

Fractal methods and *Markov random field* methods were developed into texture descriptors, and while these methods may be good for texture synthesis, they do not map well to texture classification, since both Fractal and Markov random field methods use random fields, thus there are limitations when applied to real-world textures that are not random.

1990s—Optimizations and Refinements to Texture Metrics

In 1993, Lam and Ip[41,47] used pyramid segmentation methods to achieve spatial invariance, where an image is segmented into homogenous regions using Voronoi polygon tessellation and irregular pyramid segmentation techniques around Q points taken from a binary thresholded image; five shape descriptors are calculated for each polygon: area, perimeter, roundness, orientation, and major/minor axis ratio, combined into texture descriptors.

Local binary patterns (LBP) were developed in 1994 by Ojala et al.[173] as a novel method of encoding both pattern and contrast to define texture [43,44,15,16]; since then, hundreds of researchers have added to the LBP literature in the areas of theoretical foundations, generalization into 2D and 3D, domain-specific interest point descriptors used in face detection, and spatio-temporal applications to motion analysis [42]. LBP research remains quite active at this time. LBPs are covered in detail in Chapter 6. There are many applications for the powerful LBP method as texture metric, a feature descriptor, and an image processing operator, the latter which was discussed in Chapter 2.

2000 toToday—More Robust Invariant Texture Metrics and 3D Texture

Feature metrics research is investigating texture metrics that are invariant to scale, rotation, lighting, perspective, and so on to approach the capabilities of human texture discrimination. In fact, texture is used interchangeably as a feature descriptor in some circles. The work by Pun and Lee[45] is an example of development of rotational invariant texture metrics, as well as scale invariance. Invariance attributes are discussed in the general taxonomy in Chapter 5.

The next wave of metrics being developed increasingly will take advantage of 3D depth information. One example is the surface shape metrics developed by Spence [46] in 2003, which provide a bump-map type metric for affine invariant texture recognition and texture description with scale and perspective invariance. Chapter 6 also discusses some related 3D feature descriptors.

Statistical Methods

The topic of statistical methods is vast, and we can only refer the reader to selected literature as we go along. One useful and comprehensive resource is the online NIST National Institute of Science and Technology Engineering Statistics Handbook,[1] including examples and links to additional resources and tools.

Statistical methods may be drawn upon at any time to generate novel feature metrics. Any feature, such as pixel values or local region gradients, can be expressed statistically by any number of methods. Simple methods, such as the histogram shown in Figure 3-1, are invaluable. Basic statistics such as minimum, maximum, and average values can be seen easily in the histogram shown in Chapter 2 (Figure 2-22). We survey several applications of statistical methods to computer vision here.

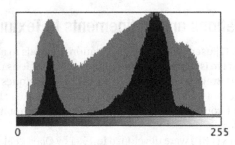

0   255

Figure 3-1. *Histogram with linear scale values (black) and log scale values (gray), illustrating how the same data is interpreted differently based on the chart scale*

---

[1]See the NIST online resource for engineering statistics: http://www.itl.nist.gov/div898/handbook/

Texture Region Metrics

Now we look in detail at the specific metrics for feature description based on texture. Texture is one of the most-studied classes of metrics. It can be thought of in terms of the surface—for example, a burlap bag compared to silk fabric. There are many possible textural relationships and signatures that can be devised in a range of domains, with new ones being developed all the time. In this section we survey some of the most common methods for calculating texture metrics:

- Edge metrics

- Cross-correlation

- Fourier spectrum signatures

- Co-occurrence matrix, Haralick features, extended SDM features

- Laws texture metrics

- Tessellation

- Local binary patterns (LBP)

- Dynamic textures

Within an image, each image region has a *texture signature,* where texture is defined as a common structure and pattern within that region. Texture signatures may be a function of position and intensity relationships, as in the spatial domain, or be based on comparisons in some other function basis and feature domain, such as frequency space using Fourier methods.

Texture metrics can be used to both segment and describe regions. Regions are differentiated based on texture homogeneousness, and as a result, texture works well as a method for region segmentation. Texture is also a good metric for feature description, and as a result it is useful for feature detection, matching, and tracking.

Appendix B contains several ground truth datasets with example images for computing texture metrics, including the CUReT reflectance and texture database from Columbia University. Several key papers describe the metrics used against the CUReT dataset [21,48–50] including the appearance of a surface as a bi-directional reflectance distribution function (BRDF) and a bi-directional texture function (BTF).

These metrics are intended to measure texture as a function of direction and illumination, to capture coarse details and fine details of each surface. If the surface texture contains significant subpixel detail not apparent in single pixels or groups of pixels, the BRDF reflectance metrics can capture the *coarse reflectance* details. If the surface contains pixel-by-pixel difference details, the BTF captures the *fine texture* details.

Edge Metrics

Edges, lines, contours, or ridges are basic textural features [316,317]. A variety of simple metrics can be devised just by analyzing the edge structure of regions in an image. There are many edge metrics in the literature, and a few are illustrated here.

Computing edges can be considered on a continuum of methods from interest point to edges, where the interest point may be a single pixel at a gradient maxima or minima, with several connected gradient maxima pixels composed into corners, ridges line segments, or a contours. In summary, a *gradient point* is a degenerate edge, and an edge is a collection of connected gradient points.

The edge metrics can be computed locally or globally on image regions as follows:

- Compute the gradient $g(d)$ at each pixel, selecting an appropriate gradient operator $g()$ and select the appropriate kernel size or distance d to target either micro or macro edge features.

- The distance d or kernel size can be varied to achieve different metrics; many researchers have used 3x3 kernels.

- Compute edge orientation by binning gradient directions for each edge into a histogram; for example, use 45 degree angle increment bins for a total of 8 bins at degrees 0,45,90,135,180,225,270.

Several other methods can be used to compute edge statistics. The representative methods are shown here; see also Shapiro and Stockton [517] for a standard reference.

Edge Density

Edge density can be expressed as the average value of the gradient magnitudes g_m in a region.

$$E_d = \frac{g_m(d)}{\text{pixels in region}}$$

Edge Contrast

Edge contrast can be expressed as the ratio of the average value of gradient magnitudes to the maximum possible pixel value in the region.

$$E_c = \frac{E_d}{\text{max pixel value}}$$

Edge Entropy

Edge randomness can be expressed as a measure of the Shannon entropy of the gradient magnitudes.

$$E_e = \sum_{i=0}^{n} g_m(x_i)\log_b g_m(x_i)$$

Edge Directivity

Edge directivity can be expressed as a measure of the Shannon entropy of the gradient directions.

$$E_e = \sum_{i=0}^{n} g_d(x_i)\log_b g_d(x_i)$$

Edge Linearity

Edge linearity measures the co-occurrence of collinear edge pairs using gradient direction, as shown by edges a – b in Figure 3-2.

$$E_l = \text{cooccurrence of colinear edge pairs}$$

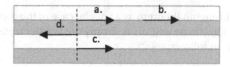

Figure 3-2. *Gradient direction of edges a,b,c,d used to illustrate relationships for edge metrics*

Edge Periodicity

Edge periodicity measures the co-occurrence of identically oriented edge pairs using gradient direction, as shown by edges a – c in Figure 3-2.

$$E_p = \text{cooccurrence of identically oriented edge pairs}$$

Edge Size

Edge size measures the co-occurrence of opposite oriented edge pairs using gradient direction, as shown by edges a – d in Figure 3-2.

$$E_s = \text{cooccurrence of opposite oriented edge pairs}$$

Edge Primitive Length Total

Edge primitive length measures the total length of all gradient magnitudes along the same direction.

$$E_t = \text{total length of gradeitn magnitudes with same direction}$$

Cross-Correlation and Auto-Correlation

Cross-correlation [34] is a metric showing similarity between two signals with a time displacement between them. *Auto-correlation* is the cross-correlation of a signal with a time-displaced version of itself. In the literature on signal processing, cross-correlation is also referred to as a *sliding inner* product or *sliding dot* product. Typically, this method is used to search a large signal for a smaller pattern.

$$f * g = \bar{f}(-t) * g(t)$$

Using the Wiener-Khinchin theorem as a special case of the general cross-correlation theorem, cross-correlation can be written as simply the Fourier transform of the absolute square of the function f_v as follows:

$$c(t) = \mathcal{F}_v\left[|f_v|^2\right](t)$$

In computer vision, the feature used for correlation may be a 1D line of pixels or gradient magnitudes, a 2D pixel region, or a 3D voxel volume region. By comparing the features from the current image frame and the previous image frame using cross-correlation derivatives, we obtain a useful texture change correlation metric.

By comparing displaced versions of an image with itself, we obtain a set of either local or global auto-correlation texture metrics. Auto-correlation can be used to detect repeating patterns or textures in an image, and also to describe the texture in terms of fine or coarse, where coarse textures show the auto-correlation function dropping of more slowly than fine textures. See also the discussion of correlation in Chapter 6 and Figure 6-20.

Fourier Spectrum, Wavelets, and Basis Signatures

Basis transforms, such as the FFT, decompose a signal into a set of basis vectors from which the signal can be synthesized or reconstructed. Viewing the set of basis vectors as a spectrum is a valuable method for understanding image texture and for creating a signature. Several basis spaces are discussed in this chapter, including Fourier, HAAR, wavelets, and Zernike.

Although computationally expensive and memory intensive, the Fast Fourier Transform (FFT) is often used to produce a frequency spectrum signature. The FFT spectrum is useful for a wide range of problems. The computations typically are limited to rectangular regions of fixed sizes, depending on the radix of the transform (see Bracewell[227]).

As shown in Figure 3-3, Fourier spectrum plots reveal definite image features useful for texture and statistical analysis of images. For example, Figure 3-10 shows an FFT spectrum of LBP pattern metrics. Note that the Fourier spectrum has many valuable attributes, such as rotational invariance, as shown in Figure 3-3, where a texture image is rotated 90 degrees and the corresponding FFT spectrums exhibit the same attributes, only rotated 90 degrees.

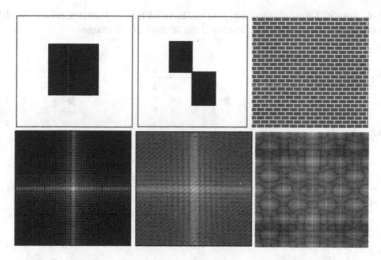

Figure 3-3. (Top row) Example images with texture. (Bottom row) Texture and shape information revealed in the corresponding FFT power spectrums

Wavelets [227] are similar to Fourier methods, and have become increasingly popular for texture analysis [311], discussed later in the section on basis spaces.

Note that the FFT spectrum as a texture metric or descriptor is rotational invariant, as shown in the bottom left image of Figure 3-3. FFT spectra can be taken over rectangular 2D regions. Also, 1D arrays such as annuli or Cartesian coordinates of the shape taken around the perimeter of an object shape can be used as input to an FFT and as an FFT descriptor shape metric.

Co-Occurrence Matrix, Haralick Features

Haralick[6] proposed a set of 2D texture metrics calculated from directional differences between adjacent pixels, referred to as *co-occurrence* matrices, or *spatial dependency matrices* (SDM), or gray level co-occurrence matrices (GLCM). A complete set of four (4) matrices are calculated by evaluating the difference between adjacent pixels in the *x, y, diagonal x and diagonal y* directions, as shown in Figure 3-4, and further illustrated with a 4x4 image and corresponding co-occurence tables shown in Figure 3-5.

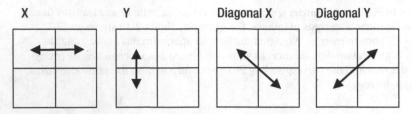

Figure 3-4. *Four different vectors used for the Haralick texture features, where the difference of each pixel in the image is plotted to reveal the texture of the image*

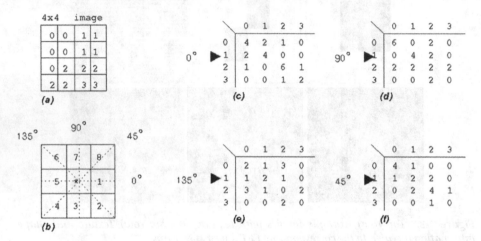

Figure 3-5. *(a) 4x4 pixel image, with gray values in the range 0-3. (b) Nearest neighbor angles corresponding to SDM tables. (c)(d)(e)(f) With neighborhood counts for each angle*

One benefit of the SDM as a texture metric is that it is easy to calculate in a single pass over the image. The SDM is also fairly invariant to rotation, which is often a difficult robustness attribute to attain. Within a segmented region or around an interest point, the SDM plot can be a valuable texture metric all by itself, therefore useful for texture analysis, feature description, noise detection, and pattern matching.

For example, if a camera has digital-circuit readout noise, it will show up in the SDM for the x direction only if the lines are scanned out of the sensor one at a time in the x direction, so using the SDM information will enable intelligent sensor processing to remove the readout noise. However, it should be noted that SDM metrics are not always useful alone, and should be qualified with additional feature information. The SDM is primarily concerned with spatial relationships, with regard to spatial orientation and frequency of occurrence. So, it is primarily a statistical measure.

The SDM is calculated in four orientations, as shown in Figure 3-4. Since the SDM is only concerned with adjacent pairs of pixels, these four calculations cover all possible spatial orientations. SDMs could be extended beyond 2x2 regions by using forming kernels extending into 5x5, 7x7, 9x9, and other dimensions.

A *spatial dependency matrix* is basically a count of how many times a given pixel value occurs next to another pixel value. Figure 3-5 illustrates the concept. For example, assume we have an 8-bit image (0. 255). If an SDM shows that pixel value x frequently occurs adjacent to pixels within the range $x+1$ to $x-1$, then we would say that there is a "smooth" texture at that intensity. However, if pixel value x frequently occurs adjacent to pixels within the range $x+70$ to $x-70$, we would say that there is quite a bit of contrast at that intensity, if not noise.

A critical point in using SDMs is to be sensitive to the varied results achieved when sampling over small vs. large image areas. By sampling the SDM over a smaller area (say 64x64 pixels), details will be revealed in the SDMs that would otherwise be obscured. The larger the size of the sample image area, the more the SDM will be populated. And the more samples taken, the more likely that detail will be obscured in the SDM image plots. Actually, smaller areas (i.e., 64x64 pixels) are a good place to start when using SDMs, since smaller areas are faster to compute and will reveal a lot about local texture.

The Haralick metrics are shown in Figure 3-6.

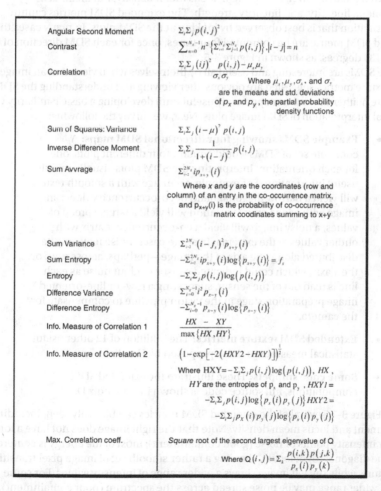

Figure 3-6. *Haralick texture metrics. (Image used by permission, © Intel Press, from Building Intelligent Systems)*

The statistical characteristics of the SDM have been extended by several researchers to add more useful metrics [26], and SDMs have been applied to 3D volumetric data by a number of researchers with good results [25].

Extended SDM Metrics

Extensions to the Haralick metrics have been developed by the author [26], primarily motivated by a visual study of SDM plots as shown in Figure 3-7. Applications for the extended SDM metrics include texture analysis, data visualization, and image recognition. The visual plots of the SDMs alone are valuable indicators of pixel intensity relationships, and are worth using along with histograms to get to know the data.

The extended SDM metrics include centroid, total coverage, low-frequency coverage, total power, relative Power, locus length, locus mean density, bin mean density, containment, linearity, and linearity strength. The extended SDM metrics capture key information that is best observed by looking at the SDM plots. In many cases the extended SDM metric are be computed four times, once for each SDM direction of 0, 45, 90, and 135 degrees, as shown in Figure 3-5.

The SDMs are interesting and useful all by themselves when viewed as an image. Many of the texture metrics suggested are obvious after viewing and understanding the SDMs; others are neither obvious nor apparently useful until developing a basic familiarity with the visual interpretation of SDM image plots. Next, we survey the following:

- **Example SDMs showing four directional SDM maps:** A complete set of SDMs would contain four different plots, one for each orientation. Interpreting the SDM plots visually reveals useful information. For example, an image with a smooth texture will yield a narrow diagonal band of co-occurrence values; an image with wide texture variation will yield a larger spread of values; a noisy image will yield a co-occurrence matrix with outlier values at the extrema. In some cases, noise may only be distributed along one axis of the image—perhaps, across rows or the x axis, which could indicated sensor readout noise as each line is read out of the sensor, suggesting a row- or line-oriented image preparation stage in the vision pipeline to compensate for the camera.

- **Extended SDM texture metrics:** The addition of 12 other useful statistical measures to those proposed by Haralick.

- **Some code snippets:** These illustrate the extended SDM computations, full source code is shown in Appendix D.

In Figure 3-7, several of the extended SDM metrics can be easily seen, including containment and locus mean density. Note that the right image does not have a lot of outliner intensity points or noise (good containment); most of the energy is centered along the diagonal (tight locus), showing a rather smooth set of image pixel transitions and texture, while the left image shows a wider range of intensity values. For some images, wider range may be noise spread across the spectrum (poor containment), revealing a wider band of energy and contrast between adjacent pixels.

100

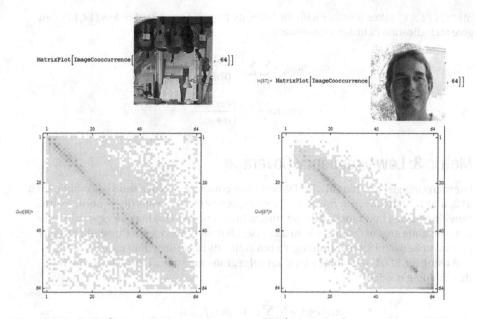

Figure 3-7. *Pair of image co-occurrence matrix plots (x-axis plots) computed over 64 bins in the bottom row corresponding to the images in the top row*

Metric 1: Centroid

To compute the centroid, for each SDM bin *p(i,j)*, the count of the bin is multiplied by the bin coordinate for *x,y* and also the total bin count is summed. The centroid calculation is weighted to compute the centroid based on the actual bin counts, rather than an unweighted "binary" approach of determining the center of the binning region based on only bin data presence. The result is the weighted center of mass over the SDM bins.

$$centroid = \sum_{i=0}^{n} \sum_{j=0}^{m} \begin{pmatrix} x = jp(i,j) \\ y = ip(i,j) \\ z = p(i,j) \end{pmatrix}$$

$$centroid_y = \frac{y}{z}$$

$$centroid_x = \frac{x}{z}$$

Metric 2: Total Coverage

This is a measure of the spread, or range of distribution, of the binning. A small coverage percentage would be indicative of an image with few gray levels, which corresponds in some cases to image smoothness. For example, a random image would have a very large coverage number, since all or most of the SDM bins would be hit. The coverage feature

101

metrics (2,3,4), taken together with the linearity features suggested below (11,12), can give an indication of image smoothness.

$$coverage_c = \sum_{i=0}^{n} \sum_{j=0}^{m} \left(\begin{array}{l} 1 \, if \, 0 < p(i,j), \\ 0 \, otherwise \end{array} \right)$$

$$coverage_t = \frac{coverage_c}{(n*m)}$$

Metric 3: Low-Frequency Coverage

For many images, any bins in the SDM with bin counts less than a threshold value, such as 3, may be considered as noise. The low-frequency coverage metric, or noise metric, provides an idea how much of the binning is in this range. This may be especially true as the sample area of the image area increases. For whole images, a threshold of 3 has proved to be useful for determining if a bin contains noise for a data range of 0-255, and using the SDM over smaller local kernel regions may use all the values with no thresholding needed.

$$coverage_c = \sum_{i=0}^{n} \sum_{j=0}^{m} if \, 0 < p(i,j) < 3 \left(\begin{array}{l} 1, \\ else \, 0 \end{array} \right)$$

$$coverage_l = \frac{coverage_c}{(n*m)}$$

Metric 4: Corrected Coverage

Corrected coverage is the total coverage with noise removed.

$$coverage_n = coverage_t - coverage_l$$

Metric 5: Total Power

The power metric provides a measure of the swing in value between adjacent pixels in an image, and is computed in four directions. A smooth image will have a low power number because the differences between pixels are smaller. Total power and relative power are inter-related, and relative power is computed using the total populated bins (z) and total difference power (t).

$$power_c = \sum_{i=0}^{n} \sum_{j=0}^{m} if \, p(i,j) \neq 0 \left(\begin{array}{l} z += 1, \\ t += |i-j| \end{array} \right)$$

$$power_t = t$$

Metric 6: Relative Power

The relative power is calculated based on the scaled total power using nonempty SDM bins t, while the total power uses all bins.

$$power_r = \frac{t}{z}$$

Metric 7: Locus Mean Density

For many images, there is a "locus" area of high-intensity binning surrounding the bin axis (locus axis is where adjacent pixels are of the same value $x=y$) corresponding to a diagonal line drawn from the upper left corner of the SDM plot. The degree of clustering around the locus area indicates the amount of smoothness in the image. Binning from a noisy image will be scattered with little relation to the locus area, while a cleaner image will show a pattern centered about the locus.

$$locus_c = \sum_{i=0}^{n} \sum_{j=0}^{m} if\ 0 < |i-j| < 7 \begin{pmatrix} z += 1, \\ d += p(i,j) \end{pmatrix}$$

$$locus_d = \frac{d}{z}$$

The locus mean density is an average of the bin values within the locus area. The locus is the area around the center diagonal line, within a band of 7 pixels on either side of the identity line ($x=y$) that passes down the center of each SDM. However, the number 7 is not particularly special, but based upon experience, it just gives a good indication of the desired feature over whole images. This feature is good for indicating smoothness.

Metric 8: Locus Length

The locus length measures the range of the locus concentration about the diagonal. The algorithm for locus length is a simple count of bins populated in the locus area; a threshold band of 7 pixels about the locus has been found useful.

```
y=length=0;
while (y < 256) {
    x=count=0;
    while (x < 256) {
        n = |y-x|;
        if (p[i,j] == 0) && (n < 7) count++;
        x++;
    }
    if (!count) length++;
    y++;
}
```

Metric 9: Bin Mean Density

This is simply the average bin count from nonempty bins.

$$density_c = \sum_{i=0}^{n} \sum_{j=0}^{m} if\ p(i,j) \neq 0\ (v = p(i,j), z+=1)$$

$$density_b = \frac{v}{z}$$

Metric 10: Containment

Containment is a measure of how well the binning in the SDM is contained within the boundaries or edges of the SDM, and there are four edges or boundaries, for example assuming a data range [0..255], there are containment boundaries along rows 0 and 255, and along columns 0 and 255. Typically, the bin count m is 256 bins, or possibly less such as 64. To measure containment, basically the perimeters of the SDM bins are checked to see if any binning has occurred, where the perimeter region bins of the SDM represent extrema values next to some other value. The left image in Figure 3-7 has lower containment than the right image, especially for the low values.

$$containment_1 = \sum_{i=0}^{m} if\ p(i,0) \neq 0\ (c_1+=1)$$

$$containment_2 = \sum_{i=0}^{m} if\ p(i,m) \neq 0\ (c_2+=1)$$

$$containment_3 = \sum_{i=0}^{m} if\ p(0,i) \neq 0\ (c_3+=1)$$

$$containment_4 = \sum_{i=0}^{m} if\ p(m,i) \neq 0\ (c_4+=1)$$

$$containment_t = 1.0 - \frac{(c_1 + c_2 + c_3 + c_4)}{4m}$$

If extrema are hit frequently, this probably indicates some sort of overflow condition such as numerical overflow, sensor saturation, or noise. The binning is treated unweighted. A high containment number indicates that all the binning took place within the boundaries of the SDM. A lower number indicates some bleeding. This feature appears visually very well in the SDM plots.

Metric 11. Linearity

The linearity characteristic may only be visible in a single orientation of the SDM, or by comparing SDMs. For example, the image in Figure 3-8 reveals some linearity variations across the set of SDMs. This is consistent with the image sensor used (older tube camera).

$$linearity_c = \sum_{j=0}^{m} if\; p(jm,j) > 1 \begin{pmatrix} z+=1, \\ l+= p(256j,j) \end{pmatrix}$$

$$linearity_{normalized} = \frac{z}{m}$$

$$linearity_{strength} = \frac{l}{z} * m^{-1}$$

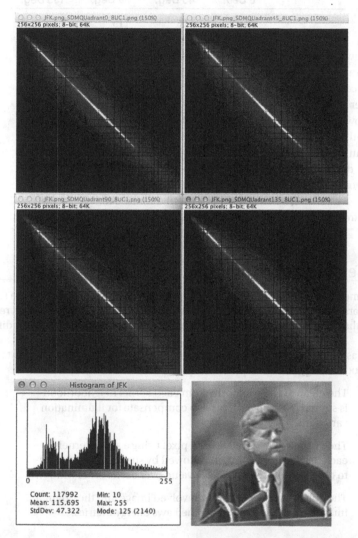

Figure 3-8. *SDMs from old tube camera showing linearity variations in the sensor, includes full set of 0, 45, 90, and 135 degree SDM's. (Public domain image from National Archives)*

105

Metric 12: Linearity Strength

The algorithm for linearity strength is shown in Metric 11. If there is any linearity present in a given angle of SDM, both linearity strength and linearity will be comparatively higher at this angle than the other SDM angles (Table 3-1).

Table 3-1. *Extended SDM Metrics from Figure 3-8*

METRIC	0 Deg.	45 Deg.	90 Deg.	135 Deg.	Ave.
xcentroid	115	115	115	115	115
ycentroid	115	115	115	115	115
low_frequency_coverage	0.075	0.092	0.103	0.108	0.095
total_coverage	0.831	0.818	0.781	0.780	0.803
corrected_coverage	0.755	0.726	0.678	0.672	0.708
total_power	2.000	3.000	5.000	5.000	3.750
relative_power	17.000	19.000	23.000	23.000	20.500
locus_length	71	72	71	70	71
locus_mean_density	79	80	74	76	77
bin_mean_density	21	19	16	16	18
containment	0.961	0.932	0.926	0.912	0.933
linearity	0.867	0.848	0.848	0.848	0.853
linearity_strength	1.526	1.557	0.973	1.046	1.276

Laws Texture Metrics

The Laws metrics [52] provide a structural approach to texture analysis, using a set of masking kernels to measure texture energy or variation within fixed sized local regions, similar to the 2x2 region SDM approach but using larger pixel areas to achieve different metrics.

The basic Laws algorithm involves classifying each pixel in the image into texture based on local energy, using a few basic steps:

1. The mean average intensity from each kernel neighborhood is subtracted from each pixel to compensate for illumination variations.

2. The image is convolved at each pixel using a set of kernels, each of which sums to zero, followed by summing the results to obtain the absolute average value over each kernel window.

3. The difference between the convolved image and the original image is measured, revealing the Laws energy metrics.

Laws defines a set of nine separable kernels to produce a set of texture region energy metrics, and some of the kernels work better than others in practice. The kernels are composed via matrix multiplication from a set of four vector masks L5, E5, S5, and R5, described below. The kernels were originally defined as 5x5 masks, but 3x3 approximations have been used also, as shown below.

```
5x5 form
L5      Level Detector      [ 1     4     6     4     1 ]
E5      Edge Detector       [-1    -2     0     2     1 ]
S5      Spot Detector       [-1     0     2     0     1 ]
R5      Ripple Detector     [ 1    -4     6    -4     1 ]

3x3 approximations of 5x5 form
L3      Level Detector      [ 1     2     1 ]
E3      Edge Detector       [-1     0     1 ]
S3      Spot Detector       [-1     2    -1 ]
R3      Ripple Detector     [*NOTE: cannot be reproduced in 3x3 form]
```

To create 2D masks, vectors *Ln, En, Sn, and Rn* (as shown above) are convolved together as separable pairs into kernels; a few examples are shown in Figure 3-9.

$$\begin{pmatrix} -1 \\ 0 \\ 1 \end{pmatrix} * [1, 2, 1] = \begin{pmatrix} -1 & -2 & -1 \\ 0 & 0 & 0 \\ 1 & 2 & 1 \end{pmatrix}$$

E3L3	E3S3	L3S3
$\begin{pmatrix} -1 & 0 & 1 \\ -2 & 0 & 2 \\ -1 & 0 & 1 \end{pmatrix}$	$\begin{pmatrix} 1 & 0 & -1 \\ -2 & 0 & 2 \\ 1 & 0 & -1 \end{pmatrix}$	$\begin{pmatrix} -1 & -2 & -1 \\ 2 & 4 & 2 \\ -1 & -2 & -1 \end{pmatrix}$
E5L5	E5S5	L5S5
$\begin{pmatrix} -1 & -2 & 0 & 2 & 1 \\ -4 & -8 & 0 & 8 & 4 \\ -6 & -12 & 0 & 12 & 6 \\ -4 & -8 & 0 & 8 & 4 \\ -1 & -2 & 0 & 2 & 1 \end{pmatrix}$	$\begin{pmatrix} 1 & 2 & 0 & -2 & -1 \\ 0 & 0 & 0 & 0 & 0 \\ -2 & -4 & 0 & 4 & 2 \\ 0 & 0 & 0 & 0 & 0 \\ 1 & 2 & 0 & -2 & -1 \end{pmatrix}$	$\begin{pmatrix} -1 & -4 & -6 & -4 & -1 \\ 0 & 0 & 0 & 0 & 0 \\ 2 & 8 & 12 & 8 & 2 \\ 0 & 0 & 0 & 0 & 0 \\ -1 & -4 & -6 & -4 & -1 \end{pmatrix}$

Figure 3-9. L3E3 kernel composition example

Note that Laws texture metrics have been extended into 3D for volumetric texture analysis.[51][52]

LBP Local Binary Patterns

In contrast to the various structural and statistical methods of texture analysis, the LBP operator [18,58] computes the local texture around each region as an LBP binary code, or *micro-texture*, allowing simple micro-texture comparisons to segment regions based on like micro-texture. (See the very detailed discussion on LBP in Chapter 6 for details and references to the literature, and especially Figure 6-6.) The LBP operator [173] is quite versatile, easy to compute, consumes a low amount of memory, and can be used for texture analysis, interest points, and feature description. As a result, the LBP operator is discussed is several places in this book.

As shown in Figure 3-10, the uniform set of LBP operators, composed of a subset of the possible LBPs that are by themselves rotation invariant, can be binned into a histogram, and the corresponding bin values are run through an FFT as a 1D array to create an FFT spectrum, which yields a robust metric with strong rotational invariance.

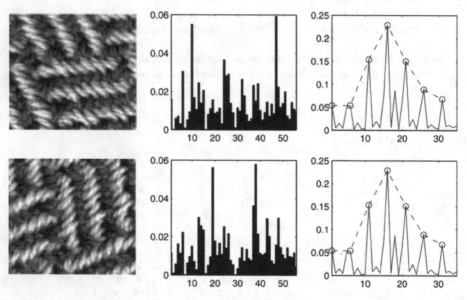

Figure 3-10. *(Left) texture images. (Center) LBP histograms. (Right) FFT spectrum plots of the histograms which reveal the rotational invariance property of the LBP histograms. Note that while the histogram binning looks different for the rotated images, the FFT spectrums look almost identical. (Image © Springer-Verlag London Limited from Computer Vision Using Local Binary Patterns)*

Dynamic Textures

Dynamic textures are a concept used to describe and track textured regions as they change and morph dynamically from frame to frame [53,13,15,14] For example, dynamic textures may be textures in motion, like sea waves, smoke, foliage blowing in the wind, fire, facial expressions, gestures, and poses. The changes are typically tracked in spatio-temporal sets

108

of image frames, where the consecutive frames are stacked into volumes for analysis as a group. The three dimensions are the XY frame sizes, and the Z dimension is derived from the stack of consecutive frames *n-2, n-1, n.*

A close cousin to dynamic texture research is the field of *activity recognition* (discussed in Chapter 6), where features are parts of moving objects that compose an activity—for example, features on arms and legs that are tracked frame to frame to determine the type of motion or activity, such as walking or running. One similarity between activity recognition and dynamic textures is that the features or textures change from frame to frame over time, so for both activity recognition and dynamic texture analysis, tracking features and textures often requires a spatio-temporal approach involving a data structure with a history buffer of past and current frames, which provides a volumetric representation to the data.

For example, VLBP and LBP-TOP (discussed in Chapter 6) provide methods for dynamic texture analysis by using the LBP constructed to operate over three dimensions in a volumetric structure, where the volume contains image frames *n-2, n-1, and n* stacked into the volume.

Statistical Region Metrics

Describing texture in terms of statistical metrics of the pixels is a common and intuitive method. Often a simple histogram of a region will be sufficient to describe the texture well enough for many applications. There are also many variations of the histogram, which lend themselves to a wide range of texture analysis. So this is a good point at which to examine histogram methods. Since statistical mathematics is a vast field, we can only introduce the topic here, dividing the discussion into image moment features and point metric features.

Image Moment Features

Image moments [518,4] are scalar quantities, analogous to the familiar statistical measures such as mean, variance, skew, and kurtosis. Moments are well suited to describe polygon shape features and general feature metric information such as gradient distributions. Image moments can be based on either scalar point values or basis functions such as Fourier or Zernike methods discussed later in the section on basis space.

Moments can describe the projection of a function onto a *basis space*—for example, the Fourier transform projects a function onto a basis of harmonic functions. Note that there is a conceptual relationship between 1D and 2D moments in the context of shape description. For example, the 1D mean corresponds to the 2D centroid, and the 1D minimum and maximum correspond to the 2D major and minor axis. The 1D minimum and maximum also correspond to the 2D bounding box around the 2D polygon shape (also see Figure 6-29).

In this work, we classify image moments under the term *polygon shape descriptors* in the taxonomy (see Chapter 5). Details on several image moments used for 2D shape description will be covered in Chapter 6, under "Object Shape Metrics for Blobs and Objects."

Common properties of moments in the context of 1D distributions and 2D images include:

- 0th order moment is the mean or 2D centroid.

- Central moments describe variation around the mean or 2D centroid.

- 1st order central moments contain information about 2D area, centroid, and size.

- 2nd order central moments are related to variance and measure 2D elliptical shape.

- 3rd order central moments provide symmetry information about the 2D shape, or skewness.

- 4th order central moments measure 2D distribution as tall, short, thin, short, or fat.

- Higher-level moments may be devised and composed of moment ratios, such as co-variance.

Moments can be used to create feature descriptors that are invariant to several robustness criteria, such as scale, rotation, and affine variations. The taxonomy of robustness and invariance criteria is provided in Chapter 5. For 2D shape description, in 1961 Hu developed a theoretical set of seven 2D planar moments for character recognition work, derived using invariant algebra, that are invariant under scale, translation, and rotation [7]. Several researchers have extended Hu's work. An excellent resource for this topic is *Moments and Moment Invariants in Pattern Recognition*, by Jan Flusser et al.[518].

Point Metric Features

Point metrics can be used for the following: (1) feature description, (2) analysis and visualization, (3) thresholding and segmentation, and (4) image processing via programmable LUT functions (discussed in Chapter 2). Point metrics are often overlooked. Using point metrics to understand the structure of the image data is one of the first necessary steps toward devising the image pre-processing pipeline to prepare images for feature analysis. Again, the place to start is by analysis of the histogram, as shown in Figures 3-1 and 3-11. The basic point metrics can be determined visually, such as minima, maxima, peaks, and valleys. False coloring of the histogram regions for data visualization is simple using color lookup tables to color the histogram regions in the images.

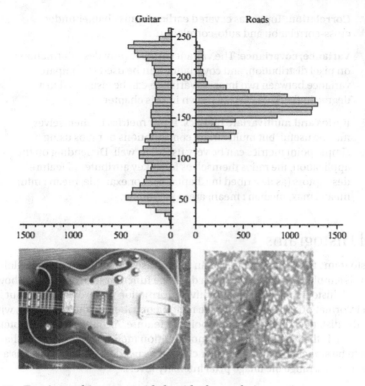

Figure 3-11. *Two image histograms side by side, for analysis*

Here is a summary of statistical point metrics:

- **Quantiles, median, rescale**: By sorting the pixel values into an ordered list, as during the histogram process, the various quartiles can be found, including the median value. Also, the pixels can be rescaled from the list and used for pixel remap functions (as described in Chapter 2).

- **Mix, max, mode**: The minimum and maximum values, together with histogram analysis, can be used to guide image pre-processing to devise a threshold method to remove outliers from the data. The mode is the most common pixel value in the sorted list of pixels.

- **Mean, harmonic mean, and geometric mean**: Various formulations of the mean are useful to learn the predominant illumination levels, dark or light, to guide image pre-processing to enhance the image for further analysis.

- **Standard deviation, skewness, and kurtosis**: These moments can be visualized by looking at the SDM plots.

- **Correlation**: Topic was covered earlier in this chapter under cross-correlation and auto-correlation.

- **Variance, covariance**: The variance metric provides information on pixel distribution, and covariance can be used to compare variance between two images. Variance can be visualized to a degree in the SDM, also as shown in this chapter.

- **Ratios and multivariate metrics**: Point metrics by themselves may be useful, but multivariate combinations or ratios using simple point metrics can be very useful as well. Depending on the application, the ratios themselves form key attributes of feature descriptors (as described in Chapter 6). For example, mean : min, mean : max, median : mean, area : perimeter.

Global Histograms

Global histograms treat the entire image. In many cases, image matching via global histograms is simple and effective, using a distance function such as SSD. As shown in Figure 3-12, histograms reveal quantitative information on pixel intensity, but not structural information. All the pixels in the region contribute to the histogram, with no respect to the distance from any specific point or feature. As discussed in Chapter 2, the histogram itself is the basis of histogram modification methods, allowing the shape of the histogram to be stretched, compressed, or clipped as needed, and then used as an inverse lookup table to rearrange the image pixel intensity levels.

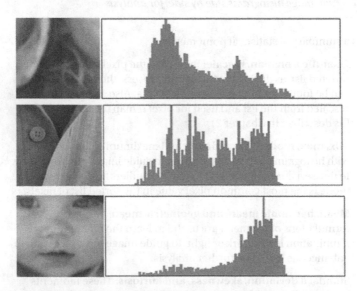

Figure 3-12. *2D histogram shapes for different images*

Local Region Histograms

Histograms can also be computed over *local regions* of pixels, such as rectangles or polygons, as well as over sets of feature attributes, such as gradient direction and magnitude or other spectra. To create a polygon region histogram feature descriptor, first a region may be segmented using morphology to create a mask shape around a region of interest, and then only the masked pixels are used for the histogram.

Local histograms of pixel intensity values can be used as attributes of a feature descriptor, and also used as the basis for remapping pixel values from one histogram shape to another, as discussed in Chapter 2, by reshaping the histogram and reprocessing the image accordingly. Chapter 6 discusses a range of feature descriptors such as SIFT, SURF, and LBP which make use of feature histograms to bin attributes such as gradient magnitude and direction.

Scatter Diagrams, 3D Histograms

The *scatter diagram* can be used to visualize the relationship or similarity between two image datasets for image analysis, pattern recognition, and feature description. Pixel intensity from two images or image regions can be compared in the scatter plot to visualize how well the values correspond. Scatter diagrams can be used for feature and pattern matching under limited translation invariance, but they are less useful for affine, scale, or rotation invariance. Figure 3-13 shows an example using a scatter diagram to look for a pattern in an image, the target pattern is compared at different offsets, the smaller the offset, the better the correspondence. In general, tighter sets of peak features indicate a strong structural or pattern correspondence; more spreading of the data indicates weaker correspondence. The farther away the pattern offset moves, the lower the correspondence.

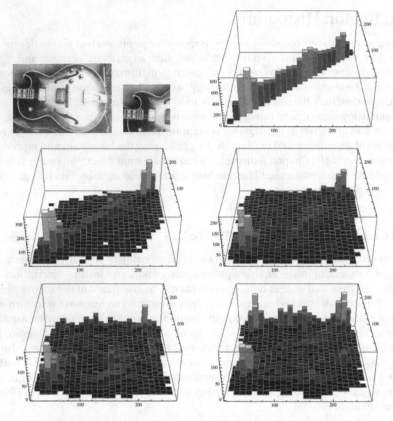

Figure 3-13. *Scatter diagrams, rendered as 3D histograms, of an image and a target pattern at various displacements. Top row: (left) image, (center) target pattern from image, (right) SDM of pattern with itself. Center row: (left) target and image offset 1,1 (right) target and image offset 8,8, Bottom row: (left) target and image offset 16,16, (right) target and image offset 32,32*

Note that by analyzing the peak features compared to the low-frequency features, correspondence can be visualized. Figure 3-14 shows scatter diagrams from two separate images. The lack of peaks along the axis and the presence of spreading in the data show low structural or pattern correspondence.

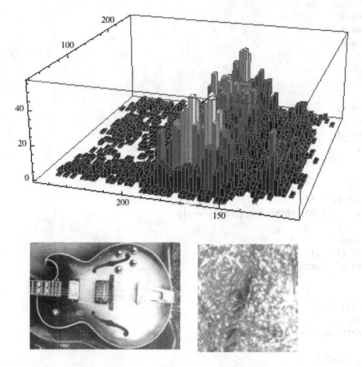

Figure 3-14. *Scatter diagram from two different images showing low correspondence along diagonal*

The scatter plot can be made, pixel by pixel, from two images, where pixel pairs form the Cartesian coordinate for scatter plotting using the pixel intensity of image 1 is used as the *x* coordinate, and the pixel intensities of image 2 as the *y* coordinate, then the count of pixel pair correspondence is binned in the scatter plot. The bin count for each coordinate can be false colored for visualization. Figure 3-15 provides some code for illustration purposes.

```
r1.x = sarea.x;
r1.y = sarea.y;
r1.z = sarea.z;
r1.dx = dx;
r1.dy = 1;
r1.dz = 1;

r2.x = darea.x;
r2.y = darea.y;
r2.z = darea.z;
r2.dx = dx;
r2.dy = 1;
r2.dz = 1;

/* INITIALIZE DATA */
for (x=0; x < 0x10000; mbin[x] = (int)0, x++);

gf = c->grain;
if (gf <= 0) gf = 1;
if (gf > dx) gf = dx;

z=0;
while (z < dz) {
    r1.y = sarea.y;
    r2.y = darea.y;
    y=0;
    while (y < dy) {

        pix_read(c->soid, &r1, data1);
        pix_read(c->doid, &r2, data2);
        for (x=0; x < dx; mbin[ ((data2[x] << 8)&0xff00) + (data1[x] & 0xff) ]++, x += gf);

        y += gf;
        r1.y += gf;
        r2.y += gf;
    }
    z += gf;
    r1.z += gf;
    r2.z += gf;
}
```

Figure 3-15. *Code to illustrate binning 8-bit data for a scatter diagram comparing two images pixel by pixel and binning the results for plotting*

For feature detection, as shown in Figure 3-12, the scatter plot may reveal enough correspondence at coarse translation steps to reduce the need for image pyramids in some feature detection and pattern matching applications. For example, the step size of the pattern search and compare could be optimized by striding or skipping pixels, searching the image at 8 or 16 pixel intervals, rather than at every pixel, reducing feature detection time. In addition, the scatter plot data could first be thresholded to a binary image, masked to show just the peak values, converted into a bit vector, and measured for correspondence using HAMMING distance for increased performance.

Multi-Resolution, Multi-Scale Histograms

Multi-resolution histograms [10] have been used for texture analysis [54], and also for feature recognition [55]. The PHOG descriptor described in Chapter 6 makes use of multi-scale histograms of feature spectra—in this case, gradient information. Note that the multi-resolution histogram provides scale invariance for feature description. For texture analysis [54], multi-resolution histograms are constructed using an image pyramid, and then a histogram is created for each pyramid level and concatenated together [10], which is referred to as a *multi-resolution histogram*. This histogram has the desirable properties of algorithm simplicity, fast computation, low memory requirements, noise tolerance, and high reliability across spatial and rotational variations. See Figure 3-16. A variation on the pyramid is used in the method of Zhao and Pietikainen [15], employing a multi-dimensional pyramid image set from a volume.

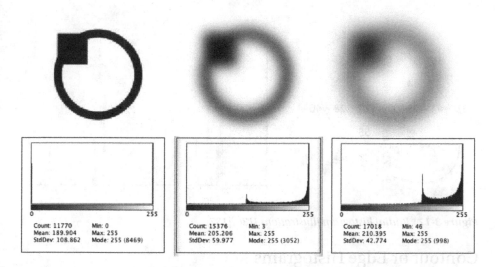

Figure 3-16. Multi-resolution histogram image sequence. Note that the multiple histograms are taken at various Gaussian blur levels in an attempt to create more invariant feature descriptors

Steps involved in creating and using multi-resolution histograms are as follows:

1. Apply Gaussian filter to image.

2. Create an image pyramid.

3. Create histograms at each level.

4. Normalize the histograms using L1 norm.

5. Create cumulative histograms.

6. Create difference histograms or DOG images (differences between pyramid levels).

7. Renormalize histograms using the difference histograms.

8. Create a feature vector from the set of difference histograms.

9. Use L1 norm as distance function for comparisons between histograms.

Radial Histograms

For some applications, computing the histogram using radial samples originating at the shape centroid can be valuable [136][137]. To do this, a line is cast from the centroid to the perimeter of the shape, and pixel values are recorded along each line and then binned into histograms. See Figure 3-17.

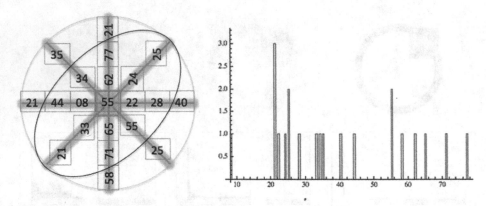

Figure 3-17. *Radial histogram illustrations [136][137]*

Contour or Edge Histograms

The perimeter or shape of an object can be the basis of a shape histogram, which includes the pixel values of each point on the perimeter of the object binned into the histogram. Besides recording the actual pixel values along the perimeter, the chain code histogram (CCH) that will be discussed in Chapter 6 shows the direction of the perimeter at connected edge point coordinates. Taken together, the CCH and contour histograms provide useful shape information.

Basis Space Metrics

Features can be described in a *basis space*, which involves transforming pixels into an alternative basis and describing features in the chosen basis, such as the frequency domain. What is a basis space and what is a transform? Consider the decimal system, which is base 10, and the binary system which is base 2. We can change numbers between the two number systems by using a transform. A Fourier transform uses sine and cosine as basis functions in frequency space, so that the Fourier transform can move pixels between the time-domain pixel space and the frequency space. Basis space moments describe the projection of a function onto a basis space [518]—for example, the Fourier transform projects a function onto a basis of harmonic functions.

Basis spaces and transforms are useful for a wide range of applications, including image coding and reconstruction, image processing, feature description, and feature matching. As shown in Figure 3-18, image representation and image coding are closely related to feature description. Images can be described using *coding methods* or *feature descriptors*, and images also can be reconstructed from the encodings or from the feature descriptors. Many methods exist to reconstruct images from alternative basis space encodings, ranging from lossless RLE methods to lossy JPEG methods; in Chapter 4, we provide illustrations of images that have been reconstructed from only local feature descriptors (see Figures 4-16 and 4-17).

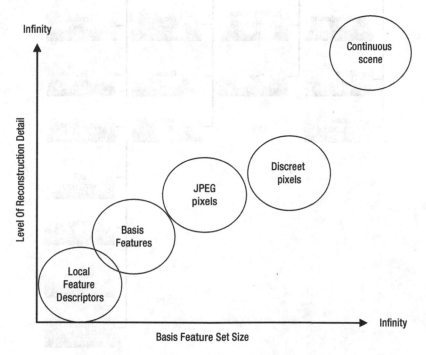

Figure 3-18. *An oversimplfiied spectrum of basis space options, showing feature set size and complexity of description and reconstruction*

As illustrated in Figure 3-18, a spectrum of basis spaces can be imagined, ranging from a continuous real function or live scene with infinite complexity, to a complete raster image, a JPEG compressed image, a frequency domain, or other basis representations, down to local feature descriptor sets. Note that the more detail that is provided and used from the basis space representation, the better the real scene can be recognized or reconstructed. So the tradeoff is to find the best representation or description, in the optimal basis space, to reach the invariance and accuracy goals using the least amount of compute and memory.

119

Transforms and basis spaces are a vast field within mathematics and signal processing, covered quite well in other works, so here we only introduce common transforms useful for image coding and feature description. We describe their key advantages and applications, and refer the reader to the literature as we go. See Figure 3-19.

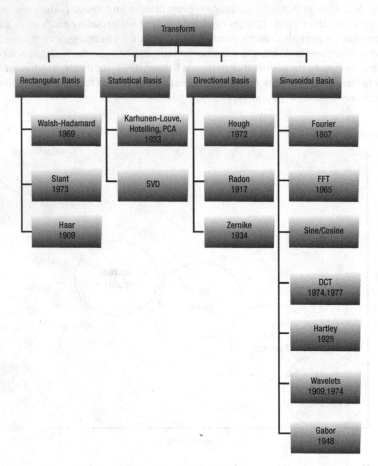

Figure 3-19. Various basis transforms used in image processing and computer vision

Since we are dealing with discrete pixels in computer vision, we are primarily interested in discrete transforms, especially those which can be accelerated with optimized software or fixed-function hardware. However, we also cover a few integral transform methods that may be slower to compute and less used. Here's an overview:

- **Global or local feature description.** It is possible to use transforms and basis space representations of images as a global feature descriptor, allowing scenes and larger objects to be recognized and compared. The 2D FFT spectrum is only one example, and it is simple to compare FFT spectrum features using SAD or SSD distance measures.

- **Image coding and compression.** Many of the transforms have proved valuable for image coding and image compression. The basic method involves transforming the image, or block regions of the image, into another basis space. For example, transforming blocks of an image into the Fourier domain allows the image regions to be represented as sine and cosine waves. Then, based on the amount of energy in the region, a reduced amount of frequency space components can be stored or coded to represent the image. The energy is mostly contained in the lower-frequency components, which can be observed in the Fourier power spectrum such as shown in Figure 2-16; the high-frequency components can be discarded and the significant lower-frequency components can be encoded, thus some image compression is achieved with a small loss of detail. Many novel image coding methods exist, such as that using a basis of scaled Laplacian features over an image pyramid.[318]

Fourier Description

The Fourier family of transforms was covered in detail in Chapter 2, in the context of image pre-processing and filtering. However, the Fourier frequency components can also be used for feature description. Using the forward Fourier transform, an image is transformed into frequency components, which can be selectively used to describe the transformed pixel region, commonly done for image coding and compression, and for feature description.

The Fourier descriptor provides several invariance attributes, such as rotation and scale. Any array of values can be fed to an FFT to generate a descriptor—for example, a histogram. A common application is illustrated in Figure 3-20, describing the circularity of a shape and finding the major and minor axis as the extrema frequency deviation from the sine wave. A related application is finding the endpoints of a flat line segment on the perimeter by fitting FFT magnitude's of the harmonic series as polar coordinates against a straight line in Cartesian space.

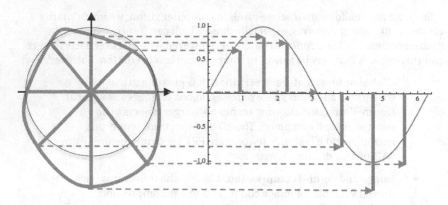

Figure 3-20. *Fourier descriptor of the odd shaped polygon surrounding the circle on the left*

In Figure 3-20, a complex wave is plotted as a dark gray circle unrolled around a sine wave function or a perfect circle. Note that the Fourier transform of the lengths of each point around the complex function yields an approximation of a periodic wave, and the Fourier descriptor of the shape of the complex wave is visible. Another example illustrating Fourier descriptors is shown in Figure 6-29.

Walsh–Hadamard Transform

The Hadamard transform [4,9] uses a series of square waves with the value of +1 or -1, which is ideal for digital signal processing. It is amenable to optimizations, since only signed addition is needed to sum the basis vectors, making this transform much faster than sinusoidal basis transforms. The basis vectors for the harmonic Hadamard series and corresponding transform can be generated by sampling Walsh functions, which make up an orthonormal basis set; thus, the combined method is commonly referred to as the Walsh-Hadamaard transform; see Figure 3-21.

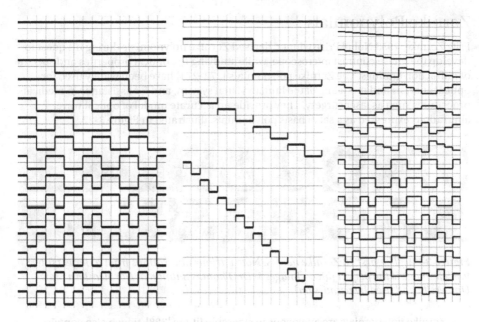

Figure 3-21. *(Left) Walsh Haramaard basis set. (Center) HAAR basis set. (Right) Slant basis set*

HAAR Transform

The HAAR transform [4,9] is similar to the Fourier transform, except that the basis vectors are HAAR features resembling square waves, and similar to wavelets. HAAR features, owing to their orthogonal rectangular shapes, are suitable for detecting vertical and horizontal images features that have near- constant gray level. Any structural discontinuities in the data, such as edges and local texture, cannot be resolved very well by the HAAR features; see Figures 3-21 and 6-22.

Slant Transform

The Slant transform [284], as illustrated in Figure 3-21, was originally developed for television signal encoding, and was later applied to general image coding [283,4]. The Slant transform is analogous to the Fourier transform, except that the basis functions are a series of slant, sawtooth, or triangle waves. The slant basis vector is suitable for applications where image brightness changes linearly over the length of the function. The slant transform is amenable to discrete optimizations in digital systems. Although the primary applications have been image coding and image compression, the slant transform is amenable to feature description. It is closely related to the Karhunen-Loeve transform and the Slant-Hadamaard transform [512].

Zernike Polynomials

Fritz Zernike, 1953 Nobel Prize winner, devised Zernike polynomials during his quest to develop the phase contrast microscope, while studying the optical properties and spectra of diffraction gratings. The Zernike polynomials [272–274] have been widely used for optical analysis and modeling of the human visual system, and for assistance in medical procedures such as laser surgery. They provide an accurate model of optical wave aberrations expressed as a set of basis polynomials, illustrated in Figure 3-22.

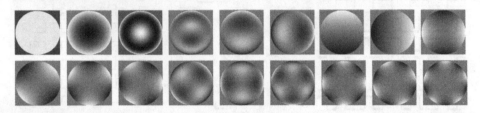

Figure 3-22. *The first 18 Zernike modes. Note various aberrations from a perfect filter; top left image is the perfect filter. (Images © Dr. Thomas Salmon at Northeastern State University and used by permission)*

Zernike polynomials are analogous to steerable filters [388], which also contain oriented basis sets of filter shapes used to identify oriented features and take moments to create descriptors. The Zernike model uses radial coordinates and circular regions, rather than rectangular patches as used in many other feature description methods.

Zernike methods are widely used in optometry to model human eye aberrations. Zernike moments are also used for image watermarking[278] and image coding and reconstruction [279,281]. The Zernike features provide scale and rotational invariance, in part due to the radial coordinate symmetry and increasing level of detail possible within the higher-order polynomials. Zernike moments are used in computer vision applications by comparing the Zernike basis features against circular patches in target images [276,277].

Fast methods to compute the Zernike polynomials and moments exist [275,280,282], which exploit the symmetry of the basis functions around the x and y axes to reduce computations, and also to exploit recursion.

Steerable Filters

Steerable filters are loosely considered as basis functions here, and can be used for both filtering or feature description. Conceptually similar to Zernike polynomials, steerable filters [388,400] are composed by synthesizing steered or oriented linearly combinations of chosen basis functions, such as quadrature pairs of Gaussian filters and oriented versions of each function, in a simple transform.

Many types of filter functions can be used as the basis for steerable filters [389,390]. The filter transform is created by combining together the basis functions in a filter bank, as shown in Figure 3-23. Gain is selected for each function, and all filters in the bank are summed, then adaptively applied to the image. Pyramid sets of basis functions can be created to operate over scale. Applications include convolving oriented steerable filters with target image regions to determine filter response strength, orientation and phase. Other applications include filtering images based on orientation of features, contour detection, and feature description.

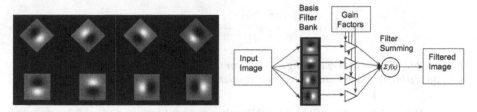

Figure 3-23. *(Left) Steerable filters basis set showing eight orientations of the first-order Gaussian filter. (Right) How steerable filters can be combined for directional filtering. Filter images generated using ImageJ Fiji SteerableJ plugin from Design of Steerable Filters for Feature Detection Using Canny-Like Criteria, M. Jacob, M. Unser, PAMI 2004*

For feature description, there are several methods that could work—for example, convolving each steerable basis function with an image patch. The highest one or two filter responses or moments from all the steerable filters can then be chosen as the set-ordinal feature descriptor, or all the filter responses can be used as a feature descriptor. As an optimization, an interest point can first be determined in the patch, and the orientation of the interest point can be used to select the one or two steerable filters closest to the orientation of the interest point; then the closest steerable filers are used as the basis to compute the descriptor.

Karhunen-Loeve Transform and Hotelling Transform

The Karhunen-Loeve transform (KLT)[4,9] was devised to describe a continuous random process as a series expansion, as opposed to the Fourier method of describing periodic signals. Hotelling later devised a discrete equivalent of the KLT using principal components. "KLT" is the most common name referring to both methods.

The basis functions are dependent on the eigenvectors of the underlying image, and computing eigenvectors is a compute-intensive process with no established fast transform known. The KLT is not separable to optimize over image blocks, so the KLT is typically used for PCA on small datasets such as feature vectors used in pattern classification, clustering, and matching.

Wavelet Transform and Gabor Filters

Wavelets, as the name suggests, are short waves or wave-lets [334]. Think of a wavelet as a short-duration pulse such as a seismic tremor, starting and ending at zero, rather than a continuous or resonating wave. Wavelets are convolved with a given signal, such as an image, to find similarity and statistical moments. Wavelets can therefore be implemented like convolution kernels in the spatial domain. See Figure 3-24.

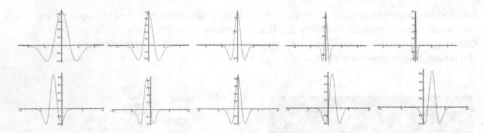

Figure 3-24. *Wavelet concepts using a "Mexican top hat" wavelet basis. (Top) A few scaled Mexican top hats derived from the mother wavelet. (Bottom) A few translated wavelets*

Wavelet analysis is a vast field [291,292] with many applications and useful resources available, including libraries of wavelet families and analysis software packages [289]. Fast wavelet transforms (FWTs) exist in common signal and image processing libraries. Several variants of the wavelet transform include:

- Discrete wavelet transform (DWT)

- Stationary wavelet transform (SWT)

- Continuous wavelet transform (CWT)

- Lifting wavelet transform (LWT)

- Stationary wavelet packet transform (SWPT)

- Discrete wavelet packet transform (DWPT)

- Fractional Fourier transform (FRFT)

- Fractional wavelet transform (FRWT)

Wavelets are designed to meet various goals, and are crafted for specific applications; there is no single wavelet function or basis. For example, a set of wavelets can be designed to represent the musical scale, where each note (such as middle C) is defined as having a duration of an eighth note wavelet pulse, and then each wavelet in the set is convolved across a signal to locate the corresponding notes in the musical scale.

When designing wavelets, the mother wavelet is the basis of the wavelet family, and then daughter wavelets are derived using translation, scaling, or compression of the mother wavelet. Ideally, a set of wavelets are overlapping and complementary so as to decompose data with no gaps and be mathematically reversible.

Wavelets are used in transforms as a set of nonlinear basis functions, where each basis function can be designed as needed to optimally match a desired feature in the input function. So, unlike transforms which use a uniform set of basis functions—as the Fourier transform uses sine and cosine functions—wavelets use a dynamic set of basis functions that are complex and nonuniform in nature. See Figure 3-25.

Figure 3-25. *Various 2D wavelet shapes: (left to right) Top hat, Shannon, Dabechies, Smylet, Coiflett*

Wavelets have been used as the basis for scale and rotation invariant feature description [288], image segmentation [285,286], shape description [287], and obviously image and signal filtering of all the expected varieties, denoising, image compression, and image coding. A set of application-specific wavelets could be devised for feature description.

Gabor Functions

Wavelets can be considered an extension of the earlier concept of Gabor functions [333,293], which can be derived for imaging applications as a set of 2D oriented bandpass filters. Gabor's work was centered on the physical transmission of sound and problems with Fourier methods involving time-varying signals like sirens that could not be perfectly represented as periodic frequency information. Gabor proposed a more compact representation than Fourier analysis could provide, using a concept called *atoms* that recorded coefficients of the sound that could be transmitted more compactly.

Hough Transform and Radon Transform

The Hough transform [228–230] and the Radon transform [299] are related, and the results are equivalent, in the opinion of many;[295][300] see Figure 3-26. The Radon transform is an integral transform, while the Hough transform is a discrete method, therefore much faster. The Hough method is widely used in image processing, and can be accelerated using a GPU [298] with data parallel methods. The Radon algorithm is slightly more accurate and perhaps more mathematically sound, and is often associated with x-ray tomography applied to reconstruction from x-ray projections. We focus primarily on the Hough transform, since it is widely available in image processing libraries.

Figure 3-26. *Line detection: (Left) Original image. (Center) Radon Transform. (Right) Hough Transform. The brightness of the transform images reveals the relative strength of the accumulators, and the sinusoidal line intersections indicate the angular orientation of features*

Key applications for the Hough and Radon transforms are shape detection and shape description of lines, circles, and parametric curves. The main advantages include:

- Robust to noise and partial occlusion

- Fill gaps in apparent lines, edges, and curves

- Can be parameterized to handle various edge and curve shapes

The disadvantages include:

- Look for one type or parameterization of a feature at a time, such as a line

- Co-linear segments are not distinguished and lumped together

- May incorrectly fill in gaps and link edges that are not connected

- Length and position of lines are not determined, but this can be done in image space

The Hough transform is primarily a global or regional descriptor and operates over larger areas. It was originally devised to detect lines, and has been subsequently generalized to detect parametric shapes [301], such as curves and circles. However, adding more parameterization to the feature requires more memory and compute. Hough features can be used to mark region boundaries described by regular parametric curves and lines. The Hough transform is attractive for some applications, since it can tolerate gaps in the lines or curves and is not strongly affected by noise or some occlusion, but morphology and edge detection via other methods is often sufficient, so the Hough transform has limited applications.

The input to the Hough transform is a gradient magnitude image, which has been thresholded, leaving the dominant gradient information. The gradient magnitude is used to build a map revealing all the parameterized features in the image—for example, lines at a given orientation or circles with a given diameter. For example, to detect lines, we map each gradient point in the pixel space into the Hough parameter space, parameterized as a single point (d,θ) corresponding to all lines with orientation angle θ at distance d from the origin. Curve and circle parameterization uses different variables [301]. The parameter space is quantized into cells or accumulator bins, and each accumulator is updated by summing the number of gradient lines passing through the same Hough points. The accumulator method is modified for detecting parametric curves and circles. Thresholding the accumulator space and re-projecting only the highest accumulator values as overlays back onto the image is useful to highlight features.

Summary

This chapter has provided a selected history of global and regional metrics, with the treatment of local feature metrics deferred until Chapters 4 and 6. Some historical context is provided on the development of structural and statistical texture metrics, as well as basis spaces useful for feature description, and several common regional and global metrics. A wide range of topics in texture analysis and statistical analysis have been surveyed with applications to computer vision.

Since it is difficult to cleanly partition all the related topics in image processing and computer vision, there is some overlap of topics in here and in Chapters 2, 4,5, and 6.

CHAPTER 4

■ ■ ■

Local Feature Design Concepts, Classification, and Learning

"Science, my boy, is made up of mistakes, but they are mistakes which it is useful to make, because they lead little by little to the truth."

— *Jules Verne,* Journey to The Center of The Earth

In this chapter we examine several concepts related to local feature descriptor design—namely local patterns, shapes, spectra, distance functions, classification, matching, and object recognition. The main focus is *local feature metrics,* as shown in Figure 4-1. This discussion follows the general vision taxonomy that will be presented in Chapter 5, and includes key fundamentals for understanding interest point detectors and feature descriptors, as will be surveyed in Chapter 6, including selected concepts common to both detector and descriptor methods. Note that the opportunity always exists to modify as well as mix and match detectors and descriptors to achieve the best results.

Vision Pipeline Stages

Sensor Processing
Image Pre-Processing
Global Metrics
Local Feature Metrics
Classification, Learning
Augment, Render, Control

Figure 4-1. *Various stages in the vision pipeline; this chapter will focus on local feature metrics and classification and learning*

Local Features

We focus on the design of *local feature descriptors* and how they are used in training, classification, and machine learning. The discussion follows the feature taxonomy as is presented in Chapter 5 and as is illustrated in Figure 5-1. The main elements are: (1) *shape* (for example, rectangle or circle); (2) *pattern* (either dense sampling or sparse sampling); and (3) *spectra* (binary values, scalars, sparse codes, or other values). A dense patterned feature will use each pixel in the local region, such as each pixel in a rectangle, while a sparse feature will use only selected pixels from the region.

In addition to the many approaches to shape and pattern, there are numerous approaches taken for the spectra, ranging from gradient-based patch methods to sparse local binary pattern methods. The main topics covered here include:

- **Detectors**, used to locate interesting features in the image.

- **Descriptors**, used to describe the regions surrounding interesting features.

- **Descriptor attributes**, such as feature robustness and invariance.

- **Classification**, used to create databases of features and optimal feature matching.

- **Recognition**, used to match detected features in target images against trained features.

- **Feature learning**, or machine learning methods.

Based on the concepts presented this chapter, the vision taxonomy offered in Chapter 5 provides a way to summarize and analyze the feature descriptors and their attributes, thereby enabling limited comparison between the different approaches.

Detectors, Interest Points, Keypoints, Anchor Points, Landmarks

A *detector* finds interesting features in the image. The terminology in the literature for discussing an "interesting feature" includes several interchangeable terms, such as *keypoint, landmark, interest point,* or *anchor point,* all of which refer to features such as corners, edges, or patterns that can be found repeatedly with high likelihood. In Chapter 6, we will survey many detector methods, along with various design approaches. In some cases, the keypoint detector is used to determine the orientation vector of the surrounding feature descriptor—for example, by computing the overall gradient orientation of the corner. The uncertain or low-quality keypoints are commonly filtered out prior to feature description. Note that many keypoint methods operate on smaller pixel regions, such as 3x3 for the LBP and 7x7 for FAST.

The keypoint location itself may not be enough for feature matching; however, some methods discussed here rely on *keypoints only,* without a feature descriptor. Feature description provides more information around each keypoint, and may be computed over larger regions and multiple scales, such as SIFT and ORB.

Descriptors, Feature Description, Feature Extraction

A feature *descriptor* can be computed at each key point to provide more information about the pixel region surrounding the keypoint. However, in methods that compute features across a fixed-size pixel grid such as the Viola Jones method [146], no interest point is necessary, since the grid defines the descriptor region. Feature description typically uses some combination of color or gray scale intensity channels, as well as local information such as gradients and colors. Feature description takes place over a shape, such as a square or circle. In some cases, pixel point-pair sample patterns are used to compute or compare selected pixel values to yield a *descriptor vector*—for example, as shown later, in Figure 4-8.

Typically, an interest point provides some amount of invariance and robustness—for example, in scale and rotation. In many cases, the orientation of the descriptor is determined from the interest point, and the descriptor provides other invariance attributes. Combining the interest point with the descriptor provides a larger set of invariance attributes. And if several descriptors are associated together from the same object, object recognition is possible.

For example, a descriptor may contain multivariate, multidimensional, and multigeometric quantities calculated over several intensity channels, multiple geometric scales, and multiple perspectives. A *multivariate* descriptor may contain RGBD data (red, green, blue, and Z depth data); a *multidimensional* descriptor may contain feature descriptions at various levels of zoom across an image pyramid; and a *multigeometry* descriptor may contain a set of feature descriptions computed across affine transforms of the local image patch or region.

There is no right or wrong method for designing features; many approaches are taken. For example, a set of metrics including region shape, region texture, and region color of an object may be helpful in an application to locate fruit, while another application may not need color or shape and can rely instead on sets of interest points, feature descriptors, and their spatial relationships. In fact, combining several weaker descriptor methods into a multivariate descriptor is often the best approach.

Computing feature descriptors from an image is commonly referred to as *feature extraction.*

Sparse Local Pattern Methods

While some methods describe features densely within regular sampling grids across an image, such as the PHOG [191] method discussed in Chapter 6, other methods such as FREAK [130] use *sparse local patterns* to sample pixels anchored at interest points to create the descriptor. Depending on the method, the shapes may be trained, learned, or chosen by design, and many topologies of shapes and patterns are in current use.

To frame the discussion on sparse local pattern and descriptor methods, notice that there is a contrast with global and regional descriptor methods, which typically do *not* rely on sparse local patterns. Instead, global and regional methods typically use dense sampling of larger shapes such as rectangles or other polygons. For example, polygon shape descriptors, as will be discussed in Chapter 6, may delineate or segment the feature region using dense methods such as mathematical morphology and region segmentation. Global and regional descriptor metrics, such as texture metrics, histograms, or SDMs discussed in Chapter 3, are typically computed across cohesive, dense regions rather than sparse regions.

133

Local Feature Attributes

This section discusses how features are chosen to provide the desired attributes of feature goodness, such as invariance and robustness.

Choosing Feature Descriptors and Interest Points

Both the interest point detector and the feature description method must be chosen to work well together, and to work well for the type of images being processed. Robustness attributes such as contrast, scale, and rotation must be considered for both the detector and the descriptor pair. As shown in Appendix A, each interest point detector is best designed to find specific types of features, and therefore no single method is good for all types of images.

For example, FAST and Harris methods typically find many small *mono-scale* interest points, while other methods, such as that used in SIFT find fewer, larger and finely tuned *multi-scale* interest points. Some tuning of the interest point detector parameters is expected, so as to make them work at all, or else some pre-processing of the images maybe needed to help the detector find the interest points in the first place. (Chapter 6 provides a survey of interest point methods and background mathematical concepts.)

Feature Descriptors and Feature Matching

Feature description is foundational to *feature matching*, leading to image understanding, scene analysis, and object tracking. The central problems in feature matching include how to determine if a feature is differentiated from other similar features, and if the feature is part of a larger object.

The method of determining a feature match is critical, for many reasons; these reasons include compute cost, memory size, repeatability, accuracy, and robustness. While a perfect match is ideal, in practice a relative match is determined by a *distance function*, where the incoming set of feature descriptors is compared with known feature descriptors. But we'll discuss several distance functions later in this chapter.

Criteria for Goodness

Measuring the goodness of features can be done *one attribute at a time*. A general list of goodness attributes for feature landmarks is provided later, in Table 4-2. Note that this list is primarily about invariance and robustness: these are the key concepts, since performance can be tuned using various optimization methods, as will be discussed in Chapter 8. Of course, in a given application some attributes of goodness are more important than others; this is discussed in Chapter 7, in connection with ground truth data.

How do we know a feature is *good* for an application? We may divide the discussion between the interest point methods and the descriptor method, and the combined robustness and invariance attributes provided by both (see Table 4-1). The interest point at which the feature is anchored is critical, since if the anchor is not good and cannot be easily and repeatedly found, the resulting descriptor is calculated at a suboptimal location.

Table 4-1. *Some Attributes for Good Feature Descriptors and Interest Points. (See also Figure 5-2 for the general robustness criteria)*

Good Feature Metric Attributes	Details
Scale invariance	Should be able to find the feature at different scales
Perspective invariance	Should be able to find the feature from different perspectives in the field of view
Rotational invariance	The feature should be recognized in various rotations within the image plane
Translation invariance	The feature should be recognized in various positions in the FOV
Reflection invariance	The feature should be recognized as a mirror image of itself
Affine invariance	The feature should be recognized under affine transforms
Noise invariance	The feature should be detectable in the presence of noise
Illumination invariance	The feature should be recognizable in various lighting conditions including changes in brightness and contrast
Compute efficiency	The feature descriptor should be efficient to compute and match
Distinctiveness	The feature should be distinct and detectable, with a low probability of mis-match, amenable to matching from a database of features
Compact to describe	The feature should not require large amounts of memory to hold details
Occlusion robustness	The feature or set of features can be described and detected when parts of the feature or feature set are occluded
Focus or blur robustness	The feature or set of features can be detected at varying degrees of focus (i.e, image pyramids can provide some of this capability)
Clutter and outlier robustness	The feature or set of features can be detected in the presence of outlier features and clutter

Note that in many cases, image pre-processing is key to creating a good feature (Figure 4-1). If the image data has problems that can be corrected or improved, the feature description should be done after the image pre-processing. Note that many feature description methods rely on local image enhancements during descriptor creation, such as Gaussian blur of regions around keypoints for noise removal, so image pre-processing should complement the descriptor method. Each pre-processing method has drawbacks and advantages; see Table 2-1 and Chapter 2 for information on image pre-preprocessing.

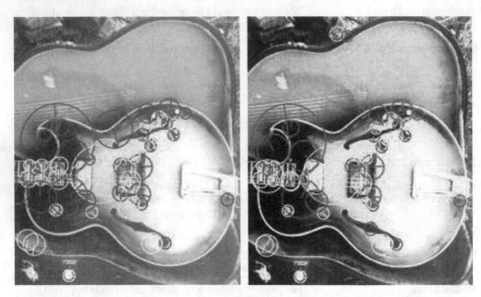

Figure 4-2. *(Left) SURF feature descriptors calculated over original image. (Right) Image has been pre-processed using histogram equalization prior to feature extraction and therefore a different but overlapping set of features is found*

Repeatability, Easy vs. Hard to Find

Ideally the feature will be easy to find in an image, meaning that the feature description contains sufficient information to be robust under various conditions (as shown in Table 4-1), such as contrast and brightness variations, scale, and rotation. *Repeatability* applies particularly to interest point detection, so the choice of interest point detector method is critical. (Appendix A contains example images showing interesting nonrepeatability anomalies for several common interest point detectors.)

Some descriptors, such as SIFT [161,178], are known to be robust under many imaging conditions. This is not too surprising, since SIFT is designed to be discriminating over multiple dimensions, such as scale and rotation, using carefully composed sets of local region gradients with a weighting factor applied to increase the importance of gradients closer to the center of the feature. But the robustness and repeatability come at a compute cost. SIFT [161,178] is one of the most computationally expensive methods; however, Chapter 6 surveys various SIFT optimizations and variations.

Distinctive vs. Indistinctive

A descriptor is distinctive if:

- The feature can be differentiated from other, similar feature regions of the image.

- Different feature vectors are unique in the feature set.

- The feature can be matched effectively using a suitable distance function.

A feature is indistinct if similar features cannot be distinguished; this may be caused by a lack of suitable image pre-processing, insufficient information in the descriptor, or an unsuitable distance function chosen for the matching stage. Of course, adding information into a simpler descriptor to make the descriptor a hybrid multivariate or multi-scale descriptor may be all that is needed to improve distinctiveness. For example, color information can be added to distinguish between skin tones.

Relative and Absolute Position

Positional information, such as coordinates, can be critical for feature goodness. For example, to associate features together using constraints on the corner position of human eyes, interest point coordinates are needed. These enable more accurate identification and location of the eyes by using, as part of an intelligent matching process, the distance and angles between the eye corner locations.

With the increasing use of depth sensors, simply providing the Z or depth location of the feature in the descriptor itself may be enough to easily distinguish a feature from the background. Position in the depth field is a powerful bit of information, and since computer vision is often concerned with finding 3D information in a 2D image field, the Z depth information can be an invaluable attribute for feature goodness.

Matching Cost and Correspondence

Feature matching is a measurement of the correspondence between two or more features using a *distance function* (discussed next in this section). Note here that feature matching has a cost in terms of memory and compute time. For example, if a feature descriptor is composed of an array of 8-bit bytes, such as an 18x18 pixel correlation template, then the feature matching cost is the compute time and memory required to compare two 18x18 (324) pixel regions against each other, where the matching method or distance function used may be SAD, SSD, or similar difference metric. Another example involves local binary descriptors such as the LBP (linear binary patterns), which are stored as bit vectors, where the matching cost is the time to perform the Hamming distance function, which operates by comparing two binary vectors via Boolean XOR followed by a bit count to provide the match metric.

In general, distance functions are well-known mathematical functions that are applied to computer vision; however, some are better suited than others in terms of computability and application to a specific vision task. For example, SSD, SAD, cosine distance, and Hamming distance metrics have been implemented in silicon as computer machine language instructions in some architectures, owing to their wide applicability. So choosing a distance function that is accelerated in silicon can be an advantage.

The feature database is another component of the matching cost, so the organization of the database and feature search contribute to the cost. We briefly touch on this topic later in this chapter.

Distance Functions

This section provides a general discussion of distance functions used for clustering, classification, and feature matching. Note that distance functions can be taken over several dimensions—for example, 2D image arrays for feature descriptor matching, 3D voxel volumes for point cloud matching, and multidimensional spaces for multivariate descriptors. Since this is a brief overview, a deeper treatment is available by Pele[548].

Note that kernel machines [361,362], discussed later in this chapter, provide an automated framework to classify a feature space and substitute chosen distance function kernels.

Early Work on Distance Functions

In 1968, Rosenfeld and Pfaltz[121] developed novel methods for determining the distance between image features, which they referred to as "a given subset of the picture," where the feature shapes used in their work included diamonds, squares, and triangles. The distance metrics they studied include some methods that are no longer in common use today:

- Hexagonal distance from a single point (Cartesian array)

- Hexagonal distance from a single point (staggered array)

- Octagonal distance from a single point

- City block distance from blank areas

- Square distances from blank areas

- Hexagonal distance from blank areas

- Octagonal distance from blank areas

- Nearest integer to Euclidean distance from a single point

This early work by Rosenfeld and Pfaltz is fascinating, since the output device used to render the images was ASCII characters printed on a CRT terminal or line printer, as shown in Figure 4-3.

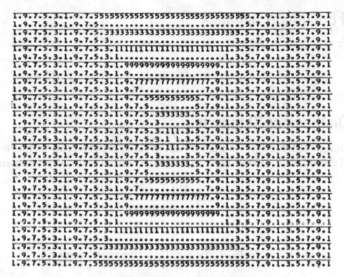

"Square" distances (d_2) from a single point.

Figure 4-3. An early Rosenfeld and Pfaltz rendering that illustrates a distance function (square distance in this case) using a line printer as the output device. (Image © reprinted from Rosenfeld and Pfaltz, Pattern Recognition (Oxford: Pergamon Press, 1968), 1:33-61. Used with permission from Elsevier)

Euclidean or Cartesian Distance Metrics

The Euclidean distance metrics include basic Euclidean geometry identities in Cartesian coordinate spaces; in general, these are simple and obvious to use.

Euclidean Distance

This is the simple distance between two points.

$$EuclideanDistance\big[\{a,b\},\{x,y\}\big] = \sqrt{(a-x)^2 + (b-y)^2}$$

Squared Euclidean Distance

This is faster to compute, and omits the square root.

$$SquaredEuclideanDistance\big[\{a,b\},\{x,y\}\big] = (a-x)^2 + (b-y)^2$$

Cosine Distance or Similarity

This is angular distance, or the normalized dot product between two vectors to yield similarity of vector angle; also useful for 3D surface normal and viewpoint matching.

$$cos(\theta) = \frac{A.B}{\|A\|\,\|B\|}$$

$$CosineDistance\big[\{a,b\},\{x,y\}\big] = 1 - \frac{ax+by}{\sqrt{a^2+b^2}\,\sqrt{x^2+y^2}}$$

Sum of Absolute Differences (SAD) or L1 Norm

The difference between vector elements is summed and taken as the total distance between the vectors. Note that SAD is equivalent to Manhattan distance.

$$SAD(d_1,d_2) = \sum_{i=0}^{n1}\sum_{j=0}^{n2}(d_1[i,j]-d_2[i,j])$$

Sum of Squared Differences (SSD) or L2 Norm

The difference between vector elements is summed and squared and taken as the total distance between the vectors; commonly used in video decoding for motion estimation.

$$SSD(d_1,d_2) = \sum_{i=0}^{n1}\sum_{j=0}^{n2}(d_1[i,j]-d_2[i,j])^2$$

Correlation Distance

This is the correlation difference coefficient between two vectors, similar to cosine distance.

$$C[u,v] = \frac{1 - (u - Mean[u]) \cdot (v - Mean[v])}{\|u - Mean[u]\| \|v - Mean[v]\|}$$

$$[\{a,b\},\{x,y\}] = \frac{\left(a + \frac{1}{2}(-a-b)\right)\left(x + \frac{1}{2}(-x-y)\right) + \left(\frac{1}{2}(-a-b)+b\right)\left(\frac{1}{2}(-x-y)+y\right)}{\sqrt{Abs\left[a + \frac{1}{2}(-a-b)\right]^2 + Abs\left[\frac{1}{2}(-a-b)+b\right]^2}\sqrt{Abs\left[x + \frac{1}{2}(-x-y)\right]^2 Abs\left[\frac{1}{2}(-x-y)+y\right]^2}}$$

Hellinger Distance

An effective alternative to Euclidean distance, yielding better performance and accuracy for histogram-type distance metrics, as reported in the ROOTSIFT [178] optimization of SIFT. Hellinger distance is defined for L1 normalized histogram vectors as:

$$H(x,y) = \sum_{i=1}^{n} \sqrt{x_i y_i}$$

Grid Distance Metrics

These metrics calculate distance analogous to paths on grids. Therefore the distance is measured as grid steps.

Manhattan Distance

Also known as city block difference or rectilinear distance, this measures distance via the route along a grid; there may be more than one path along a grid with equal distance.

$$ManhattanDistance\left[\{a,b\},\{x,y\}\right] = Abs(a-x) + Abs(b-y)$$

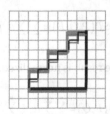

Chebyshev Distance

Also known as chessboard difference, this measures the greatest difference along a grid between two vectors. Note in the illustration below that each side of the triangle would have a Chebyshev distance, or length of 5, but in Euclidean space, one of the lines, the hypotenuse, is longer than the others.

$$ChebyshevDistance\big[\{a,b\},\{x,y\}\big] = Max[Abs(a-x), Abs(b-y)]$$

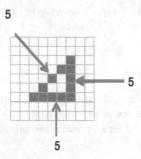

Statistical Difference Metrics

These metrics are based on statistical features of the vectors, and therefore the distance metrics need not map into a Euclidean space.

Earth Movers Distance (EMD) or Wasserstein Metric

Earth movers distance measures the cost to transform a multidimensional vector, such as a histogram, into another vector. The analogy is an earth mover (bulldozer) moving dirt between two groups of piles to make the piles of dirt in each group the same size. The EMD assumes there is a ground distance between the features in the vector—for example, the distance between bins in a histogram. The EMD is computed to be the minimal cost for the transform, which integrates the distance moved d * the amount moved f, subject to a few constraints [130].

$$COST(P,Q,F) = \sum_{i=1}^{m}\sum_{j=1}^{n} d_{ij} f_{ij}$$

Once the cost is computed, the result is normalized.

$$EMD(P,Q) = \sum_{i=1}^{m}\sum_{j=1}^{n} d_{ij} f_{ij} \sum_{i=1}^{m}\sum_{j=1}^{n} f_{ij}$$

The EMD has a high compute cost and can be useful for image analysis, but EMD is not an efficient metric for feature matching.

Mahalanobis Distance

Also known as quadratic distance, this computes distance using mean and covariance; it is scale invariant.

$$d_{ij} = \left(\left(\overline{x}_i - \overline{x}_j \right)^T S^{-1} \left(\overline{x}_i - \overline{x}_j \right) \right)^{\frac{1}{2}}$$

$$SSD(d_1,d_2) = \sum_{i=-n1}^{n1} \sum_{j=-n2}^{n2} f\left((x+i,y+j) - g(x+i-d_1,y_j-d_2) \right)^2$$

where $\overline{x}_i$ = mean of feature vector 1, and $\overline{x}_j$ = mean of feature vector 2.

Bray Curtis Distance

This is equivalent to a ratio of the sums of absolute differences and sums, such as a ratio of norms of Manhattan distances. Bray Curtis dissimilarity is sometimes used for clustering data.

$$BrayCurtisDistance\left[\{a,b,c\},\{x,y,z\} \right] = \frac{Abs(a-x)+Abs(b-y)+Abs(c-z)}{Abs(a+x)+Abs(b+y)+Abs(c+z)}$$

Canberra Distance

This measures the distance between two vectors of equal length:

$$CanberraDistance\left[\{a,b\},\{x,y\} \right] = \frac{Abs(a-x)}{Abs(a)+Abs(x)} + \frac{Abs(b-y)}{Abs(b)+Abs(y)}$$

Binary or Boolean Distance Metrics

These metrics rely on set comparisons and Boolean algebra concepts, which makes this family of metrics attractive for optimization on digital computers.

L0 Norm

The L0 norm is a count of non-zero elements in a vector and is used in the Hamming Distance metric and other binary or Boolean metrics.

$$\|x\|_0 = \#(i \mid x_i \neq 0)$$

Hamming Distance

This measures the binary difference or agreement between vectors of equal length—for example, string or binary vectors. Hamming distance for binary bit vectors can be efficiently implemented in digital computers with either complete machine language instructions or as as an XOR operation followed by a bit count operation. Hamming distance is a favorite for matching local binary descriptors, such as LBP, FREAK, CENSUS, BRISK, BRIEF, and ORB.

> *String distance:* 5 = 0001100111 = compare "Hel**lo**Th**ere**" and
> "Hel**ps**Th**ing**"
>
> *Binary distance:* 3 = 10100010 = (**01**0011**10**) XOR (**11**0011**00**)
>
> **Bit count of (u XOR v)**

Jaccard Similarity and Dissimilarity

The ratio of pairwise similarity of a binary set (0,1 or true, false) over the number of set elements. Set 1 below contains two bits with the same pairwise value as Set 2, so the similarity is 2/5 and the dissimilarity is 3/5. Jaccard similarity can be combined with Hamming distance.

> *Set 1:* {1,0,1,1,0}
>
> *Set 2:* {1,1,0,1,1}
>
> *Jaccard Similarity:* 2 / 5 = .4
>
> **Jaccard Dissimilarity:** **3 / 5 = .6**

Descriptor Representation

This section discusses how information is represented in the descriptors, including coordinates spaces useful for feature description and matching, with some discussion of multimodal data and feature pyramids.

Coordinate Spaces, Complex Spaces

There are many coordinate systems used in computer vision, so being able to transform data between coordinate systems is valuable. Coordinate spaces are analogous to basis spaces. Often, choosing the right coordinate system provides advantages for feature representation, computation, or matching. Complex spaces may include multivariate collections of scalar and vector variables, such as gradients, color, binary patterns, and statistical moments of pixel regions. See Figure 4-4.

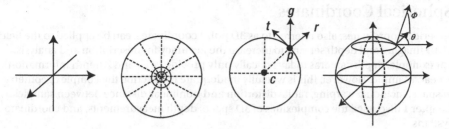

Figure 4-4. *Coordinate spaces, Cartesian, polar, radial, and spherical*

Cartesian Coordinates

Images are typically captured in the time domain in a Cartesian space, and for many applications translating to other coordinate spaces is needed. The human visual system views the world as a complex 3D spherical coordinate space, and humans can, through a small miracle, map the 3D space into approximate or relative Cartesian coordinates. Computer imaging systems capture data and convert it to Cartesian coordinates, but depth perception and geometric accuracy are lost in the conversion. (Chapter 1 provided a discussion of depth-sensing methods and 3D imaging systems, including geometric considerations.)

Polar and Log Polar Coordinates

Many descriptors mentioned later in Chapter 6 use a circular descriptor region to match the human visual system. Therefore, polar coordinates are logical candidates to bin the feature vectors. For example, the GLOH [144] method uses polar coordinates for histogram gradient binning, rather than Cartesian coordinates as used in the original SIFT [161] method. GLOH can be used as a retrofit for SIFT and has proved to increase accuracy [144]. Since the circular sampling patterns tend to provide better rotational invariance, polar coordinates and circular sampling are a good match for descriptor design.

Radial Coordinates

The RIFF descriptor (described later in Chapter 6) uses a local radial coordinate system to describe rotationally invariant gradient-based feature descriptors. The radial coordinate system is based on a radial gradient transform (RGT) that normalizes vectors for invariant binning.

As shown in Figures 4-4 and 6-27, the RGT creates a local coordinate system within a patch region c, and establishes two orthogonal basis vectors (r,t) relative to any point p in the patch, r for the radial vector, and t for the tangential vector. The measured gradients g at all points p are projected onto the radial coordinate system (r,t), so that the gradients are represented in a locally invariant fashion relative to the interest point c at the center of the patch. When the patch is rotated about c, the gradients rotate also, and the invariant representation holds.

Spherical Coordinates

Spherical coordinates, also referred to as 3D polar coordinates, can be applied to the field of 3D imaging and depth sensing to increase the accuracy for description and analysis. For example, depth cameras today typically only provide (x,y), and Z depth information for each sample. However, this is woefully inadequate to describe the complex geometry of space, including warping, radial distortion and nonlinear distance between samples. Chapter 1 discussed the complexities of 3D space, depth measurements, and coordinate systems.

Gauge Coordinates

The G-SURF methods [188] use a differential geometry concept [190] of a local region Gauge coordinate system to compute the features. Gauge coordinates are local to the image feature, and they carry advantages for geometrical accuracy. Gauge derivatives are rotation and translation invariant.

Multivariate Spaces, Multimodal Data

Multivariate spaces combine several quantities, such as Tensor spaces which combine scalar and vector values, and are commonly used in computer vision. While raw image data may be scalar values only, many feature descriptors compute local gradients at each pixel, so the combination of pixel scalar value and gradient vector forms a tensor or multivariate space. For example, color spaces (see Chapter 2) may represent color as a set of scalar and vector quantities, such as the hue, saturation, and value (HSV) color space illustrated in Figure 2-9, where the vectors include *HS* with *H* hue as the vector angle and *S* saturation as the vector magnitude. *V* is another vector with two purposes, first as the axis origin for the *HS* vector and second as the color intensity or gray scale vector *V*. It is often useful to convert raw *RGB* data into such color spaces for ease of analysis—for example, to be able to uniformly change the color intensity of all colors together so as to affect brightness or contrast.

In general, by increasing the dimensions of the feature space, more discrimination and robustness can be added. For example, the LBP pattern as described later in Chapter 6 can be extended into multiple variables by adding features such as a rotational invariant representation (RILBP); or by replicating the LBP across *RGB* color cannels as demonstrated in the color LBP descriptor; or by extending the LBP pattern into spatio-temporal 3-space, like the LBP-TOP to add geometric distortion invariance.

Multimodal sensor data is becoming widespread with the proliferation of mobile devices that have built-in GPS, compass, temperature, altimeter, inertial and other sensors. An example of a multimodal, multivariate descriptor is the SIFT-GAFD [245] method, as illustrated in Figure 4-5, which adds accelerometer information in the form of a gravity vector to the SIFT descriptor. The gravity vector is referred to as *global orientation*, and the SIFT local pixel region gradient is referred to as the *local orientation*.

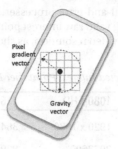

Figure 4-5. *Multimodal descriptor using accelerometer data in the form of a gravity vector, in a feature descriptor as used in the SIFT-GAFD method [245]. The gravity vector of global orientation can be used for feature orientation with respect to the environment*

Feature Pyramids

Many feature descriptors are computed in a mono-scale fashion using pixel values at a given scale only, and then for feature detection and matching the feature is searched for in a scale space image pyramid. However, by computing the descriptor at multiple scales and storing multiple scaled descriptors together in a *feature pyramid*, the feature can be detected on mono-scale images with scale variance without using a scale space pyramid.

For interest point and feature descriptor methods, *scale invariance* can be addressed either by: (1) scaling the images prior to searching, as in the scale space pyramid methods discussed later in this chapter; or (2) scaling and pyramiding multiple scales of the feature in the descriptor. Shape-based methods are by nature more scale invariant than interest point and feature descriptor methods, since shape-based methods depend on larger polygon structures and shape metrics.

Descriptor Density

Depending on the image data, there will be a different number of good interest points and features, since some images have more pronounced texture. And depending on the detector method used, images with high texture structure, or wider pixel intensity range differences, will likely generate more interest points than images with low contrast and smooth texture.

A good rule of thumb is that between .1 and 1 percent of the pixels in an image can yield raw, unfiltered interest points. The more sensitive detectors such as FAST and the Harris detector family are at the upper end of this range (see Appendix A). Of course, detector parameters are tuned to reduce unwanted detection for each application.

Interest Point and Descriptor Culling

In fact, even though the interest point looks good, the corresponding descriptor computed at the interest point may not be worth using and will be discarded in some cases. Both interest points and descriptors are culled. So tuning the detector and

descriptor together are critical trial-and-error processes. Using our base assumption of .
1 to 1 percent of the pixels yielding valid raw interest points, we can estimate the possible
detected interest points based on video resolution, as shown in Table 4-2.

Table 4-2. *Possible Range of Detected Interest Points per Image*

	480p NTSC	1080p HD	2160p 4kUHD	4320p 8kUHD
Resolution	640 x 480	1920 x 1080	3840 × 2160	7680 x 4320
Pixels	307200	2073600	8294400	33177600
Interest points	300 – 3k	2k – 21k	8k – 83k	33k – 331k

Depending on the approach, the detector may be run only at mono-scale or across a
set of scaled images in an image pyramid scale space. For scale space search methods, the
interest point detector is run at each pixel in each image in the pyramid. What methods can
be used to cull interest points to reduce the interest point density to a manageable number?

One method to select the best interest points is to use an *adaptive detector tuning
method* (as discussed in Chapter 6 under "Interest Point Tuning"). Other approaches
include only choosing interest points at a given threshold distance apart—for example,
an interest point that cannot be adjacent to another interest point within a five-pixel
window, with the best candidate point selected within the threshold.

Another method is to vary the search strategy as discussed in this chapter—for
example, search for features at a lower resolution of the image pyramid, identify the best
features, and record their positions, and perhaps search at higher levels of the pyramid
to confirm the feature location, then compute the descriptors. This last method has the
drawback of missing fine-grain features by default, since features may only be present at
full image resolution.

Yet another method is to look for interest points every other pixel or within grid-sized
regions. All of the above methods are used in practice, and other methods exist besides.

Dense vs. Sparse Feature Description

A *dense* descriptor makes use of all the pixels in the region or patch. By "dense" we mean
that the kernel sampling pattern includes all the pixels, since a sparse kernel may select
specific pixels to use or ignore. SIFT and SURF are classic examples of dense descriptors,
since all pixels in rectangular regions contribute to the descriptor computation.

Many feature description methods, especially local binary descriptor methods, are
making use of *sparse patterns*, where selected pixels are used from a region rather than
all the pixels. The FREAK descriptor demonstrates one of the most ingenious methods
of sparse sampling by modeling the human visual system, using a circular search region,
and leveraging the finer resolution sampling closer to the center of the region, as well as
tuning a hierarchy of local sampling patterns of increasing resolution for optimal results.
Not only can sparse features potentially use less memory and reduce computations,
but the sparse descriptor can be spread over a wider area to compensate for feature
anomalies that occur in smaller regions.

Descriptor Shape Topologies

For this discussion, we view descriptor shape *topology* with an eye toward surveying the various shapes of the pixel regions used for descriptor computations. Part of the topology is the shape or boundary, and part of the topology is the choice of dense vs. sparse sampling patterns, discussed later in this chapter. Sampling and pattering methods range from the simple rectangular regions up to the more complex sparse local binary descriptor patterns. As will be discussed in Chapter 6, both 2D and 3D descriptors are being designed to use a wide range of topologies. Let's look at a few topological design considerations, such as patch shape, sub-patches, strips, and deformable patches.

Which shape is better? The answer is subjective and we do not attempt to provide absolute answers, just offer a survey.

Correlation Templates

An obvious shape is the simple rectangular regions commonly used by correlation template matching methods. The descriptor is thus the *mugshot,* or actual image in the template region. To select sub-spaces within the rectangle, a mask can be used—for example, it could be a circular mask inside the bounding rectangle to mask off peripheral pixels from consideration.

Patches and Shape

The literature commonly refers to the feature shape as a *patch*, and usually a rectangular shape is assumed. Patch shapes are commonly rectangular owing to the ease of coding 2D array memory access. Circular patches are widely used in the local binary descriptor methods.

However, many descriptors also compute features *over multiple patches* or regions, not just a single patch. Here are some common variations on patch topology.

Single Patches, Sub-Patches

Many descriptors limit the patch count to a single 2D patch. This is true of most common descriptors that are surveyed in Chapter 6. However, some of the local binary descriptors use a set of integral image *sub-patches* at specific points within the larger patch—for example, BRIEF uses a 5x5 integral image sub-patch at each sample point in the local binary pattern, within the larger 31x31 pixel patch region, so the value of each sub-patch becomes the value used for the point-pair comparison. The goal is to filter the values at each point to remove noise.

Deformable Patches

Rather than use a rigid shape, such as a fixed-size rectangle or a circle, feature descriptors can be designed with deformation in mind, such as scale deformations [345,346], and affine or homographic deformation [220], to enable more robust matching. Examples include the DeepFlow [344,394] deep matching method, and RFM2.3, as will be discussed in Chapter 6. Also, the D-NETS [135] method, using the fully connected or sparse connected topology, can be considered to be deformable in terms of invariance of the placement of the strip patterns; see Figure 4-7 and the discussion of D-nets in Chapter 6. Many feature learning methods discussed later in this chapter also use deformed features for training.

Fixed descriptor shapes, such as rigid rectangles and circles, can detect motion under a rigid motion hypothesis, where the entire descriptor is expected to move with some amount of variance, such as in scale or affine transformation. However, for activity recognition and motion, a more deformable descriptor model is needed, and DeepFlow [344,394] bridges the gap between descriptor matching methods and optical flow matching methods, using deformable patches and deep matching along the lines of deep learning networks.

Multi-Patch Sets

The SIFT descriptor uses multi-patch sets of three patches from adjacent DoG images taken from the scale space pyramid structure, as shown in Figure 6-15. Several other methods, such as the LBP-TOP and VLBP shown in Figure 6-12, use sets of patches spread across a volume structure. LBP-TOP uses patches from adjacent planes, and the VLBP uses intersecting patches in 3-space. Dynamic texture methods use sets of three adjacent patches from spatio-temporal image frame sets, as frame n-2, frame n-1, and frame-0 (current frame).

TPLBP, FPLBP

The three-patch LBP TPLBP and four-patch LBP FPLBP [244] utilize novel multi-patch sampling patterns to add sparse local structure into a composite LBP descriptor. As shown in Figure 4-6, the three-patch LBP uses a radial set of LBP patterns composed using alternating sets of three patches, and the four-patch LBP uses a more distributed pairing of patches over a wider range.

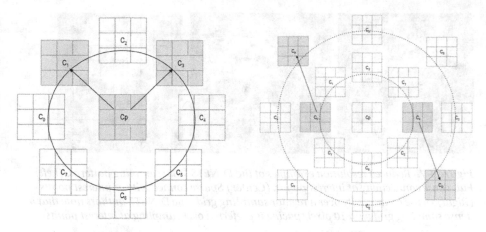

Figure 4-6. *Novel multi-patch sets developed by Wolf et. al [244]. (Left) The TPLBP compares the values from three-patch sets around the ring to compute the LBP code, eight sets total, so there is one set for each LBP bit. (Right) The four-patch LBP uses four patches to computed bits using two symmetrically distributed patches from each ring, to produce each bit in the LBP code. The radius of each ring is a variable, the patch pairing is a variable, and the number of patches per ring is a variable; here, there are eight patches per ring*

Strip and Radial Fan Shapes

Radial fans or spokes originating at the feature interest point location or shape centroid can be used as the descriptor sampling topology—for example, with Fourier shape descriptors (as discussed in Chapter 6; see especially Figure 6-29).

D-NETS Strip Patterns

The D-NETS method developed by Hundelshausen and Sukthankar[135] uses a connected graph-shaped descriptor pattern with variations in the sampling pattern possible. The authors suggest that the method is effective using three different patterns, as shown in Figure 4-7:

1. Fully connected graph at interest points

2. Sparse or iterative connected graph at interest points

3. Densely sampled graph over a chosen grid

Figure 4-7. *Reduced resolution examples of the D-NETS [135] sampling patterns. (Left)*
Full dense connectivity at interest points. (Center) Sparse connectivity at interest points.
(Right) Dense connectivity over a regular sampling grid. The D-NETS authors note that a
dense sampling grid with 10 pixel spacing is preferred over sampling at interest points

The descriptor itself is composed of a set of *d-tokens,* which are strips of raw pixel values rather than a value from a patch region: the strip is the region, and various orientations of lines are the pattern. The sampling along the strip is between 80 and 20 percent of the strip length rather than the entire length, omitting the endpoints, which is claimed to reduce the contribution of noisy interest points. The sampled points are combined into a set *s* of uniform chunks of pixels and normalized and stored into a discrete d-token descriptor.

Object Polygon Shapes

The object and polygon shape methods scan globally and regionally to find the shapes in the entire image frame or region. The goal is to find an object or region that is cohesive. A discussion of the fundamental methods for segmentation polygon shapes for feature descriptors is provided here, including:

- Morphological object boundary methods

- Texture or regional structural methods

- Superpixel or pixel similarity methods

- Depth map segmentation

Chapter 6 provides details on a range of object shape factors and metrics used to statistically describe the features of polygon shape. Note that this topic is often discussed in the literature as "image moments"; a good source of information is Flusser et.al.[518].

Morphological Boundary Shapes

One method for defining polygon shapes is to use morphology. Morphological segmentation is a common method for region delineation, either as a binary object or as a gray scale object. Morphological shapes are sometimes referred to as *blobs*. In both binary and gray scale cases, thresholding is often used as a first step toward defining the object boundary, and morphological reshaping operations such as ERODE and DILATE are used to grow, shrink, and clean up the shape boundary. Morphological segmentation is threshold- and edge-feature driven. (Chapter 3 provided a discussion of the methods used for morphology and thresholding.)

Texture Structure Shapes

Region texture is also used to segment polygon shapes. Texture segmentation is a familiar image-processing method for image analysis and classification, and is an ideal method for segmentation in a nonbinary fashion. Texture reveals structure that simple thresholding ignores. As shown in Figure 6-6, the LBP operator can detect local texture, and the texture can be used to segment regions such as sky, water, and land. Texture segmentation is based on local image pixel relationships. (Several texture segmentation methods were surveyed in Chapter 3.)

Super-Pixel Similarity Shapes

Segmenting a region using super-pixel methods is based on the idea of collapsing similar pixels together—for example, collapsing pixels together with similar colors into a larger shape. The goal is to segment the entire image region into super-pixels. Super-pixel methods are based on similarity. (Several super-pixel processing methods were discussed in Chapter 3.)

Local Binary Descriptor Point-Pair Patterns

Local binary descriptor shapes and sampling patterns, such as those employed in FREAK, BRISK, ORB, and BRIEF, are good examples to study in order to understand the various tradeoffs and design approaches. We will examine local binary shape and pattern concepts here. (Chapter 6 provides a more detailed survey of each descriptor.)

Local binary descriptors use a *point-pair sampling method*, where pairs of pixels are assigned to each other for a binary comparison. Note that a drawback of local binary descriptors and point-pair comparisons is that small changes in the image pixel values in the local region may manifest as *binary artifacts*. Seemingly insignificant changes in a set of pixel values may cause problems during matching that are pronounced for: (1) noisy images, and (2) images with constant gray level. However, each local binary descriptor method attempts to mitigate the binary artifact problems. For example, BRISK (see Figure 4-10 later) and ORB (see Figure 4-11 later) compute a *filtered region* surrounding each interest point to reduce the noise component prior to the binary comparison.

Another method to mitigate the binary artifact problem of constant gray level is used in a modification of the LBP method called the local trinary pattern operator, or LTP [522] (see also reference[173], Section 2.9.3), which uses *trinary values* of *{-1, 0, 1}* to describe regions. A threshold band is established for the LTP to describe near-constant gray values as 0, values above the threshold band as 1, and values below the threshold band as -1. The LTP can be used to describe both smooth regions of constant gray level and contrasted regions in the standard LBP. In addition, the compare threshold for point-pairs can be tuned to compensate for noise, illumination, and contrast, as employed in nearly all local binary descriptor methods.

Figure 4-8 (left image) illustrates a hypothetical descriptor pattern to include selected pixels as the black values, while the center left image shows a strip-oriented shape and pattern where the descriptor calculates the descriptor over pixels along a set of line segments with no particular symmetry like the DNETS [135] method.

 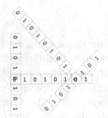 

Figure 4-8. *illustrating various descriptor patterns and shapes. (Left) Sparse. (Center left) Nets or strips. (Center right) Kernels. (Right) Radial spokes*

In Figure 4-8 also, the center right image illustrates a convolution kernel where the filter shape and filter goal are specified, while the right image is a blob shape using radial pixel sampling lines originating at the shape centroid and terminating on the blob perimeter. Note that a 1D Fourier descriptor can be computed from an array containing the length of each radial line segment from the centroid to the perimeter to describe shape, or just an array of raw pixel values can be kept, or else D-nets can be computed.

A feature descriptor may be designed by using one or more shapes and patterns together. For example, the hypothetical descriptor pattern in Figure 4-8 (left image) uses one pattern for pixels close to the interest point, another pattern uses pixels farther away from the center to capture circular pattern information, and another pattern covers a few extrema points. An excellent example of tuned sampling patterns is the FREAK descriptor, discussed next.

FREAK Retinal Patterns

The FREAK [130] descriptor shape, also discussed in some detail in Chapter 6, uses local binary patterns based on the human retinal system, as shown in Figure 4-9, where the density of the receptor cells in the human visual system is greater in the center and decreases with distance from center. FREAK follows a similar pattern when building the local binary descriptors, referred to as a *coarse-to-fine* descriptor pattern, with fine detail in the center of the patch and coarse detail moving outward. The coarse-to-fine method also allows for the descriptor to be matched in coarse-to-fine segments. The coarse part is matched first, and if the match is good enough, the fine feature components are matched as well.

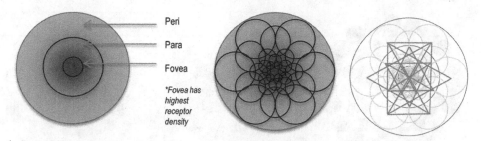

Figure 4-9. *(Left) The human visual system concentration of receptors in the center Fovea region with less receptor density moving outward to periphery vision regions of Para and Peri. (Center) FREAK [130] local binary pattern sampling regions, six regions in each of six overlapping distance rings from the center, size of ring denotes compare point averaging area. (Right) Hypothetical example of a FREAK-style point-pair pattern*

FREAK descriptors can be built with several patterns within this framework. For FREAK, the actual pattern shape and point-pairing are designed during a training phase where the best point-pair patterns are learned using a method similar to ORB [134] to find point-pairs with high variance. The pattern is only constrained by the training data; only 45 point-pairs are used from the 32x31 image patch region.

As illustrated in Figure 4-9, the pairs of points at the end of each line segment are compared, the set of compare values are composed into a binary descriptor vector using 16 bytes, and a cascade of four separate 16-byte coarse-to-fine patterns are included in the descriptor set. Typically, the coarse pattern alone effectively rejects bad matches, and the finer patterns are used to qualify only the closest matches.

Brisk Patterns

The BRISK descriptor [131] point-pair sampling shape is symmetric and circular, composed of 60 total points arranged in four concentric rings, as shown in Figure 4-10. Surrounding each of the 60 points is a sampling region shown in blue, the sampling regions increase in size with distance from the center, and also proportional to the distance between sample points. Within the sampling regions, Gaussian smoothing is applied to the pixels and a local gradient is calculated over the smoothed region.

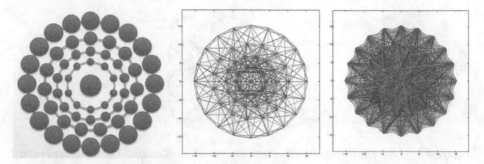

Figure 4-10. *(Left) BRISK concentric sampling grid pattern. (Center) Short segment pairs. (Right) Long distance pairs. Note that the size of the region (left image) for each selected point increases in diamter with distance from the center, and the binary comparison is computed from the center point of each Gaussian-sampled circular region, rather than from each solitary center point. (Center and right images used by permission © Josh Gleason[143])*

Like other local binary descriptors, BRISK compares pairs of points to form the descriptor. The point- pairs are specified in two groups: (1) *long segments,* which are used together with the region gradients to determine angle and direction of the descriptor, the angle is used to rotate the descriptor area, and then the pair–wise sampling pattern is applied;(2) *short segments,* which can be pair-wise compared and composed into the 512-bit binary descriptor vector.

ORB and BRIEF Patterns

ORB [134] is based in part on the BRIEF descriptor [132,133], thus the name **Ori**ented **B**rief, since ORB adds orientation to the BRIEF method and provides other improvements as well. For example, ORB also improves the interest point method by qualifying FAST corners using Harris corner methods, and improves corner orientation using Rosin's method [61] in order to steer the BRIEF descriptor to improve rotational invariance (BRIEF is known to be sensitive to rotation).

ORB also provides a very good point-pair training method, which is an improvement over BRIEF. In BRIEF, as shown in Figure 4-11, the sample points are specified in a random distribution pattern based on a Gaussian distribution about the center point within the 31x31 patch region; the chosen number of sample points is 256. Selected sample point-pairs are compared to each other to form the binary descriptor vector. The value of each point is calculated via an integral image method to smooth a 5x5 region into the point value.

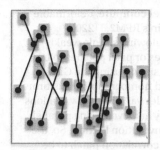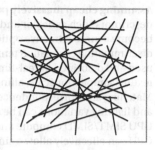

Figure 4-11. *(Left) An ORB style pattern at greatly reduced point pair count resolution, using < 32 points instead of the full 256 points. (Right) A BRIEF style pattern using randomized point-pairs*

To learn the descriptor point-pair sample and compare pattern, ORB uses a training algorithm to find uncorrelated points in the training set with high variance, and selects the best 256 points to define the pairwise sampling patterns used to create the binary feature vector. So the shape and pattern are nonsymmetric, as shown in Figure 4-11, similar to some DNETS patterns. The ORB point-pair patterns are dependent on the training data.

Note in Figure 4-11 that a BRIEF style pattern (right image) uses random point-pairs. Several methods for randomizing point-pairs are suggested by the developers [132]. The ORB pattern shown in Figure 4-11 is based on choosing point-pairs that have high statistical variance within a bounding 31x31 image patch, where the smaller 5x5 gray image patch regions are centered at the chosen interest points. Then each 5x5 region is smoothed using an integral image method to yield a single value for the point.

Descriptor Discrimination

How discriminating is a descriptor? By *discrimination* we mean how well the descriptor can uniquely describe and differentiate between other features. Depending on the application, more or less discrimination is needed, thus it is possible to *over-describe* a feature by providing more information and invariance than is useful, or to *under-describe* the feature by limiting the robustness and invariance attributes. Feature descriptor discrimination for a given set of robustness criteria may be important and interesting, but discrimination is not always the right problem to solve in some cases.

The need for increased discrimination in the descriptor can be balanced in favor of using a cascade of simple descriptors like correlation templates under the following assumptions.

1. **Assuming cheap massively parallel compute**, deformable descriptors such as Taylor and Rosin's RFM2.3 [220] become a more attractive option, allowing simple weakly discriminating correlation templates or pixel patches to be used and deformed in real-time in silicon using the GPU texture sampler for scale, affine and homographic transforms. Matching and correspondence under various pose variations and lighting variations can be easily achieved using parallel GPU SIMT/SIMD compute and convolution kernels. So, the GPU can effectively allow a simple correlation patch to be warped and contrast enhanced to be used as a deformable descriptor and compared against target features.

2. **Assuming lots of fast and cheap memory**, such as large memory cache systems, many nondiscriminating descriptors or training patterns can be stored in the database in the memory cache. Various weighting schemes such as those used in neural networks and convolutional networks can be effectively employed to achieve desired correspondence and quality. Also, other boosting schemes can be employed in the classifier, such as the Adaboost method, to developed strong classifiers from weakly discriminating data.

In summary, both highly discriminating feature descriptors and cascades of simple weakly discriminating feature descriptors may be the right choice for a given application, depending on the target system.

Spectra Discrimination

One dimension of feature discrimination is the chosen descriptor spectra or values used to represent the feature. We refer to *spectra* simply as values within a spectrum or over a continuum. A feature descriptor that only uses a single spectra, such as a histogram of intensity values, will have discrimination to intensity distributions, with no discrimination for other attributes such as shape or affine transforms. For example, a feature descriptor may increase the level of discrimination by combining a multivariate set of spectra such as *RGB* color, depth, and local area gradients of color intensity.

It is well known [248] that the human visual system discriminates and responds to gradient information in a scale and rotationally invariant manner across the retina, as demonstrated in SIFT and many other feature description methods. Thus the use of gradients is a common and preferred spectra for computer vision.

Spectra may be taken over a range of variables, where simple scalar ranges of values are only one type of spectra:

1. Gray scale intensity

2. Color channel intensity

3. Basis function domains (frequency domain, HAAR, etc.)

4. 2D or 3D gradients

5.   3D surface normals

6.   Shape factors and morphological measures

7.   Texture metrics

8.   Area integrals

9.   Statistical moments of regions

10.   Hamming codes from local binary patterns

Each of the above spectra types, along with many others that could be enumerated, can be included in a multivariate feature descriptor to increase discrimination. Of course, discrimination requirements for a chosen application will guide the design of the descriptor. For example, an application that identifies fruit will be more effective using color channel spectra for fruit color, shape factors to identify fruit shapes, and texture metrics for skin texture.

One way to answer the question of discrimination is to look at the information contained in the descriptor. Does the descriptor contain multivariate collections of spectra, and how many invariance attributes are covered, such as orientation or scale?

Region, Shapes, and Pattern Discrimination

Shape and pattern of the feature descriptor are important dimensions affecting discrimination. Each feature shape has advantages and disadvantages depending on the application. Surprisingly, even a single pixel can be used as a feature descriptor shape (see Figure 1-7). Let's look at other dimensions of discrimination.

Shapes and patterns may be classified as follows:

1.   A single pixel (discussion of single pixel description methods to follow)

2.   A line of pixels

3.   A rectangular region of pixels

4.   A polygon shape or region of pixels

5.   A pattern or set of unconnected pixels, such as foveal patterns

The shape of the descriptor determines attributes of discrimination. For example, a rectangular descriptor will be limited in the rotational invariance attribute compared to a circular shaped descriptor. Also, a smaller shape for the descriptor limits the range to a smaller area, and also limits scale invariance. A larger size descriptor area carries more pixels which can increase discrimination.

Descriptor shape, pixel sampling pattern, sampling region size, and pixel metrics have been surveyed by several other researchers [128–130]. In this section, we dig deeper and wider into specific methods used for feature descriptor tuning, paying special attention to local binary feature descriptors, which hold promise for low power and high performance.

Geometric Discrimination Factors

The shape largely determines the amount of rotational invariance possible. For example, a rectangular shape typically begins to fall off in rotational discrimination at around 15 degrees, while a circular pattern typically performs much better under rotational variations. Note that any poorly discriminating shape or pattern descriptor can be enhanced and made more discriminating by incorporating more than one shape or pattern into the descriptor vector.

A shape and pattern such as a HAAR wavelet, as used in the Viola Jones method, integrates all pixels in a rectangular region, yielding the composite value of all the pixels in the region. Thus there is no local fine-detail pattern information contained in the descriptor, leading to very limited local area discrimination and poor rotational invariance or discrimination.

Another example of poor rotational discrimination is the rectangular correlation template method, which compares two rectangular regions pixel by pixel. However, several effective descriptor methods use a rectangular-shaped region.

In general, rectangles are a limitation to rotational invariance. However, SURF uses a method of determining the dominant orientation of the rectangular HAAR wavelet features within a circular neighborhood to achieve better rotational invariance. And SIFT uses a method to improve rotational invariance and accuracy by applying a circular weighting function to the rectangular regions during the binning stage.

It should also be noted that descriptors with low discrimination are being used very effectively in targeted applications, such as correlation methods for motion estimation in video encoding. In this case, the rectangle shape is a great match to the encoding problem and lends itself to highly optimized fixed function hardware implementations, since frame-to-frame motion can be captured very well in rectangular regions, and there is typically little rotation or scale change from frame to frame for at 30 Hz frame rates, just translation.

With this discussion in mind, descriptor discrimination should be *fitted* appropriately to the application, since adding discrimination comes at a cost of compute and memory.

Feature Visualization to Evaluate Discrimination

Another way to understand discrimination is to use the feature descriptor itself to reconstruct images from the descriptor information alone, where we may consider the collection of descriptors to be a compressed or encoded version of the actual image. Image compression, encoding, and feature description are related; see Figure 3-18. Next, we examine a few examples of image reconstruction from the descriptor information alone.

Discrimination via Image Reconstruction from HOG

Figure 4-12 visualizes a reconstruction using the HOG descriptor [106]. The level of detail is coarse and follows line and edge structure that matches the intended use of HOG. One key aspect of the discrimination provided by HOG is that no image smoothing is used on the image prior to calculating the descriptor. The HOG research shows that smoothing the image results in a *loss of discrimination*. Dalal and Triggs[106] highlight their deliberate intention to avoid image smoothing to preserve image detail.

Figure 4-12. *Discrimination via a visualization of the HOG description. (Image (c) Carl Vodrick, used by permission.) See also "HOGgles: Visualizing Object Detection Features, Carl Vondrick, Aditya Khosla, Tomasz Malisiewicz, Antonio Torralba, Massachusetts Institute of Technology, Oral presentation at ICCV 2013"*

However, some researchers argue that noise causes problems when calculating values such as local area gradients and edges, and further recommend that noise be eliminated from the image by smoothing prior to descriptor calculations; this is the conventional wisdom in many circles. Note that there are many methods to filter noise without resorting to extreme Gaussian-style smoothing, convolution blur, and integral images, which distort the image field.

Some of the better noise-filtering methods include speckle removal filters, rank filtering, bilateral filters, and many other methods that were discussed in Chapter 2. If the input image is left as is, or at least the best noise filtering methods are used, the feature descriptor will likely retain more discrimination power for fine-grained features.

Discrimination via Image Reconstruction from Local Binary Patterns

As shown in Figure 4-13, d'Angelo and Alehi[127] provide visualizations of images reconstructed from the FREAK and BRIEF local binary descriptors. The reconstruction is rendered entirely from the descriptor information alone, across the entire image. BRIEF uses a more random pattern to compare points across a region, while FREAK uses a trained and more foveal and symmetrical pattern with increased detail closer to the center of the region. And d'Angelo and Alehi[127] note that the reconstruction results are similar to Laplacian filtered versions of the original image, which helps us understand that the discrimination of these features appears to be structurally related to detailed edge and gradient information.

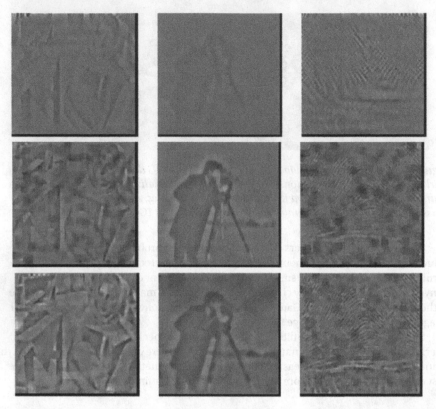

Figure 4-13. *Images reconstructed using local binary descriptors using 512 point-pairs. (Top row) BRIEF. (Middle row) Randomized FREAK (more similar to BRIEF). (Bottom row) Binary FREAK using the foveal pattern Images (c) Alexandre Alehi, used by permission*

The d'Angelo and Alehi reconstruction method [127] creates an image from a set of overlapping descriptor patches calculated across the original image. To reconstruct the image, the descriptors are first reconstructed using a novel method to render patches, and then the patches are merged by averaging the overlapping regions to form an image, where the patch merge size may vary as desired. For example, note that Figure 4-13 uses 32x32 patches for the Barbara images in the left column, and a 64x64 patch size for the cameraman in the center column. Also note that Barbara is not reconstructed with the same discrimination as the cameraman, whose image contains finer details.

Discrimination via Image Reconstruction from SIFT Features

Another method of approximate image reconstruction [105] proves the discrimination capabilities of SIFT descriptors; see Figure 4-14. The reconstruction method for this research starts by taking an unknown image containing a scene such as a famous building, finding the set of Hessian-affine region detectors in the image, extracting associated SIFT feature descriptors, and then saving a set of elliptical image patch regions around the SIFT descriptors.

Figure 4-14. *Image reconstruction of common scenes using combined SIFT descriptors taken from several views of the same object, images (c) Herve Jegou, used by permission*

Next, an image database containing similar and, it is hoped, matching images of the same scene are searched to find the closest matching SIFT descriptors at Hessian-affine interest points. Then a set of elliptical patch regions around each SIFT descriptor is taken. The elliptical patches found in the database are warped into a synthesized image based on a priori interest region geometric parameters of the scenes.

The patches are stitched together via stacking and blending overlapping patches and also via smooth interpolation. Any remaining holes are filled by smooth interpolation. One remarkable result of this method is the demonstration that an image can be reconstructed from a set of patches from different images at different orientations, since the feature descriptors are similar; and in this case, the discrimination of the SIFT descriptor is demonstrated well.

Accuracy, Trackability

Accuracy can be measured in terms of specific feature attributes or robustness criteria; see Tables 4-1 and 7-4. A given descriptor may outperform another descriptor in one area and in not another. In the research literature, the accuracy and performance of each new feature descriptor is usually benchmarked against the standby methods SIFT and SURF. The feature descriptor accuracy is measured using commonly accepted ground truth datasets designed to measure robustness and invariance attributes. (See Appendix B for a survey of standard ground truth datasets, and Chapter 7 for a discussion about ground truth dataset design.)

A few useful accuracy studies are highlighted here, illustrating some of the ways descriptor and interest point accuracy can be measured. For instance, one of the most comprehensive surveys of earlier feature detector and descriptor accuracy and invariance is provided by Mikolajczyk and Schmid[144], covering a range of descriptors including GLOH, SIFT, PCA-SIFT, Shape Context, spin images, Hessian Laplacian GLOH, cross correlation, gradient moments, complex filters, differential invariants, and steerable filters.

In Gauglitz et al.[145], there are invariance metrics for zoom, pan, rotation, perspective distortion, motion blur, static lighting, and dynamic lighting for several feature metrics, including Harris, Shi-Tomasi, DoG, Fast Hessian, FAST, and CenSurE, which are discussed in Chapter 6. There are also metrics for a few classifiers, including randomized trees and FERNS, which are discussed later in this chapter. Figure 4-15 provides some visual comparisons of feature detector and interest point accuracy from Gauglitz [145].

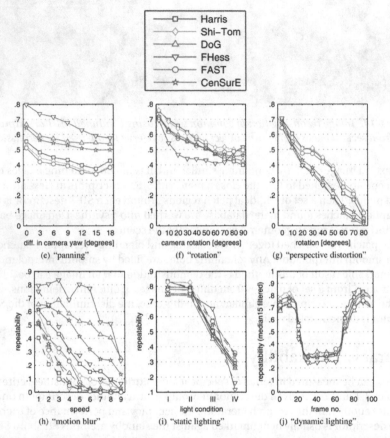

Figure 4-15. *Accuracy of feature descriptors over various invariance criteria. (From Gauglitz et al. [145], images © Springer Science +Business Media, LLC, used by permission)*

Turning to the more recent local binary descriptors, Alehi et. al. [130] provide a set of comparisons where FREAK is shown to be superior in accuracy to BRISK, SURF, and SIFT on a particular dataset and set of criteria developed by Mikolajczyk and Schmid [144] for feature accuracy over attributes such as viewpoint, blur, JPEG compression, brightness, rotation, and scale. In Rublee et. al. [120], ORB is shown to have better rotational invariance than SIFT, SURF, and BRIEF. In summary, local binary descriptors are proving to be attractive in terms of robustness, accuracy, and compute efficiency.

Accuracy Optimizations, Sub-Region Overlap, Gaussian Weighting, and Pooling

Various methods are employed to optimize feature descriptor accuracy, and a few methods are discussed here. For example, descriptors often use overlapping sampling pattern sub-regions, as shown in the FREAK descriptor pattern in Figure 4-9. By overlapping sampling regions and treating boundaries carefully, accuracy seems to be better in most all cases [161,178]. Overlapping regions makes sense intuitively, since each point in a region is related to surrounding points. The value of pattern sub-region overlapping in feature description seems obvious for local binary pattern type descriptors and spectra descriptor variants such as SURF and others [181,144]. When the sampling regions used in the descriptor do not overlap, recognition rates are not as accurate [130].

Gaussian weighting is another effective method for increasing accuracy to reduce noise and uncertainty in measurements. For example, the SIFT [161,178] descriptor applies a Gaussian-based weighting factor to each local area gradient in the descriptor region to favor gradients nearer the center and reduce the weighting of gradients farther away. In addition, the SIFT weighting is applied in a circularly symmetric pattern, which adds some rotational invariance; see Figure 6-17.

Note that Gaussian weighting is different from Gaussian filtering; a Gaussian filter both reduces noise and eliminates critical fine details in the image, but such filtering has been found to be counterproductive in the HOG method [106]. A Gaussian weighting factor, such as used by SIFT on the gradient bins, can simply be used to qualify data rather than change the data. In general, a weighting factor can be used to scale the results and fine-tune the detector or descriptor. The sub-region overlap in the sampling pattern and Gaussian weighting schemes are complementary.

Accuracy can be improved by relying on groups of nearby features together rather than just a single feature. For example, in convolutional networks, several nearby features may be pooled for a joint decision to increase accuracy via chosen robustness or invariance criteria [347]. The pooling concept may also be referred to as *neighborhood consensus* or *semi-local constraints* in the literature, and it can involve joint constraints, such as the angle and distance among a combined set of local features [348–350].

Sub-Pixel Accuracy

Some descriptor and recognition methods can provide sub-pixel accuracy in matching the feature location [147–151]. Common methods to compute sub-pixel accuracy include cross-correlation, sum-absolute difference, Gaussian fitting, Fourier methods, and rigid body transforms and ICP. In general, sub-pixel accuracy is not a common feature in popular, commercial applications and is needed only in high-end applications like industrial inspection, aerospace, and military systems.

For example, SIFT provides sub-pixel accuracy for the location of keypoints. Digital correlation methods and template matching are well known and used in industrial applications for object tracking, and can be extended to compute correlations over a range of one-pixel offset areas to yield a set of correlations that can be fit into a curve and interpolated to find the highest match to yield sub-pixel accuracy.

Sub-pixel accuracy is typically limited to translation. Rotation and scale are much more difficult to quantify in terms of sub-pixel accuracy. Typical sub-pixel accuracy results for translation only achieve better than ¼ pixel resolution, but resolution accuracy can be finer grained, and in some methods translation accuracy is claimed to be as high as $1/20^{th}$ of a pixel using FFT registration methods [151].

Also, stereo disparity methods benefit from improved sub-pixel accuracy, especially at long ranges, since the granularity of Z distance measurements increases exponentially with distance. Thus the calculated depth field contains coarser information as the depth field increases, and the computed depth field is actually nonlinear in Z. Therefore, sub-pixel accuracy in stereo and multi-view stereo disparity calculations is quite desirable and necessary for best accuracy.

Search Strategies and Optimizations

As shown in Figure 5-1, a feature may be sparse, covering a local area, or it may cover a regional or global area. The search strategy used to isolate each of these feature types is different. For a global feature, there is no search strategy: the entire frame is used as the feature. For a regional descriptor, a region needs to be chosen or segmented (discussed in Chapter 2). For sparse local features, the search strategy becomes important. Search strategies for sparse local regions fall into a few major categories, as follows (also included in the taxonomy in Chapter 5).

Dense Search

In a dense search, each pixel in the image is checked. For example, an interest point is calculated at each pixel, the interest points are then qualified and sorted into a candidate list, and a feature descriptor is calculated for each candidate. Dense search is used by local binary descriptors and common descriptors such as SIFT.

In stereo matching and depth sensing, each pixel is searched in a dense manner for calculating disparity and closest points. For example, stereo algorithms use a dense search for correspondence to compute disparity, line by line and pixel by pixel; monocular depth-sensing methods such as PTAM [327] use a dense search for interest points, followed by a sparse search for known features at predicted locations.

Dense methods may also be applied across an image pyramid, where the lower resolution pyramids are usually searched first and finer-grain pyramids are searched later. Dense methods in general are preferred for accuracy and robustness when feature locations are not known and cannot be predicted.

Grid Search

In grid search methods, the image is divided into a regular grid or tiles, and features are located based on the tiles. A novel grid search method is provided in the OpenCV library, using a grid search adapter (discussed in Chapter 6 and Appendix A). This allows for repeated trial searches within a grid region for the best features, and has the capability of adjusting detector parameters before each trial run. One possible disadvantage of a grid search from the perspective of accuracy is that features do not line up into grids, so features can be missed or truncated along the grid boundary, decreasing accuracy and robustness overall.

Grid search can be used in many ways. For example, a regular grid is used as anchor points with the grid topology of D-NETS, as illustrated in Figure 4-7. Or, a grid is used to form image tile patches and a descriptor is computed for each tile, such as in the HOG method, as shown in Figure 4-12. Also the Viola Jones method [146] computes HAAR features on a grid.

Multi-Scale Pyramid Search

The idea behind the multi-scale image pyramid search is either to accelerate searching by starting at a lower resolution or to truly provide multi-scale images to allow for features to be found at appropriate scale. Methods to reduce image scale include pixel decimation, bilinear interpolation, and other multi-sampling methods. Scale space is a popular method for creating image pyramids, and many variations are discussed in the next section; see Figure 4-16.

Figure 4-16. *A five-octave scale pyramid. The image is from Albrecht Durer's Apocalypse woodcuts, 1498. Note that many methods use non-octave pyramid scales [120]*

However, the number of detected features falls off rapidly as the pyramid levels increase, especially for scale space pyramids, which have been Gaussian filtered, since Gaussian filters reduce image texture detail. Also, fewer pixels are present to begin with at higher pyramid levels, so a pyramid scale interval smaller than octaves is sometimes used. See reference[160] for a good discussion of image pyramids.

Scale Space and Image Pyramids

Often, instead of using simple pixel decimation and pixel interpolation to reduce image scale, a *scale space* [524,523] pyramid representation, originally proposed by Lindberg[547], is built up using Gaussian filtering methods to decrease the scaling artifacts and preserve blob-like features. Scale space is a more formal method of defining a multi-scale set of images, typically using a Gaussian kernel *g()* convolved with the image *f(x,y)*, as follows:

$$g(x,y:t) = \frac{1}{2\pi t} e^{-(x^2+y^2)/2t}$$

$$L(.,.;t) = g(.,.:t) * f(.,.),$$

or by an equivalent method:

$$\partial_t L = \frac{1}{2} \nabla^2 L,$$

with the initial state $L(x,y;0) = f(x,y),$

A good example of Gaussian filter design for scale space is described in the SURF method [160]. Gaussian filters implemented as kernels with increasing size are applied to the original image at octave-spaced subsampling intervals to create the scale space images—for example, starting with a 9x9 Gaussian filter and increasing to 15x15, 21x21, 27x27, 33x33, and 39x39; see Figure 4-17.

Figure 4-17. *Scale space Gaussian images at scales of 0, 2, 4, 16, 32, 64. Image is from Albrecht Durer's Apocalypse woodcuts, 1498*

One drawback of scale space is the loss of localization and lack of accuracy in higher levels of the image pyramid. In fact, some features are simply missing from higher levels of the image pyramid, owing to a lack of resolution and to the Gaussian filtering. The best example of effective scale space feature matching may be SIFT, which provides for the 1st pyramid image in the scale to be double the original resolution to mitigate scale space problems, and also provides a good multi-scale descriptor framework. See also Figure 4-18.

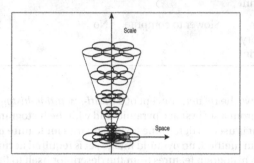

Figure 4-18. Scale and space

Image pyramids are analogous to texture *mip-maps* used in computer graphics. Variations on the image pyramid are common. Octave and non-octave pyramid spacings are used, with variations on the filtering method also. For example, the SIFT method [161,178] uses a five-level octave scale *n/2* image pyramid with Gaussians filtered images in a scale space. Then, the Difference of Gaussians (DoG) method is used to capture the interest point extrema maxima and minima in the adjacent images in the pyramid. SIFT uses a double-scale first pyramid level with linear interpolated pixels at 2x original magnification to help preserve fine details. This technique increases the number of stable keypoints by about four times, which is quite significant. In the ORB [120] method, a non-octave scale space is built around a scale over a five-level pyramid, which has closer resolution gradations between pyramid levels than an octave scale of two times.

Feature Pyramids

An alternative to scale space pyramids and pyramid searching is to use *feature-space pyramiding*, and build a set of multi-scale feature descriptors stored together in the database. In this approach, the descriptor itself contains the pyramid, and no scale space or image pyramid is needed. Instead, feature searching occurs directly from the mono-scale target image to the multi-scale features. The RFM method [220] discussed in Chapter 6 goes even further and includes *multi-perspective* transformed versions of each patch for each descriptor. In Table 4-3, note that the multi-scale features can be used to match directly on the target images, while the mono-scale features are better to use on an image pyramid.

Table 4-3. *Some Tradeoffs in Using a Mono-Scale Feature and a Multi-Scale Feature*

Feature Scale	Feature Size	Feature Description Compute Time	Image Pyramid Used for Matching	Mono-Scale Images Used for Matching
Mono-scale feature	Smaller memory footprint	Faster to compute	Yes	No
Multi-scale feature	Larger memory footprint	Slower to compute	No	Yes

Figure 3-16 shows the related concept of a *multi-resolution histogram* [152], created from image regions from a scale space pyramid and with the histograms concatenated in the descriptor that is used to determine texture metrics for feature matching. So in the multi-scale histogram method, no pyramid image set is required at run time; rather, the pyramid search uses histogram features from the descriptor itself to find correspondence with the mono-scale target image.

A wide range of scalar and other metrics can be composed into a multi-scale feature pyramid, such as image intensity patches, color channel intensity patches, gradient magnitude, and gradient orientations. Histograms of textural features have been found useful as affine-invariant metrics as a part of a wider feature descriptor [152].

Sparse Predictive Search and Tracking

In a sparse predictive search pipeline, specific features at known locations, found in previous frames, are searched for in the next frame at the expected positions. For example, in the PTAM [327] algorithm for monocular depth sensing, a sparse 3D point cloud and camera pose are created from sequential video frames from a single camera by locating a set of interest points and feature descriptors. For each new frame, a *prediction* is made of the coordinates where the same interest points and feature detectors might be in the new image, using the prior camera pose matrix. Then, for the new frame, a search or tracking loop is started to locate a *small number* of the predicted interest points using a pyramid coarse to fine search strategy. The predicted interest points and features are searched for within a range around where each is predicted to be, and the camera pose matrix is updated based on the new coordinates where the features are found. Then, a *larger number* of points are predicted using the updated camera pose and a search and tracking loop is entered over a finer scale pyramid image in the set. This process iterates to find points and refine the pose matrix.

Tracking Region-Limited Search

One example of a region-limited search is a video conferencing system that tracks the location of the speaker using stereo microphones to calculate the coarse location via triangulation. Once the coarse speaker position is known, the camera is moved to view the speaker, and only the face region is of interest for further fine positional location adjustments, auto-zoom, auto-focus, and auto-contrast enhancements. In this application, the entire image does not need to be searched or processed for face features. Instead, the center of the FOV is the region where the search is limited to locate the face. For example, if the image is taken from an HD camera with 1920x1080 resolution, only a limited region in the center of the image, perhaps 512x512 pixels, needs to be processed to locate the face features.

Segmentation Limited Search

A segmented region can define the search area, such as a region with specific texture, or pixels of a specific color intensity. In a morphological vision pipeline, regions may be segmented in a variety of ways, such as thresholding and binary erosion + dilation to create binary shapes. Then the binary shapes can be used as masks to segment the corresponding gray scale image regions under the masks for feature searching. Image segmentation methods were covered in Chapter 2.

Depth or Z Limited Search

With the advent of low-cost commercial depth sensors appearing on mobile consumer devices, the Z dimension is available for limiting search ranges. See Figure 4-19. For example, by segmenting out the background of an image using depth, the foreground features are more easily segmented and identified, and search can be limited by depth segments. Considering how much time is spent in computer vision to extract 3D image information from 2D images, we can expect depth cameras to be used in novel ways to simplify computer vision algorithms.

Figure 4-19. *Segmentation of image regions based on a depth map. Depth image from Middlebury Data set: (Source: D. Scharstein and C. Pal "Learning conditional random fields for stereo" CVPR Conference, 2007. Courtesy of authors)*

Computer Vision, Models, Organization

This section contains a high- level overview of selected examples to illustrate how feature metrics are used within computer vision systems. Here, we explore how features are selected, learned, associated together to describe real objects, classified for efficient searching and matching, and used in computer vision pipelines. This section introduces machine learning, but only at a high level using selected examples. A good reference on machine learning is found in [546] by Prince. A good reference for computer vision models, organization, applications, and algorithms is found in Szelinski [324].

Several terms are chosen and defined in this section for the discussion of computer vision models, namely *feature space, object models*, and *constraints*. The main topics for this section include:

- Feature spaces and selection of optimal features

- Object recognition via object models containing features and constraints

- Classification and clustering methods to optimize pattern matching

- Training and learning

■ **Note**   Many of the methods discussed in computer vision research journals and courses are borrowed from other tangent fields and applied, for example, machine learning and statistical analysis. In some cases computer vision is driving the research in such tangent fields. Since these fields are well established and considered beyond the scope of this work, we provide only a brief topical introduction here, with references for completeness [546,324].

Feature Space

The collection and organization of all features, attributes, and other information necessary to describe objects may be called the *feature space*. Features are typically organized and classified into a feature space during a training or learning phase using ground truth data as a training set. The selected features are organized and structured in a database or a set of data structures, such as trees and lists, to allow for rapid search and feature matching at run time.

The feature space may contain one or more types of *descriptors* using spectra such as histograms, binary pattern vectors, as multivariate composite descriptors. In addition, the feature space contains *constraints* used to associate sets of features together to identify objects and classes of objects. A feature space is unique to any given application, and is built according to the types of features used and the requirements of the application; there is no standard method.

The feature space may contain several *parameters* for describing objects; for example:

- **Several types of feature descriptors**, such as SIFT and simple color histograms.

- **Cartesian coordinates** for each descriptor relative to training images.

- **Orientations** of each descriptor.

- **Name of training image** associated with each descriptor.

- **Multimodal information**, such as GPS, temperatures, elevation, acceleration.

- **Feature sets** or lists of associated descriptors.

- **Constraints** between the descriptors in a set, such as the relative distance from each other, relative distance thresholds, angular relationships between descriptors, or relative to a reference point.

- **Object models** to collect and associate parameters for each object.

- **Classes** or associations of objects of the same type, such as automobiles.

- **Labels** for objects or constraints.

Object Models

An *object model* describes real objects or classes of objects using parameters from the feature space. For example, an object may contain all parameters required to describe a specific automobile, such as feature descriptor sets, labels, and constraints. A class of objects may associate and label all objects of the same class, such as an automobile of any type. There is no standard or canonical object model to follow, so in this section we describe the overall attributes of computer vision objects and how to model them.

Object models may be composed of sets of individual features; constraints on the related features, such as position or orientation of features within an object model; and perhaps other multimodal information for the objects or descriptors, such as GPS information or time stamps, as shown in Figure 4-20. The object model can be created using a combination of supervised and unsupervised learning methods [403]; we survey several methods later in this chapter.

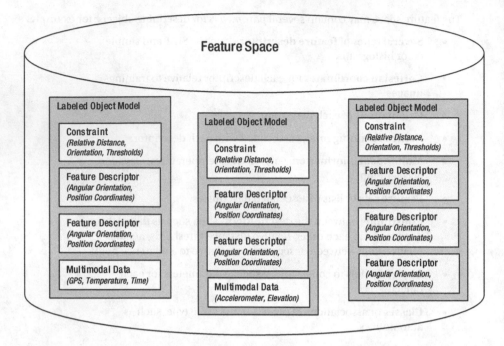

Figure 4-20. *Simplified hypothetical feature space showing organization and association of features, constraints, and objects*

One early attempt to formulate object models is known as *parts-based models*, suggested in 1973 by Fischler and Elschlager[530]. These describe and recognize larger objects by first recognizing their parts—for example, a face being composed of parts such as eyes, nose, and mouth. There are several variations on parts-based models; see references[531–533], for example. Machine learning methods are also used to create the object models [546], and are discussed later in this section.

A simple object model may be composed of only image histograms of whole images, the name or label of each associated image, and possibly a few classification parameters such as the subject matter of the image, GPS location, and date. To identify unknown target images, a histogram of the target image is taken and compared against image histograms from the database. Correspondence is measured using a suitable distance metric such as SAD. In this simple example, brute-force searching or a hash table index may be used to check each histogram in the database against target image histograms, and perhaps other parameters from the object model may be matched along with the histograms, such as the GPS coordinates. No complex machine learning classification, clustering, data reductions, or organization of the database need be done, since the search method is brute-force. However, finding correspondence will become progressively slower as more images are added to the database. And the histogram all by itself is not very discriminative and offers little invariance.

Constraints

Key to object recognition, *constraints* are used to associate and qualify features and related attributes as objects. Features alone are probably insufficient to recognize an object without additional qualification, including *neighborhood consensus* or *semi-local constraints* involving joint constraints, such as the angle and distance among a combined set of local features [348–350]. Constraints associate object model elements together to describe and recognize a larger object [365,366,379], such as by minimum feature count thresholds required to ensure that a proper subset of object features are found together, or by using multimodal data constraints such as GPS position, or by voting.

Since there are many approaches for creating constraints, we can only illustrate the concept. For example, Lowe[161] shows recognition examples illustrating how SIFT features can be used to recognize objects containing many tens of distinct features, in some cases using as few as two or three good features. This allows for perspective and occlusion invariance if some of the features describing the object cannot be found, taking into consideration feature orientation and scale as constraints. Another example is wide baseline stereo matching, which requires position and distance constraints on feature pairs in L/R image assuming that the scale and orientation of L/R feature pairs is about equal; in this case, translation would be constrained to be within a range based on depth.

Selection of Detectors and Features

Feature detectors are selected based on a combination of variables, such as the feature detector *design method* and the types of invariance and performance desired. Several approaches or design methods are discussed next.

Manually Designed Feature Detectors

Some feature detectors, such as polygon shape descriptors and sparse local features like SURF, are manually designed and chosen using the intuition, experience, and test results of the practitioner to address the desired invariance attributes for an application. This involves selecting the right spectra to describe the features, determining the shape and pattern of the feature, and choosing the types of regions to search. However, some detectors are statistically and empirically designed, which we cover next.

Statistically Designed Feature Detectors

Statistical methods are used to design and create feature detectors. For example, the binary sampling patterns used in methods such as ORB and FREAK are created from the training dataset based on the statistical characteristics of the possible interest point comparison pairs. Typically, ORB ranks each detected interest point feature pair combination to find terms that are uncorrelated with high variance. This is a statistical sorting or training process to design the feature patterns and tune them for a specific ground truth dataset. See Figure 4-11 for more details on ORB, and see the discussions of FREAK and ORB earlier in this chapter as well.

SIFT also uses statistical methods to determine, from a training set, the best interest points, dominant orientation of each interest point, and scale of each interest point.

Learned Features

Many systems learn a unique codebook of features, using sparse coding methods to identify a unique set of basis features during a training phase against selected ground truth data. The learned basis features are specific to the application domain or training data, and the chosen detectors and descriptors may simply be pixel regions used as correlation templates. However, any descriptor may be used, such as SIFT. Neural network and convolutional network approaches are popularly used for feature learning, as well as sparse coding methods, which are discussed later in this chapter.

Overview of Training

A machine vision system is *trained* to recognize desired features, objects, and activities. However, training can be quite complex and is covered very well in the field of machine learning and statistical analysis (which we do not cover in any detail). Training may be supervised and assisted by an expert, or unsupervised as in the deep learning methods discussed later in this section. Here, we provide an overview of common steps and provide references for more detail. One of the simplest examples of training would be to take image histograms associated with each type of image—for example, a set of histograms that describe a face, animal, or automobile taken from different images.

Training involves collecting a training set of images appropriate for the application domain, and then determining which detectors and descriptors can be tuned to yield the best results. In some cases, the feature descriptor itself may be trainable and designed to match the training data, such as the local binary pattern descriptors ORB, BRIEF, and FREAK, which can use variable pixel sampling patterns optimized and learned from the training data.

In feature learning systems, the entire feature set is learned from the training set. Feature learning methods employ a range of descriptor methods such as simple correlation temples containing pixel regions, or SIFT descriptors. The learned feature set is reduced by keeping only the features that are significantly different from features already in the set. Feature learning methods are covered later in this chapter.

To form larger objects during training, sets of features are associated together using constraints, such as geometric relationships like angles or distances between features, or the count of features of a given value within a specific region. Objects are determined during training, which involves running detectors and descriptors against chosen ground truth data to find the features, and then determining the constraints to represent objects as a composite set of features. Activities can be recognized by tracking features and their positions within adjacent frames, so activity can be considered a type of meta-object and stored in a database as well.

In any case, the features obtained through the training phase are *classified* into a searchable feature space using a wide range of statistical and machine learning methods. Training, classification, and learning are discussed at a high level later in this chapter.

Classification of Features and Objects

Classification is another term for recognition, and it includes feature space organization and training. A *classifier* is a term describing a method or system for learning structure from data and recognizing objects. Several approaches are taken for automatically building classifiers, including support vector machines (SVMs), kernel machines, and neural networks.

In general, the size of the training set or ground truth dataset is key to classifier accuracy [336–338]. During system training, first a training set with ground truth data is used to build up the classifier. The machine learning community provides a wealth of guidance on training, so we defer to established sources. Key journals to dig deeper into machine learning and testing against ground truth data include NIPS and IEEE PAMI, the latter which goes back to 1979. Machine learning and statistical methods are used to guide the selection, classification, and organization of features during training. If no classification of the feature space is made, the feature match process follows a slow brute-force linear search of new features against known features.

Key classification problems discussed in this section include:

- **Group Distance and Clustering** of similar features using a range of nearest–neighbor methods to assist in organization, fitting, error minimization, searching and matching, and enabling similarity constraints such as geometric proximity, angular relationships, and multimodal cues.

- **Dimensionality Reductions** to avoid over-fitting, cleaning the data to remove outliers and spurious data, and reducing the size of the database.

- **Boosting and Weighting** to increase the accuracy of feature matching.

- **Constraints** describing relationships between descriptors composing an object, such as pose estimators and threshold accept/reject filters.

- **Structuring the Database** for rapid matching vs. brute-force methods.

Group Distance: Clustering, Training, and Statistical Learning

We refer to *group distance* and *clustering* in this discussion, sometimes interchangeably, as methods to describe similarities and differences between groups of data atoms, such as feature descriptors. Applications of group distance and clustering include error minimization, regression, outlier removal, classification, training, and feature matching.

According to Estivill-Castro[351], *clustering* is impossible to define in a mathematical sense, since there are so many diverse methods and approaches to describe a cluster. See Table 4-3 for a summary of related methods. However, we will discuss clustering here in the context of computer vision to address data organization, pattern matching, and describing object model constraints (while attempting to not ruffle the feathers of mathematical purists who use different terminology).

To identify similar features in a group, a wide range of clustering algorithms or group distance algorithms are used [353], which may also be referred to as *error minimization* and *regression methods* in some literature. Features are clustered together for computer vision to help solve fundamental problems, including object modeling, finding similar patterns during matching, organizing and classifying similar data, and dimensionality reductions.

One way to describe a cluster is by *similarity*—for example, describing a cluster of related features under some distance metric or regression method. In this sense, clustering overlaps with distance functions: Euclidean distance for position, cosine distance for orientation, and Hamming distance for binary feature vector comparisons are examples. However, distance functions between two points are differentiated in this discussion from group distance functions, clusters, and group distributions.

Efficiently organizing similar data in feature space for searching and classification is a form of clustering. It can be based on similarity or distance measures of feature vectors or on object constraint similarity, and it is required to speed up feature searching and matching. However, commercial databases "and brute-force search" may be used as-is for feature descriptors, with no attempt made to optimize. Custom data structures can be built for optimizations via trees, pyramids, lists, and hash tables. (We refer the reader to standard references in computer science covering data organization and searching; see the classic texts *The Art of Computer Programming* by Donald Knuth or *Data structure and Algorithms* by Aho, Ullman, and Hopcroft.)

Another aspect of clustering is the feature space dimension and topology. Since some feature spaces are multivariate and multidimensional, containing scalars and tensors, any strict definition of clustering, error minimization, regression, or distance is difficult; it really depends on the space in which similarity is to be measured.

Group Distance: Clustering Methods Survey, KNN, RANSAC, K-Means, GMM, SVM, Others

A spectrum of alternatives may be chosen for clustering and learning similarities between groups of data atoms, starting at the low end with basic C library searching and sorting functions, and reaching the high end with statistical and machine learning methods such as kernel machines and support vector machines (SVMs) to build complete classifiers. Kernel machines allow various similarity functions to be substituted into a common framework to enable simplified comparison of similarity methods and classification.

Table 4-4 is a summary of selected clustering methods, with a few key references for the interested reader.

Table 4-4. *Clustering, Classification, and Machine Learning Methods*

Group Distance Criteria	Methods & References	Description
Distance	K-Nearest Neighbor [364]	Uses a chosen distance function, cluster based on simple distance to k-nearest neighbors in the training set.
Consensus Models	RANSAC [380] PROSAC [363] Levenberg-Marquardt [401]	Use random sample consensus to estimate model parameters from contaminated data sets.
Centroid Models	K-Means [354], Voroni Tesselation, Delauney Triangulation Hierarchical K-Means, Nister trees [387]	Use a centroid of distribution as the base of the cluster, which can be very slow for large datsasets; can be formulated in a hierarchical tree structure using vocabulary words (Nister method) for much better performance.
Connectivity of Clusters	Hierarchical Clustering [355]	Builds connectivity between other clusters.
Density Models	DBSCAN [395][352] OPTICS [396]	Locate distributions with maxima and minima density compared to surrounding data.
Distribution Models	Gaussian Mixture Models [356]	Iterative methods of finding maximum likelihood of model parameters.
Neural Methods	Neural Networks [360]	Neural methods defy a single definition, but typically use one or more inputs; adaptive weight factors for each input that can be learned and trained, a neural function to act on the inputs and weights, a bias factor for the neural function; produce one or more outputs.
Bayesian	Naïve Bayesian [383] Randomize Trees [384] FERNS [307]	Learning model recording probabilistic relationships between variables.

(continued)

Table 4-4. (*continued*)

Group Distance Criteria	Methods & References	Description
Probabilistic, Semantic	[232] Latent Semantic Analysis (pLSA) Latent Dirichlet Allocation (LDA) Hidden Markov Models, HMM [385][386]	Learning model based on probabilistic relationships between variables.
Kernel Methods, Kernel Machines	Kernel Machines [361][1] Various Kernels [362] PCA [357][358] *SVM is a well-known instance of a kernel machine.	Reduce a distribution to a set of uncorrelated, ranked principal components in a Euclidean space for ease of matching and clustering.
Support Vector Machines	SVM [377,359]	An SVM may produce structured or multivariate output to classify input.

[1]http://www.kernel-machines.org/

Classification Frameworks, REIN, MOPED

Training and classification fall into the following general categories:

- **Supervised.** A human will assist during the training process to make sure the results are correct.

- **Unsupervised.** The classifier can be trained automatically from feature data and parameters [403].

Putting all the pieces together, we see that training the classifiers may be manual or automated, simple or complex, depending on the complexity of the objects and the range of feature metrics used.

An SVM or kernel machine may be the ideal solution, or the problem may be simpler. For example, a machine vision system to identify fruit may contain a classifier for each type of fruit, with features including simple color histograms, shape factors such as area and perimeter and Fourier descriptors, and surface texture metrics, with constraints to associate and quantify all the features for each type of fruit. The training process would involve imaging several pieces of fruit of each type; developing canonical descriptors for color, shape, and surface texture; and devising a top-level classifier perhaps discriminating first on color, next surface texture, and finally shape. A simpler fruit classifier may contain just a set of image histograms of accurate color measurements for each fruit object, and may work well enough if each piece of fruit is imaged with a high-precision color camera against a black conveyor belt background in a factory.

While most published research is based on a wide range of nonstandard classification methods designed for specific applications or to demonstrate research results, some work is being done toward more standardized classification frameworks.

One noteworthy example of a potentially standard classifier framework developed for robot navigation and object recognition is the REIN method [397], which allows the mixing and matching of detectors, descriptors, and classifiers for determining constraints. REIN provides a plug-in architecture and interfaces to allow for any algorithms, such as OpenCV detectors and descriptors, to be combined in parallel or serial pipelines. Two classification methods are available in REIN as plug-in modules for concurrent use: *Binarized Gradient Grid Pyramids* are introduced as a new method [397], and *View Point Feature Histograms* [398] are also used.

The REIN pipeline provides interfaces for (1) *attention operators* to identify interesting 3D points and reduce the search space; (2) *detectors* for creating feature descriptors; and (3) *pose estimators* to determine geometric constraints for applications like robot motion such as grasping. REIN is available for research as open source; see reference[397].

Another research project, MOPED [399], provides a regular architecture for robotic navigation, including object and pose recognition. MOPED includes optimizations to use all available CPU and GPU compute resources in parallel. Moped provides optimized versions of SIFT and SURF for GPGPU, and makes heavy use of SSE instructions for pose estimation.

Kernel Machines

In machine learning, a *kernel machine* [362] is a framework allowing a set of methods for statistically clustering, ranking, correlating, and classifying patterns or features to be automated. One common example of a kernel machine is the support vector machine (SVM) [341].

The framework for a kernel machine maps descriptor data into a feature space, where each coordinate in the feature space corresponds to a descriptor. Within the feature space, feature matching and feature space reductions can be efficiently carried out using *kernel functions*. Various kernel functions are used within the kernel machine framework, including RBF kernels, Fisher kernels, various polynomial kernels, and graph kernels.

Once the feature descriptors are transformed into the feature space, comparisons, reductions, and clustering may be employed. The key advantage of a kernel machine is that the kernel methods are interchangeable, allowing for many different kernels to be evaluated against the same feature data. There is an active kernel machine community (see kernel-machines.org).

Boosting, Weighting

Boosting [381] is a machine learning concept that allows a set of classifiers to be used together, organized into combinatorial networks, pipelines, or cascades, and with learned weights applied to each classifier. This results in a higher, synergistic prediction and recognition capability using the combined weighted classifiers. Boosting is analogous to the weighting factors used for neural network inputs; however, boosting methods go further to combine networks of classifiers to create a single, strong classifier.

181

We will illustrate boosting from the Viola Jones method [146,186] also discussed in Chapter 6, which uses the ADA-BOOST training method to create a cascaded pattern matching and classification network by generating strong classifiers from many weak learners. This is done through dynamic weighting factors determined in a training phase, and the method of using weighting factors is called *boosting*.

The idea of boosting is to first start out by equally weighting the detected features—in this case, HAAR wavelets—and then matching the detected features against the set of expected features; for example, those features detected for a specific face. Each set of weighted features is a classifier. Classifiers that fail to match correctly are called *weak learners*. For each weak learner during the training phase, new weighting factors are applied to each feature to make the classifier match correctly. Finally, all weak learners are combined linearly into a *cascaded classifier,* which is like a pipeline or funnel of weak classifiers designed to reject bad features early in the pipeline.

The training can take many hours, days or weeks and requires some supervision. While ADA-BOOST solved binary classification problems, the method can be extended into multiclass classification [382].

Selected Examples of Classification

We call out a few noteworthy and popular classification approaches here, which are also listed in Table 4-5.

Table 4-5. *Comparison of Various Interest Point, Descriptor, and Classifier Concepts*

Technique	FERNS	SIFT	FREAK	Convolutional Network	Polygon Shape Factors
Sparse Keypoints	x	x	x	x	
Feature Descriptor		x	x	x	x
Multi-Scale Representation	x	x		x	
Coarse to Fine Descriptor			x		
Deep Learning Network				x	
Sparse Codebook				x	

Note: The FERNS method does not rely on a local feature descriptor, and instead relies on a classifier using constraints between interest points.

Randomized trees is a method using hierarchical patch classifiers [384] based on Bayesian probability methods, taking a set of simple patch features deformed by random homography parameters. Ozuysal et al.[307] further develop the randomized tree method with optimizations using non-hierarchical organization in the form of *FERNS,* using binary probability tests for patch classifier membership. Matches are evaluated using a naïve Bayesian approach.

FERNS training [307] involves combining training data from multiple viewpoints of each patch to add scale and perspective invariance, using trees with 11 levels and 11 versions of each patch, warped using randomized affine deformation parameters; some Gaussian noise and smoothing are also applied to the deformed patches. Keypoints are then located in each deformed patch, and the keypoints found in the most deformed patches are selected for the training set. The FERNS keypoints use maxima of Laplacian filters at three scales and retain only the strongest 400 keypoints. The Laplacian keypoints do not include orientation or fine-scale estimation. FERNS does not use descriptors, just the strongest Laplacian keypoints computed over the 11 deformed images in each set.

While K-means [354] methods can be very slow, an optimization using hierarchical Nister Trees [387] is a highly scalable alternative for indexing massive numbers of quantized or clustered local descriptors in a hierarchical vocabulary tree. The method is reported to be very discriminative and has been tested on large datasets.

Binary Histogram Intersection Minimization (BHIM) [322] uses pairs of multi-scale local binary patterns (MSLBP) [322] to form pairwise-coupled classifiers based on strong divergence between pairs of MSLBP features. Histogram intersection on pairs of MSLBP features use a distance function such as SAD to find the largest divergence of histogram distance. The BHIM classifier is then composed of a list of "pairs" of MSLBP histograms with large divergence, and MSLBPs are matched into the classifier. BHIM uses features created across multiple scales of training data. It is reported by the authors to be at least as accurate as ADA-BOOST, and the MSLBP features are reported to be more discriminant than LBPs.

Alehi et al.[391] develop a method for classification and matching using a cascaded set of coarse to fine grids of region descriptors called *object descriptors* (ODs). The target application is tracking objects across a set of cameras, such as traffic cameras in a metropolitan area. Each OD is a collection of multi-scale descriptors computed in equal-size regions over multi-scale grids; the grids range over six scales with a 25 percent scaling factor difference. Any existing descriptor method can be used in the OD method, such as SIFT, SURF, or correlation templates. The authors [391] claim improved performance by cascading descriptors in an OD compared with using existing descriptors.

Feature Learning, Sparse Coding, Convolutional Networks

Feature learning methods create a set of basis features (we use the term *basis features* loosely here) derived from the ground truth data during a training phase. The basis features are collected into a set. There are several related approaches taken to create the set, discussed in this section.

Terminology: Codebooks, Visual Vocabulary, Bag of Words, Bag of Features

Several related approaches and terminologies are used in the feature learning literature, including variations such as *sparse coding, codebooks, bag of words*, and *visual vocabularies*. However, for the novice, there is some conceptual overlap in the various approaches and the terminology is subtle, describing minor variations in methods used to learn the features and build the classification networks; see references[114–119]. The sparse codes are analogous to basis features. Many researchers in the areas of activity recognition [69,75] are using sparse codebooks and extending the field of research.

We describe some of the terminology and concepts, including:

- Dictionaries, codebooks, visual vocabularies, bags of words, bags of features, and feature alphabet, containing sets of features.

- Sparse codes, sparse coding, and minimal sets of features or codes.

- Multi-layered sparse coding and deep belief networks, containing multi-layered classification networks for hierarchical matching; these are composed of small, medium, and large scale features— perhaps ten or more layers of scale.

- Single-layer sparse coding, with no hierarchy of features, which may be built on top of a multi-scale descriptor such as SIFT.

- Unsupervised feature learning, including various methods of learning the best features for a given application from the ground truth dataset; feature learning has received much attention recently in the Neural Information Processing Systems (NIPS) community, especially as applied to convolutional networks.

Sparse Coding

Some early work in the area of sparse coding for natural images can be found in the work of Olshausen and Field [126], which forms the conceptual basis. To create a *sparse codebook*, first an image feature domain is chosen, such as face recognition or automobile recognition. Then a set of *basis items* (patches, vectors, or functions) are selected and put into a codebook based on a chosen uniqueness function. The sparse coding goal is to contain the smallest set of unique basis items required to achieve the accuracy and performance goals for the system.

When adding a new feature to the codebook during the training stage, candidate features are compared against the features already in the codebook to determine feature uniqueness, using a suitable distance function and empirical threshold. If the feature is sufficiently unique, as measured by the distance function and a threshold, the new feature is added to the codebook.

In work by Bo, Ren, and Fox[124], the training phase involves using objects such as a cup, which is positioned on a small rotating table. Multiple images are taken of the object from a number of viewpoints and distances to achieve perspective invariance, which then yields a set of patches taken from a variety of poses, from which the unique sparse codewords are created and added to the codebook. See also references[124,237,225,226]. Related work includes a histogram of sparse codes descriptor or HSC [125], as described in Chapter 7, used to retrofit a HOG descriptor.

Visual Vocabularies

Visual vocabularies are analogous to word vocabularies and they share common research [231]. In the area of document analysis, content is analyzed and described based on the histogram of unique word counts in the document. Of course, the histogram can be trimmed and remapped to reduce the quantization and binning. Visual vocabularies follow the same method as word vocabulary methods, representing images globally by the frequency of visual words, as illustrated in Figure 4-21, where visual word methods use feature descriptors of many types.

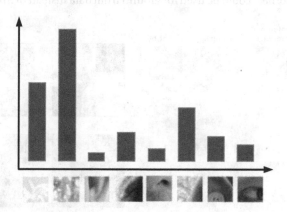

Figure 4-21. *Hypothetical, simplified illustration representing a set of visual words, and a histogram showing frequency of use of each visual word in a given image*

To build the visual vocabularies, unique features descriptors are extracted and collected from ground truth images. To be included in the vocabulary, the new feature must have significant statistical differences from the existing features in the vocabulary, so features are added to the vocabulary only if they exceed a difference threshold function.

To quantize the visual vocabulary features for determining their uniqueness, clustering and classification methods are performed on the feature set, and candidate features are selected that are unique so as to reduce the feature space and assist in matching speed. Various statistical methods may be employed to reduce the feature space, such as K-means, KNN, SVM, Bayes, and others.

To collect the visual features, practitioners are using all possible methods of feature description and image search, including sampling the image at regular grids and at interest points, as well as scale space searches. The features used in the vocabularies range from simple rectangular pixel regions, to SIFT features, and everything in between. Applications for the visual vocabularies range from analyzing spatio-temporal images for activity recognition [232,235] to image classification [233,234,118,116,235].

Learned Detectors via Convolutional Filter Masks

As illustrated in Figure 4-22, Richardson and Olson[122] developed a method of learning optimal convolutional filters as an interest point detector with applications to stereo visual odometry. This method uses combinations of DCT and HAAR basis features composed together, using random weights to form a set of candidate 8x8 pixel basis functions, each of which is tested against a target feature set resembling 2D barcodes known as AprilTags [527]. Each 8x8 pixel candidate is measure against the AprilTags to find the best convolution masks for each tag to form the basis set. Of course, other target features such as corners could be used for ground truth data instead of AprilTags.

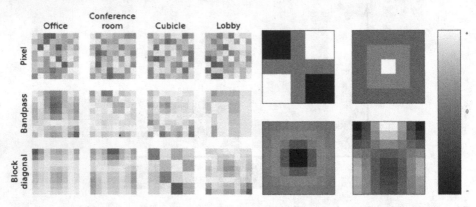

Figure 4-22. *(Left) The optimal learned convolution filters for an image of an Office, a conference room, cubicle, and lobby; gray scale values represent filter coefficient magnitudes. (Right) Comparable corner detectors in the top row, difference of Gaussian in the bottom left, and a custom filter which is preferred by the author. (Images © Andrew Richardson and Edwin Olson, used by permission)*

Using the learned convolution masks, the steps in feature detection are as follows: (1) convolve each masks at chosen pixels to get a response; (2) compare convolution response against a threshold; (3) suppress non-extrema response values using a 3x3 spatial filter window. The authors report good accuracy and high performance on the order of a FAST detector, but with the benefit of higher performance for the combined detection and non-maximal suppression stage as feature counts increase.

Convolutional Neural Networks, Neural Networks

Convolutional neural networks, pioneered by Lecun [339] and others, are one method of implementing machine learning algorithms based on neural network theory [360]. Convolutional networks are showing great success in academia and industry [340] for image classification and feature matching.

Convolutional neural networks are one method of modeling a neural network. The main compute elements in the convolutional network are many optimized convolutions in parallel, as well as fast local memory between the compute units. The run-time classification performance can be quite fast, especially for hardware-optimized implementations [528].

As shown in Figure 4-23 at a high level, one method of modeling each neuron and a network of neurons includes a set of inputs, a set of weighting factors applied to each input, a combinatorial function, and an output. Many neural models exist that map into convolutional networks, we refer the reader to the experts, see Lecun [339]. Neural networks have been devised using several models, but this topic is outside the scope of this work [360]; see the NIPS community research for more.

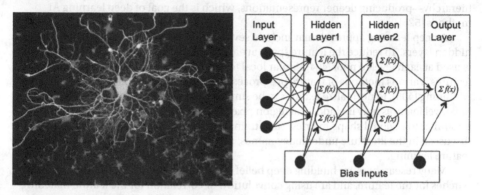

Figure 4-23. *(Left) Neurons from a human brain. (Right) One of many possible models of an artificial neural network [360]. Note that each neuron may have several inputs, several outputs, a bias factor, and input/output weight factors (not shown). Human neuron Image on left @ Gerry Shaw, used by permission*

Neural networks are multi-level, containing several layers and interconnections. As shown in the hypothetical neural network in Figure 4-23, a bias input is provided to each neural function as a weighting factor. Some neural network configurations use individual weights applied to each individual input, so the weighting factors act as convolution kernel coefficients. In terms of convolutional networks, the neural network paradigm can be mapped into localized patches of raw pixels as feature inputs at the lowest level. For example, the patch size may be 1 pixel or a 5x5 patch of pixels, each input having a convolutional weighting factor.

Learned weighting factors [85,339] are determined in the networks to use as convolution kernel values applied to each pixel in the patch. The output of a layer is referred to as a *feature map*. The weighting factors are learned in the network, and may be back-propagated to tune the system during training.

A standard introduction to convolutional networks is provided by Lecun [339]. During the learning process, a key goal is to preserve only the unique features and reduce the feature space; for this reason, sparse coding is used. Learned features are composed into a multi-layer structure of scaled high-level, mid-level, and low-level features in a *deep learning* approach [339,340] containing 10 or more scale layers. Networks and pixel input areas may overlap into adjacent convolutional kernels.

Deep Learning, Pooling, Trainable Feature Hierarchies

Local feature descriptors are often concerned with matching at a specific scale or perhaps even a few scales. However, trainable feature hierarchy methods [402,339] are being developed that classify features using a hierarchy, or *deep set,* of features containing low-level features at fine scales, intermediate, or medium scale features, and high-level features at coarse scales—perhaps eight or more layers in the feature detection hierarchy—producing deeper representations, which is the goal of deep learning AI methods [525].

A deep learning approach may include several layers of neural networks, including hidden layers. To reduce the feature space at each level of the hierarchy, feature learning is used at each level to pool [404] similar local features, preserving only the unique features. Various methods of feature pre-processing are used for pooling, such as feature whitening [405], to normalize features to be similar under contrast or variance. The low-level features may include local region pixel details, and the high-level features may be similar to regional shape metrics. Such trainable feature classification networks are discussed in the literature under many names, such as deep belief networks [526] and feature learning.

Many researchers are building deep belief networks relying on rectangular pixel patches for the feature, and are using convolution or correlation for the feature matching method. Convolutional networks using deep learning are deployed in many successful commercial applications, such as speech recognition, or face, person, and gender recognition. They have also been used to win several competitions [340]. Convolutional networks using deep learning are reported to increase in accuracy as the resolution of features decreases toward a finer scale, which increases the depth of the network. Training is reported to take several days [340], using a bank of dedicated GPUs.

One interesting example is the work of Bo, Ren and Fox [242], where a hierarchical matching pursuit HMP method (deep method) is employed to learn features in an unsupervised framework and add to a sparse codebook with two levels. RGB-D data channels are used to compute the descriptors, including separate descriptors for gray scale or intensity, *RBG* color, *Z* or depth from a depth camera, and the 3D surface normal from the depth data. A few different descriptor sizes are used, including 16x16 patches sampled with 4-pixel overlap for higher-level matching, and a set of nonoverlapping 5x5 patches for lower levels. The features are pooled as a part of the feature learning process.

Summary

In this chapter, we surveyed background concepts and ideas used to create local feature descriptors and interest point detectors. The key concepts and ideas were also developed into the vision taxonomy suggested in Chapter 5. Distance functions were covered here, as well as useful coordinate systems. We examined the shape and pattern of local descriptors, with an emphasis on local binary descriptors such as ORB, FREAK, and BRISK to illustrate the concepts.

Feature descriptor discrimination was illustrated using image reconstructions from feature descriptor data alone. Search strategies were discussed, such as scale space pyramids and multi-level search, as well as other methods such as grid limited search. Computer vision system models were covered, including concepts such as feature space, object models, feature constraints, statistically designed features, and feature learning. Classification and training were illustrated using several methods, including kernel machines, convolutional networks, and deep learning. Several references to the literature were provided for the interested reader to dig deeper. Practical observations and considerations for designing vision systems were also provided.

In summary, this chapter provided useful background concepts to keep in mind when reading the local feature descriptor survey in Chapter 6, since the concepts discussed here were taken mainly from the current local descriptor methods in use; however, some additional observations and directions for future research were suggested in this chapter as well.

CHAPTER 5

■ ■ ■

Taxonomy of Feature Description Attributes

"for the Entwives desired order, and plenty, and peace (by which they meant that things should remain where they had set them)."

—*J. R. R. Tolkien,* Lord of the Rings

This chapter develops a general *Vision Metrics Taxonomy* for feature description, so as to collect summary descriptor attributes for high-level analysis. The taxonomy includes a set of general *robustness criteria* for feature description and ground truth datasets. The material presented and discussed in this book follows and reflects this taxonomy. By developing a standard vocabulary in the taxonomy, terms and techniques are intended to be consistently communicated and better understood. The taxonomy is used in the survey of feature descriptor methods in Chapter 6 to record *'what'* practitioners are doing.

As shown in Figure 5-1, the Vision Metrics Taxonomy is based on feature descriptor dimensions using three axes—shape and pattern, spectra, and density—intended to create a simple framework for analysis and discussion. A few new terms and concepts have been introduced where there had been no standard, such as for the the term feature descriptor families. These have been broken down into categories of local binary descriptors, spectra descriptors, basis space descriptors, and polygon shape descriptors; these descriptor families are also discussed in detail in Chapter 4. Additionally, the taxonomy borrows some useful terminology from the literature when it exists there, including several terms for the robustness and invariance attributes.

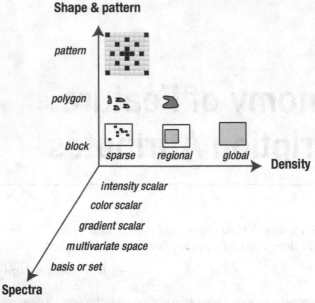

Figure 5-1. *Taxonomy for feature descriptor dimensions, including (1) feature density as global, regional, and sparse local; (2) shape and pattern of pixels used to compute the descriptor, which includes rectangles, circles, and sparse sampling patterns; (3) spectra, which includes the spectrum of information contained in the feature itself*

Why create a taxonomy that is guaranteed to be fuzzy, includes several variables, and will not perfectly express the attributes of any feature descriptor? The intent is to provide a framework to describe various design approaches used for feature description. However, the taxonomy is not intended to be used for comparing descriptors in terms of their goodness, performance, or accuracy.

The three axes of the Vision Metrics Taxonomy are:

1. **Shape and pattern:** How the pixels are taken from the target image.

2. **Density:** The extent of the image required for the descriptor, differentiating among local, regional, and global descriptors.

3. **Spectra:** The scalar and vector quantities used for the metrics, and a summary breakdown of the algorithms and computations.

Feature Descriptor Families

Feature descriptors and metrics have developed along several lines of thinking into separate families. In many cases, the research communities for the various families are working on different problems, and there is little cross-pollination or mutual interest.

For example, cell biology and medical applications are typically interested in polygon shape descriptors, also referred to in the literature as image moments. Those involved with trendy augmented reality applications for mobile phones, as discussed in the computer vision literature, may be more interested in local binary descriptors. In some cases, there are common concepts shared by feature detectors and feature descriptors, as will be discussed in detail in Chapter 6; these include the use of gradients and local binary patterns.

Based on the taxonomy shown in Figure 5-1, we divide features into the following families:

- **Local Binary Descriptors.** These sample point-pairs in a local region and create a binary coded bit vector, 1 bit per compare, amenable to Hamming distance feature matching. Examples include LBP, FREAK, ORB, BRISK, Census.

- **Spectra Descriptors.** These use a wide range of spectra values, such as gradients and region averages. There is no practical limit to the spectra that could be used with these features. One of the most common spectra used in detectors is the local region gradient, such as in SIFT. Gradients are also used in several interest point and edge detectors, such as Harris, Sobel.

- **Basis Space Descriptors.** These methods encode the feature vector into a set of basis functions, such as the familiar Fourier series of sine and cosine magnitude and phase. In addition, existing and novel basis features are being devised in the form of sparse codebooks and visual vocabularies (we use the term basis space loosely).

- **Polygon Shape Descriptors.** These take the shape of objects as measured by statistical metrics, such as area, perimeter, and centroid. Typically, the shapes are extracted using a morphological vision pipeline and regional algorithms, which can be more complex than localized algorithms for feature detectors and feature descriptors (as will be discussed in Chapter 8). *Image moments* [518] is a term often used in the literature to describe shape features.

Prior Work on Computer Vision Taxonomies

Several research papers compare and contrast various aspects of sparse local features, and the field is rich with examples of comparisons of keypoint detectors [306,93] and feature descriptors [145,107]. New feature descriptor methods and improvements are usually compared to existing methods, utilizing several robustness and invariance criteria. However, there is a lack of formal taxonomy work to highlight the subtle details affecting design and comparison. For a good survey covering state-of-the-art computer vision methods, see Szelinski [324].

It should be noted that computer vision is a huge field. Several thousand research papers are published every year, and several thousand equally interesting research papers are rejected by conference publishers. Here are a few noteworthy works that survey and organize the field of feature metrics and computer vision.

- **Affine Covariant Interest Point Detectors.** A good taxonomy is provided by Mikolajczyk et al. [153] for affine covariant interest point detectors. Also, Lindberg [150] has studied the area of scale independent interest point methods extensively. We seek a much richer taxonomy, however, to cover design principles for feature descriptors, and we have developed our taxonomy around families of descriptor methods with common design characteristics.

- **Annotated Computer Vision Bibliography.** From USC and maintained by Keith Price, this resource provides a detailed breakdown of computer vision into several branches, as well as links to some key research in the field and computer vision resources.[1]

- **CVonline: The Evolving, Distributed, Non-Proprietary, On-Line Compendium of Computer Vision.** This provides a comprehensive and detailed list of topics in computer vision. The website is maintained by Robert Fisher, and indexes the key Wikipedia articles. This may be one of the best online resources currently available.[2]

- **Local Invariant Feature Detectors: A Survey.** Prepared by Tinne Tuytelaars and Krystian Mikolajczyk [107], this reference provides a good overview of several feature description methods, as well as a discussion of literature on local features, performance and accuracy evaluations of several methods, types of methods (corner detectors, blob detectors, feature detectors), and implementation details.

Robustness and Accuracy

A key goal for computer vision is *robustness*, or the ability of a feature to be recognized under various conditions. Robustness can be broken down into several attributes. For example, detecting a feature should be robust over various criteria that are critical to a given application, such as scale, rotation, or illumination. We might also use the terms *invariant* or *invariance* to describe robustness. The end goal is accurate localization, correspondence, and robustness under invariance criteria.

However, some robustness attributes are dependent on the feature descriptor combined with other variables. For example, many local feature descriptor methods compute position and orientation based on a chosen interest point method, so the descriptor accuracy is interrelated with the interest point method. The distance function and classification method are interrelated as well, to determine final accuracy.

---

[1]http://iris.usc.edu/Vision-Notes/bibliography/contents.html.
[2]http://homepages.inf.ed.ac.uk/rbf/CVonline/CVentry.htm.

> ■ **Note**   Since it is not possible to define robustness or accuracy of a feature descriptor in isolation from the interest point method, the classifier, and the distance function, the opportunity exists to mix and match well-known detectors and descriptors, combined with various classifiers, to yield the desired robustness and accuracy.

Robustness and accuracy are a combination of the following factors:

1. **Interest point accuracy,** since many descriptors depend on the keypoint location and orientation.

2. **Descriptor accuracy,** as each descriptor method varies, and can be tuned.

3. **Classifier and distance function accuracy,** as a poor classifier and matching stage can lead to the wrong results.

Part of the challenge for an application, thus, is to define the robustness criteria, attribute by attribute, and then to define the limits and bounds of invariance sought. For example, scale invariance from 1x to 100x magnification may not be needed and hardly possible, but scale invariance from 1x to 4x may be all that is needed and much simpler to reach.

Several attributes of robustness are developed here into a robustness taxonomy. To determine actual robustness, ground truth data is needed as a basis to check the algorithms and measure results. Chapter 7 provides a background in ground truth data selection and design.

General Robustness Taxonomy

Robustness criteria can be expressed in terms of attributes and measured as invariance or robustness to those attributes. (See Chapter 7, Table 7-1, for more information on each of the robustness criteria attributes, with considerations for creating ground truth datasets.) Robustness criteria and attributes are grouped under the following group headings:

- Illumination

- Color

- Incompleteness

- Resolution and distance

- Geometric distortion

- Discrimination and uniqueness

Each robustness criterions group contains several finer-grain attributes, as illustrated in Figure 5-2.

Figure 5-2. *General robustness criteria and their attributes*

Let's take a look at these robustness attributes, along with some practical considerations for design and implementation of feature descriptors and the corresponding ground truth data to address the attributes.

Illumination

Light is the source of all imaging, and it should be the no.1 priority area for analysis and consideration when setting requirements for a given application. Illumination has several facets and is considered separately from color and color spaces. In some cases, the illumination can be corrected by changing the light source, or by adding or relocating light sources. In other cases, image pre-processing is needed to correct the illumination to prepare the image for further analysis and feature extraction.

Attention to illumination cannot be stressed enough; for example, see Figure 4-3 showing the effects of pre-processing to change the illumination in terms of increasing the contrast for feature extraction. Key illumination attributes are:

- **Uneven illumination:** image contains dark and bright regions, sometimes obscuring a feature that is dependent on a certain range of pixel intensities.

- **Brightness:** there's too much or too little total light, affecting feature detection and matching.

- **Contrast:** intensity bands are too narrow, too wide, or contained in several bands.

- **Vignette:** light is distributed unevenly, such as dark around the edges.

Color Criteria

When color is used, accuracy of color is critical. Color management and color spaces are discussed in Chapter 2, but some major considerations are:

- **Color space accuracy:** which color space should be used— RGB, YIQ, HSV, or a perceptually accurate color sapce such as CIECAM02 Jch or Jab? Each color space has accuracy and utility considerations, such as the ease of transforming colors to and from color spaces.

- **Color channels:** since cameras typically provide RGB data, extracting the gray scale intensity from the RGB data is often important. There are many methods for converting RGB color to gray scale intensity, and many color spaces to choose from.

- **Color bit depth:** color information, when used, must be accurate enough for the application. For example, 8-bit color may be suitable for most applications, unless color discrimination is necessary, so higher precision color using 10,12,14, or 16 bits per channel may be needed.

Also, depending on the camera sensor used, there will be signal characteristics, such as color sensitivity and dynamic range, which differ for each color channel. For demanding color-critical applications, the camera sensor should be well understood and have a known method of calibration. Individual colors may need to be compensated during image pro-processing. (See Chapter 1 for a discussion of camera sensors.)

Incompleteness

Features are not always presented in the image from frame to frame the way they are expected, or in the way they were learned. The features may appear to be incomplete. Key attributes of incompleteness include:

- **Clutter:** the feature is obscured by surrounding image features, and the feature aliases and blends into the surrounding pixels.

- **Occlusion:** the feature is partially hidden; in many cases the application will encounter occluded features or sets of features.

- **Outliers, proximity:** sometimes only features in certain regions are used, and outlying features must be detected and ignored.

- **Noise:** can come from rain, bad image sensors, and many other sources. A constant problem, noise can be compensated for, if it is understood, using a wide range of filter methods during pre-processing.

- **Motion blur:** if it is measured and understood, motion blur can be compensated for using filtering during pre-processing.

- **Jitter, judder:** a motion artifact, jitter or judder can be corrected, but not always; this can be a difficult robustness criteria to meet.

Resolution and Accuracy

Robustness regarding resolution, scale, and distance is often a challenge for computer vision. This is especially true when using feature metrics that rely on discrete pixel sizes over which the pixel area varies with distance. For example, feature metrics that rely on pixel neighborhood structure alone do not scale well or easily, such as correlation templates and most local region kernel methods. Other descriptors, such as those based on shape factors, may provide robustness that pixel region structures cannot achieve. Depending on the application, more than one descriptor method may be required to handle resolution and scale.

To meet the challenge of resolution and distance robustness, various methods are employed in practice, such as scale-space image pyramid collections and feature-space pyramids, which contain multi-scale representations of the feature. Key criteria for resolution and distance robustness include:

- **Location accuracy or position:** how close does the metric need to provide coordinate location under scale, rotation, noise and other criteria? Is pixel acuracy or sub-pixel accuracy needed? Regional accuracy methods of feature description cannot determine positional accuracy as well; for example, methods that use HAAR-like features and integral images can suffer the most, since in computing the HAAR rectangle, all pixels in the rectangle are summed together, throwing away discrimination of individual pixel locations. Pixel-accurate feature accuracy can also be challenging, since as features move and rotate they distort, and the pixel sampling artifacts create uncertainty.

- **Shape and thickness distortion:** distance, resolution, and rotation combine to distort the pixel sample shapes, so a feature may appear to be thicker than it really is or thinner. Distortion is a type of sampling artifact.

- **Focal plane or depth:** depending on distance, the pixel area covered by each pixel changes size. In this case, depth sensors can provide some help when used along with RGB or other sensors.

- **Pixel depth resolution:** for example, processing color chanels to preserve the bit accuracy using float or unsigned short int as a minimum can be required.

Geometric Distortion

Perhaps the most common distortion of image features is geometric, since geometric distortions take many forms as the camera moves and as objects move. Geometric attributes for robustness include the following:

- **Scale:** distance from viewpoint, a commonly addressed robustness criteria.

- **Rotation:** important in many applications, such as industrial inspection.

- **Geometric warp:** key area of research in the fields of activity recognition and dynamic texture analysis, as discussed in Chapters 4 and 6.

- **Reflection:** flipping the image by 180 degrees.

- **Radial distortion:** a key problem in depth sensing and also for 2D camera geometry in general, since depth fields are not uniform or simple; see Chapter 1.

- **Polar distortion:** a key problem in depth sensing geometry; see Chapter 1.

Efficiency Variables, Costs and Benefits

We consider efficiency to be related to compute, memory, and total invariance attributes provided. How efficient is a feature descriptor or feature metric? How much compute is needed to create the metric? How much memory is needed to store the metric? How accurate is the metric? How much robustness and invariance are provided vs. the cost of compute and memory? To answer the above questions is very difficult and depends on how the entire vision pipeline is implemented for an application, as well as the compute resources available. The Vision Metrics Taxonomy provides information to pursue such questions, but as always pursuing the wrong questions may lead to the wrong answers.

Discrimination and Uniqueness

The selection of optimal, discriminating features is achieved using a variety of methods. For example, local feature detector methods filter out only the most discriminating or unique candidates based on criteria such as corner strength; then descriptors are computed at the selected interest points as patches or other shapes; and finally the resulting descriptor is either accepted or rejected based on uniqueness criteria. Uniqueness is also the key criterion for creating sparse codebooks discussed in Chapter 4.

Discrimination can be measured by the ability to recreate an image from only the descriptor information, as discussed in Chapter 4. A descriptor with too little information to adequately recreate an image may be considered weak or non discriminating.

General Vision Metrics Taxonomy

To understand feature metrics, we develop a Vision Metrics Taxonomy composed of summary criteria. Each criterion is selected with a practical, engineering perspective in mind to provide information for evaluation and implementation in specific terms, such as algorithm, spectra, memory size, and other attributes. The basic categories of the Vision Metrics Taxonomy are shown in Table 5-1, and also summarized here as a list, and each list item is discussed in separate sections in this chapter:

- Feature Descriptor Family

- Spectra Dimension

- Spectra Value

- Interest Point

- Storage Format

- Data Types

- Descriptor Memory
- Feature Shape
- Feature Pattern
- Feature Density
- Feature Search Method
- Pattern Pair Sampling
- Pattern Region Size
- Distance Function
- Run-Time Compute

Table 5-1. *Vision Metrics Taxonomy*

Vision Metric Taxonomy		
Feature Descriptor Family	**Interest Point**	**Pattern Pair Sampling**
Local Binary Descriptor	Point, edge, or corner	Center – boundary pair
Spectra Descriptor	Contour based, perimeter	Random pair points
Basis Space Descriptor	Other	Foveal centered trained pairs
Polygon Shape Descriptor	No interest point	Trained pairs
Spectra Dimensions	**Storage Format**	Symmetric pairs
Single variate	Spectra vector	**Pattern Region Size**
Multivariate	Bit vector	Bounding box (x size, y size)
Spectra Value	Multivariate collection	**Distance function**
Orientation Vector	**Data Types**	Euclidean distance
Sensor, accelerometer data	Float	Squared Euclidean distance
Multigeometry	Integer	Cosine similarity
Multi-scale	Fixed point	Correlation distance
Fourier magnitude	**Descriptor Memory**	Manhattan distance
Fourier phase	Fixed length or variable length	Chessboard or Chebychev distance
Other basis function	Byte count range	Earth movers distance
Morphological shape metrics	**Feature Shape**	SAD L1 Norm
Learned binary descriptors	Rectangle block patch	SSD L2 Norm
Dictionary, codebook, vocabulary	Symmetric polygon region	Mahalanobis distance
Region histogram 2D	Irregular segmented region	Bray Curtis difference
3D histogram	Volumetric region	Canberra distance
Log polar bins	Deformable	L0 Norm
Cartesian bins	**Feature Search Method**	Hamming distance
Region sum	Coarse to fine image pyramid	Jaccard similarity
Region average	Scale space pyramid	**Run-Time Compute**
Region statistical	Pyramid scale	Compute complexity % of SIFT
Binary pattern	Dense sliding window	**Feature Density**
DoG (1-bit)	Dense grid block search	Global
DoG (multi-bit)	Window search	Regional
Bit vector of values	Grid block search	Sparse
Gradient magnitude	Sparse at interest points	**Feature Pattern**
Gradient direction	Sparse at predicted points	Rectangular kernel
3D surface normals	Sparse in segmented regions	Binary compare pattern
Line segment metric	Depth segmented regions (Z)	DNET line sample strip set
Gray scale info	Super-pixel search	Radial line sampling pattern
Color space info	Sub-pixel search	Perimeter or contour edge
	Double-scale 1st pyramid level	Sample weighting pattern

Many of the background concepts used in the taxonomy are discussed in Chapter 4, where attributes about the internal structure and goals of common features are analyzed. In addition, this taxonomy is illustrated in the Feature Metric Evaluation (FME) information tables later in this chapter. A small subset of the taxonomy is used in the Chapter 6 survey of feature descriptors to record summary information. The taxonomy in Table 5-1 is a guideline for collecting and summarizing information. No judgment on goodness or performance is recorded or implied.

Feature Descriptor Family

As described at the beginning of this chapter, feature descriptors are classified in this taxonomy as follows:

- Local Binary Descriptors

- Spectra Descriptors

- Basis Space Descriptors

- Polygon Shape Descriptors

Spectra Dimensions

The spectra or values recorded in the feature descriptor vary, and may include one or more types of information or spectra. We divide the categories as follows:

- **Single variate:** stores a single value such as an integral image or region average, or just a simple set of pixel gradients.

- **Multivariate:** multiple spectra are stored; for example, a combination of spectra such as color information, gradient magnitude and direction, and other values.

Spectra Type

The spectral type of feature descriptor is a major axis in this taxonomy, as shown in Figure 5-1. Here are common spectra, which have been discussed in Chapter 3 and will be discussed in Chapter 6 as well.

- **Gradient magnitude:** a measure of local region texture or difference, used by a wide range of patch-based feature descriptor methods. It is well known [248] that the human visual system responds to gradient information in a scale and rotationally invariant manner across the retina, as demonstrated in SIFT and many other feature description methods, thus the use of gradients is a preferred method for computer vision.

- **Gradient direction:** some descriptor methods compute a gradient direction and others do not. A simple region gradient direction method is used by several feature descriptors and edge detection methods, including Sobel and SIFT, to provide rotational invariance.

- **Orientation vector:** some descriptors are oriented and others are not. Orientation can be computed by methods other than a simple gradient—for example, SURF uses a method of sampling many gradient directions to compute the dominant gradient orientation of the entire patch region as the orientation vector. In the RIFF method, a radial relative orientation is computed. In the SIFT method, any orientations detected within 80 percent of the dominant orientation will result in an additional interest point being generated, so the same descriptor may allow multiple interest points differing only in orientation.

- **Sensor data:** data such as accelerometer or GPS information is added to the descriptor. In the GAFD method, a gravity vector computed from an accelerometer is used for orientation.

- **Multigeometry:** multiple geometric transforms of the descriptor data that are stored together in the descriptor, such as several different perspective transforms of the same data as used in the RFM2.3 descriptor; the latter contains the same patch computed over various geometric transforms to increase the scale, rotation, and geometric robustness.

- **Multiscale:** instead of relying on a scale-space pyramid, the descriptor stores a copy of several scaled representations. The multi-resolution histogram method described in Chapter 4 is one such method of approximating feature description over a range of scales, where scale is approximated using a range of Gaussian blur functions, and their resulting histograms are stored as the multi-scale descriptor.

- **Fourier magnitude:** both the sine and cosine basis functions from the Fourier series can be used in the descriptor—for example, in the polygon shape family of descriptors as illustrated in Figure 6-29. The magnitude of the sine or cosine alone is a revealing shape factor, without the phase, as illustrated in Figure 6-6, which shows the histogram of LBPs run through a Fourier series to produce the power spectrum. This illustrates how the LBP histogram power spectrum provides rotational invariance. Other methods related to Fourier series may use alternative arrangements of the computation, such as the discrete cosine transform (DCT), which uses only the cosine component and is amenable to integer computations and hardware acceleration as commonly done for media applications.

- **Fourier phase:** phase information has been shown to be valuable for creating a blur-invariant feature descriptor, as demonstrated in the LPQ method discussed in Chapter 6.

- **Other basis functions:** can be used for feature description. Wavelets are commonly used in place of Fourier methods owing to greater control over the function window and tuning of the basis functions derived from the mother wavelet into the family of related wavelets. See Chapter 2 for a discussion of wavelets compared to other basis functions.

- **Morphological shape metrics:** predominantly used in the polygon shape descriptor family, composed of shape factors, and referred to as *image moments* in some literature. They are computed over the gross features of a polygon image region such as area, perimeter, centroid, and many others. The vision pipeline and image pre-processing used for polygon shape description may include morphological and texture operators, rather than local interest point and descriptor computations.

- **Learned binary descriptors:** created by running ground truth data through a training step, such as developed in ORB and FREAK, to create a set of statistically optimized binary sampling point-pair patterns.

- **Dictionary, codebook, vocabulary from feature learning methods:** build up a visual vocabulary, dictionary, or sparse codebook as a sparse set of unique features using a wide range of descriptor methods, such as simple images correlation patches or SIFT descriptors. When combined as a sparse set, these are representative of the features found in a set of ground truth data for an application domain, such as automobile recognition or face recognition.

- **Region histogram 2D:** used for several types of information, such as binning gradient direction, as in CARD, RFM2.3, and SURF; or for binning linear binary patterns, such as the LBP. The SIFT method of histogramming gradient information uses a fairly large histogram bin region, which provides for some translation invariance, similar to the human visual system treatment of the 3D position of gradients across the retina [248].

- **3D histogram:** used in methods such as used in SIFT, which represents gradient magnitude and orientation together as a 3D histogram.

- **Cartesian bins:** a common method of binning local region information into the descriptor simply based on the Cartesian position of pixels in a patch—for example, histogramming the pixel intensity magnitude of each point in the region.

- **Log polar bins:** instead of binning local region feature information in Cartesian rectangular arrangements, some descriptors such as GLOH use a log polar coordinate system to prepare values for histogram binning, with the goal of adding better rotational invariance to the descriptor.

- **Region sum:** such as an integral image, a method used to quickly sum the local region pixel values, or HAAR feature. The region sum is stored into the feature representing the total value of all the pixels in the region. Note that region summation may be good for coarse-feature description of an area, but the summation process eliminates fine local texture detail.

- **Region average:** average value of the pixels in a region area, also referred to as a box filter, which may be computed from a convolution operation, scaled integral image, or by simply adding up the pixel values in the array.

- **Region statistical:** such as region moments, like standard deviation, variance, or max or min values.

- **Binary pattern:** such as a vector of binary values, or bits—for example, stored as a result of local pixel pair compare computations of local neighborhood pixel values as used in the local binary descriptor family, such as LBP, Census, and ORB.

- **DoG (1-bit quantized):** as used in the FREAK descriptor, a set of DoG or bandpass filter features of different sizes, taken over a local binary region in a retinal sampling pattern similar to the human visual system, compared in pairs, and quantized to a single bit in a histogram vector.

- **DoG (multi-bit):** a type of bandpass filter that is implemented using many variations, where a Gaussian blur filter is applied to the image, then the image is subtracted from (a) a shifted copy of itself, (b) a copy of itself at another Gaussian blur level, or (3) a copy of itself at another image scale as in the SIFT descriptor method.

- **Bit vector of values:** a bit string containing a sequence of values quantized to a single bit, such as a threshold.

- **3D surface normals:** the analog to 2D gradients except in 3D, used in the HON4D method [198] to describe the surface of a 3D object location in the feature descriptor.

- **Line segment metric:** as in the CCH method, used to describe the line segments composing an object perimeter. Or, as used as a shape factor for objects where the length of a set of radial line segments originating at the centroid and extending to the perimeter are recorded in the descriptor, which can be fed into a Fourier transform to yield a power spectrum signature, as shown in Figure 6-29.

- **Color space info:** some descriptors do not take advantage of color information, which in many cases can provide added discrimination and accuracy. Both the use of simple RGB channels, such as in the RGB-D methods [75,118], or using color space conversions into more accurate spaces are invaluable. For example, face recognition has problems distinguishing faces from different cultures, and since the skin tone varies across regions, the color value can be measured and added to the descriptor. However, several descriptors make use of color information, such as S-LBP, which operates in a colorimetric, accurate color space such as CIE-Lab, or the F-LBP, which computes a Fourier spectrum of color distance from the center pixel to adjacent pixels, as well as color variants of SIFT and many others.

- **Gray scale info:** the gray scale or color intensity value is the default spectra in almost all descriptors. However, the method used to create the gray scale from color, and the image pre-processing used to prepare intensity for analysis and measurement, are critical for the vision pipeline and were discussed in Chapter 2.

Interest Point

The use of interest points is optional with feature description. Some methods do not use interest points, and sample the image on a fixed grid rather than at every pixel, such as the Viola Jones method using HAAR-like features. It is also possible to simply create a feature descriptor for every pixel rather than just at interest points, but since the performance impact is considerable, interest points are typically used to find the best location for a feature first.

Several methods for finding interest points are surveyed and discussed in Chapter 6. Categories of interest points for the taxonomy include:

- **Point, edge, or corner:** these methods typically start with locating the local region maxima and minima; methods used include gradients, local curvature, Harris methods, blob detectors, and edge detectors.

- **Contour based, perimeter:** some methods do not start feature description at maxima and minima, and instead look for structure in the image, such as a contour or perimeter, and this is true mainly for the morphological shape based methods.

- **Other:** there are other possibilities for determining interest point location, such as prediction of likely interest point or feature positions, or using grid or tile regions.

- **No interest point:** some methods do not use any interest points at all.

Storage Formats

Storage formats are a practical matter for memory efficiency and engineering real systems and designing data structures. Knowing the storage format can guide efforts during engineering and optimization toward various programming constructs, instruction sets, and memory architecture.

For example, both CPU and GPGPU graphics processors often provide dedicated silicon to support various storage format organizations, such as scatter and gather operations, and sparse and dense data structure support. Understanding the GPGPU capabilities can provide guidelines for designing the storage format, as discussed in Chapter 8. Storage format summary:

- **Spectra vector:** may be a set of histograms, a set of color values, a set of basis vectors.

- **Bit vector:** local binary patterns use bit vector data types, some programming languages include bit vector constructs, and some instruction sets include bit vector handling instructions.

- **Multivariate collection:** a set of values such as statistical moments or shape factors.

Data Types

The data types used for feature description are critical for accuracy, memory use, and compute. However, it is worth noting that data types can be changed as a tradeoff for accuracy in some cases. For example, converting floating point to fixed point or integer computations may be more memory efficient, as well as power efficient, since a floating point silicon ALU complex occupies almost four times more die space, thus consuming more power than an integer ALU. The data type summary includes:

- **Float:** many applications require floating point for accuracy. For example, a Fourier transform of images requires at least 64 bits double precision (larger images require more precision); other applications like target tracking may require 32-bit floating point for precision trajectory computations.

- **Integer:** pixel values are commonly represented with 8 bit values, with 16 bits per pixel common as image sensors provide better data. At least 32-bit integers are needed for many data structures and numerical results, such as integral images.

- **Fixed point:** this is an alternative representation to floating point, which saves data space and can be implemented more efficiently in silicon. Most modern GPUs support several fixed-point formats, and some CPUs as well. Fixed-point formats include 8-,16-, and 24-bit representations. Accuracy may be close enough using fixed point, depending on the application. In addition to fixed-point data types, GPUs and some processors also provide various normalized data types (see manufacturer information).

Descriptor Memory

The total descriptor memory size is part of the efficiency of the descriptor, and compute performance is another component. A descriptor with a large memory footprint, few invariance attributes and heavy compute is inefficient. We are interested in memory size as a practical matter. Key memory-related attributes include:

- **Fixed length or variable length:** some descriptors allows for alternative representations.

- **Byte count:** the length of all data in the descriptor.

Feature Shapes

A range of shapes are used for the pixel sampling pattern; shapes are surveyed in Chapter 4 including the following methods:

- **Rectangle block patch:** simple x, y, dx, dy range.

- **Symmetric polygon region:** may be an octagon, as in the CenSurE method, or a circular region, like FREAK or DAISY.

- **Irregular segmented region:** such as computed using morphological methods following segmented regions or thresholded perimeter.

- **Volumetric region:** some features make use of stacks of images resembling a volume structure. As shown in Figure 6-12, the VLBP or Volume LBP and the LBP-TOP make use of volumetric data structures. The dynamic texture methods and activity recognition methods often use sets of three adjacent patches from the current frame plus 2 past frames, organized in a spatio-temporal image frame history, similar to a volume.

- **Deformable:** most features use a rigid shape, such as a fixed-size rectangle or a circle; however, some descriptors are designed with deformation in mind, such as scale deformations [345,346], and affine or homographic deformation [220], to enable more robust matching.

Feature Pattern

Feature pattern is a major axis in this taxonomy, as shown in Figure 5-3, since it affects memory architecture and compute efficiency.

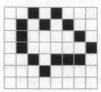 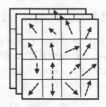

Figure 5-3. *Feature shapes. (Left to right) Rectangular patch, symmetric polygon region, irregular segmented region, and volumetric region*

Feature shape and pattern are related. Shape refers to the boundary, and pattern refers to the sampling method. Patterns include:

- **Rectangular kernel:** some methods use a kernel to define which elements in the region are included in the sample; see Figure 5-3 (left image) showing a kernel that does not use the corner pixels in the region; see also Figure 4-10.

- **Binary compare pattern:** such as FREAK, ORB, and BRISK, where specific pixels in a region are paired to form a complex sampling pattern.

- **DNET line sample strip set:** where points along a line segment are sampled densely; see Figure 4-8.

- **Radial line sampling pattern:** where points on radial line segments originating at a center point are sampled densely; for example, used to compute Fourier descriptors for polygon region shape; see Figure 6-29.

- **Perimeter or contour edge:** where points around the edge of a shape or region are sampled densely.

- **Sample weighting pattern:** as shown in Figure 6-17, SIFT uses a circular weighting pattern in the histogram bins to decrease the contribution of points farther away from the center of the patch. The D-NETS method uses binary weighting of samples along the line strips, favoring points away from the endpoints and ignoring points close to the end points. Weighting patterns can provide invariance to noise and occlusion.

See Chapter 4 for more illustrations in the section on patches and shapes.

Feature Density

As shown in Figure 5-1, feature density is a major axis in this taxonomy. The amount of the image used for the descriptor is referred to in this taxonomy as *feature density*. For example, some descriptors are intended to use smaller regions of local pixels, anchored at interest points, and to ignore the larger image. Other methods use larger regions. Density categories include:

- **Global:** covers the entire image, each pixel in the image.

- **Regional:** covers fairly large regions of the image, typically on a grid, or around a segmented structure or region, not anchored at interest points.

- **Sparse:** may be taken at interest points, or in small regions at selected points such as random points in the BRIEF descriptor, trained points such as FREAK and ORB, or a sparse sampling grid as in the RFM2.3 descriptor.

Feature Search Methods

The method used for searching for features in the image is a significant for feature descriptor design. The search method determines a lot about the design of the descriptor, and the compute time required in the vision pipeline. We list several search variations here, and more detailed descriptions and illustrations are provided in Chapter 4. Note that a feature descriptor can make use of multiple search criteria. Feature search related information is summarized as follows:

- **Coarse-to-fine image pyramid:** or multi-scale search, using a pyramid of coarser resolution copies of the original.

- **Scale space pyramid:** the scale space pyramid is a variation of the regular coarse-to-fine image pyramid, where a Gaussian blur function is computed over each pyramid scale image [547] to create a more uniform search space; see Figure 4-17.

- **Pyramid scale factor:** captures pyramid scale intervals, such as octaves or other scales—for example, ORB uses a ~1.41x scale.

- **Dense sliding window:** where the search is made over each pixel in the image, often within a sliding rectangular region centered at each pixel.

- **Grid block search:** where the image is divided into a fixed grid or tiles, so the search can be faster but does not discriminate as well as dense methods. For example, see Figure 6-17 describing the PHOG method, which computes descriptors at different grid resolutions across the entire image.

- **Window search:** limited dense search to particular regions, such as in stereo matching between two L/R frames where the correspondence search range is limited to expected locations.

- **Sparse at interest points:** where a corner detector or other detector is used to determine where valid features may be found.

- **Sparse at predicted points:** such as in tracking and mapping algorithms like PTAM, where the location of interest points is predicted based on motion or trajectory, and then a feature search begins at the predicted points.

- **Sparse in segmented regions:** for example, when morphological shape segmentation methods or thresholding segmentation methods define a region, and a second pass is made through the region looking for features.

- **Depth segmented regions (Z):** when depth camera information is used to threshold the image into foreground and background, and only the foreground regions are searched for features.

- **Super-pixel search:** similar to the image pyramid method, but a multi-scale representation of the image is created by combining pixel values together using super-pixel integration methods, as discussed in Chapter 2.

- **Sub-pixel search:** where sub-pixel accuracy is needed—for example, with region correlation, so several searches are made around a single pixel, with sub-pixel offsets computed for each compare, and in some cases geometric transforms of the pattern are made prior to feature matching.

- **Double-scale first pyramid level:** In the SIFT scale-space pyramid method, the lowest level of the pyramid is computed from a doubled 2x linear interpolated version of the full-scale image, which has the effect of preserving high-frequency information in the lowest level of the image pyramid, and increasing the number of stable keypoints by about four times, which is quite significant. Otherwise, computing the Gaussian blur across the original image would have the effect of throwing away most of the high-frequency details.

Pattern Pair Sampling

For local binary patterns, pattern pair sampling design is one of the key areas of innovation. Pairs of points are compared using a function such as (center pixel < kernel pixel) using a compare region threshold, and then the result of the comparison forms the binary descriptor vector. Note that many local binary descriptor method were discussed and illustrated in Chapter 4, to illustrate variations in point-pair sampling configuration and compare functions. The vision taxonomy for point-pair sampling includes:

- **Center – boundary pair:** such as in the LBP family and Census transform.

- **Random pair points:** such as in BRIEF, and semi-random in ORB.

- **Foveal centered trained pairs:** such as in FREAK and Daisy.

- **Trained pairs:** many methods train the point-pairs using ground truth data to meet objective criteria, such as FREAK and ORB.

- **Symmetric pairs:** such as BRISK, which provides short and long line segments spaced symmetrically for point-pair comparisons.

Pattern Region Size

The size of the local pattern region is a critical performance factor, even though memory access is likely from fast-register files and cache. For example, if we are performing a convolution of a 3x3 pattern region, there are nine multiplies per kernel, and possibly one summary multiply to scale the results, for a total of 10 multiplies per pixel. For each multiply we have two memory reads, one for the pixel and one for the kernel value; and we have ten memory writes, one for each multiply. A 640x480 image has 307200 pixels, and assuming 8 bits per pixel gray scale only, per frame we end up with 3,072,000 multiplies, 60,720,000 memory reads, and 307200 writes for the result. Larger kernel sizes and larger image sizes of course add more compute.

There are many ways to optimize the performance, which we will cover in Chapter 8 on vision pipeline engineering. For this attribute, we are interested in the following:

- **Bounding box (x size, y size):** for example, the bounding box around a rectangular region, circular region, or polygon shape region.

Distance Function

Computing the pattern matching or correspondence is one of the key performance criteria for a good descriptor. Feature matching is a tradeoff between accuracy and performance, with the key variables being the numeric type and size of the feature descriptor vectors, the distance function, and the number of patterns and search optimizations in the feature database. Choosing a feature descriptor amenable to fast matching is a good goal.

In general, the fastest distance functions are the binary family and Hamming distance, which is used in the local binary descriptor family. Distance functions are enumerated here; see Chapter 4 for details.

Euclidean or Cartesian Distance Family

- Euclidean distance

- Squared Euclidean distance

- Cosine similarity

- SAD L1 Norm

- SSD L2 Norm

- Correlation distance
- Hellinger distance

Grid Distance Family

- Manhattan distance
- Chessboard or Chebychev distance

Statistical Distance Family

- Earth movers distance
- Mahalanobis distance
- Bray Curtis difference
- Canberra distance

Binary or Boolean Distance Family

- L0 Norm
- Hamming distance
- Jaccard similarity

Feature Metric Evaluation

This section addresses the question of how to summarize feature descriptor information at a high level from the Vision Metrics Taxonomy into a practical Feature Metric Evaluation Framework (FME) from an engineering and design perspective.

■ **Note** The FME is intended as a template to capture high-level information for basic analysis.

Efficiency Variables, Costs and Benefits

Efficiency can be measured for a feature descriptor in simple terms, such as the benefit of the compute cost and memory used vs. what is provided in the way of accuracy, discrimination, robustness, and invariance. How much value does the method provide for the time, space, and power cost? Efficiency metrics include:

- **Costs:** compute, memory, time, power

- **Benefits:** accuracy, robustness, and invariance attributes provided

- **Efficiency:** benefits vs. costs

The effectiveness of the data contained in the descriptor varies—for example, a large memory footprint to contain a descriptor with little invariance is not efficient, and a high compute cost for small amounts of invariance and accuracy also reveals low efficiency. We could say that an efficient feature representation contains the least number of bytes and lowest compute cost providing the greatest amount of discrimination, robustness, and accuracy. Local binary descriptors have demonstrated the best efficiency for many robustness attributes.

Image Reconstruction Efficiency Metric

For a visual comparison of feature descriptor efficiency, we can also reconstruct an image from the feature descriptors, and then visually and statistically analyze the quality of the reconstruction vs. the compute and memory cost. Detailed feature descriptors can provide good visualization and reconstruction of the original image from the descriptor data only. For example, Figure 4-15 shows how the HOG descriptor captures oriented gradients using 32780 bytes per 64x128 region, Figure 4-16 shows image reconstruction illustrating how BRIEF and FREAK capture edge information similar to Laplacian or other edge filters using 64 bytes per descriptor, and Figure 4-17 shows SIFT image reconstruction using 128 bytes per descriptor.

Although we do not include image reconstruction efficiency in the FME, this topic was covered in Chapter 4, under the discussion of discrimination.

Example Feature Metric Evaluations

Here area few examples showing how the Vision Metrics Taxonomy and the FME can be used to collect summary descriptor information.

SIFT Example

We use SIFT as an example baseline, since SIFT is widely recognized and carefully designed.

VISION METRIC TAXONOMY FME

Name:	*SIFT*
Feature Family:	*Spectra*
Spectra dimensions:	*Multivariate*
Spectra:	*Gradient magnitude and direction, DoG Scale Space Maxima*
Storage format:	*Orientation and position, gradient orientation histograms*
Data type:	*Float, integer*
Descriptor Memory:	*128 bytes for descriptor histogram*
Feature shape:	*Rectangular region*
Search method:	*Dense sliding window in 2D & 3D 3x3x3 image pyramid*
Feature density:	*Local*
Feature pattern:	*Rectangular and pyramid-cubic*
Pattern pair sampling:	*-*
Pattern region size:	*16x16*
Distance function:	*Euclidean distance*

GENERAL ROBUSTNESS ATTRIBUTES

Total:	*5 (scale, illumination, rotation, affine transforms, noise)*

LBP Example

The LBP is a very simple feature detector with many variations, used for texture analysis and feature description. We use the most basic form of 3x3 LBP here as an example.

VISION METRIC TAXONOMY FME

Name:	*LBP*
Feature Family:	*Local Binary*
Spectra dimensions:	*Single-variate*
Spectra:	*Pixel pair compares with center pixel*
Storage format:	*Binary Bit Vector*
Data type:	*Integer*
Descriptor Memory:	*1 byte*
Feature shape:	*Square centered at center pixel*
Search method:	*Dense sliding window*
Feature density:	*Local*
Feature pattern:	*Rectangular kernel*
Pattern pair sampling:	*Center - boundary pairs*
Pattern region size:	*3x3 or more*
Distance function:	*Hamming distance*

GENERAL ROBUSTNESS ATTRIBUTES

Total:	*3 (brightness, contrast, rotation using RILBP)*

Shape Factors Example

This example uses binary thresholded polygon regions. For this hypothetical example, the pre-processing steps begin with adaptive binary thresholding and morphological shape definition operations, and the measurement steps begin with pixel neighborhood based perimeter following to defined the perimeter edge, followed by centroid computation from perimeter points, followed by determination of 36 radial line segments originating at the centroid reaching to the perimeter. Then each line segment is analyzed to find the shape factors including major/minor axis the Fourier descriptor. The measurements assume a single binary object is being measured, and real-world images may contain at many objects.

We also assume the memory footprint as follows: angular samples taken around 360 degrees, starting at centroid, at 10 degree increments for 36 angular samples, 36 floats for FFT spectrum magnitude, 36 integers for line segment length array, 4 integers for major/minor axis orientation and length, 4 integers for bounding box (x, y, dx, dy), 1 integer for perimeter length, 2 integers for centroid coordinates, TOTAL $36*4 + 36*2 + 4*2 + 4*2 + 1*2 * 2*2 = 238$, assuming 2 byte short integers and 4-byte floats are used.

VISION METRIC TAXONOMY FME

Name:	*Shape Factors*
Feature Family:	*Polygon Shape*
Spectra dimensions:	*Multivariate*
Spectra:	*Perimeter following, area, perimeter, centroid, other image moments*
Storage format:	*complex data structure*
Data type:	*Float, integer*
Descriptor Memory:	*Variable, several hundred bytes possible*
Feature shape:	*Polygon shapes, rectangular bounding box region*
Search method:	*Dense, recursive*
Feature density:	*Regional*
Feature pattern:	*Perimeter contour or edge*
Pattern pair sampling:	*-*
Pattern region size:	*Entire image*
Distance function:	*Multiple methods, multiple comparisons*

GENERAL ROBUSTNESS ATTRIBUTES

Total:	*8 or more (scale, rotation, occlusion, shape, affine, reflection, noise, illumination)*

Summary

In this chapter, a taxonomy is proposed as shown in Figure 5-1 to describe feature description dimensions as shape, pattern, and spectra. This taxonomy is used to divide the families of feature description methods into polygon shape descriptors, local binary descriptors, and basis space descriptors. The taxonomy is used throughout the book. Also, a general vision metrics taxonomy is proposed for the purpose of summarizing high-level feature descriptor design attributes, such as type of spectra, descriptor pixel region size, distance function, and search method. In addition, a general robustness taxonomy is developed to quantify feature descriptor goodness, one attribute at a time, based on invariance and robustness criteria attributes, including illumination, scale, rotation, and perspective. Since feature descriptor methods are designed to address only some of the invariance and robustness attributes, each attribute should be considered separately when evaluating a feature descriptor for a given application. In addition, the robustness attributes can be applied to the design of ground truth datasets, as discussed in Chapter 7. Finally, the vision metrics taxonomy and the robustness taxonomy are combined to form a feature metric evaluation (FME) table to record feature descriptor attributes in summary form. A simple subset of the FME is used to review the attributes of several feature descriptor methods surveyed in Chapter 6.

CHAPTER 6

███

Interest Point Detector and Feature Descriptor Survey

"Who makes all these?"

—Jack Sparrow, *Pirates of the Caribbean*

Many algorithms for computer vision rely on locating interest points, or keypoints in each image, and calculating a feature description from the pixel region surrounding the interest point. This is in contrast to methods such as correlation, where a larger rectangular pattern is stepped over the image at pixel intervals and the correlation is measured at each location. The interest point is the *anchor point*, and often provides the scale, rotational, and illumination invariance attributes for the descriptor; the descriptor adds more detail and more invariance attributes. Groups of interest points and descriptors together describe the actual objects.

However, there are many methods and variations in feature description. Some methods use features that are not anchored at interest points, such as polygon shape descriptors, computed over larger segmented polygon-shaped structures or regions in an image. Other methods use interest points only, without using feature descriptors at all. And some methods use feature descriptors only, computed across a regular grid on the image, with no interest points at all.

Terminology varies across the literature. In some discussions, interest points may be referred to as *keypoints*. The algorithms used to find the interest points maybe referred to as *detectors*, and the algorithms used to describe the features may be called *descriptors*. We use the terminology interchangeably in this work. Keypoints may be considered a set composed of (1) interest points, (2) corners, (3) edges or contours, and (4) larger features or regions such as blobs; see Figure 6-1. This chapter surveys the various methods for designing local interest point detectors and feature descriptors.

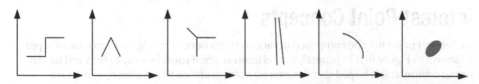

Figure 6-1. *Types of keypoints, including corners and interest points. (Left to right) Step, roof, corner, line or edge, ridge or contour, maxima region*

217

Interest Point Tuning

What is a good keypoint for a given application? Which ones are most useful? Which ones should be ignored? Tuning the detectors is not simple. Each detector has different parameters to tune for best results on a given image, and each image presents different challenges regarding lighting, contrast, and image pre-processing. Additionally, each detector is designed to be useful for a different class of interest points, and must be tuned accordingly *to* filter the results down to a useful set of good candidates for a specific feature descriptor. Each feature detector will work best with certain descriptors, see appendix A.

So, the keypoints are further filtered to be useful for the chosen feature descriptor. In some cases, a keypoint is not suitable for producing a useful feature descriptor, even if the keypoint has a high score and high response. If the feature descriptor computed at the keypoint produces a descriptor score that is too weak, for example, the keypoint and corresponding descriptor should both be rejected. OpenCV provides several novel methods for working with detectors, enabling the user to try different detectors and descriptors in a common framework, and automatically adjust the parameters for tuning and culling as follows:

- **DynamicAdaptedFeatureDetector.** This class will tune supported detectors using an *adjusterAdapter()* to only keep a limited number of features, and iterate the detector parameters several times and redetect features in an attempt to find the best parameters, keeping only the requested number of best features. Several OpenCV detectors have an *adjusterAdapter()* provided, some do not; the API allows for adjusters to be created.

- **AdjusterAdapter.** This class implements the criteria for culling and keeping interest points. Criteria may include KNN nearest neighbor matching, detector response or strength, radius distance to nearest other detected points, number of keypoints within a local region, and other measures that can be included for culling keypoints for which a good descriptor cannot be computed.

- **PyramidAdaptedFeatureDetector.** This class can be used to adapt detectors that do not use a scale-space pyramid, and the adapter will create a Gaussian pyramid and detect features over the pyramid.

- **GridAdaptedFeatureDetector.** This class divides an image into grids and adapts the detector to find the best features within each grid cell.

Interest Point Concepts

An interest point may be composed of various types of corner, edge, and maxima shapes, as shown in Figure 6-1. In general, a good interest point must be easy to find and ideally fast to compute; it is hoped that the interest point is at a good location to compute a feature descriptor. The interest point is thus the qualifier or *keypoint* around which a feature may be described.

There are various concepts behind the interest point methods currently in use, as this is an active area of research. One of the best analyses of interest point detectors is found in Mikolajczyk et al.[153], with a comparison framework and taxonomy for affine covariant interest point detectors, where *covariant* refers to the elliptical shape of the interest region, which is an affine deformable representation. Scale invariant detectors are represented well in a circular region. Maxima region and blob detectors can take irregular shapes. See the response of several detectors against synthetic interest point and corner alphabets in Appendix A.

Commonly, detectors use *maxima and minima points*, such as gradient peaks and corners; however, edges, ridges, and contours are also used as keypoints, as shown in Figure 6-2. There is no superior method for interest point detection for all applications. A simple taxonomy provided by Tuytelaars and Van Gool [529] lists edge-based region methods (EBR), maxima or intensity-based region methods (IBR), and segmentation methods to find shape-based regions (SBR) that may be blobs or features with high entropy.

Figure 6-2. *Candidate edge interest point filters. (Left to right) Laplacian, derivative filter, and gradient filter*

Corners are often preferred over edges or isolated maxima points, since the corner is a structure and can be used to compute an angular orientation for the feature. Interest points are computed over color components as well as gray scale luminance. Many of the interest point methods will first apply some sort of Gaussian filter across the image and then perform a gradient operator. The idea of using the Gaussian filter first is to reduce noise in the image, which is otherwise amplified by gradient operators.

Each detector locates features with different degrees of invariance to attributes such as rotation, scale, perspective, occlusion, and illumination. For evaluations of the quality and performance of interest point detection methods measured against various robustness and invariance criteria on standardized datasets, see Mikolajczyk and Schmidt [144] and Gauglitz et al.[145]. One of the key challenges for interest point detection is scale invariance, since interest points change dramatically in some cases over scale. Lindberg [212] has extensively studied the area of scale independent interest point methods.

Affine invariant interest points have been studied in detail by Mikolajcyk and Schmid [107,141,144,153,306,311]. In addition, Mikolajcyk and Schmid [519] developed an affine-invariant version of the Harris detector. As shown in [541], it is often useful to combine several interest point detection methods to form a hybrid, for example, using the Harris or Hessian to locate suitable maxima regions, and then using the Laplacian to select the best scale attributes. Variations are common, Harris-based and Hessian-based detectors may use scale-space methods, while local binary detector methods do not use scale space.

A few fundamental concepts behind many interest point methods come from the field of linear algebra, where the local region of pixels is treated as a matrix. Additional concepts come from other areas of mathematical analysis. Some of the key math useful for locating interest points includes:

- **Gradient Magnitude.** This is the first derivative of the pixels in the local interest region, and assumes a direction. This is an unsigned positive number.

$$(\partial f(x,y)/\partial x))^2 + (\partial f(x,y)/\partial y))^2$$

- **Gradient Direction.** This is the angle or direction of the largest gradient angle from pixels in the local region in the range $+\pi$ to $-\pi$.

$$\tan^{-1}(\partial f(x,y)/\partial y)/\partial f(x,y)/\partial x))$$

- **Laplacian.** This is the second derivative and can be computed directionally using any of three terms:

$$(\partial^2 f(x,y)/\partial x^2$$

$$(\partial^2 f(x,y)/\partial y^2$$

$$(\partial^2 f(x,y)/\partial x \partial y)$$

However, the Laplacian operator ignores the third term and computes a signed value of average orientation.

$$(\partial f(x,y)/\partial x))^2 + (\partial f(x,y)/\partial y))^2$$

- **Hessian Matrix or Hessian.** A square matrix containing second-order partial derivatives describing surface curvature. The Hessian has several interesting properties useful for interest point detection methods discussed in this section.

- **Largest Hessian.** This is based on the second derivative, as is the Laplacian, but the Hessian uses all three terms of the second derivative to compute the direction along which the second derivative is maximum as a signed value.

- **Smallest Hessian.** This is based on the second derivative, is computed as a signed number, and may be a useful metric as a ratio between largest and smallest Hessian.

- **Hessian Orientation, largest and smallest values.** This is the orientation of the largest second derivative in the range $+\pi$ to $-\pi$, which is a signed value, and it corresponds to an orientation without direction. The smallest orientation can be computed by adding or subtracting $\pi/2$ from the largest value.

- **Determinant of Hessian, Trace of Hessian, Laplacian of Gaussian.**
  All three names are used to describe the trace characteristic of a
  matrix, which can reveal geometric scale information by the absolute
  value, and orientation by the sign of the value. The eigenvalues of a
  matrix can be found using determinants.

- **Eigenvalues, Eigenvectors, Eigenspaces.** Eigen properties are
  important to understanding vector direction in local pixel region
  matrices. When a matrix acts on a vector, and the vector orientation
  is preserved, and when the sign or direction is simply reversed,
  the vector is considered to be an eigenvector, and the matrix factor
  is considered to be the eigenvalue. An eigenspace is therefore all
  eigenvectors within the space with the same eigenvalue. Eigen
  properties are valuable for interest point detection, orientation,
  and feature detection. For example, Turk and Petland [158] use
  eigenvectors reduced into a smaller set of vectors via PCA for face
  recognition, in a method they call Eigenfaces.

Interest Point Method Survey

We will now look briefly at algorithms and computational methods for some common
interest point detector methods including:

- Laplacian of Gaussian (LOG)

- Moravac corner detector

- Harris and Stephens corner detection

- Shi and Tomasi corner detector (improvement on Harris method)

- Difference of Gaussians (DoG; an approximation of LOG)

- Harris methods, Harris-/Hessian-Laplace,
  Harris-/Hessian-Affine

- Determinant of Hessian (DoH)

- Salient regions

- SUSAN

- FAST, FASTER, AGAST

- Local curvature

- Morphological interest points

- MSER (discussed in the section on polygon shape descriptors)

- *NOTE: many feature descriptors, such as SIFT, SURF, BRISK
  and others, provide their own detector method along with the
  descriptor method, see Appendix A.

Laplacian and Laplacian of Gaussian

The Lapacian operator, as used in image processing, is a method of finding the derivative or maximum rate of change in a pixel area. Commonly, the Laplacian is approximated using standard convolution kernels that add up to zero, such as:

$$L1 = \begin{pmatrix} -1 & -1 & -1 \\ -1 & 8 & -1 \\ -1 & -1 & -1 \end{pmatrix}$$

$$L2 = \begin{pmatrix} -1 & 0 & -1 \\ 0 & 4 & 0 \\ -1 & 0 & -1 \end{pmatrix}$$

The Laplacian of Gaussian (LOG) is simply the Laplacian performed over a region that has been processed using a Gaussian smoothing kernel to focus edge energy; see Gun [155].

Moravac Corner Detector

The Moravic corner detection algorithm is an early method of corner detection whereby each pixel in the image is tested by correlating overlapping patches surrounding each neighboring pixel. The strength of the correlation in any direction reveals information about the point: a corner is found when there is change in all directions, and an edge is found when there is no change along the edge direction. A flat region yields no change in any direction. The correlation difference is calculated using the SSD between the two overlapping patches. Similarity is measured by the near-zero difference in the SSD. This method is compute intensive; see Moravac [330].

Harris Methods, Harris-Stephens, Shi-Tomasi, and Hessian-Type Detectors

The Harris or Harris-Stephens corner detector family [156,365] provides improvements over the Moravic method. The goal of the Harris method is to find the direction of fastest and lowest change for feature orientation, using a covariance matrix of local directional derivatives. The directional derivative values are compared with a scoring factor to identify which features are corners, which are edges, and which are likely noise. Depending on the formulation of the algorithm, the Harris method can provide high rotational invariance, limited intensity invariance, and in some of the formulations of the algorithm, scale invariance is provided such as the Harris-Laplace method using scale space [519] [212]. Many Harris family algorithms can be implemented in a compute-efficient manner.

Note that corners have an ill-defined gradient, since two edges converge at the corner, but near the corner the gradient can be detected with two different values with respect to x and y—this is a basic idea behind the Harris corner detector.

Variations on the Harris method include:

- The Shi, Tomasi and Kanade corner detector [157] is an optimization on the Harris method, using only the minimum eigenvalues for discrimination, thus streamlining the computation considerably.

- The Hessian (Hessian-Affine) corner detector [153] is designed to be affine invariant, and it uses the basic Harris corner detection method but combines interest points from several scales in a pyramid, with some iterative selection criteria and a Hessian matrix.

- Many other variations on the basic Harris operator exist, such as the Harris–Hessian–Laplace [331], which provides improved scale invariance using a scale selection method, and the Harris-/Hessian–Affine method [306,153].

Hessian Matrix Detector and Hessian-Laplace

The Hessian Matrix method, also referred to as Determinant of Hessian (DoH) method, is used in the popular SURF algorithm [160]. It detects interest objects from a multi-scale image set where the determinant of the Hessian matrix is at a maxima and the Hessian matrix operator is calculated using the convolution of the second-order partial derivative of the Gaussian to yield a gradient maxima.

The DoH method uses integral images to calculate the Gaussian partial derivatives very quickly. Performance for calculating the Hessian Matrix is therefore very good, and accuracy is better than many methods. The related Hessian-Laplace method [331,306] also operates on local extrema, using the determinant of the Hessian at multiple scales for spatial localization, and the Laplacian at multiple scales for scale localization.

Difference of Gaussians

The Difference of Gaussians (DoG) is an approximation of the Laplacian of Gaussians, but computed in a simpler and faster manner using the difference of two smoothed or Gaussian filtered images to detect local extrema features. The idea with Gaussian smoothing is to remove noise artifacts that are not relevant at the given scale, which would otherwise be amplified and result in false DoG features. The DoG features are used in the popular SIFT method [161], and as shown later in Figure 6-15, the simple difference of Gaussian filtered images is taken to identify maxima regions.

Salient Regions

Salient regions [162,163] are based on the notion that interest points over a range of scales should exhibit local attributes or entropy that are "unpredictable" or "surprising" compared to the surrounding region. The method proceeds as follows:

1. The Shannon entropy E of pixel attributes such as intensity or color are computed over a scale space, where Shannon entropy is used the measure of unpredictability.

2. The entropy values are located over the scale space with maxima or peak values M. At this stage, the optimal scales are determined as well.

3. The probability density function (PDF) is computed for magnitude deltas at each peak within each scale, where the PDF is computed using a histogram of pixel values taken from a circular window of desired radius from the peak.

4. Saliency is the product of E and M at each peak, and is also related to scale. So the final detector is salient and robust to scale.

SUSAN, and Trajkovic and Hedly

The SUSAN method [164,165] is dependent on segmenting image features based on local areas of similar brightness, which yields a bimodal valued feature. No noise filtering and no gradients are used. As shown in Figure 6-3, the method works by using a center nucleus pixel value as a comparison reference against which neighbor pixels within a given radius region are compared, yielding a set of pixels with similar brightness, called a Univalue Segment Assimilating Nucleus (USAN).

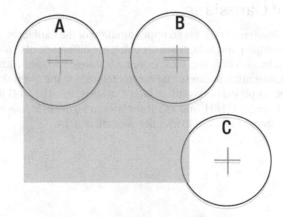

Figure 6-3. *SUSAN method of computing interest points. The dark region of the image is a rectangle intersecting USAN's A, B, and C. USAN A will be labeled as an edge, USAN B will be labeled as a corner, and USAN C will be labeled as neither an edge nor a corner*

Each USAN contains structural information about the image in the local region, and the size, centroid, and second-order moments of each USAN can be computed. The SUSAN method can be used for both edge and corner detection. Corners are determined by the ratio of pixels similar to the center pixel in the circular region: a low ratio around 25 percent indicates a corner, and a higher ratio around 50 percent indicates an edge. SUSAN is very robust to noise.

The Trajkovic and Hedly method [214] is similar to SUSAN, and discriminates among points in USAN regions, edge points, and corner points.

SUSAN is also useful for noise suppression, and the bilateral filter [302], discussed in Chapter 2, is closely related to SUSAN. SUSAN uses fairly large circular windows; several implementations use 37 pixel radius windows. The FAST [138] detector is also similar to SUSAN, but uses a smaller 7x7 or 9x9 window and only some of the pixels in the region instead of all of them; FAST yields a local binary descriptor.

Fast, Faster, AGHAST

The FAST methods [138] are derived from SUSAN with respect to a bimodal segmentation goal. However, FAST relies on a connected set of pixels in a circular pattern to determine a corner. The connected region size is commonly 9 or 10 out of a possible 16; either number may be chosen, referred to as FAST9 and FAST10. FAST is known to be efficient to compute and fast to match; accuracy is also quite good. FAST can be considered a relative of the local binary pattern LBP.

FAST is not a scale-space detector, and therefore it may produce many more edge detections at the given scale than a scale-space method such as used in SIFT.

As shown in Figure 6-4, FAST uses binary comparison with each pixel in a circular pattern against the center pixel using a threshold to determine if a pixel is less than or greater than the center pixel The resulting descriptor is stored as a contiguous bit vector in order from 0 to 15. Also, due to the circular nature of the pixel compare pattern, it is possible to retrofit FAST and store the bit vector in a rotational-invariant representation, as demonstrated by the RILBP descriptor discussed later in this chapter; see Figure 6-11.

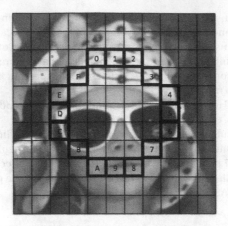

Figure 6-4. *The FAST detector with a 16-element circular sampling pattern grid. Note that each pixel in the grid is compared against the center pixel to yield a binary value, and each binary value is stored in a bit vector*

Local Curvature Methods

Local curvature methods [208–212] are among the early means of detecting corners, and some local curvature methods are the first known to be reliable and accurate in tracking corners over scale variations [210]. Local curvature detects points where the gradient magnitude and the local surface curvature are both high. One approach taken is a differential method, computing the product of the gradient magnitude and the level curve curvature together over scale space, and then selecting the maxima and minima absolute values in scale and space. One formulation of the method is shown here.

$$\tilde{\alpha}\,(x,y;t) = L_x^2 L_{yy} + L_y^2 L_{xx} - 2L_x L_y L_{xy}$$

Various formulations of the basic algorithm can be taken depending on the curvature equation used. To improve scale invariance and noise sensitivity, the method can be modified using a normalized formulation of the equation over scale space, as follows:

$$\tilde{\alpha}_{norm}\,(x,y;t) = t^{2\gamma}\,(L_x^2 L_{yy} + L_y^2 L_{xx} - 2L_x L_y L_{xy})$$

where

$$\gamma = .875$$

At larger scales, corners can be detected with less sharp and more rounded features, while at lower scales or at unity scale sharper corners over smaller areas are detected. The Wang and Brady method [213] also computes interest points using local curvature on the 2D surface, looking for inflexion points where the surface curvature changes rapidly.

Morphological Interest Regions

Interest points can be determined from a pipeline of morphological operations, such as thresholding followed by combinations or erosion and dilation to smooth, thin, grown, and shrink pixel groups. If done correctly for a given application, such morphological features can be scale and rotation invariant. Note that the simple morphological operations alone are not enough; for example, erode left unconstrained will shrink regions until they disappear. So intelligence must be added to the morphology pipeline to control the final region size and shape. For polygon shape descriptors, morphological interest points define the feature, and various image moments are computed over the feature, as described in Chapter 3 and also in the section on polygon shape descriptors later in this chapter.

Morphological operations can be used to create interest regions on binary, gray scale, or color channel images. To prepare gray scale or color channel images for morphology, typically some sort of pre-processing is used, such as pixel remapping, LUT transforms, or histogram equalization. (These methods were discussed in Chapter 2.) For binary images and binary morphology approaches, binary thresholding is a key pre-processing step. Many binary thresholding methods have been devised, ranging from simple global thresholds to statistical and structural kernel-based local methods.

Note that the morphological interest region approach is similar to the maximally stable extrema region (MSER) feature descriptor method discussed later in the section on polygon shape descriptors, since both methods look for connected groups of pixels at maxima or minima. However, MSER does not use morphology operators.

A few examples of morphological and related operation sequences for interest region detection are shown in Figure 6-5, and many more can be devised.

Figure 6-5. *Morphological methods to find interest regions. (Left to right) Original image, binary thresholded and segmented image using Chan Vese method, skeleton transform, pruned skeleton transform, and distance transform image. Note that binary thresholding requires quite a bit of work to set parameters correctly for a given application*

Feature Descriptor Survey

This section provides a survey and observations about a few representative feature descriptor methods, with no intention to directly compare descriptors to each other. In practice, the feature descriptor methods are often modified and customized. The goal of this survey is to examine a range of feature descriptor approaches from each feature descriptor family from the taxonomy that was presented in Chapter 5:

- Local binary descriptors
- Spectra descriptors
- Basis space descriptors

- Polygon shape descriptors

- 3D, 4D, and volumetric descriptors

For key feature descriptor methods, we provide here a summary analysis:

- **General Vision Taxonomy and FME:** covering feature attributes including spectra, shape, and pattern, single or multivariate, compute complexity criteria, data types, memory criteria, matching method, robustness attributes, and accuracy.

- **General Robustness Attributes:** covering invariance attributes such as illumination, scale, perspective, and many others.

No direct comparisons are made between feature descriptors here, but ample references are provided to the literature for detailed comparisons and performance information on each method.

Local Binary Descriptors

This family of descriptors represents features as binary bit vectors. To compute the features, image pixel point-pairs are compared and the results are stored as binary values in a vector. Local binary descriptors are efficient to compute, efficient to store, and efficient to match using Hamming distance. In general, local binary pattern methods achieve very good accuracy and robustness compared to other methods.

A variety of local sampling patterns are used with local binary descriptors to set the pairwise point comparisons; see the section in Chapter 4 on local binary descriptor point-pair patterns for a discussion on local binary sampling patterns. We start this section on local binary descriptors by analyzing the local binary pattern (LBP) and some LBP variants, since the LBP is a powerful metric all by itself and is well known.

Local Binary Patterns

Local binary patterns (LBP) were developed in 1994 by Ojala et al. [173] as a novel method of encoding both pattern and contrast to define texture [169,170–173]. LBP's can be used as an image processing operator. The LBP creates a descriptor or texture model using a set of histograms of the local texture neighborhood surrounding each pixel. In this case, local texture is the feature descriptor.

The LBP metric is simple yet powerful; see Figure 6-6. We cover some level of detail on LBPs, since there are so many applications for this powerful texture metric as a feature descriptor as well. Also, hundreds of researchers have added to the LBP literature [173] in the areas of theoretical foundations, generalizations into 2D and 3D, applied as a descriptor for face detection, and also applied to spatio-temporal applications such as motion analysis. LBP research remains quite active at this time. In addition, the LBP is used as an image processing operator, and has been used as a feature descriptor retrofit in SIFT with excellent results, described in this chapter.

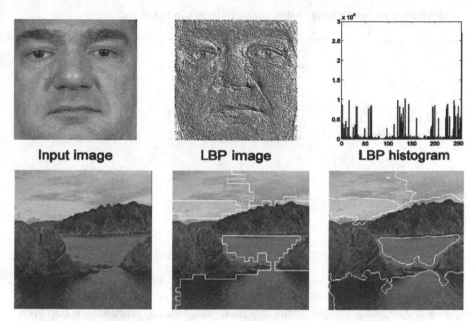

Figure 6-6. *(Above) A local binary pattern representation of an image where the LBP is used as an image processing operator, and the corresponding histogram of cumulative LBP features. (Bottom) Segmentation results using LBP texture metrics. (Images courtesy and © Springer Press, from Computer Vision Using Local Binary Patterns, by Matti Pietikäinen and Janne Heikkilä [173])*

In its simplest embodiment, LBP has the goal of creating a binary coded neighborhood descriptor for a pixel. It does this by comparing each pixel against its neighbors using the > operator and encoding the compare results *(1,0)* into a binary number, as shown later in Figure 6-8. LPB histograms from larger image regions can even be used as signals and passed into a 1D FFT to create a feature descriptor. The Fourier spectrum of the LBP histogram is rotational invariant; see Figure 6-6. The FFT spectrum can then be concatenated onto the LBP histogram to form a multivariate descriptor.

As shown in Figure 6-6, the LBP is used as an image processing operator, region segmentation method, and histogram feature descriptor. The LBP has many applications. An LBP may be calculated over various sizes and shapes using various sizes of forming kernels. A simple 3x3 neighborhood provides basic coverage for local features, while wider areas and kernel shapes are used as well.

Assuming a 3x3 LBP kernel pattern is chosen, this means that there will be 8 pixel compares and up to 2^8 combinations of results for a 256-bin histogram possible. However, it has been shown [18] that reducing the 8-bit 256-bin histogram to use only 56 LBP bins based on *uniform patterns* is the optimal number. The 56 bins or uniform patterns are chosen to represent only two contiguous LBP patterns around the circle, which consists of two connected contiguous segments rather than all 256 possible pattern combinations [173,15]. The same uniform pattern logic applies to LBPs of dimension larger than 8 bits. So, uniform patterns provide both histogram space savings and feature compare-space optimization, since fewer features need be matched (56 instead of all 256).

LPB feature recognition may follow the steps shown in Figure 6-7.

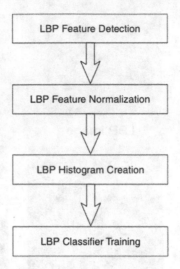

Figure 6-7. LBP feature flow for feature detection. (Image used by permission, © Intel Press, from Building Intelligent Systems)

The LBP is calculated by assigning a binary weighting value to each pixel in the local neighborhood and summing up the pixel compare results as binary values to create a composite LBP value. The LBP contains region information encoded in a compact binary pattern, as shown in Figure 6-8, so the LBP is thus a binary coded neighborhood texture descriptor.

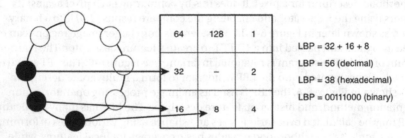

Figure 6-8. Assigned LBP weighting values. (Image used by permission, © Intel Press, from Building Intelligent Systems)

Assuming a 3x3 neighborhood is used to describe the LBP patterns, one may compare the 3x3 rectangular region to a circular region, suggesting 360 degree directionality at 45 degree increments, as shown in Figure 6-9.

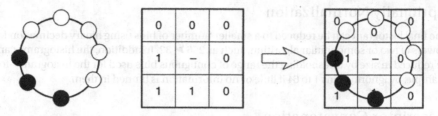

Figure 6-9. *The concept of LBP directionality. (Image used by permission, © Intel Press, from Building Intelligent Systems)*

The steps involved in calculating a 3x3 LBP are illustrated in Figure 6-10.

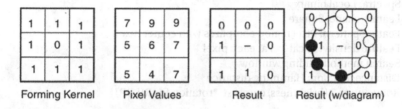

| Forming Kernel | Pixel Values | Result | Result (w/diagram) |

LBP Calculations | Binary Bit Values Summed

[0,0] 6 > [−1,−1] 7 = 0   **LBP = 0**
[0,0] 6 > [−1,0] 9 = 0   **LBP = 00**
[0,0] 6 > [−1,1] 9 = 0   **LBP = 000**
[0,0] 6 > [0,−1] 5 = 1   **LBP = 0001**
[0,0] 6 > [0,+1] 7 = 0   **LBP = 00010**
[0,0] 6 > [+1,−1] 5 = 1   **LBP = 000101**
[0,0] 6 > [+1,−1] 4 = 1   **LBP = 0001011**
[0,0] 6 > [+1,−1] 7 = 0   **LBP = 00010110**

LBP Descriptor = 00010110 (0 × 16 is the Hex Representation of the Binary Value)

Figure 6-10. *LBP neighborhood comparison. (Image used by permission, © Intel Press, from Building Intelligent Systems)*

Neighborhood Comparison

Each pixel is compared to its neighbors according to a forming kernel that allows selection of neighbors for the comparison. In Figure 6-10, all pixels are used in the forming kernel (all 1s). If the neighbor is > than the center pixel, the binary pattern is 1, otherwise it is 0.

Histogram Composition

Each LBP descriptor over an image region is recorded in a histogram to describe the cumulative texture feature. Uniform LBP histograms would have 56 bins, since only single-connected regions are histogrammed.

Optionally Normalization

The final histogram can be reduced to a smaller number of bins using binary decimation for powers of two or some similar algorithm, such as 256 ➤ 32. In addition, the histograms can be reduced in size by thresholding the range of contiguous bins used for the histogram—for example, by ignoring bins 1 to 64 if little or no information is binned in them.

Descriptor Concatenation

Multiple LBPs taken over overlapping regions may be concatenated together into a larger histogram feature descriptor to provide better discrimination.

LBP Summary Taxonomy

> Spectra: Local binary
> Feature shape: Square
> Feature pattern: Pixel region compares with center pixel
> Feature density: Local 3x3 at each pixel
> Search method: Sliding window
> Distance function: Hamming distance
> Robustness: 3 (brightness, contrast, *rotation for RILBP)

Rotation Invariant LBP (RILBP)

To achieve rotational invariance, the rotation invariant LBP (RILBP) [173] is calculated by circular bitwise rotation of the local LBP to find the minimum binary value. The minimum value LBP is used as a rotation invariant signature and is recorded in the histogram bins. The RILBP is computationally very efficient.

To illustrate the method, Figure 6-11 shows a pattern of three consecutive LBP bits; in order to make this descriptor rotation invariant, the value is *left-shifted* until a minimum value is reached.

Original	<< 1	<< 2	<< 3	<< 4	<< 5	<< 6	<< 7 *minimum*
00010110	00101100	01011000	10110000	01100001	11000010	10000101	00001011

Figure 6-11. *Method of calculating the minimum LBP by using circular bit shifting of the binary value to find the minimum value. The LBP descriptor is then rotation invariant. (Image used by permission, © Intel Press, from Building Intelligent Systems)*

Note that many researchers [171, 172] are extending the methods used for LBP calculation to use refinements such as local derivatives, local median or mean values, trinary or quinary compare functions, and many other methods, rather than the simple binary compare function, as originally proposed.

Dynamic Texture Metric Using 3D LBPs

Dynamic textures are visual features that morph and change as they move from frame to frame; examples include waves, clouds, wind, smoke, foliage, and ripples. Two extensions of the basic LBP used for tracking such dynamic textures are discussed here: VLBP and LBP-TOP.

Volume LBP (VLBP)

To create the VLBP [175] descriptor, first an image volume is created by stacking together at least three consecutive video frames into a volume 3D dataset. Next, three LBPs are taken centered on the selected interest point, one LBP from each parallel plane in the volume, into a summary volume LBP or VLBP, and the histogram of each orthogonal LBP is concatenated into a single dynamic descriptor vector, the VLBP. The VLPB can then be tracked from frame to frame and recalculated to account for dynamic changes in the texture from frame to frame. See Figure 6-12.

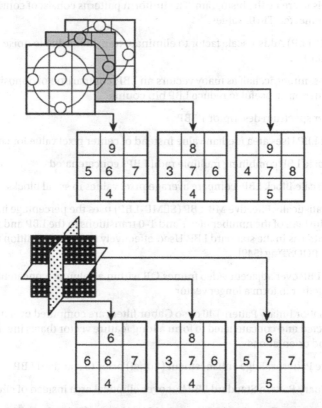

Figure 6-12. *(Top) VLBP method [175] of calculating LBPs from parallel planes. (Bottom) LBP-TOP method [176] of calculating LBPs from orthogonal planes. (Image used by permission, © Intel Press, from Building Intelligent Systems)*

LPB-TOP

The LBP-TOP [176] is created like the VLBP, except that instead of calculating the three individual LBPs from parallel planes, they are calculated from orthogonal planes in the volume (x,y,z) intersecting the interest point, as shown in Figure 6-12. The 3D composite descriptor is the same size as the VLBP and contains three planes' worth of data. The histograms for each LBP plane are also concatenated for the LBP-TOP like the VLBP.

Other LBP Variants

As shown in Table 6-1, there are many variants of the LBP [173]. Note that the LBP has been successfully used as a replacement for SIFT, SURF, and also as a texture metric.

Table 6-1. *LBP Variants (from reference [173])*

ULBP (Uniform LBP) Uses only 56 uniform bins instead of the full 256 bins possible with 8-bit pixels to create the histogram. The uniform patterns consist of contiguous segments of connected TRUE values.

RLBP (ROBUST LBP) Adds + scale factor to eliminate transitions due to noise (p1 - p2 + SCALE)

CS-LBP Circle-symmetric, half as many vectors an LBP, comparison of opposite pixel pairs vs. w/center pixel, useful to reduce LBP bin counts

LBP-HF Fourier spectrum descriptor + LBP

MLBP Median LBP Uses area median value instead of center pixel value for comparison

M-LBP Multiscale LBP combining multiple radii LBPs concatenated

MB-LBP Multiscale Block LBP; compare average pixel values in small blocks

SEMB-LBP: Statistically Effective MB-LBP (SEMB-LBP) uses the percentage in distributions, instead of the number of 0-1 and 1-0 transitions in the LBP and redefines the uniform patterns in the standard LBP. Used effectively in face recognition using GENTLE ADA-BOOSTing [549]

VLBP Volume LBP over adjacent video frames OR within a volume - concatenate histograms together to form a longer vector

LGBP (Local Gabor Binary Pattern) 40 or so Gabor filters are computed over a feature, LBPs are extracted and concatenated to form a long feature vector that is invariant over more scales and orientations

LEP Local Edge Patterns: Edge enhancement (Sobel) prior to standard LBP

EBP Elliptic Binary Pattern Standard LBP but over elliptical area instead of circular

EQP Elliptical Quinary Patterns - LBP extended from binary (2) level resolution to quinary (5) level resolution (-2,-1, 0,-1,2)

(*continued*)

Table 6-1. (*continued*)

LTP - LBP extended over Ternary range to deal with near constant areas (-1, 0, 1)

LLBP Local line Binary Pattern - calculates LBP over line patterns (cross shape) and then calculates a magnitude metrics using SQRT of SQUARES of each X/Y dimension

TPLBP- [x5]three LBPs are calculated together: the basic LBP for the center pixel, plus two others around adjacent pixels so the total descriptor is a set of overlapping LBP's,

FPLBP- [x5]four LBPs are calculated together: the basic LBP for the center pixel, plus two others around adjacent pixels so the total descriptor is a set of overlapping LBP's, XPLBP –

NOTE: The TPLBP and FPLBP method can be extended to 3,4,n dimensions in feature space. LARGE VECTORS.

TBP - Ternary (3) Binary pattern, like LBP, but uses three levels of encoding (1,0,-1) to effectively deal with areas of equal or near equal intensity, uses two binary patterns (one for + and one for -) concatenated together

ETLP - Elongated Ternary Local Patterns (elliptical + ternary [5] levels

FLBP - Fuzzy LBP where each pixel contributes to more than one bin

PLBP - Probabilistic LBP computes magnitude of difference between each pixel & center pixel (more compute, more storage)

SILTP - Scale invariant LBP using a 3 part piece-wise comparison function to compensate and support intensity scale invariance to deal with image noise

tLBP - Transition Coded LBP, where the encoding is clockwise between adjacent pixels in the LBP

dLBP - Direction Coded LBP - similar to CSLBP, but stores both maxima and comparison info (is this pixel greater, less than, or maxima)

CBP - Centralized Binary pattern - center pixel compared to average of all nine kernel neighbors

S-LBP Semantic LBP done in a colorimetric-accurate space (like CIE LAB etc.) over uniform connected LBP circular patterns to find principal direction + arc length used to form a 2D histogram as the descriptor.

F-LBP - Fourier Spectrum of color distance from center pixel to adjacent pixels

LDP - Local Derivate Patterns (higher order derivatives) - basic

LBP is the first order directional derivative, which is combined with additional nth order directional derivatives concatenated into a histogram, more sensitive to noise of course

BLBP - Baysian LBP - combination of LBP and LTP together using Baysian methods to optimize towards a more robust pattern

---

(*continued*)

Table 6-1. (*continued*)

FLS - Filtering, Labeling and Statistical Framework for LBP comparison, translates LBP's or any type of histogram descriptor into vector space allowing efficient comparison "A Bayesian Local Binary Pattern Texture Descriptor"

MB-LBP Multiscale Block LBP - compare average pixel values in small blocks instead of individual pixels, thus a 3x3 pixel PBL will become a 9x9 block LBP where each block is a 3x3 region. The histogram is calculated by scaling the image and creating a rendering at each scale and creating a histogram of each scaled image and concatenating the histograms together.

PM-LBP Pyramid Based MultiStructured LBP - used 5 templates to extract different structural info at varying levels 1) Gaussian filters, 4 anisotrophic filters to detect gradient directions

MSLBF - Multiscale Selected Local Binary Features

RILBP - Rotation Invariant LBP rotates the bins (binary LBP value) until maximum value is achieved, the max value is considered rotational invariant. This is the most widely used method for LBP rotational invariance.

ALBP - Adaptive LBP for rotational invariance, instead of shifting to a maximal value as in the standard LBP method, find the dominant vector orientation and shift the vector to the dominant vector orientation

LBPV - Local binary pattern variance - uses local area variance to weight pixel contribution to the LBP, align features to principal orientations, determine non-dominant patterns and reduce their contribution.

OCLBP - Opponent Color LBP - describes color and texture together - each color channel LBP is converted, then opposing color channel LBP's are converted by using one color as the center pixel and another color as the neighborhood, so 9 total histograms are computed but only size are used R G B RG RG RB

SDMCLBP - SDM (co -LBP images for each color are used as the basis for generating occurrence matrices, and then Haralick features are extracted from the images to form a multi dimensional feature space.

MSCLBP - Multi Scale Color Local Binary Patterns (concatenate 6 histograms together)- USES COLOR SPACE COMPONENTS

HUE-LBP OPPONENT-LBP (ALL 3 CHANNELS) nOPPONENT-LBP (COMPUTED OVER 2 CHANNELS), light intensity change, intensity shift, intensity change+shift, color-change color-shift, DEFINE SIX NEW OPERATORS: transformed color LBP (RGB) [subtract mean, divide by STD DEV], opponent LBP, nOpponent LBP, Hue LBP, RGB-LBP, nRGB-LBP [x8] "Multi-scale Color Local Binary Patterns for Visual Object Classes Recognition", Chao ZHU, Charles-Edmond BICHOT, Liming CHEN

3D histograms - 3DRGBLBP [best performance, high memory footprint] - 3D histogram computed over RGB-LBP color image space using uniform pattern minimization to yield 10 levels or patterns per color yielding a large descriptor: 10 x 10 x 10 = 1000 descriptors.

Census

The Census transform [177] is basically an LBP, and like a population census, it uses simple greater-than and less-than queries to count and compare results. Census records pixel comparison results made between the center pixel in the kernel and the other pixels in the kernel region. It employs comparisons and possibly a threshold, and stores the results in a binary vector. The Census transform also uses a feature called the *rank value scalar*, which is the number of pixel values less than the center pixel. The Census descriptor thus uses both a bit vector and a rank scalar.

CENSUS Summary Vision Taxonomy

> Spectra: Local binary + scalar ranking
> Feature shape: Square
> Feature pattern: Pixel region compares with center pixel
> Feature density: Local 3x3 at each pixel
> Search method: Sliding window
> Distance function: Hamming distance
> Robustness: 2 (brightness, contrast)

Modified Census Transform

The Modified Census trasform (MCT) [205] seeks to improve the local binary pattern robustness of the original Census transform. The method uses an ordered comparison of each pixel in the 3x3 neighborhood against the mean intensity of all the pixels of the 3x3 neighborhood, generating a binary descriptor bit vector with bit values set to an intensity lower than the mean intensity of all the pixels. The bit vector can be used to create an MCT image using the MCT value for each pixel. See Figure 6-13.

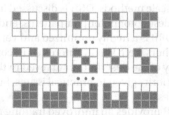

Figure 6-13. *Abbreviated set of 15 out of a possible 511 possible binary patterns for a 3x3 MCT. The structure kernels in the pattern set are the basis set of the MCT feature space comparison. The structure kernels form a pattern basis set which can represent lines, edges, corners, saddle points, semi-circles, and other patterns*

As shown in Figure 6-13, the MCT relies on the full set of possible 3x3 binary patterns ($2^9 - 1$ or 511 variations) and uses these as a kernel index into the binary patterns as the MCT output, since each binary pattern is a unique signature by itself and highly discriminative. The end result of the MCT is analogous to a nonlinear filter that assigns the output to any of the $2^9 - 1$ patterns in the kernel index. Results show that the MCT results are better than the basic CT for some types of object recognition [205].

BRIEF

As described in Chapter 4, in the section on local binary descriptor point-pair patterns, and illustrated in Figure 4-11, the BRIEF [132,133] descriptor uses a random distribution pattern of 256 point-pairs in a local 31x31 region for the binary comparison to create the descriptor. One key idea with BRIEF is to select random pairs of points within the local region for comparison.

BRIEF is a local binary descriptor and has achieved very good accuracy and performance in robotics applications [203]. BRIEF and ORB are closely related; ORB is an oriented version of BRIEF, and the ORB descriptor point-pair pattern is also built differently than BRIEF. BRIEF is known to be not very tolerant of rotation.

BRIEF Summary Taxonomy

Spectra: Local binary
Feature shape: Square centered at interest point
Feature pattern: Random local pixel point-pair compares
Feature density: Local 31x31 at interest points
Search method: Sliding window
Distance function: Hamming distance
Robustness: 2 (brightness, contrast)

ORB

ORB [134] is an acronymn for Oriented BRIEF, and as the name suggests, ORB is based on BRIEF and adds rotational invariance to BRIEF by determining corner orientation using FAST9, followed by a Harris corner metric to sort the keypoints; the corner orientation is refined by intensity centroids using Rosin's method [61]. The FAST, Harris, and Rosin processing are done at each level of an image pyramid scaled with a factor of 1.4, rather than the common octave pyramid scale methods. ORB is discussed in some detail in Chapter 4, in the section on local binary descriptor point-pair patterns, and is illustrated in Figure 4-11.

It should be noted that ORB is a highly optimized and very well engineered descriptor, since the ORB authors were keenly interested in compute speed, memory footprint, and accuracy. Many of the descriptors surveyed in this section are primarily research projects, with less priority given to practical issues, but ORB focuses on optimizing and practical issues.

Compared to BRIEF, ORB provides an improved training method for creating the local binary patterns for pairwise pixel point sampling. While BRIEF uses random point pairs in a 31x31 window, ORB goes through a training step to find uncorrelated point pairs in the window with high variance and means ~ .5, which is demonstrated to work better. For details on visualizing the ORB patterns, see Figure 4-11.

For correspondence search, ORB uses multi-probe locally sensitive hashing (MP-LSH), which searches for matches in neighboring buckets when a match fails, rather than renavigating the hash tree. The authors report that MP-LSH requires fewer hash tables, resulting in a lower memory footprint. MP-LSH also produces more uniform hash bucket sizes than BRIEF. Since ORB is a binary descriptor based on point-pair comparisons, Hamming distance is used for correspondence.

ORB is reported to be an order of magnitude faster than SURF, and two orders of magnitude faster than SIFT, with comparable accuracy. The authors provide impressive performance results in a test of over 24 NTSC resolution images on the Pascal dataset [134].

ORB*	SURF	SIFT
15.3ms	217.3ms	5228.7ms

Results reported as measured in reference [134].

ORB Summary Taxonomy

> Spectra: Local binary + orientation vector
> Feature shape: Square
> Feature pattern: Trained local pixel point-pair compares
> Feature density: Local 31x31 at interest points
> Search method: Sliding window
> Distance function: Hamming distance
> Robustness: 3 (brightness, contrast, rotation, *limited scale)

BRISK

BRISK [131,143] is a local binary method using a circular-symmetric pattern region shape and a total of 60 point-pairs as line segments arranged in four concentric rings, as shown in Figure 4-10 and described in detail in Chapter 4. The method uses point-pairs of both short segments and long segments, and this provides a measure of scale invariance, since short segments may map better for fine resolution and long segments may map better at coarse resolution.

The brisk algorithm is unique, using a novel FAST detector adapted to use scale space, reportedly achieving an order of magnitude performance increase over SURF with comparable accuracy. Here are the main computational steps in the algorithm:

- Detects keypoints using FAST or AGHAST based selection in scale space.

- Performs Gaussian smoothing at each pixel sample point to get the point value.

- Makes three sets of pairs: long pairs, short pairs, and unused pairs (the unused pairs are not in the long pair or the short pair set; see Figure 4-12).

- Computes gradient between long pairs, sums gradients to determine orientation.

- Uses gradient orientation to adjust and rotate short pairs.

- Creates binary descriptor from short pair point-wise comparisons.

BRISK Summary Taxonomy

> Spectra: Local binary + orientation vector
> Feature shape: Square
> Feature pattern: Trained local pixel point-pair compares
> Feature density: Local 31x31 at FAST interest points
> Search method: Sliding window
> Distance function: Hamming distance
> Robustness: 4 (brightness, contrast, rotation, scale)

FREAK

FREAK [130] uses a novel foveal-inspired multiresolution pixel pair sampling shape with trained pixel pairs to mimic the design of the human eye as a coarse-to-fine descriptor, with resolution highest in the center and decreasing further into the periphery, as shown in Figure 4-9. In the opinion of this author, FREAK demonstrates many of the better design approaches to feature description; it combines performance, accuracy, and robustness. Note that FREAK is fast to compute, has good discrimination compared to other local binary descriptors such as LBP, Census, BRISK, BRIEF, and ORB, and compares favorably with SIFT.

The FREAK feature training process involves determining the point-pairs for the binary comparisons based on the training data, as shown in Figure 4-9. The training method allows for a range of descriptor sampling patterns and shapes to be built by weighting and choosing sample points with high variance and low correlation. Each sampling point is first smoothed from the local region using variable-sized radius approximations to create Gaussian kernels over circular regions. The circular regions are designed with some overlap to adjacent regions, which improves accuracy.

The feature descriptor is thus designed in a coarse-to-fine cascade of four groups of 16 byte coarse-to-fine descriptors containing pixel-pair binary comparisons stored in a vector. The first 16 bytes, the coarse of highest resolution set in the cascade, is normally sufficient to find 90 percent of the matching features and to discard nonmatching features. FREAK uses 45 point pairs for the descriptor from a 31x31 pixel patch sampling region.

By storing the point-pair comparisons in four cascades of decreasing resolution pattern vectors, the matching process proceeds from coarse to fine, mimicking the human visual system's saccadic search mechanism, allowing for accelerated matching performance when there is early success or rejection in the matching phase. In summary, the FREAK approach works very well.

FREAK Summary Taxonomy

> Spectra: Local binary coarse-to-fine + orientation vector
> Feature shape: Square
> Feature pattern: 31x31 region pixel point-pair compares
> Feature density: Sparse local at AGAST interest points
> Search method: Sliding window over scale space
> Distance function: Hamming distance
> Robustness: 6 (brightness, contrast, rotation, scale, viewpoint, blur)

Spectra Descriptors

Compared to the local binary descriptor group, the spectra group of descriptors typically involves more intense computations and algorithms, often requiring floating point calculations, and may consume considerable memory. In this taxonomy and discussion, *spectra* is simply a quantity that can be measured or computed, such as light intensity, color, local area gradients, local area statistical features and moments, surface normals, and sorted data such 2D or 3D histograms of any spectral type, such as histograms of local gradient direction. Many of the methods discussed in this section use local gradient information.

Local binary descriptors, as discussed in the previous section, are an attempt to move away from more costly spectral methods to reduce power and increase performance. Local binary descriptors in many cases offer similar accuracy and robustness to the more compute-intensive spectra methods.

SIFT

The Scale Invariant Feature Transform (SIFT) developed by Lowe [161,178] is the most well-known method for finding interest points and feature descriptors, providing invariance to scale, rotation, illumination, affine distortion, perspective and similarity transforms, and noise. Lowe demonstrates that by using several SIFT descriptors together to describe an object, there is additional invariance to occlusion and clutter, since if a few descriptors are occluded, others will be found [161]. We provide some detail here on SIFT since it is well designed and well known.

SIFT is commonly used as a benchmark against which other vision methods are compared. The original SIFT research paper by author David Lowe was initially rejected several times for publication by the major computer vision journals, and as a result Lowe filed for a patent and took a different direction. According to Lowe, "By then I had decided the computer vision community was not interested, so I applied for a patent and intended to promote it just for industrial applications."[1] Eventually, the SIFT paper was published and went on to become the most widely cited article in computer vision history!

SIFT is a complete algorithm and processing pipeline, including both an interest point and a feature descriptor method. SIFT includes stages for selecting center-surrounding circular weighted Difference of Gaussian (DoG) maxima interest points in scale space to create scale-invariant keypoints (a major innovation), as illustrated in Figure 6-14. Feature descriptors are computed surrounding the scale-invariant keypoints. The feature extraction step involves calculating a binned Histogram Of Gradients (HOG) structure from local gradient magnitudes into Cartesian rectangular bins, or into log polar bins using the GLOH variation, at selected locations centered around the maximal response interest points derived over several scales.

---

[1]http://yann.lecun.com/ex/pamphlets/publishing-models.html

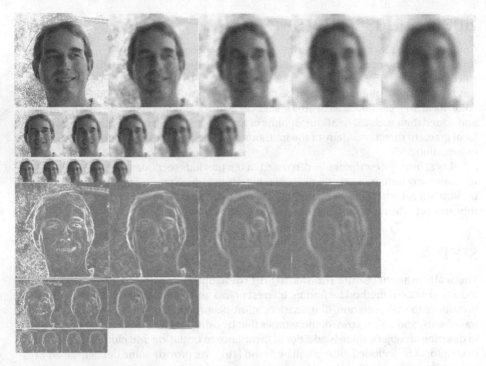

Figure 6-14. *(Top) Set of Gaussian Images obtained by convolution with a Gaussian kernel and the corresponding set of DoG images. (Bottom) In octave sets. The DOG function approximates a LOG gradient, or tunable bypass filter. Matching features against the various images in the scaled octave sets yields scale invariant features*

The descriptors are fed into a matching pipeline to find the nearest distance ratio metric between closest match and second closest match, which considers a primary match and a secondary match together and rejects both matches if they are too similar, assuming that one or the other may be a false match. The local gradient magnitudes are weighted by a strength value proportional to the pyramid scale level, and then binned into the local histograms. In summary, SIFT is a very well thought out and carefully designed multi-scale localized feature descriptor.

A variation of SIFT for color images is known as CSIFT [179].

Here is the basic SIFT descriptor processing flow (note: the matching stage is omitted since this chapter is concerned with feature descriptors and related metrics):

Create a Scale Space Pyramid

An octave scale *n/2* image pyramid is used with Gaussian filtered images in a scale space. The amount of Gaussian blur is proportional to the scale, and then the Difference of Gaussians (DoG) method is used to capture the interest point extrema maxima and minima in adjacent images in the pyramid. The image pyramid contains five levels. SIFT also uses a double-scale first pyramid level using pixels at two times the original magnification to help preserve fine details. This technique increases the number of stable keypoints by about four times, which is quite significant. Otherwise, computing the Gaussian blur across the original image would have the effect of throwing away the high-frequency details. See Figure 6-15 and 6-16.

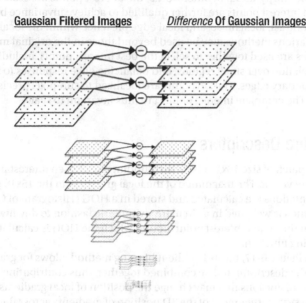

Figure 6-15. *SIFT DoG as the simple arithmetic difference between the Gaussian filtered images in the pyramid scale*

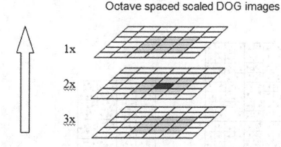

Figure 6-16. *SIFT interest point or keypoint detection using scale invariant extrema detection, where the dark pixel in the middle octave is compared within a 3x3x3 area against its 26 neighbors in adjacent DOG octaves, which includes the eight neighbors at the local scale plus the nine neighbors at adjacent octave scales (up or down)*

Identify Scale-Invariant Interest Points

As shown in Figure 6-16, the candidate interest points are chosen from local maxima or minima as compared between the 26 adjacent pixels in the DOG images from the three adjacent octaves in the pyramid. In other words, the interest points are scale invariant.

The selected interest points are further qualified to achieve invariance by analyzing local contrast, local noise, and local edge presence within the local 26 pixel neighborhood. Various methods may be used beyond those in the original method, and several techniques are used together to select the best interest points, including local curvature interpolation over small regions, and balancing edge responses to include primary and secondary edges. The keypoints are localized to sub-pixel precision over scale and space. The complete interest points are thus invariant to scale.

Create Feature Descriptors

A local region or patch of size 16x16 pixels surrounding the chosen interest points is the basis of the feature vector. The magnitude of the local gradients in the 16x16 patch and the gradient orientations are calculated and stored in a HOG (Histogram of Gradients) feature vector, which is weighted in a circularly symmetric fashion to downweight points farther away from the center interest point around which the HOG is calculated using a Gaussian weighting function.

As shown in Figure 6-17, the 4x4 gradient binning method allows for gradients to move around in the descriptor and be combined together, thus contributing invariance to various geometric distortions that may change the position of local gradients, similar to the human visual system treatment of the 3D position of gradients across the retina [248]. The SIFT HOG is reasonably invariant to scale, contrast, and rotation. The histogram bins are populated with gradient information using trilinear interpolation, and normalized to provide illumination and contrast invariance.

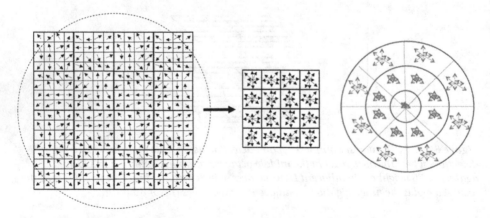

Figure 6-17. *(Left and center) Gradient magnitude and direction binned into histograms for the SIFT HOG. (Right) GLOH descriptors*

SIFT can also be performed using a variant of the HOG descriptor called the Gradient Location and Orientation Histogram (GLOH), which uses a log polar histogram format instead of the Cartesian HOG format; see Figure 6-17. The calculations for the GLOH log polar histogram are straightforward, as shown below from the Cartesian coordinates used for the Cartesian HOG histogram, where the vector magnitude is the hypotenuse and the angle is the arctangent.

$$m(x, y) = \sqrt{(L(x + 1, y) - L(x - 1, y))^2 + (L(x, y + 1) - L(x, y - 1))^2}$$

$$\theta(x, y) = TAN^{-1}(L(x, y + 1) - L(x, y - 1)) / (L(x + 1, y) - L(x - 1, y))$$

As shown in Figure 6-17, SIFT HOG and GLOH are essentially 3D histograms, and in this case the histogram bin values are gradient magnitude and direction. The descriptor vector size is thus 4x4x8=128 bytes. The 4x4 descriptor (center image) is a set of histograms of the combined eight-way gradient direction and magnitude of each 4x4 group in the left image, in Cartesian coordinates, while the GLOH gradient magnitude and direction are binned in polar coordinate spaced into 17 bins over a greater binning region. SIFT-HOG (left image) also uses a weighting factor to smoothly reduce the contribution of gradient information in a circularly symmetric fashion with increasing distance from the center.

Overall compute complexity for SIFT is high [180], as shown in Table 6-2. Note that feature description is most compute-intensive owing to all the local area gradient calculations for orientation assignment and descriptor generation including histogram binning with trilinear interpolation. The gradient orientation histogram developed in SIFT is a key innovation that provides substantial robustness.

Table 6-2. *SIFT Compute Complexity (from Vinukonda [180])*

SIFT Pipeline Step	Complexity	Number of Operations
Gaussian blurring pyramid	$\ominus N^2 U^2 s$	$4N^2 W^2 s$
Difference of Gaussian pyramid	$\ominus s N^2$	$4N^2 s$
Scale-space extrema detection	$\ominus s N^2$	$104 s N^2$
Keypoint detection	$\ominus \alpha s N^2$	$100 s \alpha N^2$
Orientation assignment	$\ominus s N^2 (1 - \alpha\beta)$	$48 s N^2$
Descriptor generation	$\ominus (x^2 N^2 (\alpha\beta + \gamma))$	$\ominus 1520 x^2 (\alpha\beta + \gamma) N^2$

The resulting feature vector for SIFT is 128 bytes. However, methods exist to reduce the dimensionality and vary the descriptor, which are discussed next.

SIFT Summary Taxonomy

Spectra: Local gradient magnitude + orientation
Feature shape: Square, with circular weighting
Feature pattern: Square with circular-symmetric weighting
Feature density: Sparse at local 16x16 DoG interest points
Search method: Sliding window over scale space
Distance function: Euclidean distance (*or Hellinger distance
with RootSIFT retrofit)
Robustness: 6 (brightness, contrast, rotation, scale, affine
transforms, noise)

SIFT-PCA

The SIFT-PCA method developed by Ke and Suthankar [183] uses an alternative feature
vector derived using principal component analysis (PCA), based on the normalized
gradient patches rather than the weighted and smoothed histograms of gradients, as used
in SIFT. In addition, SIFT-PCA reduces the dimensionality of the SIFT descriptor to a
smaller set of elements. SIFT originally was reported using 128 vectors, but using
SIFT-PCA the vector is reduced to a smaller number such as 20 or 36.

The basic steps for SIFT-PCA are as follows:

1. Construct an eigenspace based on the gradients from the local
   41x41 image patches resulting in a 3042 element vector; this
   vector is the result of the normal SIFT pipeline.

2. Compute local image gradients for the patches.

3. Create the reduced-size feature vector from the eigenspace
   using PCA on the covariance matrix of each feature vector.

SIFT-PCA is shown to provide some improvements over SIFT in the area of
robustness to image warping, and the smaller size of the feature vector results in faster
matching speed. The authors note that while PCA in general is not optimal as applied to
image patch features, the method works well for the SIFT style gradient patches that are
oriented and localized in scale space [183].

SIFT-GLOH

The Gradient Location and Orientation Histogram (GLOH) [144] method uses polar
coordinates and radially distributed bins rather than the Cartesian coordinate style
histogram binning method used by SIFT. It is reported to provide greater accuracy and
robustness over SIFT and other descriptors for some ground truth datasets [144]. As shown in
Figure 6-17, GLOH uses a set of 17 radially distributed bins to sum the gradient information
in polar coordinates, yielding a 272-bin histogram. The center bin is not direction oriented.
The size of the descriptor is reduced using PCA. GLOH has been used to retrofit SIFT.

SIFT-SIFER Retrofit

The Scale Invariant Feature Detector with Error Resilience (SIFER) [224] method provides alternatives to the standard SIFT pipeline, yielding measurable accuracy improvements reported to be as high as 20 percent for some criteria. However, the accuracy comes at a cost, since the performance is about twice as slow as SIFT. The major contributions of SIFER include improved scale-space treatment using a higher granularity image pyramid representation, and better scale-tuned filtering using a cosine modulated Gaussian filter.

The major steps in the method are shown in Table 6-3. The scale-space pyramid is blurred using a cosine modulated Gaussian (CMG) filter, which allows each scale of the octave to be subdivided into six scales, so the result is better scale accuracy.

Table 6-3. *Comparison of SIFT, SURF, and SIFER Pipelines (adapted from [224])*

	SIFT	SURF	SIFER
Scale Space Filtering	Gaussian 2nd derivative	Gaussian 2nd derivative	Cosine Modulated Gaussian
Detector	LoG	Hessian	Wavelet Modulus Maxima
Filter approximation level	OK accuracy	OK accuracy	Good accuracy
Optimizations	DoG for gradient	Integral images, constant time	Convolution, constant time
Image up-sampling	2x	2x	Not used
Sub-sampling	Yes	Yes	Not used

Since the performance of the CMG is not good, SIFER provides a fast approximation method that provides reasonable accuracy. Special care is given to the image scale and the filter scale to increase accuracy of detection, thus the cosine is used as a bandpass filter for the Gaussian filter to match the scale as well as possible, tuning the filter in a filter bank over scale space with well-matched filters for each of the six scales per octave. The CMG provides more error resilience than the SIFT Gaussian second derivative method.

SIFT CS-LBP Retrofit

The SIFT-CSLBP retrofit method [202,173] combines the best attributes of SIFT and the center symmetric LBP (CS-LBP) by replacing the SIFT gradient calculations with much more compute-efficient LBP operators, and by creating similar histogram-binned orientation feature vectors. LBP is computationally simpler both to create and to match than the SIFT descriptor.

The CS-LBP descriptor begins by applying an adaptive noise-removal filter (a Weiner filter is the variety used in this work) to the local patch for adaptive noise removal, which preserves local contrast. Rather than computing all 256 possible 8-bit local binary patterns, the CS-LBP only computes 16 center symmetric patterns for reduced dimensionality, as shown in Figure 6-18.

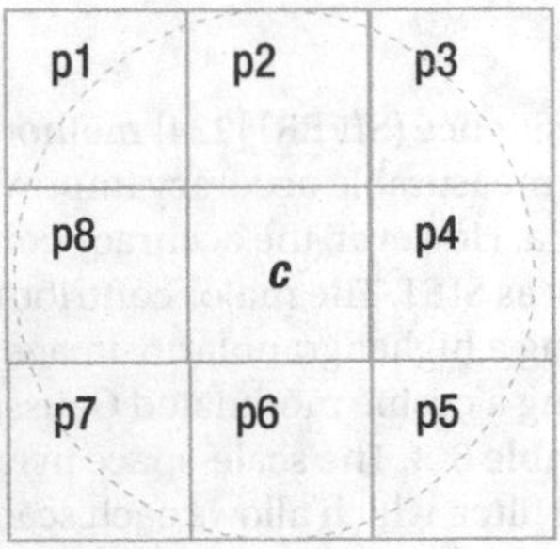

p1	p2	p3
p8	c	p4
p7	p6	p5

LPB=
$s(p1 - c)^0 +$
$s(p2 - c)^1 +$
$s(p3 - c)^2 +$
$s(p4 - c)^3 +$
$s(p5 - c)^4 +$
$s(p6 - c)^5 +$
$s(p7 - c)^6 +$
$s(p8 - c)^7$

CS-LPB=
$s(p1 - p5)^0 +$
$s(p2 - p6)^1 +$
$s(p3 - p7)^2 +$
$s(p4 - p8)^3$

Figure 6-18. *CS-LBP sampling pattern for reduced dimensionality*

Instead of weighting the histogram bins using the SIFT circular weighting function, no weighting is used, which reduces compute. Like SIFT, the CS-LBP binning method uses a 4x4 region Cartesian grid; simpler bilinear interpolation for binning is used, rather than trilinear, as in SIFT. Overall, the CS-LCP retrofit method simplifies the SIFT compute pipeline and increases performance with comparable accuracy; greater accuracy is reported for some datasets. See Table 6-4.

Table 6-4. *SIFT and CSLBP Retrofit Performance (as per reference [202])*

	Feature extraction	Descriptor construction	Descriptor normalization	Total ms time
CS-LBP 256	0.1609	0.0961	0.007	0.264
CS-LBP 128	0.1148	0.0749	0.0022	0.1919
SIFT 128	0.4387	0.1654	0.0025	0.6066

RootSIFT Retrofit

The RootSift method [174] provides a set of simple, key enhancements to the SIFT pipeline, resulting in better compute performance and slight improvements in accuracy, as follows:

- **Hellinger distance:** RootSIFT uses a simple performance optimization of the SIFT object retrieval pipeline using Hellinger distance instead of Euclidean distance for correspondence. All other portions of the SIFT pipeline remain the same; k-means is still employed to build the feature vector set, and other approximate nearest neighbor methods may still be used as well for larger feature vector sets. The authors claim a simple modification to SIFT code to perform the Hellinger distance optimization instead of Euclidean distance can be a simple set of one-line changes to the code. Other enhancements in RootSIFT are optional, discussed next.

- **Feature augmentation:** This method increases total recall. Developed by Turcot and Lowe [332], it is applied to the features. Feature vectors or visual words from similar views of the same object in the database are associated into a graph used for finding correspondence among similar features, instead of just relying on a single feature.

- **Discriminative query expansion (DQE):** This method increases query expansion during training. Feature vectors within a region of proximity are associated by averaging into a new feature vector useful for requeries into the database, using both positive and negative training data in a linear SVM; better correspondence is reported in reference [174].

By combining the three innovations described above into the SIFT pipeline, performance, accuracy, and robustness are shown to be significantly improved.

CenSurE and STAR

The Center Surround Extrema or CenSurE [185,184,145] method provides a true multi-scale descriptor, creating a feature vector using full spatial resolution at all scales in the pyramid, in contrast to SIFT and SURF, which find extrema at subsampled pixels that compromises accuracy at larger scales. CenSurE is similar to SIFT and SURF, but some key differences are summarized in Table 6-5. Modifications have been made to the original CenSurE algorithm in OpenCV, which goes by the name of STAR descriptor.

Table 6-5. *Major Differences between CenSurE and SIFT and SURF (adapted from reference [185])*

	CenSurE	SIFT	SURF
Resolution	Every pixel	Pyramid sub-sampled	Pyramid sub-sampled
Edge filter method	Harris	Hessian	Hessian
Scale space extrema method	Laplace, Center Surround	Laplace, DOG	Hessian, DOB
Rotational invariance	Approximate	yes	no
Spatial resolution in scale	Full	subsampled	Subsampled

The authors have paid careful attention to creating methods which are computationally efficient, memory efficient, with high performance and accuracy [185]. CenSurE defines an optimized approach to find extrema by first using the Laplacian at all scales, followed by a filtering step using the Harris method to discard corners with weak responses.

The major innovations of CenSurE over SIFT and SURF are as follows:

1. Use of bilevel center-surround filters, as shown in Figure 6-19, including Difference of Boxes (DoB), Difference of Octagons (DoO) and Difference of Hexagons (DoH) filters, octagons and hexagons are more rotationally invariant than boxes. DoB is computationally simple and may be computed with integral images vs. the Gaussian scale space method of SIFT. The DoO and DoH filters are also computed quickly using a modified integral image method. Circle is the desired shape, but more computationally expensive.

Figure 6-19. *CenSurE bilevel center surround filter shape approximations to the Laplacian using binary kernel values of 1 and -1, which can be efficiently implemented using signed addition rather than multiplication. Note that the circular shape is the desired shape, but the other shapes are easier to compute using integral images, especially the rectangular method*

2. To find the extrema, the DoB filter is computed using a seven-level scale space of filters at each pixel, using a 3x3x3 neighborhood. The scale space search is composed using center-surround Haar-like features on non-octave boundaries with filter block sizes [1,2,3,4,5,6,7] covering 2.5 octaves between [1 and 7] yielding five filters. This scale arrangement provides more discrimination than an octave scale. A threshold is applied to eliminate weak filter responses at each level, since the weak responses are likely not to be repeated at other scales.

3. Nonrectangular filter shapes, such as octagons and hexagons, are computed quickly using combinations of overlapping integral image regions; note that octagons and hexagons avoid artifacts caused by rectangular regions and increase rotational invariance; see Figure 6-19.

4. CenSurE filters are applied using a fast, modified version of the SURF method called Modified Upright SURF (MU-SURF) [188,189], discussed later with other SURF variants, which pays special attention to boundary effects of boxes in the descriptor by using an expanded set of overlapping sub-regions for the HAAR responses.

CenSurE Summary Taxonomy

Spectra: Center-surround shaped bi-level filters
Feature shape: Octagons, circles, boxes, hexagons
Feature pattern: Filter shape masks, 24x24 largest region
Feature density: Sparse at Local interest points
Search method: Dense sliding window over scale space
Distance function: Euclidean distance
Robustness: 5 (brightness, contrast, rotation, scale, affine transforms)

Correlation Templates

One of the most well known and obvious methods for feature description and detection is simply to take an image of the complete feature and search for it by direct pixel comparison—this is known as *correlation*. Correlation involves stepping a sliding window containing a first pixel region template across a second image region template and performing a simple pixel-by-pixel region comparison using a method such as sum of differences (SAD); the resulting score is the correlation.

Since image illumination may vary, typically the correlation template and the target image are first intensity normalized, typically by subtracting the mean and dividing by the standard deviation; however, contrast leveling and LUT transform may also be used. Correlation is commonly implemented in the spatial domain on rectangular windows, but can be used with frequency domain methods as well [4,9].

Correlation is used in video-based target tracking applications where translation as orthogonal motion from frame-to-frame over small adjacent regions predominates. For example, video motion encoders find the displacement of regions or blocks within the image using correlation, since usually small block motion in video is orthogonal to the Cartesian axis and maps well to simple displacements found using correlation. Correlation can provide sub-pixel accuracy between 1/4 to 1/20 of a pixel, depending on the images and methods used; see reference [151]. For video encoding applications, correlation allows for the motion vector displacements of corresponding blocks to be efficiently encoded and accurately computed. Correlation is amenable to fixed function hardware acceleration.

Variations on correlation include cross-correlation (sliding dot product) normalized cross-correlation (NCC), zero-mean normalized cross-correlation (ZNCC), and texture auto correlation (TAC).

In general, correlation is a good detector for orthogonal motion of a constant-sized mono-space pattern region. It provides sub-pixel accuracy, has limited robustness and accuracy over illumination, but little to no robustness over rotation or scale. However, to overcome these robustness problems, it is possible to accelerate correlation over a scale space, as well as various geometric translations, using multiple texture samplers in a graphics processor in parallel to rapidly scale and rotate the correlation templates. Then, the correlation matching can be done either via SIMD SAD instructions or else using the fast fixed function correlators in the video encoding engines.

Correlation is illustrated in Figure 6-20.

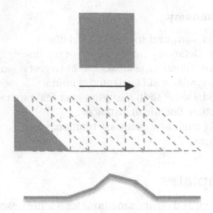

Figure 6-20. *Simplified model of digital correlation using a triangular template region swept past a rectangular region. The best correlation is shown at the location of the highest point*

Correlation Summary Taxonomy

> Spectra: Correlation
> Feature shape: Square, rectangle
> Feature pattern: Dense
> Feature density: Variable sized kernels
> Search method: Dense sliding window
> Distance function: SSD typical, others possible
> Robustness: 1 (illumination, sub-pixel accuracy)

HAAR Features

HAAR-like features [4,9] were popularized in the field of computer vision by the Viola Jones [186] algorithm. HAAR features are based on specific sets of rectangle patterns, as shown in Figure 6-21, which approximate the basic HAAR wavelets, where each HAAR feature is composed of the average pixel value of pixels within the rectangle. This is efficiently computed using integral images.

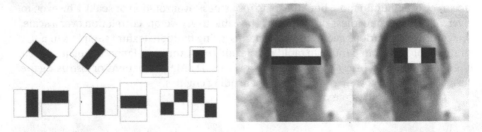

Figure 6-21. *Example HAAR-like features*

By using the average pixel value in the rectangular feature, the intent is to find a set of small patterns in adjacent areas where brighter or darker region adjacency may reveal a feature—for example, a bright cheek next to a darker eye socket. However, HAAR features have drawbacks, since rectangles by nature are not rotation invariant much beyond 15 degrees. Also, the integration of pixel values within the rectangle destroys fine detail.

Depending on the type of feature to be detected, such as eyes, a specific set of HAAR feature is chosen to reveal eye/cheek details and eye/nose details. For example, HAAR patterns with two rectangles are useful for detecting edges, while patterns with three rectangles can be used for lines, and patterns with an inset rectangle or four rectangles can be used for single-object features. Note that HAAR features may be a rotated set.

Of course, the scale of the HAAR patterns is an issue, and since a given HAAR feature only works with an image of appropriate scale. Image pyramids are used for HAAR feature detection, along with other techniques for stepping the search window across the image in optimal grid sizes for a given application. Another method to address feature scale is to use a wider set of scaled HAAR features to perform the pyramiding in the feature space rather than the image space. One method to address HAAR feature granularity and rectangular shape is to use overlapping HAAR features to approximate octagons and hexagons; see the CenSurE and STAR methods in Figure 6-19.

HAAR features are closely related to wavelets [227,334]. Wavelets can be considered as an extension of the earlier concept of Gabor functions [333,187]. We provide only a short discussion of wavelets and Gabor functions here; more discussion was provided in Chapter 2. Wavelets are an *orthonormal* set of small duration functions. Each set of wavelets is designed to meet various goals to locate short-term signal phenomenon. There is no single wavelet function; rather, when designing wavelets, a mother wavelet is first designed as the basis of the wavelet family, and then daughter wavelets are derived using translation and compression of the mother wavelet into a basis set. Wavelets are used as a set of nonlinear basis functions, where each basis function can be designed as needed to optimally match a desired feature in the input function. So, unlike transforms which use a uniform set of basis functions like the Fourier transform, composed of SIN and COS functions, wavelets use a dynamic set of basis functions that are complex and nonuniform in nature. Wavelets can be used to describe very complex short-term features, and this may be an advantage in some feature detection applications.

However, compared to integral images and HAAR features, wavelets are computationally expensive, since they represent complex functions in a complex domain. HAAR 2D basis functions are commonly used owing to the simple rectangular shape and computational simplicity, especially when HAAR features are derived from integral images.

HAAR Summary Taxonomy

> Spectra: Integral box filter
> Feature shape: Square, rectangle
> Feature pattern: Dense
> Feature density: Variable-sized kernels
> Search method: Grid search typical
> Distance function: Simple difference
> Robustness: 1 (illumination)

Viola Jones with HAAR-Like Features

The Viola Jones method [186] is a feature detection pipeline framework based on HAAR-like features using a perceptron learning algorithm to train a detector matching network that consists of three major parts:

1. Integral images used to rapidly compute HAAR-like features.

2. The ADA-BOOST learning algorithm to create a strong pattern matching and classifier network by combining strong classifiers with good matching performance with weak classifiers that have been "boosted" by adjusting weighting factors during the training process.

3. Combining classifiers into a detector cascade or funnel to quickly discard unwanted features at early stages in the cascade.

Since thousands of HAAR pattern matches may be found in a single image, the feature calculations must be done quickly. To make the HAAR pattern match calculation rapidly, the entire image is first processed into an integral image. Each region of the image is searched for known HAAR features using a sliding window method stepped at some chosen interval, such as every n pixels, and the detected features are fed into a classification funnel known as a *HAAR* Cascade Classifier. The top of the funnel consists of feature sets which yield low false positives and false negatives, so the first-order results of the cascade contain high-probability regions of the image for further analysis. The HAAR features become more complex progressing deeper into the funnel of the cascade. With this arrangement, images regions are rejected as soon as possible if the desired HAAR features are not found, minimizing processing overhead.

A complete HAAR feature detector may combine hundreds or thousands of HAAR features together into a final classifier, where not only the feature itself may be important but also the spatial arrangements of features—for example, the distance and angular relationships between features could be used in the classifier.

SURF

The Speeded-up Robust Features Method (SURF) [160] operates in a scale space and uses a fast Hessian detector based on the determinant maxima points of the Hessian matrix. SURF uses a scale space over a 3x3x3 neighborhood to localize bloblike interest point features. To find feature orientation, a set of HAAR-like feature responses are computed in the local region surrounding each interest point within a circular radius, computed at the matching pyramid scale for the interest point.

The dominant orientation assignment for the local set of HAAR features is found, as shown in Figure 6-22, using a sliding sector window of size $\pi / 3$. This sliding sector window is rotated around the interest point at intervals. Within the sliding sector region, all HAAR features are summed. This includes both the horizontal and vertical responses, which yield a set of orientation vectors; the largest vector is chosen to represent dominant feature orientation. By way of comparison, SURF integrates gradients to find the dominant direction, while SIFT uses a histogram of gradient directions to record orientation.

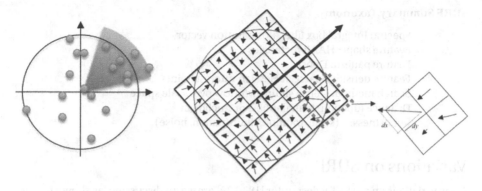

Figure 6-22. *(Left) The sliding sector window used in SURF to compute the dominant orientation of the HAAR features to add rotational invariance to the SURF features. (Right) The feature vector construction process, showing a grid containing a 4x4 region subdivided into 4x4 sub-regions and 2x2 subdivisions*

To create the SURF descriptor vector, a rectangular grid of 4x4 regions is established surrounding the interest point, similar to SIFT, and each region of this grid is split into 4x4 sub-regions. Within each sub-region, the HAAR wavelet response is computed over 5x5 sample points. Each HAAR response is weighted using a circularly symmetric Gaussian weighting factor, where the weighting factor decreases with distance from the center interest point, which is similar to SIFT. Each feature vector contains four parts:

$$v = \left(\sum d_x , \sum d_y , \sum |d_x|, \sum |d_y| \right)$$

The wavelet responses d_x and d_y for each sub-region are summed, and the absolute value of the responses $|d_x|$ and $|d_y|$ provide polarity of the change in intensity. The final descriptor vector is 4x4x4: 4x4 regions with four parts per region, for a total vector length of 64. Of course, other vector lengths can be devised by modifying the basic method.

As shown in Figure 6-22, the SURF gradient grid is rotated according to the dominant orientation, computed during the sliding sector window process, and then the wavelet response is computed in each square region relative to orientation for binning into the feature vector. Each of the wavelet directional sums d_x, d_y $|d_x|$, $|d_y|$ is recorded in the feature vector.

The SURF and SIFT pipeline methods are generally comparable in implementation steps and final accuracy, but SURF is one order of magnitude faster to compute than SIFT, as compared in an ORB benchmarking test [134]. However, the local binary descriptors, such as ORB, are another order of magnitude faster than SURF, with comparable accuracy for many applications [134]. For more information, see the section earlier in this chapter on local binary descriptors.

SURF Summary Taxonomy

> Spectra: Integral box filter + orientation vector
> Feature shape: HAAR rectangles
> Feature pattern: Dense
> Feature density: Sparse at Hessian interest points
> Search method: Dense sliding window over scale space
> Distance function: Mahalanobis or Euclidean
> Robustness: 4 (scale, rotation, illumination, noise)

Variations on SURF

A few variations on the SURF descriptor [188,189] are worth discussing, as shown in Table 6-6. Of particular interest are the G-SURF methods [188], which use a differential geometry concept [190] of a local region gauge coordinate system to compute the features. Since gauge coordinates are not global but, rather, local to the image feature, gauge space features carry advantages for geometrical accuracy.

Table 6-6. *SURF Variants (as discussed in Alcantarilla et. Al [188])*

SURF	Circular Symmetric Gaussian Weighting Scheme, 20x20 grid
U-SURF [189]	Faster version of SURF, only upright features are used; no orientation. Like M-SURF except calculated upright "U" with no rotation of the grid, uses a 20x20 grid, no overlapping HAAR features, modified Gaussian weighting scheme, bilinear interpolation between histogram bins.
M-SURF MU-SURF [189]	Circular symmetric Gaussian weighting scheme computed in two steps instead of one as for normal SURF, 24x24 grid using overlapping HAAR features, rotation orientation left out in MU-SURF version.
G-SURF, GU-SURF [188]	Instead of HAAR features, substitutes 2nd order gauge derivatives in Gauge coordinate space, no Gaussian weighting, 20x20 grid. Gauge derivatives are rotation and translation invariant, while the HAAR features are simple rectangles, and rectangles have poor rotational invariance, maybe +/-15 degrees at best.
MG-SURF [188]	Same as M-SURF, but uses gauge derivatives.
NG-SURF [188]	N = No Gaussian weighting as in SURF; same as SURF but no Gaussian weighting applied, allows for comparison between gauge derivate features and HAAR features.

Histogram of Gradients (HOG) and Variants

The Histogram of Gradients (HOG) method [106] is intended for image classification, and relies on computing local region gradients over a dense grid of overlapping blocks, rather than at interest points. HOG is appropriate for some applications, such as person detection, where the feature in the image is quite large.

HOG operates on raw data; while many methods rely on Gaussian smoothing and other filtering methods to prepare the data, HOG is designed specifically to use all the raw data without introducing filtering artifacts that remove fine details. The authors show clear benefits using this approach. It's a tradeoff: *filtering artifacts* such as smoothing vs. *image artifacts* such as fine details. The HOG method shows preferential results for the raw data. See Figure 4-12, showing a visualization of a HOG descriptor.

Major aspects in the HOG method are as follows:

- Raw RGB image is used with no color correction or noise filtering, using other color spaces and color gamma adjustment provided little advantage for the added cost.

- Prefers a 64x128 sliding detector window; 56x120 and 48x112 sized windows were also tested. Within this detector window, a total of 8x16 8x8 pixel block regions are defined for computation of gradients. Block sizes are tunable.

- For each 8x8 pixel block, a total of 64 local gradient magnitudes are computed. The preferred method is simple line and column derivatives *[-1,0,1]* in *x/y*; other gradient filter methods are tried, but larger filters with or without Gaussian filtering degrade accuracy and performance. Separate gradients are calculated for each color channel.

- Local gradient magnitudes are binned into a 9-bin histogram of edge orientations, quantizing dimensionality from 64 to 9, using bilinear interpolation; <9 bins produce poorer accuracy, >9 bins does not seem to matter. Note that either rectangular R-HOG or circular log polar C-HOG binning regions can be used.

- Normalization of gradient magnitude histogram values to unit length to provide illumination invariance. Normalization is performed in groups, rather than on single histograms. Overlapping 2x2 blocks of histograms are used within the detector window; the block overlapping method reduces sharp artifacts, and the 2x2 region size seems to work best.

- For the 64x128 pixel detector window method, a total of 128 8x8 pixel blocks are defined. Each 8x8 block has four cells for computing separate 9-bin histograms. The total descriptor size is then 8x16x4x9=4608.

Note that various formulations of the sliding window and block sizes are used for dealing with specific application domains. See Figure 4-12, showing a visualization of HOG descriptor computed using 7x15 8x8 pixel cells. Key findings from the HOG [106] design approach include:

- The abrupt edges at fine scales in the raw data are required for accuracy in the gradient calculations, and post-processing and normalizing the gradient bins later works well.

- L2 style block normalization of local contrast is preferred and provides better accuracy over global normalization; note that the local region blocks are overlapped to assist in the normalization.

- Dropping the L2 block normalization stage during histogram binning reduces accuracy by 27 percent.

- HOG features perform much better than HAAR-style detectors, and this makes sense when we consider that a HAAR wavelet is an integrated directionless value, while gradient magnitude and direction over the local HOG region provides a richer spectra.

HOG Summary Taxonomy

Spectra: Local region gradient histograms
Feature shape: Rectangle or circle
Feature pattern: Dense 64x128 typical rectangle
Feature density: Dense overlapping blocks
Search method: Grid over scale space
Distance function: Euclidean
Robustness: 4 (illumination, viewpoint, scale, noise)

PHOG and Related Methods

The Pyramid Histogram of Oriented Gradients (PHOG) [191] method is designed for global or regional image classification, rather than local feature detection. PHOG combines regional HOG features with whole image area features using spatial relationships between features spread across the entire image in an octave grid region subdivision; see Figure 6-23.

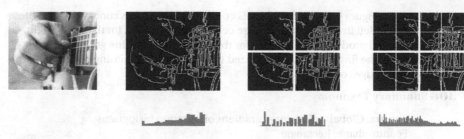

Figure 6-23. *Set of PHOG descriptors computed over the whole image, using octave grid cells to bound the edge information. (Center Left) A single histogram. (Center right) Four histograms shown concatenated together. (Right) Sixteen histograms shown concatenated*

PHOG is similar to related work using a coarse-to-fine grid of region histograms called Spatial Pyramid Matching by Lazebni, Schmid, and Ponce [534], using histograms of oriented edges and SIFT features to provide multi-class classification. It is also similar to earlier work on pyramids of concatenated histogram features taken over a progressively finer grid, called Pyramid Match Kernel and developed by Grauman and Darrell [535], which computes correspondence using weighted, multi-resolution histogram intersection. Other related earlier work using multi-resolution histograms for texture classification are described in reference [55].

The PHOG descriptor captures several feature variables, including:

- **Shape features,** derived from local distribution of edges based on gradient features inspired by the HOG method [106].

- **Spatial relationships,** across the entire image by computing histogram features over a set of octave grid cells with blocks of increasingly finer size over the image.

- **Appearance features,** using a dense set of SIFT descriptors calculated across a regularly spaced dense grid. PHOG is demonstrated to compute SIFT vectors for color images; results are provided in [191] for the HSV color space.

A set of training images is used to generate a set of PHOG descriptor variables for a class of images, such as cars or people. This training set of PHOG features is reduced using K-means clustering to a set of several hundred visual words to use for feature matching and image classification.

Some key concepts of the PHOG are illustrated in Figure 6-23. For the feature shape, the edges are computed using the Canny edge detector, and the gradient orientation is computed using the Sobel operator. The gradient orientation binning is linearly interpolated across adjacent histogram bins by gradient orientation (HOG), each bin represents the angle of the edge. A HOG vector is computed for each size of grid cell across the entire image. The final PHOG descriptor is composed of a weighted concatenation of all the individual HOG histograms from each grid level. There is no scale-space smoothing between the octave grid cell regions to reduce fine detail.

As shown in Figure 6-23, the final PHOG contains all the HOGs concatenated. Note that for the center left image, the full grid size cell produces 1 HOG, for the center right, the half octave grid produces 4 HOGs, and for the right image, the fine grid produces 16 HOG vectors. The final PHOG is normalized to unity to reduce biasing due to concentration of edges or texture.

PHOG Summary Taxonomy

> Spectra: Global and regional gradient orientation histograms
> Feature shape: Rectangle
> Feature pattern: Dense grid of tiles
> Feature density: Dense tiles
> Search method: Grid regions, no searching
> Distance function: l2 norm
> Robustness: 3 (image classification under some invariance to illumination, viewpoint, noise)

Daisy and O-Daisy

The Daisy Descriptor [214.309] is inspired by SIFT and GLOH-like descriptors, and is devised for dense-matching applications such as stereo mapping and tracking, reported to be about 40 percent faster than SIFT. See Figure 6-24. Daisy relies on a set of radially distributed and increasing size Gaussian convolution kernels that overlap and resemble a flower-like shape (Daisy).

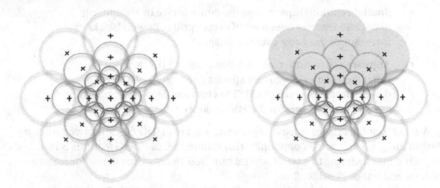

Figure 6-24. *(Left) Daisy pattern region, which is composed of four sets of eight overlapping concentric circles, with increasing Gaussian blur in the outer circles, where the radius of each circle is proportional to the Gaussian kernel region standard deviation. The overlapping circular regions provide a degree of filtering against adjacent region transition artifacts. (Right) A hypothetical binary occlusion mask; darker regions indicate points that may be occluded and "turned off" in the descriptor during matching*

Daisy does not need local interest points, and instead computes a descriptor densely at each pixel, since the intended application is stereo mapping and tracking. Rather than using gradient magnitude and direction calculations like SIFT and GLOH, Daisy computes a set of convolved orientation maps based on a set of oriented derivatives of Gaussian filters to create eight orientation maps spaced at equal angles.

As shown in Figure 6-24, the size of each filter region and the amount of blur in each Gaussian filter increase with distance away from the center, mimicking the human visual system by maintaining a sharpness and focus in the center of the field of view and decreasing focus and resolution farther away from the center. Like SIFT, Daisy also uses histogram binning of the local orientation to form the descriptor.

Daisy is designed with optimizations in mind. The convolution orientation map approach consumes fewer compute cycles than the gradient magnitude and direction approach of SIFT and GLOH, yet yields similar results. The Daisy method also includes optimizations for computing larger Gaussian kernels by using a sequential set of smaller kernels, and also by computing certain convolution kernels recursively. Another optimization is gained using a circular grid pattern instead of the rectangular grid used in SIFT, which allows Daisy to vary the rotation by rotating the sampling grid rather than re-computing the convolution maps.

As shown in Figure 6-24 (right image), Daisy also uses binary occlusion masks to identify portions of the descriptor pattern to use or ignore in the feature matching distance functions. This is a novel feature and provides for invariance to occlusion.

An FPGA optimized version of Daisy, called O-Daisy [217], provides enhancements for increased rotational invariance.

Daisy Summary Taxonomy

> Spectra: Gaussian convolution values
> Feature shape: Circular
> Feature pattern: Overlapping concentric circular
> Feature density: Dense at each pixel
> Search method: Dense sliding window
> Distance function: Euclidean
> Robustness: 3 (illumination, occlusion, noise)

CARD

The Compact and Realtime Descriptor (CARD) method [218] is designed with performance optimizations in mind, using learning-based sparse hashing to convert descriptors into binary codes supporting fast Hamming distance matching. A novel concept from CARD is the lookup-table descriptor extraction of histograms of oriented gradients from local pixel patches, as well as the lookup-table binning into Cartesian or log polar bins. CARD is reported to achieve significantly better rotation and scale robustness compared to SIFT and SURF, with performance at least ten times better than SIFT and slightly better than SURF.

CARD follows the method of RIFF [222][219] for feature detection, using FAST features located over octave levels in the image pyramid. The complete CARD pyramid includes intermediate levels between octaves for increased resolution. The pyramid levels are computed at intervals of $1/\sqrt{2}$, with level 0 being the full image. Keypoints are found using a Shi-Tomasi [157] optimized Harris corner detector.

Like SIFT, CARD computes the gradient at each pixel, and can use either Cartesian coordinate binning, or log polar coordinate binning like GLOH; see Figure 6-17. To avoid the costly biliner interpolation of gradient information into the histogram bins, CARD instead optimizes this step by rotating the binning pattern before binning, as shown in Figure 6-25. Note that the binning is further optimized using lookup tables, which contain function values based on principal orientations of the gradients in the patch.

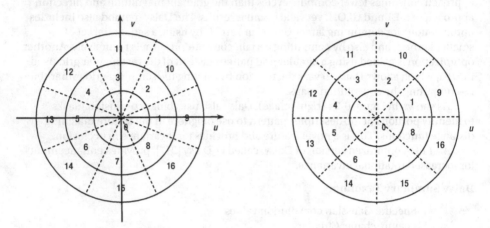

Figure 6-25. *CARD patch pattern containing 17 log polar coordinate bins, with image on left rotated to optimize binning*

As shown in Figure 6-25, to speed up binning, instead of rotating the patch based on the estimated gradient direction to extract and bin a rotationally invariant descriptor, as done in SIFT and other methods, CARD rotates the binning pattern over the patch based on the gradient direction and then performs binning, which is much faster. Figure 6-25 shows the binning pattern unrotated on the right, and rotated by $\pi/8$ on the left. All binned values are concatenated and normalized to form the descriptor, which is 128 bits long in the most accurate form reported [218].

CARD Summary Taxonomy

> Spectra: Gradient magnitude and direction
> Feature shape: Circular, variable sized based on pyramid scale and principal orientation
> Feature pattern: Dense
> Feature density: Sparse at FAST interest points over image pyramid

Search method: Sliding window
Distance function: Hamming
Robustness: 3 (illumination, scale, rotation)

Robust Fast Feature Matching

Robust Feature Matching in 2.3us developed by Taylor, Rosten and Drummond [220] (RFM2.3) (this *acronym is coined here by the author*) is a novel, fast method of feature description and matching, optimized for both compute speed and memory footprint. RFM2.3 stands alone among the feature descriptors surveyed here with regard to the combination of methods and optimizations employed, including sparse region histograms and binary feature codes. One of the key ideas developed in RFM2.3 is to compute a descriptor for multiple views of the same patch by creating a set of scaled, rotated, and affine warped views of the original feature, which provides invariance under affine transforms such as rotation and scaling, as well as perspective.

In addition to warping, some noise and blurring is added to the warped patch set to provide robustness to the descriptor. RFM2.3 is one of few methods in the class of deformable descriptors [344-346]. FAST keypoints in a scale space pyramid are used to locate candidate features, and the warped patch set is computed for each keypoint. After the warped patch set has been computed, FAST corners are again generated over each new patch in the set to determine which patches are most distinct and detectable, and the best patches are selected and quantized into binary feature descriptors and saved in the pattern database.

As shown in Figure 6-26, RFM2.3 uses a sparse 8x8 sampling pattern within a 16x16 region to capture the patch. A sparse set of 13 pixels in the 8x8 sampling pattern is chosen to form the index into the pattern database for the sparse pattern. The index is formed as a 13-bit integer, where each bit is set to 1 if the pixel value is greater than the patch mean value, limiting the index to 2^{13} or 8192 entries, so several features in the database may share the same index. However, feature differences can be computed very quickly using Hamming distance, so the index serves mostly as a database key for organizing like-patches. A training phase determines the optimal set of index values to include in the feature database, and the optimal patterns to save, since some patterns are more distinct than others. Initially, features are captured at full resolution, but if few good features are found at full resolution, additional features are extracted at the next level of the image pyramid.

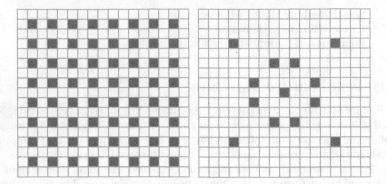

Figure 6-26. *RFM2.3 (Left) Descriptor sparse sampling pattern. (Right) Sparse descriptor using 13 samples used to build the feature index into the database*

The descriptor is modeled during training as a 64-value normalized intensity distribution function, which is reduced in size to compute the final descriptor vector in two passes: first, the 64 values are reduced to a five-bin histogram of pixel intensity distribution; second, when training is complete, each histogram bin is binary encoded with a 1 bit if the bin is used, and a 0 bit if the bin is rarely used. The resulting descriptor is a compressed, binary encoded bit vector suitable for Hamming distance.

RFM2.3 Summary Taxonomy

> Spectra: Normalized histogram patch intensity encoded into
> binary patch index code
> Feature shape: Rectangular, multiple viewpoints
> Feature pattern: Sparse patterns in 15x15 pixel patch
> Feature density: Sparse at FAST9 interest points
> Search method: Sliding window over image pyramid
> Distance function: Hamming
> Robustness: 4 (illumination, scale, rotation, viewpoint)

RIFF, CHOG

The Rotation Invariant Fast Features (RIFF) [222][219] method is motivated by tracking and mapping applications in mobile augmented reality. The basis of the RIFF method includes the development of a radial gradient transform (RGT), which expresses gradient orientation and magnitude in a compute-efficient and rotationally invariant fashion. Another contribution of RIFF is a tracking method, which is reported to be more accurate than KLT with 26x better performance. RIFF is reported to be 15x faster than SURF.

RIFF uses a HOG descriptor computed at FAST interest points located in scale space, and generally follows the method of the author's previous work in CHOG [223] (compressed HOG) for reduced dimensionality, low bitrate binning. Prior to binning the HOG gradients, a radial gradient transform (RGT) is used to create a rotationally invariant gradient format. As shown in Figure 6-27 (left image), the RGT uses two orthogonal basis vectors (r,t) to form the radial coordinate system that surrounds the patch center point c, and the HOG gradient g is projected onto (r,t) to express as the rotationally invariant vector $(g^T r, g^T t)$. A vector quantizer and a scalar quantizer are both suggested and used for binning, illustrated in Figure 6-27.

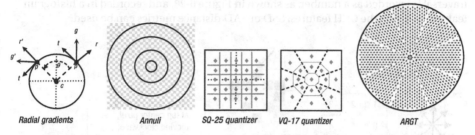

Radial gradients   Annuli   SQ-25 quantizer   VQ-17 quantizer   ARGT

Figure 6-27. *Concepts behind the RIFF descriptor [222][219], based partially on CHOG [223]*

As shown in Figure 6-27 (right image) the basis vectors can be optimized by using gradient direction approximations in the approximated radial gradient transform (ARGT), which is optimized to be easily computed using a simple differences between adjacent, normalized pixels along the same gradient line, and simple 45 degree quantization. Also note in Figure 6-27 (center left image), that the histogramming is optimized by sampling every other pixel within the annuli regions, and four annuli regions are used for practical reasons as a tradeoff between discrimination and performance. To meet real-time system performance goals for quantizing the gradient histogram bins, RIFF uses a 5x5 scalar quantizer rather than a vector quantizer.

In Figure 6-27 (left image), the gradient projection of g at point c onto a radial coordinate system (r,t) is used for a rotationally invariant gradient expression, and the descriptor patch is centered at c. The center left image (Annuli) illustrates the method of binning, using four annuli rings, which reduces dimensionality, and sampling only the gray pixels provides a 2x speedup. The center and center right images illustrate the bin centering mechanism for histogram quantization: (1) the more flexible scalar quantizer SQ-25 and (2) the faster vector quantizer VQ-17. And the right image illustrates the radial coordinate system basis vectors for gradient orientation radiating from the center outwards, showing the more compute efficient ARGT, or approximated radial gradient transform (RGT), which does not use floating point math (RGT not shown, see [222]).

RIFF Summary Taxonomy

      Spectra: Local region histogram of approximated radial
      gradients
      Feature shape: Circular
      Feature pattern: Sparse every other pixel
      Feature density: Sparse at FAST interest points over image
      pyramid
      Search method: Sliding window
      Distance function: Symmetric KL-divergence
      Robustness: 4 (illumination, scale, rotation, viewpoint)

Chain Code Histograms

A Chain Code Histogram (CCH) [206] descriptor records the shape of the perimeter as a histogram by binning the direction of the connected components—connected perimeter pixels in this case. As the perimeter is traversed pixel by pixel, the direction of the traversal is recorded as a number, as shown in Figure 6-28, and recorded in a histogram feature. To match the CCH features, SSD or SAD distance metrics can be used.

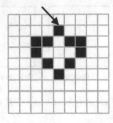

Chain code starting at top center pixel, moving clockwise: 5,4,6,7,7,1,1,1,2,4

Figure 6-28. *Chain code process for making a histogram. (Left to right) 1. The 8 possible directions that the connected perimeter may change. 2. Chain code values for each connected perimeter direction change; direction for determining the chain code value is starting from the center pixel. 3. An object with a connected perimeter highlighted by black pixels. 4. Chain code for the object following the connected perimeter starting at the top pixel. 5. Histogram of all the chain code values*

Chain code histograms are covered by U.S. Patent US4783828. CCH was invented in 1961 [206] and is also known as the Freeman chain code. A variant of the CCH is the Vertex chain code [207], which allows for descriptor size reduction and is reported to have better accuracy.

D-NETS

The D-NETS (Descriptor-NETS) [135] approach developed by Hundelshausen and Sukthankar abandons patch or rectangular descriptor regions in favor of a set of strips connected at endpoints. D-NETS allows for a family of strip patterns composed of directed graphs between a set of endpoints; it does not specifically limit the types of endpoints or strip patterns that may be used. The D-NETS paper provides a discussion of results from three types of patterns:

- **Clique D-NETS:** A fully connected network of strips linking all the interest points. While the type of interest point used may vary within the method, the initial work reports results using SIFT keypoints.

- **Iterative D-NETS**: Dynamically creates the network using a sub-set of the interest points, increasing the connectivity using a stopping criterion to optimize the connection density for obtaining desired matching performance and accuracy.

- **Densely sampled D-NETS:** This variant does not use interest points, and instead densely samples the nets over a regularly spaced grid, a 10-pixel grid being empirically chosen and preferred, with some hysteresis or noise added to the grid positions to reduce pathological sampling artifacts. The dense method is suitable for highly parallel implementations for increased performance.

For an illustration of the three D-NETS patterns and some discussion, see Figure 4-9.

Each strip is an array of raw pixel values sampled between two points. The descriptor itself is referred to as a *d-token*, and various methods for computing the d-token are suggested, such as binary comparisons among pixel values in the strip similar to FERNS or ORB, as well as comparing the 1D Fourier transforms of strip arrays, or using wavelets. The best results reported are a type of empirically engineered d-token, created as follows:

- **Strip vector sampling,** where each pixel strip vector is sampled at equally spaced locations between 10 and 80 percent of the length of the pixel strip vector; this sampling arrangement was determined empirically to ignore pixels near the endpoints.

- **Quantize** the pixel strip vector by integrating the values into a set of uniform chunks, *s,* to reduce noise.

- **Normalize** the strip vector for scaling and translation.

- **Discretize** the vector values into a limited bit range, *b*.

- **Concatenate** all uniform chunks into the d-token, which is a bit string of length *s*b*.

Descriptor matching makes use of an efficient and novel hashing and hypothesis correspondence voting method. D-NETS results are reported to be higher in precision and recall than ORB or SIFT.

D-NETS Summary Taxonomy

> Spectra: Normalized, averaged linear pixel intensity chunks
> Feature shape: Line segment connected networks
> Feature pattern: Sparse line segments between chosen points
> Feature density: Sparse along lines
> Search method: Sliding window
> Distance function: Hashing and voting
> Robustness: 5 (illumination, scale, rotation, viewpoint, occlusion)

Local Gradient Pattern

A variation of the LBP approach, the local gradient pattern (LGP) [204] uses local region gradients instead of local image intensity pair comparison to form the binary descriptor. The 3x3 gradient of each pixel in the local region is computed, then each gradient magnitude is compared to the mean value of all the local region gradients, and the binary bit value of 1 is assigned if the value is greater, and 0 otherwise. The authors claim accuracy and discrimination improvements over the basic LBP in face-recognition algorithms, including a reduction in false positives. However, the compute requirements are greatly increased due to the local region gradient computations.

LGP Summary Taxonomy

> Spectra: Local region gradient comparisons between center
> pixel and local region gradients
> Feature shape: Square
> Feature pattern: Every pixel 3x3 kernel region
> Feature density: Dense in 3x3 region
> Search method: Sliding window
> Distance function: Hamming
> Robustness: 3 (illumination, scale, rotation)

Local Phase Quantization

The local phase quantization (LPQ) descriptor [166–168] was designed to be robust to image blur, and it leverages the blur insensitive property of Fourier phase information. Since the Fourier transform is required to compute phase, there is some compute overhead; however, integer DFT methods can be used for acceleration. LPQ is reported to provide robustness for uniform blur, as well as uniform illumination changes. LPQ is reported to provide equal or slightly better accuracy on nonblurred images than LBP and Gabor filter bank methods. While mainly used for texture description, LPQ can also be used for local feature description to add blur invariance by combining LPQ with another descriptor method such as SIFT.

To compute, first a DFT is computed at each pixel over small regions of the image, such as 8x8 blocks. The low four frequency components from the phase spectrum are used in the descriptor. The authors note that the kernel size affects the blur invariance, so a larger kernel block may provide more invariance at the price of increased compute overhead.

Before quantization, the coefficients are de-correlated using a whitening transform, resulting in a uniform phase shift and 8-degree rotation, which preserves blur invariance. De-correlating the coefficients helps to create samples that are statistically independent for better quantization.

For each pixel, the resulting vectors are quantized into an 8-dimensional space, using an 8-bit binary encoded bit vector like the LBP and a simple scalar quantizer to yield 1 and 0 values. Binning into the feature vector is performed using 256 hypercubes derived from the 8-dimensional space. The resulting feature vector is a 256-dimensional 8-bit code.

LPQ Summary Taxonomy

> Spectra: Local region whitened phase using DFT -> an 8-bit binary code
> Feature shape: Square
> Feature pattern: 8x8 kernel region
> Feature density: Dense every pixel
> Search method: Sliding window
> Distance function: Hamming
> Robustness: 3 (contrast, brightness, blur)

Basis Space Descriptors

This section covers the use of basis spaces to describe image features for computer vision applications. A *basis space* is composed of a set of functions, the *basis functions*, which are composed together as a set, such as a series like the Fourier series (discussed in Chapter 3). A complex signal can be decomposed into a chosen basis space as a descriptor.

Basis functions can be designed and used to describe, reconstruct, or synthesize a signal. They require a forward transform to project values into the basis set, and an inverse transform to move data back to the original values. A simple example is transforming numbers between the base 2 number system and the base 10 number system; each basis had advantages.

Sometimes it is useful to transform a dataset from one basis space to another to gain insight into the data, or to process and filter the data. For example, images captured in the time domain as sets of pixels in a Cartesian coordinate system can be transformed into other basis spaces, such as the Fourier basis space in the frequency domain, for processing and statistical analysis. A good basis space for computer vision applications will provide forward and inverse transforms. Again, the Fourier transform meets these criteria, as well as several other basis spaces.

Basis spaces are similar to coordinate systems, since both have invertible transforms to related spaces. In some cases, simply transforming a feature spectra into another coordinate system makes analysis and representation simpler and more efficient. (Chapter 4 discusses coordinates systems used for feature representation.) Several of the descriptors surveyed in this chapter use non-Cartesian coordinate systems, including GLOH, which uses polar coordinate binning, and RIFF, which uses radial coordinate descriptors.

Fourier Descriptors

Fourier descriptors [227] represent feature data as sine and cosine terms, which can be observed in a Fourier Power Spectrum. The Fourier series, Fourier transform, and Fast Fourier transform are used for a wide range of signal analysis, including 1D, 2D, and 3D problems. No discussion of image processing or computer vision is complete without Fourier methods, so we will explore Fourier methods here with applications to feature description.

Instead of developing the mathematics and theory behind the Fourier series and Fourier transform, which has been done very well in the standard text by Bracewell [227], we discuss applications of the Fourier Power Spectrum to feature description and provide minimal treatment of the fundamentals here to frame the discussion; see also Chapter 3. The basic idea behind the Fourier series is to define a series of sine and cosine basis functions in terms of magnitude and phase, which can be summed to approximate any complex periodic signal. Conversely, the Fourier transform is used to decompose a complex periodic signal into the Fourier series set of sine and cosine basis terms. The Fourier series components of a signal, such as a line or 2D image area, are used as a Fourier descriptor of the region.

For this discussion, a *Fourier descriptor* is the selected components from a Fourier Power Spectrum—typically, we select the lower-frequency components, which carry most of the power. Here are a few examples using Fourier descriptors; note that either or both the Fourier magnitude and phase may be used.

- **Fourier Spectrum of LBP Histograms.** As shown in Figure 3-10, an LBP histogram set can be represented as a Fourier Spectrum magnitude, which makes the histogram descriptor invariant to rotation.

- **Fourier Descriptor of Shape Perimeter.** As shown in Figure 6-29, the shape of a polygon object can be described by Fourier methods using an array of perimeter to centroid line segments taken at intervals, such as 10 degrees. The array is fed into an FFT to produce a shape descriptor, which is scale and rotation invariant.

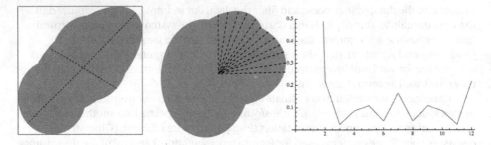

Figure 6-29. *(Left) Polygon shape major and minor axis and bounding box. (Center) Object with radial sample length taken from the centroid to the perimeter, each sample length saved in an array, normalized. (Right) Image fed into the Fourier Spectrum to yield a Fourier descriptor*

- **Fourier Descriptor of Gradient Histograms.** Many descriptors use gradients to represent features, and use gradient magnitude or direction histograms to bin the results. Fourier Spectrum magnitudes may be used to create a descriptor from gradient information to add invariance.

- **Fourier Spectrum of Radial Line Samples.** As used in the RFAN descriptor [136], radial line samples of pixel values from local regions can be represented as a Fourier descriptor of Fourier magnitudes.

- **Fourier Spectrum Phase.** The LPQ descriptor, described in this chapter, makes use of the Fourier Spectrum phase information in the descriptor, and the LPQ is reported to be insensitive to blur owing to the phase information.

Other Basis Functions for Descriptor Building

Besides the Fourier basis series, other function series and basis sets are used for descriptor building, pattern recognition, and image coding. However, such methods are usually applied over a global or regional area. See Chapter 3 for details on several other methods.

Sparse Coding Methods

In this discussion on basis space descriptors, we briefly discuss sparse coding methods, since they are analogous to a basis space. Many approaches are taken to sparse coding [530–533], using subtle differences in terminology, including *visual vocabularies* and *bag of words* methods [537]. However, sparse coding methods use a reduced set of learned feature descriptors or codes instead of basis functions. The key idea is to build a sparse codebook of basis features from the training images, and match against the sparse codebook. The sparse codes may be simple image patches or other descriptors.

A range of machine learning methods (outside the scope of this book, see [546] by Prince for more on machine learning) are used for finding the optimal sparse feature set. In addition, each sparse coding method may prefer a particular style of classification and matching. Sparse codes are associated as subsets or signatures to identify objects. Any of the local feature descriptor methods discussed in this chapter may be used as the basis for a sparse codebook. Sparse coding and related methods are discussed in more detail in Chapter 4. See the work by Aharon, Alad, and Bruckstein [536] for more details on sparse coding, as well as Fei-Fei, Fergus, and Torralba [537].

Examples of Sparse Coding Methods

As an example of the use of sparse codes for object recognition, Ren and Ramaan [125] retrofit the HOG method by replacing the HOG histogram of gradients feature with a new feature descriptor called Histograms of Sparse Codes (HSC); see Figure 6-30. Related work using sparse code books includes the Hierarchical Matching Pursuit method (HMP) [140], which builds a layered feature hierarchy of patch-level sparse codes derived from image patches to produce local features. The patch-level sparse codes from across the whole image are combined to produce image-level features. A close variation on HMP is the multipath sparse coding method [124], which effectively combines multiple sizes of smaller and medium-size patches and multiple layers of sparse coding into a single system.

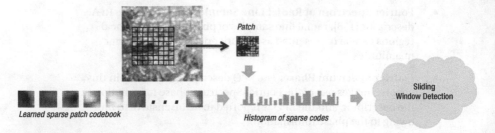

Figure 6-30. *One method of feature learning using sparse coding, showing how Histograms of Sparse Codes (HSC) are constructed from a set of learned sparse codes. The HSC method [125] is reported to outperform HOG in many cases*

Polygon Shape Descriptors

Polygon shape descriptors compute a set of *shape features* for an arbitrary polygon or blob, and the shape is described using statistical moments or image moments (as discussed in Chapter 3). These shape features are based on the perimeter of the polygon shape. The methods used to delineate image perimeters to highlight shapes prior to measurement and description are often complex, empirically tuned pipelines of image pre-processing operations, like thresholding, segmentation, and morphology (as discussed in Chapter 2). Once the polygon shapes are delineated, the shape descriptors are computed; see Figure 6-31. Typically, polygon shape methods are applicable to larger region-size features. In the literature, this topic may also be discussed as *image moments*. For a deep dive into the topic of image moments, see Flusser et. al. [518].

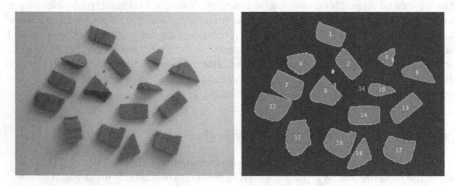

Figure 6-31. *Polygon shape descriptors. (Left) Malachite pieces. (Right) Polygon shapes defined and labeled after binary thresholding, perimeter tracing, and feature labeling. (Image processing and particle analysis performed using ImageJ Fiji)*

Polygon shape methods are commonly used in medical and industrial applications, such as automated microscopy for cell biology, and also for industrial inspection; see Figure 6-31. Commercial software libraries are available for polygon shape description, commonly referred to as *particle analysis* or *blob analysis*. See Appendix C.

MSER Method

The Maximally Stable Extremal Regions (MSER) method [194] is usually discussed in the literature as an interest region detector, and in fact it is. However we include MSER in the shape descriptor section because MSER regions can be much larger than other interest point methods, such as HARRIS or FAST.

The MSER detector was developed for solving disparity correspondence in a wide baseline stereo system. Stereo systems create a warped and complex geometric depth field, and depending on the baseline between cameras and the distance of the subject to the camera, various geometric effects must be compensated for. In a wide baseline stereo system, features nearer the camera are more distorted under affine transforms, making it harder to find exact matches between the left/right image pair. The MSER approach attempts to overcome this problem by matching on blob-like features. MSER regions are similar to morphological blobs and are fairly robust to skewing and lighting. MSER is essentially an efficient variant of the watershed algorithm, except that the goal of MSER is to find a range of thresholds that leave the watershed basin unchanged in size.

The MSER method involves sorting pixels into a set of regions based on binary intensity thresholding; regions with similar pixel value over a range of threshold values in a connected component pattern are considered maximally stable. To compute a MSER, pixels are sorted in a binary intensity thresholding loop, which sweeps the intensity value from min to max. First, the binary threshold is set to a low value such as zero on a single image channel— luminance, for example. Pixels < the threshold value are black, pixels >=are white. At each threshold level, a list of connected components or pixels is kept. The intensity threshold value is incremented from 0 to the max pixel value. Regions that do not grow or shrink or change as the intensity varies are considered maximally stable, and the MSER descriptor records the position of the maximal regions and the corresponding thresholds.

In stereo applications, smaller MSER regions are preferred and correlation is used for the final correspondence, and similarity is measured inside a set of circular MSER regions at chosen rotation intervals. Some interesting advantages of the MSER include:

- Multi-scale features and multi-scale detection. Since the MSER features do not require any image smoothing or scale space, both coarse features and fine-edge features can be detected.

- Variable-size features computed globally across an entire region, not limited to patch size or search window size.

- Affine transform invariance, which is a specific goal.

- General invariance to shape change, and stability of detection, since the extremal regions tend to be detected across a wide range of image transformations.

The MSER can also be considered as the basis for a shape descriptor, and as an alternative to morphological methods of segmentation. Each MSER region can be analyzed and described using shape metrics, as discussed later in this chapter.

Object Shape Metrics for Blobs and Polygons

Object shape metrics are powerful and yield many degrees of freedom with respect to invariance and robustness. Object shape metrics are not like local feature metrics, since object shape metrics can describe much larger features. This is advantageous for tracking from frame to frame. For example, a large object described by just a few simple object shape metrics such as area, perimeter, and centroid can be tracked from frame to frame under a wide range of conditions and invariance. For more information, see references [128,129] for a survey of 2D shape description methods.

Shape can be described by several methods, including:

- **Object shape moments and metrics:** the focus of this section.

- **Image moments:** see Chapter 3 under "Image Moments."

- **Fourier descriptors:** discussed in this chapter and Chapter 3.

- **Shape Context feature descriptor:** discussed in this section.

- **Chain code descriptor for perimeter description:** discussed in this section.

Object shape is closely related to the field of morphology, and computer methods for morphological processing are discussed in detail in Chapter 2. Also see the discussion about morphological interest points earlier in this chapter.

In many areas of computer vision research, local features seem to be favored over object shape-based features. The lack of popularity of shape analysis methods may be a reaction to the effort involved in creating pre-processing pipelines of filtering, morphology, and segmentation to prepare the image for shape analysis. If the image is not pre-processed and prepared correctly, shape analysis is not possible. (See Chapter 8 for a discussion of a hypothetical shape analysis pre-processing pipeline.)

Polygon shape metrics can be used for virtually any scene analysis application to find common objects and take accurate measurements of their size and shape; typical applications include biology and manufacturing. In general, most of the polygon shape metrics are rotational and scale invariant. Table 6-7 provides a sampling of some of the common metrics that can be derived from region shapes, both binary shapes and gray scale shapes.

Table 6-7. *Various Common Object Shape and Blob Object Metrics*

Object Binary Shape Metrics	Description
Perimeter	Length of all points around the edge of the object, including the sum of diagonal lengths ~=1.4 and adjacent lengths = 1
Area	Total area of object in pixels
Convex hull	Polygon shape or set of line segments enclosing all perimeter points

(continued)

274

Table 6-7. (*continued*)

Object Binary Shape Metrics	Description
Centroid	Center of object mass, average value of all pixel coordinates or average value of all perimeter coordinates
Fourier descriptor	Fourier spectrum result from an array containing the length of a set of radial line segments passing from centroid to perimeter at regular angles used to model a 1D signal function, the 1D signal function is fed into a 1D FFT and the set of FFT magnitude data is used as a metric for a chosen set of octave frequencies
Major/minor axis	Longest and shortest line segments passing through centroid contained within and touching the perimeter
Feret	Largest caliper diameter of object
Breadth	Shortest caliper diameter
Aspect ratio	Feret / Breadth
Circularity	4 X Pi X Area / Perimeter2
Roundness	4 X Area / (Pi X Feret2) (Can also be calculated from the Fourier descriptors)
Area equivalent diameter	sqrt((4 / Pi) X Area)
Perimeter equivalent diameter	Area/Pi
Equivalent ellipse	(Pi X Feret X Breadth) / 4
Compactness	sqrt((4 / Pi) X Area) / Feret
Solidity	Area / Convex_Area
Concavity	Convex_Area - Area
Convexity	Convex_Hull / Perimeter
Shape	Perimeter2 / Area
Modification ratio	(2 X MinR) / Feret
Shape matrix	A 2D matrix representation or plot of a polygon shape (may use Cartesian or polar coordinates; see Figure 6-32)

(*continued*)

Table 6-7. (*continued*)

Object Binary Shape Metrics	Description
Grayscale Object Shape Metrics	
SDM plots	*See Chapter 3, "Texture Metrics" section.
Scatter plots	*See Chapter 3, "Texture Metrics" section.
Statistical moments of gray scale pixel values	Minimum Maximum Median Average Average deviation Standard deviation Variance Skewness Kurtosis Entropy

Note: some of binary object metrics also apply to gray scale objects.

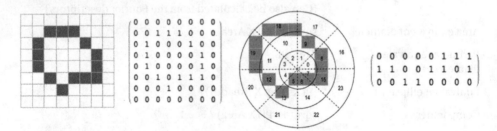

Figure 6-32. *A shape matrix descriptor [335] for the perimeter of an object. (Left two images) Cartesian coordinate shape matrix. (Right two images) polar coordinate shape matrix using three rows of eight numbered bin regions, gray boxes represent pixels to be binned. Note that multiple shape matrices can be used together. Values in matrix are set if the pixel fills at least half of the bin region, no interpolation is used*

Shape is considered to be binary; however, shape can be computed around intensity channel objects as well, using gray scale morphology. Perimeter is considered as a set of connected components. The shape is defined by a single pixel wide perimeter at a binary threshold or within an intensity band, and pixels are either on, inside, or outside of the perimeter. The perimeter edge may be computed by scanning the image, pixel by pixel, and examining the adjacent touching pixel neighbors for connectivity. Or, the perimeter may be computed from the shape matrix [335] or chain code discussed earlier in this chapter. Perimeter length is computed for each segment (pixel), where segment length = 1 for horizontal and vertical neighbors, and $\sqrt{2}$ otherwise for diagonal neighbors.

The perimeter may be used as a mask, and gray scale or color channel statistical metrics may be computed within the region. The object area is the count of all the pixels inside the perimeter. The centroid may be computed either from the average of all *(x,y)* coordinates of all points contained within the perimeter area, or from the average of all perimeter *(x,y)* coordinates.

Shape metrics are powerful. For example, shape metrics may be used to remove or excluding objects from a scene prior to measurement. For example, objects can be removed from the scene when the area is smaller than a given size, or if the centroid coordinates are outside a given range.

As shown in Figure 6-29 and Figure 2-18, the Fourier descriptor provides a rotation and scale invariant shape metric, with some occlusion invariance also. The method for determining the Fourier descriptor is to take a set of equally angular-spaced radius measurements, such as every 10 degrees, from the centroid out to points on the perimeter, and then to assemble the radius measurements into a 1D array that is run through a 1D FFT to yield the Fourier moments of the object. Or radial pixel spokes can be used as a descriptor.

Other examples of useful shape metrics, shown in Figure 6-29, include the bounding box with major and minor axis, which has longest and shortest diameter segments passing through the centroid to the perimeter; this can be used to determine rotational orientation of an object.

The SNAKES method [540] uses a spline model to fit a collection of interest points, such as selected perimeter points, into a region contour. The interest points are the spline points. The SNAKE can be used to track contoured features from frame to frame, deforming around the interest point locations.

In general, the 2D object shape methods can be extended to 3D data; however, we do not explore 3D object shape metrics here, see reference [200,201] for a survey of 3D shape descriptors.

Shape Context

The shape context method developed by Belongie, Malik, and Puzicha [239–241], describes local feature shape using a reference point on the perimeter as the Cartesian axis origin, and binning selected perimeter point coordinates relative to the reference point origin. The relative coordinates of each point are binned into a log polar histogram. Shape context is related to the earlier shape matrix descriptor [335] developed in 1985 as shown in Figure 6-32, which describes the perimeter of an object using log polar coordinates also. The shape context method provides for variations, described in several papers by the authors [239–241]. Here, we look at a few key concepts.

To begin, the perimeter edge of the object is sparsely sampled at uniform intervals, typically keeping about 100 edge sample points for coarse binning. Sparse perimeter edge points are typically distinct from interest points, and found using perimeter tracing. Next, a reference point is chosen on the perimeter of the object as the origin of a Cartesian space, and the vector angle and magnitude (r,θ) from the origin point to each other perimeter point are computed. The magnitude or distance is normalized to fit the histogram. Each sparse perimeter edge point is used to compute a tangent with the origin. Finally, each normalized vector is binned using (r,θ) into a log polar histogram, which is called the *shape context*.

An alignment transform is generated between descriptor pairs during matching, which yields the difference between targets and chosen patterns, and could be used for reconstruction. The alignment transform can be chosen as desired from affine, Euclidean, spline-based, and other methods. Correspondence uses the Hungarian method, which includes histogram similarity, and is weighted by the alignment transform strength using the tangent angle dissimilarity. Matching may also employ a local appearance similarity measure, such as normalized correlation between patches or color histograms.

The shape context method provides a measure of invariance over scale, translation, rotation, occlusion, and noise. See Figure 6-33.

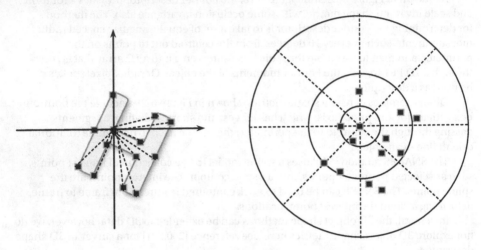

Figure 6-33. *Shape context method. (Left) Perimeter points are measured as a shape vector, both angle and distance, with respect to a chosen perimeter point as the reference Cartesian origin. (Right) Shape vectors are binned into a log polar histogram featrure descriptor*

3D, 4D, Volumetric, and Multimodal Descriptors

With the advent of more and more 3D sensors, such as stereo cameras and other depth-sensing methods, as well as the ubiquitous accelerometers and other sensors built into inexpensive mobile devices, the realm of 3D feature description and multimodal feature description is beginning to blossom.

Many 3D descriptors are associated with robotics research and 3D localization. Since the field of 3D feature description is early in the development cycle, it is not yet clear which methods will be widely adopted, so we present only a small sampling of 3D descriptor methods here. These include 3D HOG [196], 3D SIFT [195], and HON 4D [198], which are based on familiar 2D methods. We refer the interested reader to references [200,201,216] for a survey of 3D shape descriptors. Several interesting 3D descriptor metrics are available as open source in the Point Cloud Library,[2] including Radius-Based Surface Descriptors (RSD) [539], Principal Curvature Descriptors (PCD), Signatures of Histogram Orientations (SHOT) [541], Viewpoint Feature Histogram (VFH) [398], and Spin Images [538].

---

[2]http://pointclouds.org

Key applications driving the research into 3D descriptors include robotics and activity recognition, where features are tracked frame to frame as they morph and deform. The goals are to localize position and recognize human actions, such as walking, waving a hand, turning around, or jumping. See also the LBP variants for 3D: V-LBP and LBP-TOP, which are surveyed earlier in this chapter as illustrated in Figure 6-12, which are also used for activity recognition. Since the 2D features are moving during activity recognition, time is the third dimension incorporated into the descriptors. We survey some notable 3D activity-recognition research here.

One of the key concepts in the action-recognition work is to extend familiar 2D features into a 3D space that is spatio-temporal, where the 3D space is composed of 2D x,y video image sequences over time t into a volumetric representation with the form $v(x,y,t)$. In addition, the 3D surface normal, 3D gradient magnitude, and 3D gradient direction are used in many of the action-recognition descriptor methods.

3D HOG

The 3D HOG [196] is partially based on some earlier work in volumetric features [199]. The general idea is to employ the familiar HOG descriptor [106] in a 3D HOG descriptor formulation, using a stack of sequential 2D video frames or slices as a 3D volume, and to compute spatio-temporal gradient orientation on adjacent frames within the volume. For efficiency, a novel integral video approach is developed as an alternative to image pyramids based on the same line of thinking as the integral image approach use in the Viola Jones method.

A similar approach using the integral video concept was also developed in [199] using a sub-sampled space of 64x64 over 4 to 40 video frames in the volume, using pixel intensity instead of the gradient direction. The integral video method, which can also be considered an *integral volume* method, allows for arbitrary cuboid regions from stacked sequential video frames to be integrated together to compute the local gradient orientation over arbitrary scales. This is space efficient and time efficient compared to using pre-computed image pyramids. In fact, this integral video integration method is a novel contribution of the work, and may be applied to other spectra such as intensity, color, and gradient magnitude in either 2D or 3D to eliminate the need for image pyramids—providing more choices in terms of image scale besides just octaves.

The 3D HOG descriptor computations are illustrated in Figure 6-34. To find feature keypoints to anchor the descriptors, a space-time extension of the Harris operator [197] is used, then a histogram descriptor is computed from the mean of the oriented gradients in a cubic region at the keypoint. Since gradient magnitude is sensitive to illumination changes, gradient orientation is used instead to provide invariance to illumination, and it is computed over 3D cuboid regions using simple x,y,z derivatives. The mean gradient orientation of any 3D cuboid is computed quickly using the integral video method. Gradient orientations are quantized into histogram bins via projection of each vector onto the faces of a regular icosahedron 20-sided shape to combine all vectors, as shown in Figure 6-34. The 20 icosahedron faces act as the histogram bins. The sparse set of spatio-temporal features is combined into a bag of features or bag of words in a visual vocabulary.

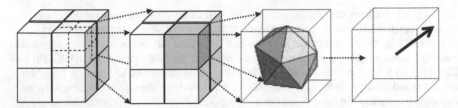

Figure 6-34. *HOG 3D descriptor computation. (Left) 2x2x2 descriptor cell block. (Left center) Gradient orientation histogram computed over 2x2x2 cell sub-blocks. (Right center) Gradient orientations quantized by projecting the vector intersection to the faces of a 20-faceted icosahedron. (Right) Mean gradient orientation computed over integral video blocks (volume vector integral)*

HON 4D

A similar approach to the 3D HOG is called HON 4D [198], which computes descriptors as Histogram of Oriented 4D Normals, where the 3D surface normal + time add up to four dimensions (4D). HON 4D uses sequences of depth images or 3D depth maps as the basis for computing the descriptor, rather than 2D image frames, as in the 3D HOG method. So a depth camera is needed. In this respect, HON 4D is similar to some volume rendering methods which compute 3D surface normals, and may be accelerated using similar methods [452,453,454].

In the HON 4D method, the surface normals capture the surface shape cues of each object, and changes in normal orientation over time can be used to determine motion and pose. Only the orientation of the surface normal is significant in this method, so the normal lengths are all normalized to unity length. As a result, the binning into histograms acts differently from the HOG style binning, so that the fourth dimension of time encodes differences in the gradient from frame to frame. The HON 4D descriptor is binned and quantized using 4D projector functions, which quantize local surface normal orientation into a 600-cell polychron, which is a geometric extension of a 2D polygon into 4-space.

Consider the discrimination of the HON 4D method using gradient orientation vs. the HOG method using gradient magnitude. If two surfaces are the same or similar with respect to gradient magnitude, the HOG style descriptor cannot differentiate; however, the HON 4D style descriptor can differentiate owing to the orientation of the surface normal used in the descriptor. Of course, computing 3D normals is compute-intensive without special optimizations considering the noncontiguous memory access patterns required to access each component of the volume.

3D SIFT

The 3D SIFT method [195] starts with the 2D SIFT feature method and reformulates the feature binning to use a volumetric spatio-temporal area $v(x,y,t)$, as shown in Figure 6-35.

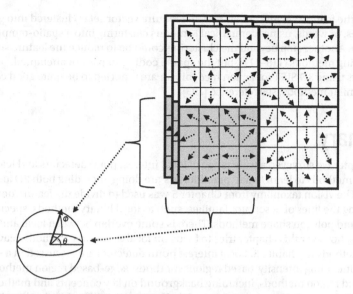

Figure 6-35. *Computation of the 3D SIFT [195] vector histogram bins as a combination of the combined gradient orientation of the sub-volumes in a volume space or 3D spatio-temporal region of three consecutive 2D image frames*

The 3D orientation of the gradient pair orientation is computed as follows:

$$m3D(x,y,t) = \sqrt{L_x^2 + L_y^2 + L_t^2}$$

$$\theta(x,y,t) = \tan^{-1}\left(\frac{L_y}{L_x}\right)$$

$$\phi(x,y,t) = \tan^{-1}\left(\frac{L_{yt}}{\sqrt{L_x^2 + L_y^2}}\right)$$

This method provides a unique two-valued (ϕ, θ) representation for each angle of the gradient orientation in 3-space at each keypoint. The binning stage is handled differently from SIFT, and instead uses orthogonal bins defined by meridians and parallels in a spherical coordinate space. This is simpler to compute, but requires normalization of each value to account for the spherical difference in the apparent size ranging from the poles to the equator.

To compute the SIFT descriptor, the 3D gradient orientation of each sub-histogram is used to guide rotation of the 3D region at the descriptor keypoint to point to 0, which provides a measure of rotational invariance to the descriptor. Each point will be represented as a single gradient magnitude and two orientation vectors (ϕ, θ) instead of one, as in 2D SIFT. The descriptor binning is computed over three dimensions into adjacent cubes instead of over two dimensions in the 2D SIFT descriptor.

Once the feature vectors are binned, the feature vector set is clustered into groups of like features, or words, using hierarchical K-means clustering into a spatio-temporal word vocabulary. Another step beyond the clustering could be to reduce the feature set using sparse coding methods [115–117], but the sparse coding step is not attempted.

Results using 3D SIFT for action recognition are reported to be quite good compared to other similar methods; see reference [195].

Summary

In this chapter we surveyed a wide range of local interest point detectors and feature descriptor methods to learn 'what' practitioners are doing, including both 2D and 3D methods. The vision taxonomy from Chapter 5 was used to divide the feature descriptor survey along the lines of descriptor families, such as local binary methods, spectra methods, and polygon shape methods. There is some overlap between local and regional descriptors, however this chapter tries to focus on local descriptor methods, leaving regional methods to Chapter 3. Local interest point detectors are discussed in a simple taxonomy including intensity-based regions methods, edge-based region methods, and shape-based region methods, including background on key concepts and mathematics used by many interest point detector methods. Some of the difficulties in choosing an appropriate interest point detector were discussed and several detector methods were surveyed.

This chapter also highlighted retrofits to common descriptor methods. For example, many descriptors are retrofitted by changing the descriptor spectra used, such as LBP vs. gradient methods, or by swapping out the interest point detector for a different method. Summary information was provided for feature descriptors following the taxonomy attributes developed in Chapter 5 to enable limited comparisons, using concepts from the analysis of local feature description design concepts presented in Chapter 4.

CHAPTER 7

Ground Truth Data, Content, Metrics, and Analysis

Buy the truth and do not sell it.

—Proverbs 23:23

This chapter discusses several topics pertaining to *ground truth data*, the basis for computer vision metric analysis. We look at examples to illustrate the importance of ground truth data design and use, including manual and automated methods. We then propose a method and corresponding ground truth dataset for measuring interest point detector response as compared to human visual system response and human expectations. Also included here are example applications of the general robustness criteria and the general vision taxonomy developed in Chapter 5 as applied to the preparation of hypothetical ground truth data. Lastly, we look at the current state of the art, its best practices, and a survey of available ground truth datasets.

Key topics include:

- Creating and collecting ground truth data: manual vs. synthetic methods

- Labeling and describing ground truth data: automated vs. human annotated

- Selected ground truth datasets

- Metrics paired with ground truth data

- Over-fitting, under-fitting, and measuring quality

- Publically available datasets

- An example scenario that compares the human visual system to machine vision detectors, using a synthetic ground truth dataset

Ground truth data may not be a cutting-edge research area, however it is as important as the algorithms for machine vision. Let's explore some of the best-known methods and consider some open questions.

What Is Ground Truth Data?

In the context of computer vision, ground truth data includes a set of images, and a set of labels on the images, and defining a model for object recognition as discussed in Chapter 4, including the count, location, and relationships of key features. The labels are added either by a human or automatically by image analysis, depending on the complexity of the problem. The collection of labels, such as interest points, corners, feature descriptors, shapes, and histograms, form a model.

A model may be trained using a variety of machine learning methods. At run-time, the detected features are fed into a classifier to measure the correspondence between detected features and modeled features. Modeling, classification, and training are statistical and machine learning problems, however, that are outside the scope of this book. Instead, we are concerned here with the content and design of the ground truth images.

Creating a ground truth dataset, then, may include condieration of the following major tasks:

- **Model design.** The model defines the composition of the objects—for example, the count, strength, and location relationship of a set of SIFT features. The model should be correctly fitted to the problem and image data so as to yield meaningful results.

- **Training set.** This set is collected and labeled to work with the model, and it contains both positive and negative images and features. Negatives contain images and features intended to generate false matches; see Figure 7-1.

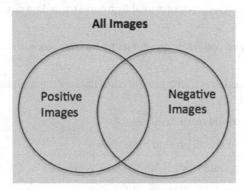

Figure 7-1. *Set of all ground truth data, composed of both positive and negative training examples*

- **Test set.** A set of images is collected for testing against the training set to verify the accuracy of the model to predict the correct matches.

- **Classifier design.** This is constructed to meet the application goals for speed and accuracy, including data organization and searching optimizations for the model.

- **Training and testing.** This work is done using several sets of images to check against ground truth.

Unless the ground truth data contains carefully selected and prepared image content, the algorithms cannot be measured effectively. Thus, *ground-truthing* is closely related to root-causing: there is no way to improve what we cannot measure and do not understand. Being able to root-cause algorithm problems and understand performance and accuracy are primary purposes for establishing ground truth data. Better ground truth data will enable better analysis.

Ground truth data varies by task. For example, in 3D image reconstruction or face recognition, different attributes of the ground truth data must be recognized for each task. Some tasks, such as face recognition, require segmentation and labeling to define the known objects, such as face locations, position and orientation of faces, size of faces, and attributes of the face, such as emotion, gender, and age. Other tasks, such as 3D reconstruction, need the raw pixels in the images and a reference 3D mesh or point cloud as their ground truth.

Ground truth datasets fall into several categories:

- **Synthetic produced**: images are generated from computer models or renderings.

- **Real produced**: a video or image sequence is designed and produced.

- **Real Selected**: real images are selected from existing sources.

- **Machine-automated annotation:** feature analysis and learning method are used to extract features from the data.

- **Human annotated**: an expert defines the location of features and objects.

- **Combined**: any mixture of the above.

Many practitioners are firmly against using synthetic datasets and insist on using real datasets. In some cases, random ground truth images are required; in other cases, carefully scripted and designed ground truth images need to be produced, similar to creating a movie with scenes and actors.

Random and natural ground truth data with unpredictable artifacts, such as poor lighting, motion blur, and geometric transformation, is often preferred. Many computer problems demand real images for ground truth, and random variations in the images are important. Real images are often easy to obtain and/or easy to generate using a video camera or even a cell phone camera. But creating synthetic datasets is not as clear; it requires knowledge of appropriate computer graphics rendering systems and tools, so the time investment to learn and use those tools may outweigh their benefits.

However, synthetic computer-generated datasets can be a way to avoid legal and privacy issues concerning the use of real images.

Previous Work on Ground Truth Data: Art vs. Science

In this section, we survey some literature on ground truth data. We also highlight several examples of automatic ground truth data labeling, as well as other research on metrics for establishing if, in fact, the ground truth data is effective. Other research surveyed here includes how closely ground truth features agree with human perception and expectations, for example, whether or not the edges that humans detect in the ground truth data are, in fact, found by the chosen detector algorithms.

General Measures of Quality Performance

Compared to other topics in computer vision, little formal or analytic work has been published to guide the *creation* of ground truth data. However, the machine learning community provides a wealth of guidance for measuring the *quality* of visual recognition between ground truth data used for training and test datasets. In general, the size of the training set or ground truth data is key to its accuracy [336–338] and the larger the better, assuming the right data is used.

Key journals to dig deeper into machine learning and testing against ground truth data include the journal IEEE PAMI for Pattern Analysis and Machine Intelligence, whose articles on the subject go back to 1979. While the majority of ground truth datasets contain real images and video sequences, some practitioners have chosen to create synthetic ground truth datasets for various application domains, such as the standard Middlebury dataset with synthetic 3D images. See Appendix B for available real ground truth datasets, along with a few synthetic datasets.

One noteworthy example framework for ground truth data, detector, and descriptor evaluation is the Mikolajczyk and Schmidt methodology (M&S), discussed later in this chapter. Many computer vision research projects follow the M&S methodology using a variety of datasets.

Measures of Algorithm Performance

Ericsson and Karlsson[102] developed a ground truth correspondence measure (GCM) for benchmarking and ranking algorithm performance across seven real datasets and one synthetic dataset. Their work focused on statistical shape models and boundaries, referred to as *polygon shape descriptors* in the vision taxonomy in Chapter 5. The goal was to automate the correspondence between shape models in the database and detected shapes from the ground truth data using their GCM. Since shape models can be fairly complex, the goal of automating model comparisons and generating quality metrics specific to shape description is novel.

Dutagaci et al.[91] developed a framework and method, including ground truth data, to measure the *perceptual* agreement between humans and 3D interest point detectors—in other words, do the 3D interest point detectors find the same interest points as the humans expect? The ground truth data includes a known set of human-labeled interest points within a set of images, which were collected automatically by an Internet scraper application. The human-labeled interest points were sorted toward a consensus set, and outliers were rejected. The consensus criterion was a radius region counting the number of humans who labeled interest points within the radius. A set of 3D interest point detectors was ran against the data and compared using simple metrics such as false positives, false negatives, and a weighted miss error. The ground truth data was used to test the agreement between humans and machine vision algorithms for 3D interest point detectors. The conclusions included observations that humans are indecisive and widely divergent about choosing interest points, and also that interest point detection algorithms are a fuzzy problem in computer vision.

Hamameh et al.[88] develop a method of automatically generating ground truth data for medical applications from a reference dataset with known landmarks, such as segmentation boundaries and interest points. The lack of experts trained to annotate the medical images and generate the ground truth data motivated the research. In this work, the data was created by generating synthetic images simulating object motion, vibrations, and other considerations, such as noise. Prestawa et al.[89] developed a similar approach for medical ground truth generation. Haltakov et al.[510] developed synthetic ground truth data from an automobile-driving simulator for testing driver assistance algorithms, which provided situation awareness using computer vision methods.

Vedaldi et al.[90] devised a framework for characterizing affine co-variant detectors, using synthetically generated ground truth as 3D scenes employing raytracing, including simulated natural and man-made environments; a depth map was provided with each scene. The goal was to characterize co-variant detector performance under affine deformations, and to design better covariant detectors as a result. A set of parameterized features were defined for modeling the detectors, including points, disks and oriented disks, and various ellipses and oriented ellipses. A large number of 3D scenes were generated, with up to 1,000 perspective views, including depth maps and camera calibration information. In this work, the metrics and ground truth data were designed together to focus on the analysis of geometric variations. Feature region shapes were analyzed with emphasis on disks and warped elliptical disks to discover any correspondence and robustness over different orientations, occlusion, folding, translation, and scaling. (The source code developed for this work is available.[1])

Rosin's Work on Corners

Research by Rosin[61,92] involved the development of an analytical taxonomy for gray scale corner properties, as illustrated in Figure 7-2. Rosin developed a methodology and case study to generate both the ground truth dataset and the metric basis for evaluating the performance and accuracy of a few well-known corner detectors. The metric is based on the receiver operating characteristic (ROC) to measure the accuracy of detectors to assess corners vs. noncorners. The work was carried out over 13,000 synthetic corner images with variations on the synthetic corners to span different orientations, subtended angles, noise, and scale. The synthetic ground truth dataset was specifically designed to enable the detection and analysis of a set of chosen corner properties, including bluntness or shape of apex, boundary shape of cusps, contrast, orientation, and subtended angle of the corner.

---

[1]See the "*VLFeat*" open-source project online (http://www.vlfeat.org").

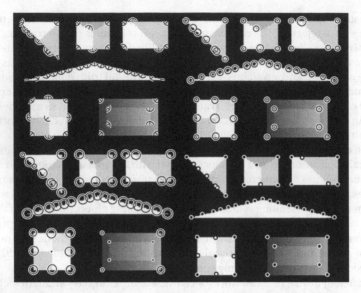

Figure 7-2. *Images illustrating the Rosin corner metrics: (Top left) Corner orientation and subtended angle. (Top right) Bluntness. (Bottom left) Contrast. (Bottom right) Black/white corner color. (Images © Paul Rosin and used by permission[61])*

A novel aspect of Rosin's work was the generation of explicit types of synthetic interest points such as corners, nonobvious corners, and noncorners into the dataset, with the goal of creating a statistically interesting set of features for evaluation that diverged from idealized features. The synthetic corners were created and generated in a simulated optical system for realistic rendering to produce corners with parameterized variations including affine transformations, diffraction, sub-sampling, and in some cases, adding noise. Rosin's ground truth dataset is available for research use, and has been used for corner detector evaluation of methods from Kitchen and Rosenfeld, Paler, Foglein, and Illingworth, as well as the Kittler Detector and the Harris & Stephens Detector.

Similar to Rosin, a set of synthetic interest point alphabets are developed later in this chapter snf tested in Appendix A, including edge and corner alphabets, with the goal of comparing human perception of interest points against machine vision methods. The synthetic interest points and corners are designed to test pixel thickness, edge intersections, shape, and complexity. The set diverges significantly from those of Rosin and others, and attempts to fill a void in the analysis of interest point detectors. The alphabets are placed on a regular grid, allowing for detmining position detection count.

Key Questions For Constructing Ground Truth Data

In this section we identify some key questions to answer for creating ground truth data, rather than provideing much specific guidance or answers. The type of work undertaken will dictates the type of guidance, for example, published research usually requires widely accepted ground truth data to allow for peer review and duplication of results. In medical or automobile industries,there may be government regulations, and also legal issues if competitors publish measurement or performance data. For example, if a company publishes any type of benchmark results against a ground truth data set comparing the results with those of competitor systems, all such data and claims should be reviewed by an attorney to avoid the complexities and penalties of commerce regulations, which can be daunting and severe.

For real products and real systems, perhaps the best guidance comes from the requirements, expectations and goals for performance and accuracy.Once a clear set of requirements are in place, then the ground truth selection process can begin.

Content: Adopt, Modify, or Create

It is useful to become familiar with existing ground truth datasets prior to creating a new one. The choices are obvious:

- Adopt an existing dataset.

- Adopt-And-Modify an existing data set.

- Create a new dataset.

Survey Of Available Ground Truth Data

Appendix B has information on several existing ground truth datasets. Take some time to get to know what is already available, and study the research papers coming out of SIGGRAPH, CVPR, IJCV, NIPS in Appendix C, and other research conferences to learn more about new datasets and how they are being used. The available datasets come from a variety of sources, including:

- Academic research organizations, usually available free of charge for academic research.

- Government datasets, sometimes with restricted use.

- Industry datasets, available from major corporations like Microsoft, sometimes can be licensed for commercial use.

Fitting Data to Algorithms

Perhaps the biggest challenge is to determine whether a dataset is a correct fit for the problem at hand. Is the detail in the ground truth data sufficient to find the boundaries and limits of the chosen algorithms and systems? "Fitting" applies to key variables such as the ground truth data, the algorithms used, the object models, classifier, and the intended use-cases. See Figure 7-3, which shows how ground truth data, image pre-processing, detector and descriptor algorithms, and model metrics should be fitted together.

Figure 7-3. *(Top left) Image pre-processing for edges shown using Shen-Castan edge detection against ground truth data. (Top right) Over-fitting detection parameters yield too many small edges. (Bottom left) Under fitting parameters yield too few edges. (Bottom right) Relaxed parameters yield reasonable edges*

Here are a few examples to illustrate the variables.

- **Data fitting:** If the dataset does not provide enough pixel resolution or bit depth, or there are insufficient unique samples in the training set, the model will be incomplete, the matching may suffer, and the data is *under-fitted* to the problem. Or, if the ground truth contains too many different types of features that will never be encoutered in the test set or in real applications. If the model resolution is 16 bits per RGB channel when only 8 bits per color channel are provided in real data, the data and model are *over-fitted* to the problem.

- **Algorithm fitting:** If scale invariance is included in the ground truth data, and the LBP operator being tested is not claimed to be scale invariant, then the algorithm is *under-fitted* to the data. If the SIFT method is used on data with no scale or rotation variations, then the SIFT algithm is *over-fitted* to the data.

- **Use-case fitting:** If the use-cases are not represented in the data and model, the data and model are *under-fitted* to the problem.

Scene Composition and Labeling

Ground truth data is composed of labeled features such as foreground, background, and objects or features to recognize. The labels define exactly what features are present in the images, and these labels may be a combination of on-screen labels, associated label files, or databases. Sometimes a randomly composed scene from the wild is preferred as ground truth data, and then only the required items in the scene are labeled. Other times, ground truth data is scripted and composed the way a scene for a movie would be.

In any case, the appropriate objects and actors in the scene must be labeled, and perhaps the positions of each must be known and recorded as well. A database or file containing the labels must therefore be created and associated with each ground truth image to allow for testing. See Figure 7-4, which shows annotated or labeled ground truth dataset images for a scene analysis of cuboids [62]. See also the Labelme database described in Appendix B, which allows contributors to provide labeled databases.

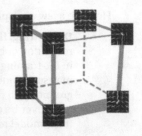

Figure 7-4. *Annotated or labeled ground-truth dataset images for scene analysis of cuboids (left and center). The labels are annotated manually into the ground- truth dataset, in yellow (light gray in B&W version) marking the cuboid edges and corners. (right) Ground-truth data contains pre-computed 3D corner HOG descriptor sets, which are matched against live detected cuboid HOG feature sets. Successful matches shown in green (dark gray in B&W version). (Images used by permission © Bryan Russel, Jianxiong Xiao, and Antonio Torralba)*

Composition

Establishing the right set of ground truth data is like asssembling a composition; several variables are involved, including:

- **Scene Content**: Designing the visual content, including fixed objects (those that do not move), dynamic objects (those that enter and leave the scene), and dynamic variables (such as position and movement of objects in the scene).

- **Lighting**: Casting appropriate lighting onto the scene.

- **Distance**: Setting and labeling the correct distance for each object to get the pixel resolution needed—too far away means not enough pixels.

- **Motion Scripting**: Determining the appropriate motion of objects in the scene for each frame; for example, how many people are in the scene, what are their positions and distances, number of frames where each person appears, and where each person enters and exits. Also, scripting scenes to enable invariance testing for changes in perspective, scale, affine geometry, occlusion.

- **Labeling**: Creating a formatted file, database, or spreadsheet to describe each labeled ground truth object in the scene for each frame.

- **Intended Algorithms**: Deciding which algorithms for interest point and feature detection will be used, what metrics are to be produced, and which invariance attributes are expected from each algorithm; for example, an LBP by itself does not provide scale invariance, but SIFT does.

- **Intended Use-Cases**: Determining the problem domain or application. Does the ground truth data represent enough real use-cases?

- **Image Channel Bit Depth, Resolution:** Setting these to match requirements.

- **Metrics**: Defining the group of metrics to measure—for example, false positives and false negatives. Creating a test fixture to run the algorithms against the dataset, measuring and recording all necessary results.

- **Analysis**: Interpreting the metrics by understanding the limitations of both the ground truth data and the algorithms, defining the success criteria.

- **Open Rating Systems:** Exploring whether there is an open rating system that can be used to report the results. For example, the Middlebury Dataset provides an open rating system for 3D stereo algorithms, and is described in Appendix B; other rating systems are published as a part of grand challenge contests held by computer vision organizations and governments, and some are reviewed in Appendix B. Open rating systems allow existing and new algorithms to be compared on a uniform scale.

Labeling

Ground truth data may simply be images returned from a search engine, and the label may just be the search engine word or phrase. Figure 7-5 shows a graph of photo connectivity for photo tourism [63–65] that is created from pseudo-random images of a well-known location, the Trevi Fountain in Rome. It is likely that in five to ten years, photo tourism applications will provide high-quality image reconstruction including textures, 3D surfaces, and rerenderings of the same location, rivaling real photographs.

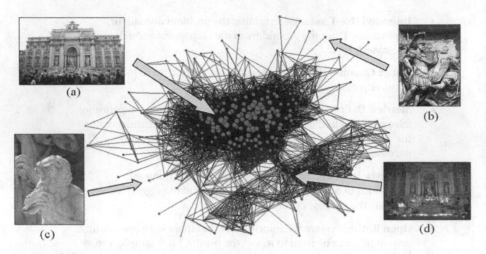

Figure 7-5. *Graph of photo connectivity (center) created from analyzing multiple public images from a search engine of the Trevi Fountain (a). Edges show photos matched and connected to features in the 3D scene, including daytime and nighttime lighting (b)(c)(d). (Images © Noah Snavely and used by permission)*

For some applications, labels and markers are inserted into the ground truth datasets to enable analysis of results, as shown in the 3D scene understanding database for cuboids in Figure 7-4. Another example later in this chapter composes scenes using *synthetic alphabets* of interest points and corners that are superimposed on the images of a regularly spaced grid to enable position verification (see also Appendix A). In some visual tracking applications, *markers* are attached to physical objects (a wrist band, for example) to establish ground truth features.

Another example is ground truth data composed to measure *gaze detection,* using a video sequence containing labels for two human male subjects entering and leaving the scene at a known location and time, walking from left to right at a known speed and depth in the scene. The object they are gazing at would be at a known location and be labeled as well.

Defining the Goals and Expectations

To establish goals for the ground truth data, questions must be asked. For instance, what is the intended use of the application requiring the ground truth data? What decisions must be made from the ground truth data in terms of accuracy and performance? How is quality and success measured? The goals of academic research and commercial systems are quite different.

Mikolajczyk and Schmid Methodology

A set of well-regarded papers by Mikolajczyk, Schmid and others [45,79,82,91,306] provides a good methodology to start with for measuring local interest points and feature detector quality. Of particular interest is the methodology used to measure scale and affine invariant interest point detectors [306] which uses natural images to start, then applies a set of known affine transformations to those images, such as homography, rotation, and scale. Interest point detectors are run against the images, followed by feature extractors, and then the matching recall and precision are measured across the transformed images to yield quality metrics.

Open Rating Systems

The computer vision community is, little by little, developing various open rating systems, which encourage algorithm comparisons and improvements to increase quality. In areas where such open databases exist, there is rapid growth in quality for specific algorithms. Appendix B lists open rating systems such as the Pascal VOC Challenge for object detection. Pascal VOC uses an open ground truth database with associated grand challenge competition problems for measuring the accuracy of the latest algorithms against the dataset.

Another example is the Middlebury Dataset, which provides ground truth datasets covering the 3D stereo algorithm domain, allowing for open comparison of key metrics between new and old algorithms, with the results published online.

Corner Cases and Limits

Finding out where the algorithms fail is valuable. Academic research is often not interested in the rigor required by industry in defining failure modes. One way to find the corner cases and limits is to run the same tests on a wide range of ground truth data, perhaps even data that is outside the scope of the problem at hand. Given the availability of publicly available ground truth databases, using several databases is realistic.

However, once the key ground truth data is gathered, it can also be useful to devise a range of corner cases—for example, by providing noisy data, intensity filtered data, or blurry data to test the limits of performance and accuracy.

Interest Points and Features

Interest points and features are not always detected as expected or predicted. Machine vision algorithms detect a different set of interst points than those humans expect. For example, Figure 7-6 shows obvious interest points missed by the SURF algorithm with a given set of parameters, which uses a method based on determinant of Hessian blob detection. Note that some interest points obvious to humans are not detected at all, some false positives occur, and some identical interest points are not detected consistently.

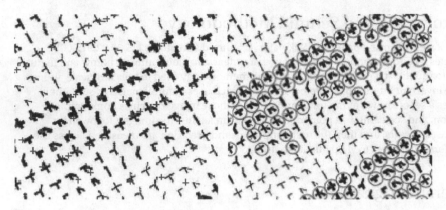

Figure 7-6. *Interest points detected on the same image using different methods: (Left) Shi-Tomasi corners marked with crosses. (Right) SURF interest points marked with circles. Results are not consistent or deterministic*

Also, real interest points change over time—for example, as objects move and rotate—which is a strong agrument for using real ground truth data vs. synthetic data to test a wide range of potential interest points for false positives and false negatives.

Robustness Criteria for Ground Truth Data

In Chapter 5, a robustness criteria was developed listing various invariance attributes, such as rotation and scale. Here, we apply the robustness criteria to the development of ground truth data.

Illustrated Robustness Criteria

Table 7-1 discusses various robustness criteria attributes, not all attributes are needed for a given application. For example, if radial distortion might be present in an optical system, then the best algorithms and corresponding metrics will be devised that are robust to radial distortion, or as mitigation, the vision pipeline must be designed with a pre-processing section to remove or compensate for the radial distortion prior to determining the metrics.

Table 7-1. *Robustness Criteria for Ground Truth Data*

Attribute	Discussion
Uneven illumination	Define range of acceptable illumination for the application; uneven illumination may degrade certain algorithms, some algorithms are more tolerant.
Brightness	Define expected brightness range of key features, and prepare ground-truth data accordingly.
Contrast	Define range of acceptable contrast for the application; some algorithms are more tolerant.
Vignette	Optical systems may degrade light and manifest as dim illumination at the edges. Smaller the features are localized better and may be able to overcome this situation; large features that span areas of uneven light are affected more.
Color accuracy	Inaccurate color space treatment may result in poor color performance. Colorimetry is important; consider choosing the right color space (RGB, YIQ, Lab, Jab, etc.) and use the right level of bit precision for each color, whether 8/16 bits is best.
Clutter	Some algorithms are not tolerant of clutter in images and rely on the scene to be constructed with a minimal number of subjects. Descriptor pixel size may be an issue for block search methods— too much extraneous detail in a region may be a problem for the algorithm.
Occlusion and clipping	Objects may be occluded or hidden or clipped. Algorithms may or may not tolerate such occlusion. Some occlusion artifacts can be eliminated or compensated for using image pre-processing and segmentation methods.
Outliers and proximity	Sometimes groups of objects within a region are the subject, and outliers are to be ignored. Also, proximity of objects or features may guide classification, so varying the arrangement of features or objects in the scene may be critical.
Noise	Noise may take on regular or random patterns, such as snow, rain, single-pixel spot nose, line noise, random electrical noise affecting pixel bit resolution, etc.
Motion blur	Motion blur is an important problem for almost all real-time applications. This can be overcome by using faster frame rates and employing image pre-processing to remove the motion blur, if possible.
Jitter and judder	Common problem in video images taken from moving cameras, where each scan line may be offset from the regular 2D grid.

(*continued*)

Table 7-1. (*continued*)

Attribute	Discussion
Focal plane or depth	If the application or use-case for the algorithm assumes all depths of the image to be in focus, then using ground truth data with out-of-focus depth planes may be a good way to test the limits.
Pixel depth Resolution	If features are matched based on the value of pixels, such as gray scale intensity or color intensity, pixel resolution is an issue. For example, if a feature descriptor uses 16 bits of effective gray scale intensity but the actual use-case and ground truth data provide only 8 bits of resolution, the descriptor may be over-fitted to the data, or the data may be unrealistic for the application.
Geometric distortion	Complex warping may occur due to combinations of geometric errors from optics or distance to subject. On deformable surfaces such as the human face, surface and feature shape may change in ways difficult to geometrically describe.
Scale, projection	Near and far objects will be represented by more or less pixels, thus a multi-scale dataset may be required for a given application, as well as multi-scale feature descriptors. Algorithm sensitivity to feature scale and intended use case also dictate ground truth data scale.
Affine transforms and rotation	In some applications like panoramic image stitching, very little rotation is expected between adjacent frames—perhaps up to 15 degrees may be tolerated. However, in other applications like object analysis and tracking of parts on an industrial conveyor belt, rotation between 0 and 360 degrees is expected.
Feature mirroring, translation	In stereo correspondence, L/R pair matching is done using the assumption that features can be matched within a limited range of translation difference between L/R pairs. If the translation is extreme between points, the stereo algorithm may fail, resulting in holes in the depth map, which must be filled.
Reflection	Some applications, like recognizing automobiles in traffic, require a feature model, which incorporates a reflective representation and a corresponding ground truth dataset. Automobiles may come and go from different directions, and have a reflected right/left feature pair.
Radial distortion	Optics may introduce radial distortion around the fringes; usually this is corrected by a camera system using digital signal processors or fixed-function hardware prior to delivering the image.

Using Robustness Criteria for Real Applications

Each application requires a different set of robustness criteria to be developed into the ground truth data. Table 7-2 illustrates how the robustness criteria may be applied to a few real and diverse applications.

Table 7-2. *Robustness Criteria Applied to Sample Applications (each application with different requirements for robustness)*

General Objective Criteria Attributes	Industrial inspection of apples on a conveyor belt, fixed distance, fixed speed, fixed illumination	Automobile identification on roadway, day and night, all road conditions	Multi-view stereo reconstruction bundle adjustment
Uneven illumination	-	Important	Useful
Brightness	Useful	Important	Useful
Contrast	Useful	Important	Useful
Vignette	Important	Useful	Useful
Color accuracy	Important	Important	Useful
Clutter	-	Important	Important
Occlusion	-	Important	Important
Outliers	-	Important	Important
Noise	-	Important	Useful
Motion blur	Useful	Important	Useful
Focal plane or depth	-	Important	Useful
Pixel depth resolution	Useful	Important	important
Subpixel resolution	-	-	important
Geometric distortion (warp)	-	Useful	Important
Affine transforms	-	Important	Important
Scale	-	Important	Important
Skew	-	-	-
Rotation	Important	Useful	Useful
Translation	Important	Useful	Useful

(continued)

Table 7-2. (*continued*)

General Objective Criteria Attributes	Industrial inspection of apples on a conveyor belt, fixed distance, fixed speed, fixed illumination	Automobile identification on roadway, day and night, all road conditions	Multi-view stereo reconstruction bundle adjustment
Projective transformations	Important	Important	-
Reflection	Important	Important	-
Radial distortion	-	-	Important
Polar distortion	-	-	Important
Discrimination or uniqueness	-	Useful	-
Location accuracy	-	Useful	-
Shape and thickness distortion	-	Useful	-

As illustrated in Table 7-2, a multi-view stereo (MVS) application will hold certain geometric criteria as very important, since accurate depth maps require accurate geometry assumptions as a basis for disparity calculations. For algorithm accuracy tuning, corresponding ground truth data should be created using a well-calibrated camera system for positional accuracy of the 3D scene to allow for effective comparisons.

Another example in Table 7-2 with many variables in an uncontrolled environment is that of automobile identification on roadways—which may be concerned with distance, shape, color, and noise. For example, identifying automobiles may require ground truth images of several vehicles from a wide range of natural conditions, such as dawn, dusk, cloudy day, and full sun, and including conditions such as rainfall and snowfall, motion blur, occlusion, and perspective views. An example automobile recognition pipeline is developed in Chapter 8.

Also shown Table 7-2 is an example with a controlled environment: industrial inspection. In industrial settings, the environment can be carefully controlled using known lighting, controlling the speed of a conveyor belt, and limiting the set of objects in the scenes. Accurate models and metrics for each object can be devised, perhaps taking color samples and so forth—all of which can be done a priori. Ground truth data could be easily created from the actual factory location.

Pairing Metrics with Ground Truth

Metrics and ground truth data should go together. Each application will have design goals for robustness and accuracy, and each algorithm will also have different intended uses and capabilities. For example, the SUSAN detector discussed in Chapter 6 is often applied to wide baseline stereo applications, and stereo applications typically are not concerned much with rotational invariance because the image features are computed on corresponding stereo pair frames that have been affine rectified to align line by line. Feature correspondence between image pairs is expected within a small window, with some minor translation on the *x* axis.

Pairing and Tuning Interest Points, Features, and Ground Truth

Pairing the right interest point detectors and feature descriptors can enhance results, and many interest point methods are available and were discussed in Chapter 6. When preparing ground truth data, the method used for interest point detection should be considered for guidance.

For example, interest point methods using derivatives, such as the Laplace and Hessian style detectors, will not do very well without sufficient contrast in the local pixel regions of the images, since contrast accentuates maxima, minima and local region changes. However, a method such as FAST9 is much more suited to low-contrast images, uses local binary patterns, and is simple to tune the compare threshold and region size to detect corners and edges; but the tradeoff in using FAST9 is that scale invariance is sacrificed.

A method using edge gradients and direction, such as eigen methods, would require ground truth containing sufficient oriented edges at the right contrast levels. A method using morphological interest points would likewise require image data that can be properly thresholded and processed to yield the desired shapes.

Interest point methods also must be tuned for various parameters like strength of thresholds for accepting and rejecting candidate interest points, as well as and region size. Choosing the right interest point detector, tuning, and pairing with appropriate ground truth data are critical. The effect of tuning interest point detector parameters is illustrated in Figures 7-6 and 7-7.

Figure 7-7. *Machine corner detection using the Shi-Tomasi method marked with crosses; results are shown using different parameter settings and thresholds for the strength and pixel size of the corners*

Examples Using The General Vision Taxonomy

As a guideline for pairing metrics and ground truth data, we use the vision taxonomy developed in Chapter 5 to illustrate how feature metrics and ground truth data can be considered together.

Table 7-3 presents a sample taxonomy and classification for SIFT and FREAK descriptors, which can be used to guide selection of ground truth data and also show several similarities in algorithm capabilities. In this example, the invariance attributes built into the data can be about the same— namely scale and rotation invariance. Note that the compute performance claimed by FREAK is orders of magnitude faster than SIFT, so perhaps the ground truth data should contain a sufficient minimum and maximum number of features per frame for good performance measurements.

Table 7-3. *General Vision Taxonomy for Describing FREAK and SIFT*

Visual Metric Taxonomy Comparison		
Attribute	**SIFT**	**FREAK**
Feature Category Family	Spectra Descriptor	Local Binary Descriptor
Spectra Dimensions	Multivariate	Single Variate
Spectra Value	Orientation Vector	Orientation Vector
	Gradient Magnitude	Bit Vector Of values
	Gradient Direction	Cascade of 4 Saccadic Descriptors
	HOG, Cartesian Bins	
Interest Point	SIFT DOG over 3D Scale Pyramid	Multi-scale AGAST
Storage Format	Spectra Vector	Bit Vector
		Orientation Vector
Data Types	Float	Integer
Descriptor Memory	512 bytes, 128 floats	64 Bytes, 4 16-byte Cascades
Feature Shape	Rectangle	Circular
Feature Search Method	Coarse to Fine Image Pyramid	Sparse at interest points
	Scale Space Image Pyramid	
	Double-scale First Pyramid Level	
	Sparse at Interest Points	
Pattern Pair Sampling	*n.a.*	Foveal Centered Trained Pairs
Pattern Region Size	41x41 Bounding Box	31x31 Bounding Box (may vary)
Distance Function	Euclidean Distance	Hamming Distance
Run-Time Compute	100% (SIFT is the baseline)	.1% of SIFT

(continued)

Table 7-3. (*continued*)

Visual Metric Taxonomy Comparison		
Attribute	**SIFT**	**FREAK**
Feature Density	Sparse	Sparse
Feature Pattern	Rectangular kernel Sample Weighting Pattern	Binary compare pattern
Claimed Robustness	Scale	Scale
	Rotation	Rotation
*Final robustness is a combination of interest point method, descriptor method, and classifier	Noise	Noise
	Affine Distortion	
	Illumination	

Synthetic Feature Alphabets

In this section, we create synthetic ground truth datasets for interest point algorithm analysis. We create alphabets of *synthetic interest points* and *synthetic corner points*. The alphabets are *synthetic*, meaning that each element is designed to perfectly represent chosen binary patterns, including points, lines, contours, and edges.

Various pixel widths or thickness are used for the alphabet characters to measure fine and coarse feature detection. Each pattern is registered at known pixel coordinates on a grid in the images to allow for detection accuracy to be measured. The datasets are designed to enable comparison between human interest point perception and machine vision interest point detectors.

Here is a high-level description of each synthetic alphabet dataset:

- **Synthetic Interest Point Alphabet.** Contains points such as boxes, triangles, circle, half boxes, half triangles, half circles, edges, and contours.

- **Synthetic Corner Point Alphabet.** Contains several types of corners and multi-corners at different pixel thickness.

- **Natural images overlaid with synthetic alphabets**. Contains both black and white versions of the interest points and corners overlaid on natural images.

■ **Note** The complete set of ground truth data is available in Appendix A.

Analysis is provided in Appendix A, which includes running ten detectors against the datasets. The detectors are implemented in OpenCV, including SIFT, SURF, ORB, BRISK, HARRIS, GFFT, FAST9, SIMPLE BLOB, MSER, and STAR. Note that the methods such as SIFT, SURF, and ORB provide both an interest point detector and a feature descriptor implementation. We are only concerned with the interest point detector portion of each method for the analysis, not the feature descriptor.

The idea of using synthetic image alphabets is not new. As shown in Figure 7-2, Rosin[61] devised a synthetic set of gray corner points and corresponding measurement methods for the purpose of quantifying corner properties via attributes such as bluntness or shape of apex, boundary shape of cusps, contrast, orientation, and subtended angle of the corner. However, the synthetic interest point and corner alphabets in this work are developed to address a different set of goals, discussed next.

Goals for the Synthetic Dataset

The goals and expectations for this synthetic dataset are listed in Table 7-4. They center on enabling analysis to determine which synthetic interest points and corners are found, so the exact count and position of each interest point is a key requirement.

Table 7-4. *Goals and Expectations for the Ground Truth Data Examples: Comparison of Human Expectations with Machine Vision Results*

Goals	Approach
Interest point and corner detectors, stress testing	Provide synthetic features easily recognized by a human; measure how well various detectors perform.
Human recognizable synthetic interest point sets	Synthetic features recognized by humans are developed spanning shapes and sizes of edges and line segments, contours and curved lines, and corners and multi-corners.
Grid positioning of interest points	Each interest point will be placed on a regular grid at a known position for detection accuracy checking.
Scale invariance	Synthetic interest points to be created with the same general shape but using different pixel thickness for scale.
Rotation invariance	Interest points will be created, then rotated in subsequent frames.
Noise invariance	Noise will be added to some interest point sets.
Duplicate interest points, known count	Interest points will be created and duplicated in each frame for determining detection and performance.
Hybrid synthetic interest points overlaid on real images	Synthetic interest points on a grid are overlaid onto real images to allow for hybrid testing.
Interest point detectors, determinism and repeatability	Detectors will include SIFT, SURF, ORB, BRISK, HARRIS, GFFT, FAST9, SIMPLE BLOB, MSER, and STAR. By locating synthetic interest points on a grid, we can compute detection counts.

The human visual system does not work like an interest point detector, since detectors can accept features which humans may not recognize. The human visual system discriminates and responds to gradient information [248] in a scale and rotationally invariant manner across the retina, and tends to look for learned features relationships among gradients and color.

Humans learn about features by observations and experience, so learned expectations play a key role interpreting visual features. *People see what they believe and what they are looking for, and may not believe what they see if they are not looking for it.* For example, Figure 7-7 shows examples of machine corner detection; a human would likely not choose all the same corner features. Note that the results are not what a human might expect, and also the algorithm parameters must be tuned to the ground truth data to get the best results.

Accuracy of Feature Detection via Location Grid

The goal of detector accuracy for this synthetic ground truth is addressed by placing synthetic features at a known position on a regular spaced grid, then after detection, the count and position are analyzed. Some of the detectors will find multiple features for a single synthetic interest point or corner. The feature grid size chosen is 14x14 pixels, and the grid extends across the entire image. See Figures 7-9 and 7-10.

Rotational Invariance via Rotated Image Set

For each ground truth set, rotated versions of each image are created in the range 0 to 90 degrees at 10 degree increments.Since the synthetic features are placed on a regularly spaced grid at known positions, the new positions under rotation are easily computed. The detected synthetic features can be counted and analyzed. See Appendix A for results.

Scale Invariance via Thickness and Bounding Box Size

The synthetic corner point features are rendered into the ground truth data with feature edge thickness ranging from 1 to 3 pixels for simulated scale variation. Some of the interest point features, such as boxes, triangles, and circles, are scaled in a bounding box ranging from 1x1 pixels to 10x10 pixels to allow for scale invariance testing.

Noise and Blur Invariance

A set of synthetic alphabets is rendered using Gaussian noise, and another set using salt-and-pepper noise to add distortion and uncertainty to the images. In addirion, by rotating the interest point alphabet at varying angles between 0 and 90 degrees, digital blur is introduced to the synthetic patterns as they are rendered, owing to the anti-aliasing interpolations introduced in the affine transform algorithms.

Repeatabilty

Each ground truth set contains a known count of synthetic features to enable detection rates to be analyzed. To enable measurement of the repeatability of each detector, there are multiple duplicate copies of each interest point feature in each image. A human would expect identical features to be detected in an identical manner; however, results in Appendix A show that some interest point detectors do not behave in a predictable manner, and some are more predictable than others.

As shown in Figure 7-6, detectors do not always find the same identical features. For example, the synthetic alphabets are provided in three versions— black on white, white on black, and light gray on dark gray—for the purpose of testing each detector on the same pattern with different gray levels and polarity. See Appendix A showing the how the detectors provide different results based on the polarity and gray level factors.

Real Image Overlays of Synthetic Features

A set of images composed of synthetic interest points and corners overlayed on top of real images is provided, sort of like markers. Why overlay interest point markers, since the state of the art has moved beyond markers to markerless tracking? The goal is to understand the limitations and behavior of the detectors themselves, so that analyzing their performance in the presence of natural and synthetic features will provide some insight.

Synthetic Interest Point Alphabet

As shown in Figures 7-8 and 7-9, an alphabet of synthetic interest points is defined across a range of pixel resolutions or thicknesses to include the following features:

- POINT / SQUARE, 1–10 PIXELS SIZE

- POINT / TRIANGLE HALF-SQUARE, 3–1 PIXELS SIZE

- CIRCLE, 3–10 PIXELS SIZE

- CIRCLE / HALF-CIRCLE, 3–10 PIXELS SIZE

- CONTOUR, 3–10 PIXELS SIZE

- CONTOUR / HALF-CONTOUR, 3–10 PIXELS SIZE

- CONNECTED EDGES

- DOUBLE CORNER, 3–10 PIXELS SIZE

- CORNER, 3–10 PIXELS SIZE

- EDGE, 3–10 PIXELS SIZE

Figure 7-8. *Portion of the synthetic interest point alphabet: points, edges, edges, and contours. (Top to bottom) White on black, black on white, light gray on dark gray, added salt and pepper noise, added Gaussian noise*

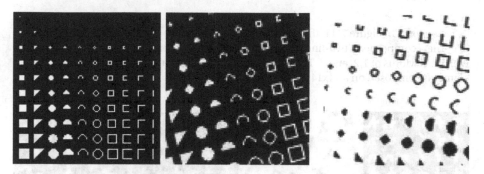

Figure 7-9. *Scaled and rotated examples of the synthetic interest point alphabet. Notice the artifacts introduced by the affine rotation, which distorts the synthetic binary patterns via anti-aliasing and sub-sampling artifacts*

The synthetic interest point alphabet contains 83 unique elements composed on a 14x14 grid, as shown in Figure 7-9. A total of seven rows and seven columns of the complete alphabet can fit inside a 1024x1024 image, yielding a total of 7x7x83=4067 total interest points.

Synthetic Corner Alphabet

The synthetic corner alphabet is shown in Figure 7-10. The alphabet contains the following types of corners and attributes:

- 2-SEGMENT CORNERS, 1,2,3 PIXELS WIDE
- 3-SEGMENT CORNERS, 1,2,3 PIXELS WIDE
- 4-SEGMENT CORNERS, 1,2,3 PIXELS WIDE

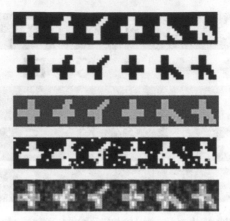

Figure 7-10. *Portion of the synthetic corner alphabet, features include 2-,3-, and 4-segment corners. (Top to bottom) White on black, black on white, light gray on dark gray, added salt and pepper noise, added Gaussian noise*

As shown in Figure 7-11, the corner alphabet contains patterns with multiple types of corners composed of two-line segments, three-line segments, and four-line segments, with pixel widths of 1,2, and 3. The synthetic corner alphabet contains 54 unique elements composed on a 14x14 pixel grid.

Figure 7-11. *Synthetic corner points image portions*

Each 1024x1024 pixel image contains 8x12 complete alphabets composed of 6x9 unique elements each, yielding 6x9x12x8=5184 total corner points per image. The full dataset includes rotated versions of each image from 0 to 90 degrees at 10 degree intervals.

Hybrid Synthetic Overlays on Real Images

We combine the synthetic interest points and corners as overlays with real images to develop a *hybrid ground truth dataset* as a more complex case.

The merging of synthetic interest points over real data will provide new challenges for the interest point algorithms and corner detectors, as well as illustrate how each detector works. Using hybrid synthetic feature overlays on real images is a new approach for ground truth data (as far as the author is aware), and the benefits are not obvious outside of curiosity. One reason the synthetic overlay approach was chosen here is to fill the gap in the literature and research, since synthetic features overlays are not normally used. See Figure 7-12.

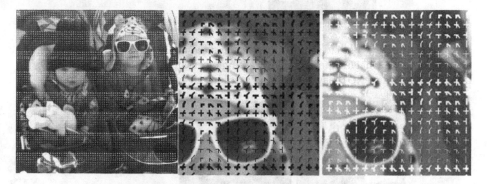

Figure 7-12. *Synthetic interest points combined with real images, used for stress testing interest point and corner detectors with unusual pixel patterns*

The hybrid synthetic and real ground truth datasets are designed with the following goals:

- Separate ground truth sets for interest points and corners, using the full synthetic alphabets overlaid on real images, to provide a range of pixel detail surrounding each interest point and corner.

- Display known positions and counts of interest points on a 14x14 grid.

- Provide color and gray scale images of the same data.

- Provide rotated versions of the same data 0 to 90 degrees at 10 degree intervals.

Method for Creating the Overlays

The alphabet can be used as a *binary mask* of 8-bit pixel values of black 0x00 and white 0xff for composing the image overlays. The following Boolean masking example is performed using Mathematica code ImageMultiply and ImageAd*d* operators.

ImageMultiply []

ImageMultiply is used to get the negatives, and then followed by ImageAdd to get the positives. Note that in other image processing tool systems, a Boolean ImageAND, ImageOR, and ImageNOT may be provided as alternatives.

ImageAdd []

Summary

We have surveyed manual and automated approaches to creating ground truth data, have identified some best practices and guidelines, have applied the robustness criteria and vision taxonomy developed in Chapter 5, and have worked through examples to create a ground truth dataset for evaluation of human perceptions compared to machine vision methods for keypoint detectors.

Here are some final thoughts and key questions for perparing ground truth data:

- **Appropriateness:** How appropriate is the ground truth dataset for the analysis and intended application? Are the use-cases and application goals built into the ground truth data and model? Is the dataset under-fitted or over-fitted to the algorithms and use-cases?

- **Public vs. proprietary:** Proprietary ground truth data is a barrier to independent evaluation of metrics and algorithms. It must be possible for interested parties to duplicate the metrics produced by various types of algorithms so they can be compared against the ground truth data. Open rating systems may be preferred, if they exist for the problem domain. But there are credibility and legal hurdles for open-sourcing any proprietary ground truth data.

- **Privacy and legal concerns:** There are privacy concerns for individuals in any images chosen to be used; images of people should not be used without their permission, and prohibitions against the taking of pictures at restricted locations should be observed. Legal concerns are very real.

- **Real data vs. synthetic data:** In some cases it is possible to use computer graphics and animations to create synthetic ground datasets. Synthetic datasets should be considered especially when privacy and legal concerns are involved, as well as be viewed as a way of gaining more control over the data itself.

CHAPTER 8

■ ■ ■

Vision Pipelines and Optimizations

"More speed, less haste . . . "

—*Treebeard,* Lord of the Rings

This chapter explores some hypothetical computer vision pipeline designs to understand HW/SW design alternatives and optimizations. Instead of looking at isolated computer vision algorithms, this chapter ties together many concepts into complete vision pipelines. Vision pipelines are sketched out for a few example applications to illustrate the use of different methods. Example applications include object recognition using shape and color for automobiles, face detection and emotion detection using local features, image classification using global features, and augmented reality. The examples have been chosen to illustrate the use of different families of feature description metrics within the *Vision Metrics Taxonomy* presented in Chapter 5. Alternative optimizations at each stage of the vision pipeline are explored. For example, we consider which vision algorithms run better on a CPU versus a GPU, and discuss how data transfer time between compute units and memory affects performance.

■ **Note**   The hypothetical examples in this chapter are sometimes sketchy, not intended to be complete. Rather, the intention is to explore design alternatives. Design choices are made in the examples *for illustration only;* other, equally valid design choices could be made to build working systems. The reader is encouraged to analyze the examples to find weaknesses and alternatives. If the reader can improve the examples, we have succeeded.

This chapter addresses the following major topics, in this order:

1. General design concepts for optimization across the SOC (CPU, GPU, memory).

2. Four hypothetical vision pipeline designs using different descriptor methods.

3. Overview of SW optimization resources and specific optimization techniques.

Stages, Operations, and Resources

A computer vision solution can be implemented into a pipeline of *stages*, as shown in Figure 8-1. In a pipeline, both parallel and sequential operations take place simultaneously. By using all available compute resources in the optimal manner, performance can be maximized for speed, power, and memory efficiency.

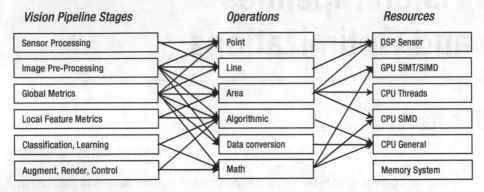

Figure 8-1. *Hypothetical assignment of vision pipeline stages to operations and to compute resources. Depending on the actual resource capabilities and optimization targets for power and performance, the assignments will vary*

Optimization approaches vary by system. For example, a low-power system for a mobile phone may not have a rich CPU SIMD instruction set, and the GPU may have a very limited thread count and low memory bandwidth, unsuitable to generic GPGPU processing for vision pipelines. However, a larger compute device, such as a rack-mounted compute server, may have several CPUs and GPUs, and each CPU and GPU will have powerful SIMD instructions and high memory bandwidth.

Table 8-1 provides more details on possible assignment of operations to resources based on data types and processor capabilities. For example, in the sensor processing stage, point line and area operations dominate the workload, as sensor data is assembled into pixels and corrections are applied. Most sensor processors are based on a digital signal processor (DSP) with wide SIMD instruction words, and the DSP may also contain a fixed-function geometric correction unit or warp unit for correcting optics problems like lens distortion. The Sensor DSP and the GPU listed in Table 8-1 typically contain a dedicated texture sampler unit, which is capable of rapid pixel interpolation, geometric warps, and affine and perspective transforms. If code is straight line with lots of branching and not much parallel operations, the CPU is the best choice.

Table 8-1. *Hypothetical Assignment of Basic Operations to Compute Resources Guided by Data Type and Parallelism (see also Zinner [495])*

Operations	Hypothetical Resources and Data Types					
	DSP uint16 int16 WarpUnit	GPU SIMT/SIMD uint16/32 int16/32 float/double TextureUnit	CPU Threads uint16/32 int16/32 float/double	CPU SIMD uint16/32 int16/32 float/double	CPU General uint16/32 int16/32 float/double	Memory System DMA
Point	x	x		x		
Line	x	x		x		
Area	x	x	x (tiles)	x		
Algorithmic Branching					x	
General Math					x	
Data Copy & Conversions						x (DMA preferred)

As illustrated in Table 8-1, the data type and data layout normally guides the selection of the best compute resource for a given task, along with the type of parallelism in the algorithm and data. Also, the programing language is chosen based on the parallelism, such as using OpenCL vs. C++. For example, a CPU may support float and double data types, but if the underlying code is SIMT and SIMD parallel oriented, calling for many concurrent thread-parallel kernel operations, then a GPU with a high thread count may be a better choice than a single CPU. However, running a language like OpenCL on multiple CPUs may provide performance as good as a smaller GPU; for performance information, see reference[544] and vendor information on OpenCL compilers. See also the section later in this chapter, "SIMD, SIMT, and SPMD Fundamentals."

For an excellent discussion of how to optimize fundamental image processing operations across different compute units and memory, see the PfeLib work by Zinner et al.[495], which provides a deep dive into the types of optimizations that can be made based on data types and intelligent memory usage.

To make the assignments from vision processing stages to operations and compute resources concrete, we look at specific vision pipelines examples later in this chapter.

Compute Resource Budgets

Prior to implementing a vision pipeline, a reasonable attempt should be made to count the cost in terms of the compute platform resources available, and determine if the application is matched to the resources. For example, a system intended for a military battlefield may place a priority on compute speed and accuracy, while an application for a mobile device will prioritize power in terms of battery life and make tradeoffs with performance and accuracy.

Since most computer vision research is concerned with breaking ground in handling relatively narrow and well-defined problems, there is limited research available to guide a general engineering discussion on vision pipeline analysis and optimizations. Instead, we follow a line of thinking that starts with the hardware resources themselves, and we discuss performance, power, memory, and I/O requirements, with some references to the literature for parallel programming and other code-optimization methods. Future research into automated tools to measure algorithm intensity, such as the number of integer and float operations, the bit precision of data types, and the number of memory transfers for each algorithm in terms of read/write, would be welcomed by engineers for vision pipeline analysis and optimizations.

As shown in Figure 8-2, the main elements of a computer system are composed of I/O, compute, and memory.

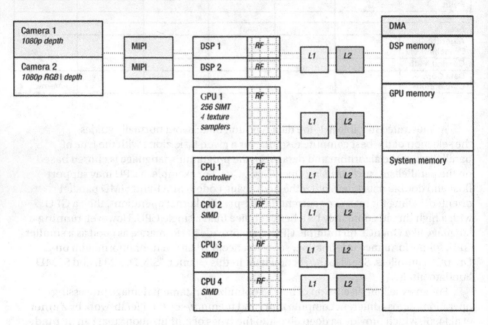

Figure 8-2. *Hypothetical computer system, highlighting compute elements in the form of a DSP, GPU, four CPU cores, DMA, and memory architecture using L1 and L2 cache and register files RF within each compute unit*

We assume suitable high bandwidth I/O busses and cache lines interconnecting the various compute units to memory; in this case, we call out the MIPI camera interface in particular, which connects directly to the DSP in our hypothetical SOC. In the case of a simple computer vision system of the near future, we assume that the price, performance, and power curves continue in the right direction to enable a *system-on-a-chip* (SOC) sufficient for most computer vision applications to be built at a low price point, approaching throw-away computing cost—similar in price to any small portable electronic gadget. This would thereby enable low-power and high-performance ubiquitous vision applications without resorting to special-purpose hardware accelerators built for any specific computer vision algorithms.

Here is a summary description of the SOC components shown in Figure 8-2:

- **Two 1080p cameras**, one for RGB and the other for a self-contained depth camera, such as a TOF sensor (as discussed in Chapter 1).

- **One small low-power controller CPU** with a reduced instruction set and no floating point, used for handling simple things like the keyboard, accelerometer updates, servicing interrupts from the DSP, and other periodic tasks, such as network interrupt handlers.

- **Three full SIMD capable CPUs** with floating point, used for heavy compute, typically thread parallel algorithms such as tiling, but also for SIMD parallel algorithms.

- **A GPU** capable of running ➤ 256 threads with full integer and floating point, and four texture samplers. A wide range of area algorithms map well to the GPU, but the programming model is SIMT kernels such as compute shaders for DirectX and OpenGL, or OpenCL.

- **A DSP** with a limited instruction set and VLIW processing capabilities well suited to pixel processing and sensor processing in general.

- **A DMA unit for fast memory transfers;** although obvious, DMA is a simple and effective method to increase memory bandwidth and reduce power.

Compute Units, ALUs, and Accelerators

There are several types of compute units in a typical system, including CPUs, GPUs, DSPs, and special-purpose hardware accelerators such as cryptography units, texture samplers, and DMA engines. Each ALU has a different instruction set tuned to the intended use, so understanding each compute unit's ALU instruction set is very helpful.

Generally speaking, computer architecture has not advanced to the point of providing any standard vision pipeline methods or hardware accelerators. That's because there are so many algorithm refinements for computer vision emerging; choosing to implement any vision accelerators in silicon is an obsolescence risk. Also, creating computer vision hardware accelerators is difficult, since applications must be portable. So developers typically choose high-level language implementations that are good enough and portable, with minimal dependencies on special purpose hardware or API's.

Instead, reliance on general-purpose languages like C++ and optimizing the software is a good path to follow to start, as is leveraging existing pixel-processing acceleration methods in a GPU as needed, such as pixel shaders and texture samplers. The standard C++ language path offers flexibility to change and portability across platforms, without relying on any vendor-specific hardware acceleration features.

In the example vision pipelines developed in this section, we make two basic assumptions. First, the DSP is dedicated to sensor processing and light image pre-processing to load-balance the system. Second, the CPUs and the GPUs are used

317

downstream for subsequent sections of the vision pipeline, so the choice of CPU vs. GPU depends on the algorithm used.

Since the compute units with programmable ALUs are typically where all the tools and attention for developers are focused, we dedicate some attention to programming acceleration alternatives later in this chapter in the "Vision Algorithm Optimizations and Tuning" section; there is also a survey of selected optimization resources and software building blocks.

In the hypothetical system shown in Figure 8-2, the compute units include general-purpose CPUs, a GPU intended primarily for graphics and media acceleration and some GPGPU acceleration, and a DSP for sensor processing. Each compute unit is programmable and contains a general-purpose ALU with a tuned instruction set. For example, a CPU contains all necessary instructions for general programming, and may also contain SIMD instructions (discussed later in this chapter). A GPU contains transcendental instructions such as square root, arctangent, and related instructions to accelerate graphics processing. The DSP likewise has an instruction set tuned for sensor processing, likely a VLIW instruction set.

Hardware accelerators are usually built for operations that are common, such as a geometric correction unit for sensor processing in the DSP and texture samplers for warping surface patches in the GPU. There are no standards yet for computer vision, and new algorithm refinements are being developed constantly, so there is little incentive to add any dedicated silicon for computer vision accelerators, except for embedded and special-purpose systems. Instead, finding creative methods of using existing accelerators may prove beneficial.

Later in this chapter we discuss methods for optimizing software on various compute units, taking advantage of the strengths and intended use of each ALU and instruction set.

Power Use

It is difficult to quantify the amount of power used for a particular algorithm on an SOC or a single compute device without very detailed power analysis; likely simulation is the best method. Typically, systems engineers developing vision pipelines for an SOC do not have accurate methods of measuring power, except crude means such as running the actual finished application and measuring wall power or battery drain.

The question of power is sometimes related to which compute device is used, such as CPU vs. GPU, since each device has a different gate count and clock rate, therefore is burning power at a different rate. Since silicon architects for both GPU and CPU designs are striving to deliver the most *performance* per *watt* per *square millimeter*, (and we assume that each set of silicon architects is equally efficient), there is no clear winner in the CPU vs. GPU power/performance race. The search to save power by using the GPU vs. the CPU might not even be worth the effort compared to other places to look, such as data organization and memory architecture.

One approach for making the power and performance tradeoff in the case of SIMD and SIMT parallel code is to use a language such as OpenCL, which supports running the same code on either a CPU or a GPU. The performance and power would then need to be measured on each compute device to quantify actual power and performance; there's more discussion on this topic later, in the "Vision Algorithm Optimizations and Tuning" section.

For detailed performance analysis using the same OpenCL code running on a specific CPU vs. a GPU, as well as clusters, see the excellent research by the National Center for Super Computing Applications[544]. Also, see the technical computing resources provided by major OpenCL vendors, such as INTEL, NVIDIA, and AMD, for details on their OpenCL compilers running the same code across the CPU vs. GPU. Sometimes the results are surprising, especially for multi-core CPU systems vs. smaller GPUs.

In general, the compute portion of the vision pipeline is not where the power is burned anyway; most power is burned in the memory subsystem and the I/O fabric, where high data bandwidth is required to keep the compute pipeline elements full and moving along. In fact, all the register files, caches, I/O busses, and main memory consume the lion's share of power and lots of silicon real estate. So memory use and bandwidth are high-value targets to attack in any attempt to reduce power. The fewer the memory copies, the higher the cache hit rates; the more reuse of the same data in local register files, the better.

Memory Use

Memory is the most important resource to manage as far as power and performance are concerned. Most of the attention on developing a vision pipeline is with the algorithms and processing flow, which is challenging enough. However, vision applications are highly demanding of the memory system. The size of the images alone is not so great, but when we consider the frame rates and number of times a pixel is read or written for kernel operations through the vision pipeline, the memory transfer bandwidth activity becomes clearer. The memory system is complex, consisting of local register files next to each compute unit, caches, I/O fabric interconnects, and system memory. We look at several memory issues in this section, including:

- Pixel resolution, bit precision, and total image size
- Memory transfer bandwidth in the vision pipeline
- Image formats, including gray scale and color spaces
- Feature descriptor size and type
- Accuracy required for matching and localization
- Feature descriptor database size

To explore memory usage, we go into some detail on a local interest point and feature extraction scenario, assuming that we locate interest points first, filter the interest points against some criteria to select a smaller set, calculate descriptors around the chosen interest points, and then match features against a database.

A reasonable first estimate is that between a lower bound and upper bound of 0.05% to 1 percent of the pixels in an image can generate decent interest points. Of course, this depends entirely on: (1) the complexity of the image texture, and (2) the interest point method used. For example, an image with rich texture and high contrast will generate more interest points than an image of a far away mountain surrounded by clouds with little texture and contrast. Also, interest point detector methods yield different results—for example, the FAST corner method may detect more corners than a SIFT scale invariant DoG feature, see Appendix A.

Descriptor size may be an important variable, see Table 8-2. A 640x480 image will contain 307,200 pixels. We estimate that the upper bound of 1 percent, or 3,072 pixels, may have decent interests points; and we assume that the lower bound of 0.05 percent is 153. We provide a second estimate that interest points may be further filtered to sort out the best ones for a given application. So if we assume perhaps only as few as 33 percent of the interest points are actually kept, then we can say that between 153*.33 and 3,072*.33 interest points are good candidates for feature description. This estimate varies widely out of bounds, depending of course on the image texture, interest point method used, and interest point filtering criteria. Assuming a feature descriptor size is 256 bytes, the total descriptor size per frame is 3072x256x.33 = 259,523 bytes maximum—that's not extreme. However, when we consider the feature match stage, the feature descriptor count and memory size will be an issue, since each extracted feature must be matched against each trained feature set in the database.

Table 8-2. *Descriptor Bytes per Frame (1% Interest Points), adapted from [141]*

Descriptor	Size in bytes	480p NTSC	1080p HD	2160p 4kUHD	4320p 8kUHD
Resolution		640 x 480	1920 x 1080	3840 × 2160	7680 × 4320
Pixels		307200	2073600	8294400	33177600
BRIEF	32	98304	663552	2654208	10616832
ORB	32	98304	663552	2654208	10616832
BRISK	64	196608	1327104	5308416	21233664
FREAK (4 cascades)	64	196608	1327104	5308416	21233664
SURF	64	196608	1327104	5308416	21233664
SIFT	128	393216	2654208	10616832	42467328
LIOP	144	442368	2985984	11943936	47775744
MROGH	192	589824	3981312	15925248	63700992
MRRID	256	786432	5308416	21233664	84934656
HOG (64x128 block)	3780	n.a.	n.a.	n.a.	n.a.

In general, local binary descriptors offer the advantage of a low memory footprint. For example, Table 8-2 provides the byte count of several descriptors for comparison, as described in Miksik and Mikolajczyk [141]. The data is annotated here to add the descriptor working memory size in bytes per frame for various resolutions.

In Table 8-2, image frame resolutions are in row 1, pixel count per frame is in row 2, and typical descriptor sizes in bytes are in subsequent rows. Total bytes for selected descriptors are in column 1, and the remaining columns show total descriptor size per frame assuming an estimated 1 percent of the pixels in each frame are used to calculate an interest point and descriptor. In practice, we estimate that 1 percent is an upper-bound estimate for a descriptor count per frame and 0.05 percent is a lower-bound estimate. Note that descriptor sizes in bytes do vary from those in the table, based on design optimizations.

Memory bandwidth is often a hidden cost, and often ignored until the very end of the optimization cycle, since developing the algorithms is usually challenging enough without also worrying about the memory access patterns and memory traffic. Table 8-2 includes a summary of several memory variables for various image frame sizes and feature descriptor sizes. For example, using the 1080p image pixel count in row 2 as a base, we see that an RGB image with 16 bits per color channel will consume:

$$2,073,600_{pixels} *3_{channels/RGB} *2_{bytes/pixel} = 12,441,600 \text{ bytes / frame}$$

And if we include the need to keep a gray scale channel I around, computed from the RGB, the total size for RGBI increases to:

$$2,073,600_{pixels} *4_{channels/RGBI} *2_{bytes/pixel} = 16,588,800 \text{ bytes / frame}$$

If we then assume 30 frames per second and two RGB cameras for depth processing + the I channel, the memory bandwidth required to move the complete 4-channel RGBI image pair out of the DSP is nearly 1GB / second:

$$12,441,600_{pixels} *4_{channels/RGBI} *_{bytes/pixel} *30_{fps} *2_{stereo} = 995,328,000_{mb/s}$$

So we assume in this example a baseline memory bandwidth of about ~1GB/second just to move the image pair downstream from the ISP. We are ignoring the ISP memory read/write requirements for sensor processing for now, assuming that clever DSP memory caching, register file design, and loop-unrolling methods in assembler can reduce the memory bandwidth.

Typically, memory coming from a register file in a compute unit transfers in a single clock cycle; memory coming from various cache layers can take maybe tens of clock cycles; and memory coming from system memory can take hundreds of clock cycles. During memory transfers, the ALU in the CPU or GPU may be sitting idle, waiting on memory.

Memory bandwidth is spread across the fast register files next to the ALU processors, and through the memory caches and even system memory, so actual memory bandwidth is quite complex to analyze. Even though some memory bandwidth numbers are provided here, it is only to illustrate the activity.

And the memory bandwidth only increases downstream from the DSP, since each image frame will be read, and possibly rewritten, several times during image pre-processing, then also read again during interest point generation and feature extraction. For example, if we assume only one image pre-processing operation using 5x5 kernels on the I channel, each I pixel is read another 25 times, hopefully from memory cache lines and fast registers.

This memory traffic is not all coming from slow-system memory, and it is mostly occurring inside the faster-memory cache system and faster register files until there is a cache miss or reload of the fast-register files. Then, performance drops by an order of magnitude waiting for the buffer fetch and register reloading. If we add a FAST9 interest point detector on the *I* channel, each pixel is read another 81 times (9x9), maybe from memory cache lines or registers. And if we add a FREAK feature descriptor over maybe 0.05 percent of the detected interest points, we add 41x41 pixel reads per descriptor to get the region (plus 45*2 reads for point-pair comparisons within the 41x41 region), hopefully from memory cache lines or registers.

Often the image will be processed in a variety of formats, such as image pre-processing the RGB colors to enhance the image, and conversion to gray scale intensity *I* for computing interest points and feature descriptors. The color conversions to and from RGB are a hidden memory cost that requires data copy operations and temporary storage for the color conversion, which is often done in floating point for best accuracy. So, several more GB/second of memory bandwidth can be consumed for color conversions. With all the memory activity, there may be cache evictions of all or part of the required images into a slower system memory, degrading into nonlinear performance.

Memory size of the descriptor, therefore, is a consideration throughout the vision pipeline. First, we consider when the features are extracted; and second, we look at when the features are matched and retrieved from the feature database. In many cases, the size of the feature database is by far the critical issue in the area of memory, since the total size of all the descriptors to match against affects the static memory storage size, memory bandwidth, and pattern match rate. Reducing the feature space into a quickly searchable format during classification and training is often of paramount importance. Besides the optimized classification methods discussed in Chapter 4, the data organization problems may be primarily in the areas of standard computer science searching, sorting, and data structures; some discussion and references were provided in Chapter 4.

When we look at the feature database or training set, memory size can be the dominant issue to contend with. Should the entire feature database be kept on a cloud server for matching? Or should the entire feature database be kept on the local device? Should a method of caching portions of the feature database on the local device from the server be used? All of the above methods are currently employed in real systems.

In summary, memory, caches, and register files exceed the silicon area of the ALU processors in the compute units by a large margin. Memory bandwidth across the SOC fabric through the vision pipeline is key to power and performance, demanding fast memory architecture and memory cache arrangement, and careful software design. Memory storage size alone is not the entire picture, though, since each byte needs to be moved around between compute units. So, careful consideration of memory footprint and memory bandwidth is critical for anything but small applications.

Often, performance and power can be dramatically improved by careful attention to memory issues alone. Later in the chapter we cover several design methods to help reduce memory bandwidth and increase memory performance, such as locking pages in memory, pipelining code, loop unrolling, and SIMD methods. Future research into minimizing memory traffic in a vision pipeline is a worthwhile field.

I/O Performance

We lump I/O topics together here as a general performance issue, including data bandwidth on the SOC I/O fabric between compute units, image input from the camera, and feature descriptor matching database traffic to a storage device. We touched on I/O issues above the discussion on memory, since pixel data is moved between various compute devices along the vision pipeline on I/O busses. One of the major I/O considerations is feature descriptor data moving out of the database at feature match time, so using smaller descriptors and optimizing the feature space using effective machine learning and classification methods is valuable.

Another type of I/O to consider is the camera input itself, which is typically accomplished via the standard MIPI interface. However, any bus or I/O fabric can be used, such as USB. If the vision pipeline design includes a complete HW/SW system design rather than software only on a standard SOC, special attention to HW I/O subsystem design for the camera and possibly special fast busses for image memory transfers to and from a HW-assisted database may be worthwhile. When considering power, I/O fabric silicon area and power exceed the area and power for the ALU processors by a large margin.

The Vision Pipeline Examples

In this section we look at four hypothetical examples of vision pipelines. Each is chosen to illustrate separate descriptor families from the Vision Metrics Taxonomy presented in Chapter 5, including global methods such as histograms and color matching, local feature methods such as FAST interest points combined with FREAK descriptors, basis space methods such as Fourier descriptors, and shape-based methods using morphology and whole object shape metrics. The examples are broken down into *stages, operations,* and *resources,* as shown in Figure 8-1, for the following applications:

- **Automobile recognition,** using shape and color

- **Face recognition,** using sparse local features

- **Image classification,** using global features

- **Augmented reality,** using depth information and tracking

None of these examples includes classification, training, and machine learning details, which are outside the scope of this book (machine learning references are provided in Chapter 4). A simple database storing the feature descriptors is assumed to be adequate for this discussion, since the focus here is on the image pre-processing and feature description stages. After working through the examples and exploring alternative types of compute resource assignments, such as GPU vs. CPU, this chapter finishes with a discussion on optimization resources and techniques for each type of compute resource.

Automobile Recognition

Here we devised a vision pipeline to recognize objects such as automobiles or machine parts by using *polygon shape descriptors* and *accurate color matching*. For example, polygon shape metrics can be used to measure the length and width of a car, while color matching can be used to measure paint color. In some cases, such as custom car paint jobs, color alone is not sufficient for identification.

For this automobile example, the main design challenges include segmentation of automobiles from the roadway, matching of paint color, and measurement of automobile size and shape. The overall system includes an RGB-D camera system, accurate color and illumination models, and several feature descriptors used in concert. See Figure 8-3. We work through this example in some detail as a way of exploring the challenges and possible solutions for a complete vision pipeline design of this type.

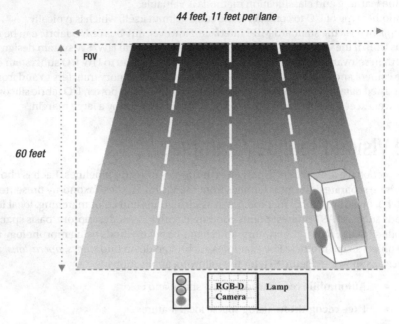

Figure 8-3. *Setting for an automobile identification application using a shape-based and color-based vision pipeline. The RGB and D cameras are mounted above the road surface, looking directly down*

We define the system with the following requirements:

- 1080p RGB color video (1920x1080 pixels) at 120 fps, horizontally mounted to provide highest resolution in length, 12 bits per color, 65 degree FOV.

- 1080p stereo depth camera with 8 bits Z resolution at 120 fps, 65 degree FOV.

- Image FOV covering 44 feet in width and 60 feet in length over four traffic lanes of oncoming traffic, enough for about three normal car lengths in each lane when traffic is stopped.

- Speed limit of 25 mph, which equals ~37 feet per second.

- Camera mounted next to overhead stoplight, with a street lamp for night illumination.

- Embedded PC with 4 CPU cores having SIMD instruction sets, one GPU, 8GB memory, 80GB disk; assumes high-end PC equivalent performance (not specified for brevity).

- Identification of automobiles in real time to determine make and model; also count of occurrences of each, with time stamp and confidence score.

- Automobile ground truth training dataset provided by major manufacturers to include geometry, and accurate color samples of all body colors used for stock models; custom colors and after-market colors not possible to identify.

- Average car sizes ranging from 5 to 6 feet wide and 12 to 16 feet long.

- Accuracy of 99 percent or better.

- Simplified robustness criteria to include noise, illumination, and motion blur.

Segmenting the Automobiles

To segment the automobiles from the roadway surface, a stereo depth camera operating at 1080p 120fps (frames per second) is used, which makes isolating each automobile from the roadway simple using depth. To make this work, a method for calibrating the depth camera to the baseline road surface is developed, allowing automobiles to be identified as being higher than the roadway surface. We sketch out the depth calibration method here for illustration.

Spherical depth differences are observed across the depth map, mostly affecting the edges of the FOV. To correct for the spherical field distortion, each image is rectified using a suitable calibrated depth function (to be determined on-site and analytically), then each horizontal line is processed, taking into consideration the curvilinear true depth distance, which is greater at the edges, to set the depth equal across each line.

Since the speed limit is 25 mph, or 37 feet per second, imaging at 120 FPS yields maximum motion blur of about 0.3 feet, or 4 inches per frame. Since the length of a pixel is determined to be 0.37 inches, as shown in Figure 8-4, the ability to compute car length from pixels is accurate within about 4 inches/0.37 inches = 11 pixels, or about 3 percent of a 12-foot-long car at 25 mph including motion blur. However, motion blur compensation can be applied during image pre-processing to each RGB and depth image to effectively reduce the motion blur further; several methods exist based on using convolution or compensating over multiple sequential images [305,492].

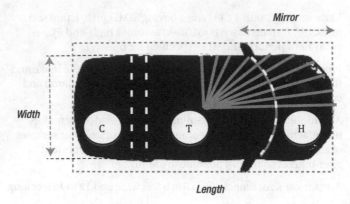

Figure 8-4. *Features used for automobile identification*

Matching the Paint Color

We assume that it is possible to identify a vehicle using paint color alone in many cases, since each manufacturer uses proprietary colors, therefore accurate colorimetry can be employed. For matching paint color, 12 bits per color channel should provide adequate resolution, which is determined in the color match stage using the CIECAM02 model and the *Jch* color space [253]. This requires development of several calibrated device models of the camera with the scene under different illumination conditions, such as full sunlight at different times of day, cloud cover, low light conditions in early morning and at dusk, and nighttime using the illuminator lamp mounted above traffic along with the camera and stop light.

The key to colorimetric accuracy is the device models' accounting for various lighting conditions. A light sensor to measure color temperature, along with the knowledge of time of day and season of the year, is used to select the correct device models for proper illumination for times of day and seasons of the year. However, dirty cars present problems for color matching; for now we ignore this detail (also custom paint jobs are a problem). In some cases, the color descriptor may not be useful or reliable; in other cases, color alone may be sufficient to identify the automobile. See the discussion of color management in Chapter 2.

Measuring the Automobile Size and Shape

For automobile size and shape, the best measurements are taken looking directly down on the car to reduce perspective distortion. As shown in Figure 8-4, the car is segmented into C (cargo), T (top), and H (hood) regions using depth information from the stereo camera, in combination with a polygon shape segmentation of the auto shape. To compute shape, some weighted combination of RGB and D images into a single image will be used, based on best results during testing. We assume the camera is mounted in the best possible location centered above all lanes, but that some perspective distortion will exist at the far ends of the FOV. We also assume that a geometric correction is applied to rectify the images into Cartesian alignment. Assuming errors introduced by the geometric corrections to rectify the FOV are negligible, the following approximate dimensional precision is expected for length and width, using the minimum car size of 5' x 12' as an example:

$$FOV\ Pixel\ Width: \quad 1080_{pixels}\ /\ (44'*12")_{inches} = each\ pixel\ is\ {\sim}0.49\ inches\ wide$$
$$FOV\ Pixel\ Length: \quad 1920_{pixels}\ /\ (60'*12")_{inches} = each\ pixel\ is\ {\sim}0.37\ inches\ long$$
$$Automobile\ Width: \quad (5'*12")\ /\ .49 = {\sim}122\ pixels$$
$$Automobile\ Length: \quad (12'*12")\ /\ .37 = {\sim}389\ pixels$$

This example uses the following shape features:

- Bounding box containing all features; width and length are used

- Centroid computed in the middle of the automobile region

- Separate width computed from the shortest diameter passing through the centroid to the perimeter

- Mirror feature measured as the distance from the front of the car; mirror locations are the smallest and largest perimeter width points within the bounding box

- Shape segmented into three regions using depth; color is measured in each region: cargo compartment (C), top (T), and hood (H)

- Fourier descriptor of the perimeter shape computed by measuring the line segments from centroid to perimeter points at intervals of 5 degrees

Feature Descriptors

Several feature descriptors are used together for identification, and the confidence of the automobile identification is based on a combined score from all descriptors. The key feature descriptors to be extracted are as follows:

- **Automobile shape factors:** Depth-based segmentation of each automobile above the roadway is used for the coarse shape outline. Some morphological processing follows to clean up the edges and remove noise. For each segmented automobile, object shape factors are computed for area, perimeter, centroid, bounding box, and Fourier descriptors of perimeter shape. The bounding box measures overall width and height, the Fourier descriptor measures the roundness and shape factors; some automobiles are more boxy, some are more curvy. (See Figure 6-32, Figure 2-18, and Chapter 6 for more information on shape descriptors. See Chapter 1 for more information on depth sensors.) In addition, the distance of the mirrors from the front of the automobile is computed; mirrors are located at width extrema around the object perimeter, corresponding to the width of the bounding box.

- **Automobile region segmentation:** Further segmentation uses a few individual regions of the automobile based on depth, namely the hood, roof, and trunk. A simple histogram is created to gather the depth statistical moments, a clustering algorithm such as K-means is performed to form three major clusters of depth: the roof will be highest, hood and trunk will be next highest, windows will be in between (top region is missing for convertibles, not covered here). The pixel areas of the hood, top, trunk, and windows are used as a descriptor.

- **Automobile color:** The predominant colors of the segmented hood, roof, and trunk regions are used as a color descriptor. The colors are processed in the *Jch* color space, which is part of the CIECAM system yielding high accuracy. The dominant color information is extracted from the color samples and normalized against the illumination model. In the event of multiple paint colors, separate color normalization occurs for each. (See Chapter 3 for more information on colorimetry.)

Calibration, Set-up, and Ground Truth Data

Several key assumptions are made regarding scene set-up, camera calibration, and other corrections; we summarize them here:

- **Roadway depth surface:** Depth camera is calibrated to the road surface as a reference to segment autos above the road surface; a baseline depth map with only the road is calibrated as a reference and used for real-time segmentation.

- **Device models:** Models for each car are created from manufacturer's information, with accurate body shape geometry and color for each make and model. Cars with custom paint confuse this approach; however, the shape descriptor and the car region depth segmentation provide a failsafe option that may be enough to give a good match—only testing will tell for sure.

- **Illumination models:** Models are created for various conditions, such as morning light, daylight, and evening light, for sunny and cloudy days; illumination models are selected based on time of day and year and weather conditions for best matching.

- **Geometric model for correction:** Models of the entire FOV for both the RGB and depth camera are devised, to be applied at each new frame to rectify the image.

Pipeline Stages and Operations

Assuming the system is fully calibrated in advance, the basic real-time processing flow for the complete pipeline is shown in Figure 8-5, divided into three primary stages of operations. Note that the complete pipeline includes an image pre-processing stage to align the image in the FOV and segment features, a feature description stage to compute shape and color descriptors, and a correspondence stage for feature matching to develop the final automobile label composed of a weighted combination of shape and color features. We assume that a separate database table for each feature in some standard database is fine.

No attempt is made to create an optimized classifier or matching stage here; instead, we assume, without proving or testing, that a brute-force search using a standard database through a few thousand makes and models of automobile objects works fine for the ALPHA version.

Note in Figure 8-5 (bottom right) that each auto is tracked from frame to frame, we do not define the tracking method here.

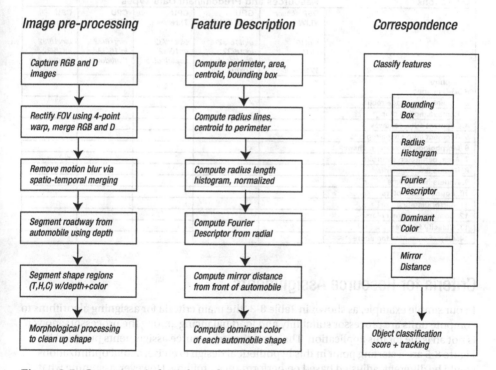

Figure 8-5. *Operations in hypothetical vision pipeline for automobile identification using polygon shape features and color*

Operations and Compute Resources

For each operation in the pipeline stages, we now explore possible mappings to the available compute resources. First, we review the major resources available in our example system, which contains 8GB of fast memory, we assume sufficient free space to map and lock the entire database in memory to avoid paging. Our system contains four CPU cores, each with SIMD instruction sets, and a GPU capable of running 128 SIMT threads simultaneously with 128GB/s memory bandwidth to shared memory for the GPU and CPU, considered powerful enough. Let's assume that, overall, the compute and memory resources are fine for our application and no special memory optimizations need to be considered. Next, we look at the coarse-grain optimizations to assign operations to compute resources. Table 8-3 provides an evaluation of possible resource assignments.

Table 8-3. *Assignment of Operations to Compute Resources*

Operations	Resources and Predominant Data Types				
	DSP *sensor* VLIW uint16 int16 WarpUnit	GPU SIMT/SIMD uint16/32 int16/32 float/double TextureUnit	CPU Threads uint16/32 int16/32 float/double	CPU SIMD uint16/32 int16/32 float/double	CPU General uint16/32 int16/32 float/double
1. Capture RGB-D images	x				
2. 4-point warp image rectify		x		x	
3. Remove motion blur		x			
4. Segment auto, roadway			x		
5. Segment auto shape regions			x		
6. Morphology to clean up shapes		x			
7. Area, perimeter, centroid					x
8. Radius line segments					x
9. Radius histograms			x		
10. Fourier descriptors			x		
11. Mirror distance			x		
12. Dominant region colors			x		
13. Classify features			x		
14. Object classification score					x

Criteria for Resource Assignments

In our simple example, as shown in Table 8-3, the main criteria for assigning algorithms to compute units are processor suitability and load balancing among the processors; power is not an issue for this application. The operation to resource assignments provided in Figure 8-5 are a starting point in this hypothetical design exercise; actual optimizations would be different, adjusted based on performance profiling. However, assuming what is obvious about the memory access patterns used for each algorithm, we can make a good guess at resource assignments based on memory access patterns. In a second-order analysis, we could also look at load balancing across the pipeline to maximize parallel uses of compute units; however, this requires actual performance measurements.

Here we will tentatively assign the tasks from Table 8-3 to resources. If we look at memory access patterns, using the GPU for the sequential tasks 2 and 3 makes sense, since we can map the images into GPU memory space first and then follow with the three sequential operations using the GPU. The GPU has a texture sampler to which we assign task 2, the geometric corrections using the four-point warp. Some DSPs or camera sensor processors also have a texture sampler capable of geometric corrections, but not in our example. In addition to geometric corrections, motion blur is a good candidate for the GPU as well, which can be implemented as an area operation efficiently in a shader. For higher-end GPUs, there may even be hardware acceleration for motion blur compensation in the media section.

Later in the pipeline, after the image has been segmented in tasks 4 and 5, the morphology stage in task 6 can be performed rapidly using a GPU shader; however, the cost of moving the image to and from the GPU for the morphology may actually be slower than performing the morphology on the CPU, so performance analysis is required for making the final design decision regarding CPU vs. GPU implementation.

In the case of stages 7 to 11, shown in Table 8-3, the algorithm for area, perimeter, centroid, and other measurements span a nonlocalized data access pattern. For example, perimeter tracing follows the edge of the car. So we will make one pass using a single CPU through the image to track the perimeter and compute the area, centroid, and bounding box for each automobile. Then, we assign each bounding box as an image tile to a separate CPU thread for computation of the remaining measurements: radial line segment length, Fourier descriptor, and mirror distance. Each bounding box is then assigned to a separate CPU thread for computation of the colorimetry of each region, including cargo, roof, and hood, as shown in Table 8-3. Each CPU thread uses C++ for the color conversions and attempts to use compiler flags to force SIMD instruction optimizations.

Tracking the automobile from frame to frame is possible using shape and color features; however, we do not develop the tracking algorithm here. For correspondence and matching, we rely on a generic database from a third party, running in a separate thread on a CPU that is executing in parallel with the earlier stages of the pipeline. We assume that the database can split its own work into parallel threads. However, an optimization phase later could rewrite and create a better database and classifier, using parallel threads to match feature descriptors.

Face, Emotion, and Age Recognition

In this example, we design a face, emotion, and age recognition pipeline that uses local feature descriptors and interest points. Face recognition is concerned with identifying the unique face of a unique person, while face detection is concerned with determining only where a face is located and interesting characteristics such as emotion, age, and gender. Our example is for face detection, and finding the emotions and age of the subject.

For simplicity, this example uses mugshots of single faces taken with a stationary camera for biometric identification to access a secure area. Using mugshots simplifies the example considerably, since there is no requirement to pick out faces in a crowd from many angles and distances. Key design challenges include finding a reliable interest point and feature descriptor method to identify the key facial landmarks, determining emotion and age, and modeling the landmarks in a normalized, relative coordinate system to allow for distance ratios and angles to be computed.

Excellent facial recognition systems for biometric identification have been deployed for several decades that use a wide range of methods, achieving accuracies of close to 100 percent. In this exercise, no attempt is made to prove performance or accuracy. We define the system with the following requirements:

- 1080p RGB color video (1920x1080 pixels) at 30 fps, horizontally mounted to provide highest resolution in length, 12 bits per color, 65 degree FOV, 30 FPS

- Image FOV covers 2 feet in height and 1.5 feet in width, enough for a complete head and top of the shoulder

- Background is a white drop screen for ease of segmentation

- Illumination is positioned in front of and slightly above the subject, to cast faint shadows across the entire face that highlight corners around eyes, lips, and nose

- For each face, the system identifies the following landmarks:

  - Eyes: two eye corners and one center of eye

  - Dominant eye color: in CIECAM02 JCH color coordinates

  - Dominant face color: in CIECAM02 JCH color coordinates

  - Eyebrows: two eyebrow endpoints and one center of eyebrow arc, used for determining emotions

  - Nose: one point on nose tip and two widest points by nostrils, used for determining emotions and gender

  - Lips: two endpoints of lips, two center ridges on upper lip

  - Cheeks: one point for each cheek center

  - Chin: one point, bottom point of chin, may be unreliable due to facial hair

  - Top of head: one point; may be unreliable due to hairstyle

  - Unique facial markings: these could include birthmarks, moles, or scars, and must fall within a bounding box computed around the face region

- A FREAK feature is computed at each detected landmark on the original image

- Accuracy is 99 percent or better

- Simplified robustness criteria to include scale only

Note that emotion, age, and gender can all be estimated from selected relative distances and proportional ratios of facial features, and we assume that an expert in human face anatomy provides the correct positions and ratios to use for a real system. See Figure 8-6.

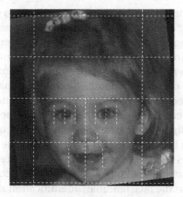 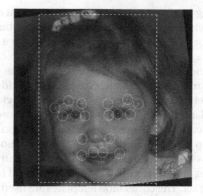

Figure 8-6. *(Left) Proportional ratios based on a bounding box of the head and face regions as guidelines to predict the location of facial landmarks. (Right) Annotated image with detected facial landmark positions and relative angles and distances measured between landmarks. The relative measurements are used to determine emotion, age, and gender*

The set of features computed for this example system includes:

1. Relative positions of facial landmarks such as eyes, eyebrows, nose, and mouth

2. Relative proportions and ratios between landmarks to determine age, sex, and emotion

3. FREAK descriptor at each landmark

4. Eye color

Calibration and Ground Truth Data

The calibration is simple: a white backdrop is used in back of the subject, who stands about 4 feet away from the camera, enabling a shot of the head and upper shoulders. (We discuss the operations used to segment the head from the background region later in this section.) Given that we have a 1080p image, we allocate the 1920 pixels to the vertical direction and the 1080 pixels to the horizontal.

Assuming the cameraman is good enough to center the head in the image so that the head occupies about 50 percent of the horizontal pixels, and about 50 percent of the vertical pixels, we have pixel resolution for the head of ~540 pixels horizontal and ~960 pixels vertical, which is good enough for our application and corresponds to the ratio of head height to width. Since we assume that average head height is about 9 inches and width as 6 inches across for male and female adults, using our assumptions for a four-foot distance from the camera, we have plenty of pixel accuracy and resolution:

$$9" / (1920_{pixels} * .5) = 0.009" \ vertical \ pixel \ size$$

$$6" / (1080_{pixels} * .5) = 0.01" \ horizontal \ pixel \ size$$

The ground truth data consists of: (1) mugshots of known people, and (2) a set of canonical eye landmark features in the form of correlation templates used to assist in locating face landmarks (a sparse codebook of correlation temlpates). There are two sets of correlation templates: one for *fine features* based on a position found using a Hessian detector, and one for *coarse features* based on a position found using a steerable filter based detector (the fine and coarse detectors are described in more detail later in this example).

Since facial features like eyes and lips are very similar among people, the canonical landmark feature correlation templates provide only rough identification of landmarks and their location. Several templates are provided covering a range of ages and genders for all landmarks, such as eye corners, eyebrow corners, eyebrow peaks, nose corners, nose bottom, lip corners, and lip center region shapes. For sake of brevity, we do not develop the ground truth dataset for correlation templates here, but we assume the process is accomplished using synthetic features created by warping or changing real features and testing them against several real human faces to arrive at the best canonical feature set. The correlation templates are used in the face landmark identification stage, discussed later.

Interest Point Position Prediction

To find the facial landmarks, such as eyes, nose, and mouth, this example application is simplified by using mugshots, making the position of facial features predictable and enabling intelligent search for each feature at the predicted locations. Rather than resort to scientific studies of head sizes and shapes, for this example we use basic proportional assumptions from human anatomy (used for centuries by artists) to predict facial feature locations and enable search for facial features at predicted locations. Facial feature ratios differ primarily by age, gender, and race; for example, typical adult male ratios are shown in Table 8-4.

Table 8-4. *Basic Approximate Face and Head Feature Proportions*

Head height	head width X 1.25
Head width	head height X .75
Face height	head height X .8
Face width	head height X .8
Eye position	eye center located 30% in from left/right edges, 50% from top
Eye length	head width X 1.25
Eye spacing	head width X .5
Nose position	25% higher than lip corners
Nose length	head height X .25
Lip corners	about eye center x, about 15% higher than chin y
Mouth/lip width	head width X .07

■ **Note** The information in Table 8-4 is synthesized for illustration purposes from elementary artists' materials and is not guaranteed to be accurate.

The most basic coordinates to establish are the bounding box for the head. From the bounding box, other landmark facial feature positions can be predicted.

Segmenting the Head and Face Using the Bounding Box

As stated earlier, the mugshots are taken from a distance of about 4 feet against a white drop background, allowing simple segmentation of the head. We use thresholding on simple color intensity as *RGBI-I,* where I = (R=G + B) / 3 and the white drop background is identified as the highest intensity.

The segmented head and shoulder region is used to create a bounding box of the head and face, discussed next. (Note: wild hairstyles will require another method, perhaps based on relative sizes and positions of facial features compared to head shape and proportions.) After segmenting the bounding box for the head, we proceed to segment the facial region and then find each landmark. The rough size of the bounding box for head is computed in two steps:

1. Find the top and left, right sides of the head— Top_{xy}, $Left_{xy}$, $Right_{xy}$—which we assume can be directly found by making a pass through the image line by line and recording the rows and columns where the background is segmented to meet the foreground of head, to establish the coordinates. All leftmost and rightmost coordinates for each line can be saved in a vector, and sorted to find the median values to use as $Right_x$ / $Left_x$ coordinates. We compute head width as:

    $$H_w = Right_x - Left_x$$

2. Find the chin to assist in computing the head height H_h. The chin is found by first predicting the location of the chin, then performing edge detection and some filtering around the predicted location to establish the chin feature, which we assume is simple to find based on gradient magnitude of the chin perimeter. The chin location prediction is made by using the head top coordinates Top_{xy} and the normal anatomical ratio of the head height H_h to head width H_w, which is known to be about 0.75. Since we know both Top_{xy} and H_w from step 1, we can predict the *x* and *y* coordinates of the chin as follows:

    $$Chin_y = (.25 * H_w) + Top_y$$
    $$Chin_x = Top_x$$

Actually, hair style makes the segmentation of the head difficult in some cases, since the hair may be piled high on top or extend widely on the sides and cover the ears. However, we can either iterate the chin detection method a few times to find the best chin, or else assume that our segmentation method will solve this problem somehow via a hair filter module, so we move on with this example for the sake of brevity.

To locate the chin position, a horizontal edge detection mask is used around the predicted location, since the chin is predominantly a horizontal edge. The coordinates of the connected horizontal edge maxima are filtered to find the lowest y coordinates of the horizontal edge set, and the median of the lowest x/y coordinates is used as the initial guess at the chin center location. Later, when the eye positions are known, the chin x position can be sanity-checked with the position of the midpoint between the eyes and recomputed, if needed. See Figure 8-7.

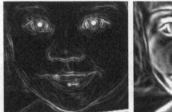

Figure 8-7. *Location of facial landmarks. (Left) Facial landmarks enhanced using largest eigenvalues of Hessian tensor [493] in FeatureJ[1]; note the fine edges that provide extra detail. (Center) Template-based feature detector using steerable filters with additional filtering along the lines of the Canny detector [400] to provide coarse detail. (Right) Steerable filter pattern used to compute center image. Both images are enhanced using contrast window remapping to highlight the edges*

The head bounding box, containing the face, is assumed to be:

$$BoundingBoxTopLeftx = Leftx$$

$$BoundingBoxTopLefty = Topy$$

$$BoundingBoxBottomRightx = Rightx$$

$$BoundingBoxBottomRighty = Chiny$$

Face Landmark Identification and Compute Features

Now that the head bounding box is computed, the locations of the face landmark feature set can be predicted using the basic proportional estimates from Table 8-4. A search is made around each predicted location to find the features; see Figure 8-6. For example, the eye center locations are ~30 percent in from the sides and about 50 percent down from the top of the head.

---

[1]FeatureJ plug-in for ImageJ used to generate eigenvalues of Hessian (FeatureJ developed by Erik Meijering).

In our system we use an image pyramid with two levels for feature searching, a coarse-level search down-sampled by four times, and a fine-level search at full resolution to relocate the interest points, compute the feature descriptors, and take the measurements. The coarse-to-fine approach allows for wide variation in the relative size of the head to account for mild scale invariance owing to distance from the camera and/or differences in head size owing to age.

We do not add a step here to rotate the head orthogonal to the Cartesian coordinates in case the head is tilted; however, this could be done easily. For example, an iterative procedure can be used to minimize the width of the orthogonal bounding box, using several rotations of the image taken every 2 degrees from -10 to +10 degrees. The bounding box is computed for each rotation, and the smallest bounding box width is taken to find the angle used to correct the image for head tilt.

In addition, we do not add a step here to compute the surface texture of the skin, useful for age detection to find wrinkles, which is easily accomplished by segmenting several skin regions, such as forehead, eye corners, and the region around mouth, and computing the surface texture (wrinkles) using an edge or texture metric.

The landmark detection steps include feature detection, feature description, and computing relative measurements of the positions and angles between landmarks, as follows:

1. Compute interest points: Prior to searching for the facial features, interest point detectors are used to compute likely candidate positions around predicted locations. Here we use a combination of two detectors: (1) the largest eigenvalue of the Hessian tensor [493], and (2) steerable filters [388] processed with an edge detection filter criteria similar to the Canny method [400], as illustrated in Figure 8-7. Both the Hessian and the Canny-like edge detectors images are followed by contrast windowing to enhance the edge detail. The Hessian style and Canny-style images are used together to vote on the actual location of best interest points during the correlation stage next.

2. Compute landmark positions using correlation: The final position of each facial landmark feature is determined using a canonical set of correlation templates, described earlier, including eye corners, eyebrow corners, eyebrow peaks, nose corners, nose bottom, lip corners, and lip center region shapes. The predicted location to start the correlation search is the average position of both detectors from step 1: (1) The Hessian approach provides fine-feature details, (2) while the steerable filter approach provides coarse-feature details. Testing will determine if correlation alone is sufficient without needing interest points from step 1.

3. Describe landmarks using FREAK descriptors: For each landmark location found in step 2, we compute a FREAK descriptor. SIFT may work just as well.

4. Measure dominant eye color using CIECAM02 JCH: We use a super-pixel method [257,258] to segment out the regions of color around the center of the eye, and make a histogram of the colors of the super-pixel cells. The black pupil and the white of the eye should cluster as peaks in the histogram, and the dominant color of the eye should cluster in the histogram also. Even multi-colored eyes will be recognized using our approach using histogram correspondence.

5. Compute relative positions and angles between landmarks: In step 2 above, correlation was used to find the location of each feature (to sub-pixel accuracy if desired [468]). As illustrated in Figure 8-6, we use the landmark positions as the basis for measuring the relative distances of several features, such as:

    a. Eye distance, center to center, useful for age and gender

    b. Eye size, corner to corner

    c. Eyebrow angle, end to center, useful for emotion

    d. Eyebrow to eye angle, ends to center positions, useful for emotion

    e. Eyebrow distance to eye center, useful for emotion

    f. Lip or mouth width

    g. Center lip ridges angle with lip corners, useful for emotion

Pipeline Stages and Operations

The pipeline stages and operations are shown in Figure 8-8. For correspondence, we assume a separate database table for each feature. We are not interested in creating an optimized classifier to speed up pattern matching; brute-force searching is fine.

Image pre-processing *Feature Description* *Correspondence*

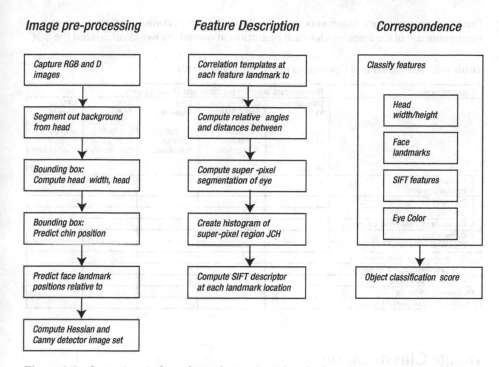

Figure 8-8. *Operations in hypothetical vision pipeline for face, emotion, and age detection using local features*

Operations and Compute Resources

For this example, there is mostly straight-line code best suited for the CPU. Following the data access patterns as a guide, the bounding box, relative distances and ratios, FREAK descriptors and correspondence are good candidates for the CPU. In some cases, separate CPU threads can be used, such as computing the FREAK descriptors at each landmark in separate threads (threads are likely overkill for this simple application). We assume feature matching using a standard database. Our application is assumed to have plenty of time to wait for correspondence.

Some operations are suited for a GPU; for example the area operations, including the Hessian and Canny-like interest point detectors. These methods could be combined and optimized into a single shader program using a single common data read loop and combined processing loop, which produce output into two images, one for each detector. In addition, we assume that the GPU provides an API to a fast, HW accelerated correlation block matcher in the media section, so we take advantage of the HW accelerated correlation.

Criteria for Resource Assignments

In this example, performance is not a problem, so the criteria for using computer resources are relaxed. In fact, all the code could be written to run in a single thread on a single CPU, and the performance would likely be fast enough with our target system assumptions.

However, the resource assignments shown in Table 8-5 are intended to illustrate reasonable use of the resources for each operation to spread the workload around the SOC.

Table 8-5. *Assignments of Operations to Compute Resources*

Operations	Resources and Predominant Data Types				
	DSP *sensor* VLIW uint16 int16 WarpUnit	GPU SIMT/SIMD uint16/32 int16/32 float/double TextureUnit	CPU Threads uint16/32 int16/32 float/double	CPU SIMD uint16/32 int16/32 float/double	CPU General uint16/32 int16/32 float/double
1. Capture RGB-D images	x				
2. Segment background from head					x
3. Bounding box					x
4. Compute Hessian and Canny		x			
5. Correlation		x			
6. Compute relative angles, distance			x		
7. Super-pixel eye segmentation					x
8. Eye segment color histogram					x
9. FREAK descriptors			x		
10. Correspondence					x
11. Object classification score					x

Image Classification

For our next example, we design a simple image classification system intended for mobile phone use, with the goal of identifying the main objects in the camera's field of view, such as buildings, automobiles, and people. For image classification applications, the entire image is of interest, rather than specific local features. The user will have a simple app which allows them to point the camera at an object, and wave the camera from side to side to establish the stereo baseline for MVS depth sensing, discussed later. A wide range of global metrics can be applied (as discussed in Chapter 3), computed over the entire image, such as texture, histograms of color or intensity, and methods for connected component labeling. Also, local features (as discussed in Chapter 6) can be applied to describe key parts of the images. This hypothetical application uses both global and local features.

We define the system with the following requirements:

- 1080p RGB color video (1920x1080 pixels) at 30 fps, 12 bits per color, 65 degree FOV, 30 FPS

- Image FOV covers infinite focus view from a mobile phone camera

- Unlimited lighting conditions (bad and good)

- Accuracy of 90 percent or better

- Simplified robustness criteria, including scale, perspective, occlusion

- For each image, the system computes the following features:

  - *Global RGBI histogram,* in RGB-I color space

  - *GPS coordinates,* since the phone has a GPS

  - *Camera pose via MVS depth sensing,* using the accelerometer data for geometric rectification to an orthogonal FOV plane (the user is asked to wave the camera while pointed at the subject, the camera pose vector is computed from the accelerometer data and relative to the main objects in the FOV using ICP)

  - *SIFT features,* ideally between 20 and 30 features stored for each image

  - *Depth map via monocular dense depth sensing,* used to segment out objects in the FOV, depth range target 0.3 meters to 30 meters, accuracy within 1 percent at 1 meter, and within 10 percent at 30 meters

  - *Scene labeling and pixel labeling,* based on attributes of segmented regions, including RGB-I color and LBP texture

Scene recognition is a well-researched field, and several grand challenge competitions are held annually to find methods for increased accuracy using established ground truth datasets, as shown in Appendix B. The best accuracy achieved for various categories of images in the challenges ranges from 50 to over 90 percent. In this exercise, no attempt is made to prove performance or accuracy.

Segmenting Images and Feature Descriptors

For this hypothetical vision pipeline, several methods for segmenting the scene into objects will be used together, instead of relying on a single method, as follows:

1. **Dense segmentation, scene parsing, and object labeling:** A depth map generated using monocular MVS is used to segment common items in the scene, including the ground or floor, sky or ceiling, left and right walls, background, and subjects in the scene. To compute monocular depth from the mobile phone device, the user is prompted by the application to move the camera from left to right over a range of arm's length covering 3 feet or so, to create a series of wide baseline stereo images for computing depth using MVS methods (as discussed in Chapter 1). MVS provides a dense depth map. Even though MVS computation is compute-intensive, this is not a problem, since our application does not require continuous real-time depth map generation – just a single depth map; 3 to 4 seconds to acquire the baseline images and generate the depth map is assumed possible for our hypothetical mobile device.

2. **Color segmentation and component labeling using super-pixels:** The color segmentation using super-pixels should correspond roughly with portions of the depth segmentation.

3. **LBP region segmentation:** This method is fairly fast to compute and compact to represent, as discussed in Chapter 6.

4. **Fused segmentation:** The depth, color, and LBP segmentation regions are combined using Boolean masks and morphology and some logic into a fused segmentation. The method uses an iterative loop to minimize the differences between color, depth, and LBP segmentation methods into a new fused segmentation map. The fused segmentation map is one of the global image descriptors.

5. **Shape features for each segmented region:** basic shape features, such as area and centroid, are computed for each fused segmentation region. Relative distance and angle between region centroids is also computed into a composite descriptor.

In this hypothetical example, we use several feature descriptor methods together for additional robustness and invariance, and some pre-processing, summarized as follows:

1. SIFT interest points across the entire image are used as additional clues. We follow the SIFT method exactly, since SIFT is known to recognize larger objects using as few as three or four SIFT features [161]. However, we expect to limit the SIFT feature count to 20 or 30 strong candidate features per scene, based on training results.

2. In addition, since we have an accelerometer and GPS sensor data on the mobile phone, we can use sensor data as hints for identifying objects based on location and camera pose alone, for example assuming a server exists to look up the GPS coordinates of landmarks in an area.

3. Since illumination invariance is required, we perform RGBI contrast remapping in an attempt to normalize contrast and color prior to the SIFT feature computations, color histograms, and LBP computations. We assume a statistical method for computing the best intensity remapping limits is used to spread out the total range of color to mitigate dark and oversaturated images, based on ground truth data testing, but we do not take time to develop the algorithm here; however, some discussion on candidate algorithms is provided in Chapter 2. For example, computing SIFT descriptors on dark images may not provide sufficient edge gradient information to compute a good SIFT descriptor, since SIFT requires gradients. Oversaturated images will have washed-out color, preventing good color histograms.

4.   The fused segmentation combines the best of all the color, LBP, and depth segmentation methods, minimizing the segmentation differences by fusing all segmentations into a fused segmentation map. LBP is used also, which is less sensitive to both low light and oversaturated conditions, providing some balance.

Again, in the spirit of a hypothetical exercise, we do not take time here to develop the algorithm beyond the basic descriptions given above.

Pipeline Stages and Operations

The pipeline stages are shown in Figure 8-9. They include an image pre-processing stage primarily to correct image contrast, compute depth maps and segmentation maps. The feature description stage computes the RGBI color histograms, SIFT features, a fused segmentation map combining the best of depth, color, and LBP methods, and then labels the pixels as connected components. For correspondence, we assume a separate database table for each feature, using brute-force search; no optimization attempted.

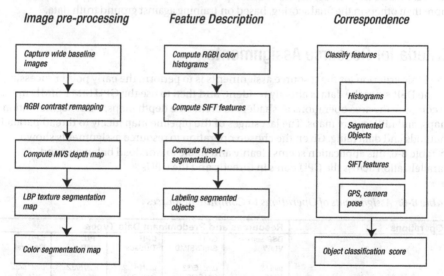

Figure 8-9. *Operations in hypothetical image classification pipeline using global features*

Mapping Operations to Resources

We assume that the DSP provides an API for contrast remapping, and since the DSP is already processing all the pixels from the sensor anyway and the pixel data is already there, contrast remapping is a good match for the DSP.

The MVS depth map computations follow a data pattern of line and area operations. We use the GPU for the heavy-lifting portions of the MVS algorithm, like left/right image pair pattern matching. Our algorithm follows the basic stereo algorithms, as discussed in Chapter 1. The stereo baseline is estimated initially from the accelerometer, then some bundle adjustment iterations over the baseline image set are used to improve the baseline estimates. We assume that the MVS stereo workload is the heaviest in this pipeline and consumes most of the GPU for a second or two. A dense depth map is produced in the end to use for depth segmentation.

The color segmentation is performed on RGBI components using a super-pixel method [257,258]. A histogram of the color components is also computed in RGBI for each superpixel cell. The LBP texture computation is a good match for the GPU since it is an area operation amenable to shader programming style. So, it is possible to combine the color segmentation and the LBP texture segmentation into the same shader to leverage data sharing in register files and avoid data swapping and data copies.

The SIFT feature description can be assigned to CPU threads, and the data can be tiled and divided among the CPU threads for parallel feature description. Likewise, the fused segmentation can be assigned to CPU threads and the data tiled also. Note that tiled data can include overlapping boundary regions or buffers, see later Figure 8-12 for an illustration of overlapped data tiling. Labeling can also be assigned to parallel CPU threads in a similar manner, using tiled data regions. Finally, we assume a brute-force matching stage using database tables for each descriptor to develop the final score, and we weight some features more than others in the final scoring, based on training against ground truth data.

Criteria for Resource Assignments

The basic criterion for the resource assignments is to perform the early point processing on the DSP, since the data is already resident, and then to use the GPU SIMT SIMD model to compute the area operations as shaders to create the depth maps, color segmentation maps, and LBP texture maps. The last stages of the pipeline map nicely to thread parallel methods and data tiling. Given the chosen operation to resource assignments shown in Table 8-6, this application seems cleanly amenable to workload balancing and parallelization across the CPU cores in threads and the GPU.

Table 8-6. *Assignments of Operations to Compute Resources*

Operations	Resources and Predominant Data Types				
	DSP *sensor* VLIW	GPU SIMT/SIMD	CPU Threads	CPU SIMD	CPU General
	uint16 int16 WarpUnit	uint16/32 int16/32 float/double TextureUnit	uint16/32 int16/32 float/double	uint16/32 int16/32 float/double	uint16/32 int16/32 float/double
1. Capture RGB wide baseline images	x				
2. RGBI contrast remapping	x				
3. MVS depth map		x			
4. LBP texture segmentation map		x			
5. Color segmentation map		x			
6. RGBI color histograms			x		
7. SIFT features			x		
8. Fused segmentation			x		
9. Labeling segmented objects			x		
10. Correspondence			x		
11. Object classification score					x

Augmented Reality

In this fourth example, we design an augmented reality application for equipment maintenance using a wearable display device such as glasses or goggles and wearable cameras. The complete system consists of a portable, wearable device with camera and display connected to a server via wireless. Processing is distributed between the wearable device and the server. (**Note:** this example is especially high level and leaves out a lot of detail, since the actual system would be complex to design, train and test.)

The server system contains all the CAD models of the machine and provides on-demand graphics models or renderings of any machine part from any viewpoint. The wearable cameras track the eye gaze and the position of the machine. The wearable display allows a service technician to look at a machine and view augmented reality overlays on the display, illustrating how to service the machine. As the user looks at a given machine, the augmented reality features identify the machine parts and provide overlays and animations for assisting in troubleshooting and repair. The system uses a combination of RGB images as textures on 3D depth surfaces and a database of 3D CAD models of the machine and all the component machine parts.

The system will have the following requirements:

- 1080p RGB color video camera (1920x1080 pixels) at 30 fps, 12 bits per color, 65 degree FOV, 30 FPS

- 1080p stereo depth camera with 8 bits Z resolution at 60 fps, 65 degree FOV; all stereo processing performed in silicon in the camera ASIC with a depth map as output

- 480p near infra-red camera pointed at eyes of technician, used for gaze detection; the near-infrared camera images better in the low-light environment around the head-mounted display

- 1080p wearable RGB display

- A wearable PC to drive the cameras and display, descriptor generation, and wireless communications with the server; the system is battery powered for mobile use with an 8-hour battery life

- A server to contain the CAD models of the machines and parts; each part will have associated descriptors pre-computed into the data base; the server can provide either graphics models or complete renderings to the wearable device via wireless

- Server to contain ground truth data consisting of feature descriptors computed on CAD model renderings of each part + normalized 3D coordinates for each descriptor for machine parts

- Simplified robustness criteria include perspective, scale, and rotation

Calibration and Ground Truth Data

We assume that the RGB camera and the stereo camera system are calibrated with correct optics to precisely image the same FOV, since the RGB camera and 3D depth map must correspond at each pixel location to enable 2D features to be accurately associated with the corresponding 3D depth location. However, the eye gaze camera will require some independent calibration, and we assume a simple calibration application is developed to learn the technician's eye positions by using the stereo and RGB cameras to locate a feature in the FOV, and then overlay an eye gaze vector on a monitor to confirm the eye gaze vector accuracy. We do not develop the calibration process here.

However, the ground truth data takes some time to develop and train, and requires experts in repair and design of the machine to work together during training. The ground truth data includes feature sets for each part, consisting of 2D SIFT features along corners, edges, and other locations such as knobs. To create the SIFT features, first a set of graphics renderings of each CAD part model is made from representative viewpoints the technician is likely to see, and then the 2D SIFT features are computed on the graphics renderings, and the geometry of the model is used to create relative 3D coordinates for each SIFT feature for correspondence.

The 2D SIFT feature locations are recorded in the database along with relative 3D coordinates, and associated into objects using suitable constraints such as angles and relative distances, see Figure 8-10. An expert selects a minimum set of features for each part during training—primarily strongest features from corners and edges of surfaces. The relative angles and distances in three dimensions between the 2D SIFT features are recorded in the database to provide for perspective, scale, and rotation invariance. The 3D coordinates for all the parts are normalized to the size of the machine. In addition, the dominant color and texture of each part surface is computed from the renderings and stored as texture and color features. This system would require considerable training and testing.

Feature and Object Description

In actual use in the field, the RGB camera is used to find the 2D SIFT, LBP and color features, and the stereo camera is used to create the depth map. Since the RGB image and depth map are pixel-aligned, each feature has 3D coordinates taken from the depth map, which means that a 3D coordinate can be assigned to a 2D SIFT feature location. The 3D angles and 3D distances between 2D SIFT feature locations are computed as constraints, and the combined LBP, color and 2D SIFT features with 3D location constraints are stored as SIFT vertex features and sent to the server for correspondence. See Figure 8-10 for an illustration of the layout of the SIFT vertex descriptors and parts objects. Note that the 3D coordinate is associated with several descriptors, including SIFT, LBP texture, ands RGB color, similar to the way a 3D vertex is represented in computer graphics by 3D location, color, and texture. During training, several SIFT vertex descriptors are created from various views of the parts, each view associated by 3D coordinates in the database, allowing for simplified searching and matching based on 3D coordinates along with the features.

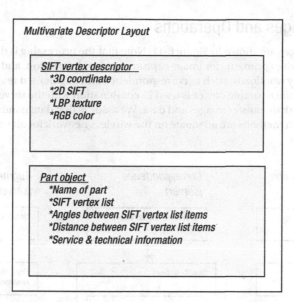

Figure 8-10. *SIFT vertex descriptor is similar to a computer graphics vertex using 3D location, color, and texture. The SIFT vertex descriptor contains the 2D SIFT descriptor from the RGB camera, the 3D coordinate of the 2D SIFT descriptor generated from the depth camera, the RGB color at the SIFT vertex, and the LBP texture at the SIFT vertex. The Part object contains a list of SIFT vertex descriptors, along with relative angles and distances between each 3D coordinate in the SIFT vertex list*

Overlays and Tracking

In the server, SIFT vertex descriptors in the scene are compared against the database to find parts object. The 3D coordinates, angles, and distances of each feature are normalized relative to the size of the machine prior to searching. As shown in Figure 8-10, the SIFT features are composed at a 3D coordinate into a SIFT vertex descriptor, with an associated 2D SIFT feature, LBP texture, and color. The SIFT vertex descriptors are associated into part objects, which contain the list of vertex coordinates describing each part, along with the relative angles and distances between SIFT vertex features.

Assuming that the machine part objects can be defined using a small set of SIFT vertex features, sizes and distance can be determined in real time, and the relative 3D information such as size and position of each part and the whole machine can be continually computed. Using 3D coordinates of recognized parts and features, augmented reality renderings can be displayed in the head-mounted display, highlighting part locations and using overlaying animations illustrating the parts to remove, as well as the path for the hand to follow in the repair process.

The near infrared camera tracks the eyes of the technician to create a 3D gaze vector onto the scene. The gaze vector can be used for augmented reality "help" overlays in the head-mounted display, allowing for gaze-directed zoom or information, with more detailed renderings and overlay information displayed for the parts the technician is looking at.

Pipeline Stages and Operations

The pipeline stages are shown in Figure 8-11. Note that the processing is divided between the wearable device (primarily for image capture, feature description, and display), and a server for heavy workloads, such as correspondence and augmented reality renderings. In this example, the wearable device is used in combination with the server, relying on a wireless network to transfer images and data. We assume that data bandwidth and data compression methods are adequate on the wireless network for all necessary data communications.

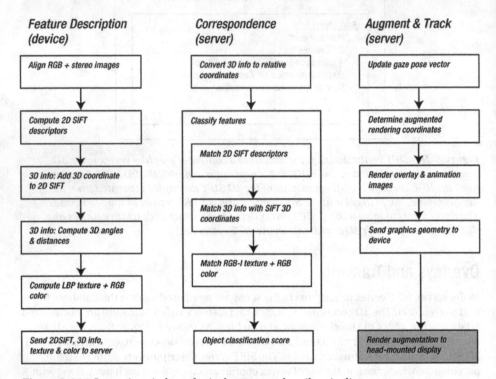

Figure 8-11. Operations in hypothetical augmented reailty pipeline

Mapping Operations to Resources

We make minimal use of the GPU for GPGPU processing and assume the server has many CPUs available, and we use the GPU for graphics rendering at the end of the pipeline. Most of the operations map well into separate CPU threads using data tiling. Note that a server commonly has many high-power and fast CPUs, so using CPU threads is a good match. See Table 8-7.

Table 8-7. *Assignments of Operations to Compute Resources*

Operations	Resources and Predominant Data Types				
	DSP *sensor* VLIW uint16 int16 WarpUnit	GPU SIMT/SIMD uint16/32 int16/32 float/double TextureUnit	CPU Threads uint16/32 int16/32 float/double	CPU SIMD uint16/32 int16/32 float/double	CPU General uint16/32 int16/32 float/double
1. Capture RGB & stereo images	Device				
2. Align RGB and stereo images		Device			
5. Compute 2D SIFT			Device		
3. Compute LBP texture			Device		
4. Compute color			Device		
5. Compute 2D SIFT			Device		
6. Compute 3D angles/distances			Device		
7. Normalize 3D coordinates					Server
8. Match 2D SIFT descriptors			Server		
9. Match SIFT vertex coordinates			Server		
10. Match SIFT vertex color & LBP			Server		
11. Object classification score					Server
12. Update gaze pose vector					Server
13. Render overlay & animation images		Server			
14. Display overlays & animations		Device *GFX pipe			

Criteria for Resource Assignments

On the mobile device, the depth map is computed in silicon on the depth camera. We use the GPU to perform the RGB and depth map alignment using the texture sampler, then perform SIFT computations on the CPU, since the SIFT computations must be done first to have the vertex to anchor and compute the multivariate descriptor information. We continue and follow data locality and perform the LBP and color computations for each 2D SIFT point in separate CPU threads using data tiling and overlapped regions. See later Figure 8-12 for an illustration of overlapped data tiling.

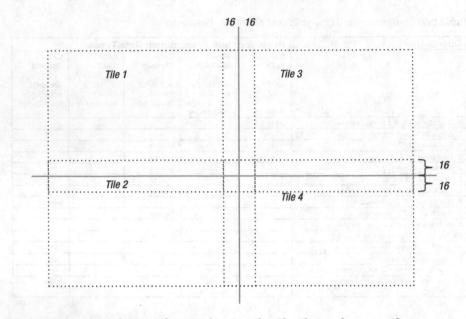

Figure 8-12. *Data tiling into four overlapping tiles. The tiles overlap a specific amount, 16 pixels in this case, allowing for area operations such as convolutions to read, not write, into the overlapped region for assembling convolution kernel data from adjacent regions. However, each thread only writes into the nonoverlapped region within its tile. Each tile can be assigned to a separate thread or CPU core for processing*

On the server, we have assigned the CAD database and most of the heavy portions of the workload, including feature matching and database access, since the server is expected to have large storage and memory capacity and many CPUs available. In addition, we wish to preserve battery life and minimize heat on the mobile device, so the server is preferred for the majority of this workload.

Acceleration Alternatives

There are a variety of common acceleration methods that can be applied to the vision pipeline, including attention to memory management, coarse-grained parallelism using threads, data-level parallelism using SIMD and SIMT methods, multi-core parallelism, advanced CPU and GPU assembler language instructions, and hardware accelerators.

There are two fundamental approaches for acceleration:

1. Follow the data

2. Follow the algorithm

Optimizing algorithms for compute devices, such as SIMD instruction sets or SIMT GPGPU methods, also referred to as *stream processing*, is oftentimes the obvious choice designers consider. However, optimizing for data flow and data residency can yield better results. For example, bouncing data back and forth between compute resources and data formats is not a good idea; it eats up time and power consumed by the copy and format conversion operations. Data copying in slow-system memory is much slower than data access in fast-register files within the compute units. Considering the memory architecture hierarchy of memory speeds, as was illustrated in Figure 8-2, and considering the image-intensive character of computer vision, it is better to find ways to follow the data and keep the data resident in fast registers and cache memory as long as possible, local to the compute unit.

Memory Optimizations

Attention to memory footprint and memory transfer bandwidth are the most often overlooked areas when optimizing an imaging or vision application. As shown in Table 8-2 and the memory discussion following, a vision pipeline moves several GB/S of data through the system between compute units and system memory. In addition, area processes like interest point detection and image pre-processing move even more data in complex routes through the register files of each compute unit, caches, and system memory.

Why optimize for memory? By optimizing memory use, data transfers are reduced, performance is improved, power costs are reduced, and battery life is increased. Power is costly; in fact, a large Internet search company has built server farms very close to the Columbia River's hydroelectric systems to guarantee clean power and reduce power transmission costs.

For mobile devices, battery life is a top concern. Governments are also beginning to issue carbon taxes and credits to encourage power reductions. Memory use, thus, is a cost that's often overlooked. Memory optimization APIs and approaches will be different for each compute platform and operating system. A good discussion on memory optimization methods for Linux is found in reference[494].

Minimizing Memory Transfers Between Compute Units

Data transfers between compute units should be avoided, if possible. Workload consolidation should be considered during the optimization and tuning stage in order to perform as much processing as possible on the same data while it is resident in register files and the local cache of a given compute unit. That is, follow the data.

For example, using a GPGPU shader for a single-area operation, then processing the same data on the CPU will likely be slower than performing all the processing on the CPU. That's because GPGPU kernels require device driver intervention to set up the memory for each kernel and launch each kernel, while a CPU program accesses code and data directly, with no driver set-up required other than initial program loading. One method to reduce the back-and-forth between compute units is to use loop coalescing and task chaining, discussed later in this section.

Memory Tiling

When dividing workloads for coarse-grained parallelism into several threads, the image can be broken into tiled regions and each tile assigned to a thread. Tiling works well for point, line, and area processing, where each thread performs the same operation on the tiled region. By allowing for an overlapped read regions between tiles, the hard boundaries are eliminated and area operations like convolution can read into adjacent tiles for kernel processing, as well as write finished results into their tile.

DMA, Data Copy, and Conversions

Often, multiple copies of an image are needed in the vision pipeline, and in some cases, the data must be converted from one type to another. Converting 12-bit unsigned color channel data stored in a 16-bit integer to a 32-bit integer allowing for more accurate numerical precision downstream in computations is one example. Also, the color channels might be converted into a chosen color space, such as RGBI, for color processing in the I component space $(R*G*B)/3 = I;$ then, the new I value is mixed and copied back into the RGB components. Careful attention to data layout and data residency will allow more efficient forward and backward color conversions.

When copying data, it is good to try using the direct memory access (DMA) unit for the fastest possible data copies. The DMA unit is implemented in hardware to directly optimize and control the I/O interconnect traffic in and out of memory. Operating systems provide APIs to access the DMA unit [494]. There are variations for optimizing the DMA methods, and some interesting reading comparing cache performance against DMA in vision applications are found in references[497,495].

Register Files, Memory Caching, and Pinning

The memory system is a hierarchy of virtual and physical memories for each processor, composed of slow fixed storage such as file systems, page files, and swap files for managing virtual memory, system memory, caches, and fast-register files inside compute units, and with memory interconnects in between. If the data to process is resident in the register files, it is processed by the ALU at processor clock rates. Best-case memory access is via the register files close to each ALU, so keeping the data in registers and performing all possible processing before copying the data is optimal, but this may require some code changes (discussed later in this section).

If the cache must be accessed to get the data, more clock cycles are burned (power is burned, performance is lost) compared to accessing the register files. And if there is a cache miss and much slower system memory must be accessed, typically many hundreds of clock cycles are required to move the memory to register files through the caches for ALU processing.

Operating systems provide APIs to lock or pin the data in memory, which usually increases the amount of data in cache, decreasing paging and swapping. (Swapping is a hidden copy operation carried out by the operating system automatically to make more room in system memory). When data is accessed often, the data will be resident in the faster cache memories, as was illustrated in Figure 8-2.

Data Structures, Packing, and Vector vs. Scatter-Gather Data Organization

The data structures used contribute to memory traffic. Data organization should allow serial access in contiguous blocks as much as possible to provide best performance. From the programming perspective, data structures are often designed with convenience in mind, and no attention is given to how the compiler will arrange the data or the resulting performance.

For example, consider a data structure with several fields composed of bytes, integers, and floating point data items; compilers may attempt to rearrange the positions of data items in the data structures, and even pack the data in a different order for various optimizations. Compilers usually provide a set of compiler directives, such as in-line pragmas and compiler switches, to control the data packing behavior; these are worth looking into.

For point processing, vectors of data are the natural structure, and the memory system will operate at peak performance in accessing and processing contiguous vectors. For area operations, rectangles spanning several lines are used, and the rectangles cause memory access patterns that can generate cache misses. Using scatter-gather operations for gathering convolution kernel data allows a large data structure to be split apart into vectors of data, increasing performance. Often, CPU and GPU memory architectures pay special attention to data-access patterns and provide hidden methods for optimizations.

Scatter-gather operations, also referred to as *vectored I/O* or *strided* memory access, can be implemented in the GPU or CPU silicon to allow for rapid read/write access to noncontiguous data structure patterns. Typically, a scatter operation writes multiple input buffers into a contiguous pattern in a single output buffer, and a gather operation analogously reads multiple input buffers into a contiguous pattern in the output buffer.

Operating systems and compute languages provide APIs for scatter-gather operations. For Linux-style operating systems, see the *readv* and *writev* function specified in the POSIX 1003.1-2001 specification. The `async_work_group_strided_copy` function is provided by OpenCL for scatter-gather.

Coarse-Grain Parallelism

A vision pipeline can be implemented using coarse-grain parallelism by breaking up the work into threads, and also by assigning work to multiple processor cores. Coarse-grained parallelism can be achieved by breaking up the compute workload into pipelines of threads, or by breaking up the memory into tiles assigned to multiple threads.

Compute-Centric vs. Data-Centric

Coarse-grain parallelism can be employed via compute-centric and data-centric approaches. For example, in a *compute-centric* approach, vision pipeline stages can be split among independent execution threads and compute units along the lines of pipeline stages, and data is fed into the next stage a little at a time via queues and FIFOs. In a *data-centric* approach, an image can be split into tiles, as was shown in Figure 8-12, and each thread processes an independent tile region.

Threads and Multiple Cores

Several methods exist to spread threads across multiple CPU cores, including reliance on the operating system scheduler to make optimum use of each CPU core and perform load balancing. Another is by assigning specific tasks to specific CPU cores. Each operating system has different controls available to tune the process scheduler for each thread, and also may provide the capability to assign specific threads to specific processors. (We discuss programming resources, languages and tools for coarse-grained threading later in this chapter.) Each operating system will provide an API for threading, such as *pthreads*. See Figure 8-13.

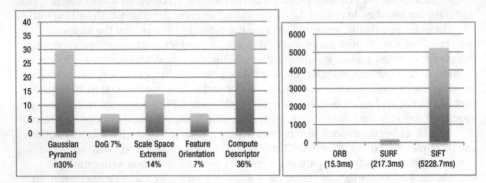

Figure 8-13. *(Left) Typical SIFT descriptor pipeline compute allocation [180]. (Right) Reported compute times [120] for ORB, SURF, and SIFT, averaged over twenty-four 640x480 images containing about 1,000 features per image. Retrofitting ORB for SIFT may be a good choice in some applications*

Fine-Grain Data Parallelism

Fine-grain parallelism refers to the data organization and the corresponding processor architectures exploiting parallelism, traditionally referred to as *array processors or vector processors*. Not all applications are data parallel. Deploying non-data-parallel code to run on a data-parallel machine is counterproductive; it's better to use the CPU and straight-line code to start.

A data-parallel operation should exhibit common memory patterns, such as large arrays of regular data like lines of pixels or tiles of pixels, which are processed in the same way. Referring back to Figure 8-1, note that some algorithms operate on vectors of points, lines, and pixel regions. These data patterns and corresponding processing operations are inherently data-parallel. Examples of point operations are color corrections and data-type conversions, and examples of area operations are convolution and morphology. Some algorithms are straight-line code, with lots of branching and little parallelism. Fine-grained data parallelism is supported directly via SIMD and SIMT methods.

SIMD, SIMT, and SPMD Fundamentals

The supercomputers of yesterday are now equivalent to the GPUs and multi-core CPUs of today. The performance of SIMD, SIMT, and SPMD machines, and their parallel programming languages, is of great interest to the scientific community. It has been developed over decades, and many good resources are available that can be applied to inexpensive SOCs today; see the National Center for Supercomputing Applications[544] for a starting point.

SIMD instructions and multiple threads can be applied when fine-grained parallelism exists in the data layout in memory and the algorithm itself, such as with point, line, and area operations on vectors. Single Instruction Multiple Data (SIMD) instructions process several data items in a vector simultaneously. To exploit fine-grained parallelism at the SIMD level, both the computer language and the corresponding ALUs should provide direct support for a rich set of vector data types and vector instructions. Vector-oriented programming languages are required to exploit data-parallelism, as shown in Table 8-8; however, sometimes compiler switches are available to exploit SIMD. Note that languages like C++ do not directly support vector data types and vector instructions, while data-parallel languages do, as shown in Table 8-8.

Table 8-8. *Common Data-Parallel Language Choices*

Language Name	Standard or Proprietary	OS Platform Support
Pixel Shader GLSL	Standard OpenGL	Several OS platforms
Pixel Shader HLSL	Direct3D	Microsoft OS
Compute Shader	Direct3D	Microsoft OS
Compute Shader	Standard OpenGL	Several OS platforms
RenderScript	Android	Google OS
OpenCL	Standard	Several OS platforms
C++ AMP	Microsoft	Microsoft OS platforms
CUDA	Only for NVIDIA GPUs	Several OS platforms
OpenMP	Standard	Several OS platforms

In some cases, the cost of SIMT outweighs its benefit, especially considering run-time overhead for data set-up and tear-down, thread management, code portability problems, and scalability across large and small CPUs and GPUs.

In addition to SIMD instructions, a method for launching and managing large groups of threads running the same identical code must be provided to exploit data-parallelism, referred to as Single Instruction Multiple Threading (SIMT), also known as Single Program Multiple Data (SPMD). The SIMT programs are referred to as *shaders*, since historically the pixel shaders and vertex shaders used in computer graphics were the first programs widely used to exploit fine-grained data parallelism. Shaders are also referred to as *kernels*.

Both CPUs and GPUs support SIMD instructions and SIMT methods—for example, using languages like OpenCL. The CPU uses the operating system scheduler for managing threads; however, GPUs use hardware schedulers, dispatchers, and scoreboarding logic to track thread execution and blocking status, allowing several threads running an identical kernel on different data to share the same ALU. For the GPU, each shader runs on the ALU until it is blocked on a memory transfer, a function call, or is swapped out by the GPU shader scheduler when its time slice expires.

Note that both C++ AMP and CUDA seem to provide language environments closest to C++. The programming model and language for SIMT programming contains a run-time execution component to marshal data for each thread, launch threads, and manage communications and completion status for groups of threads. Common SIMT languages are shown in Table 8-8.

Note that CPU and GPU execution environments differ significantly at the hardware and software level. The GPU relies on device drivers for set-up and tear-down, and fixed-function hardware scheduling, while CPUs rely on the operating system scheduler and perhaps micro-schedulers. A CPU is typically programmed in C or C++, and the program executes directly from memory and is scheduled by the operating system, while a GPU requires a shader or kernel program to be written in a SIMT SIMD-friendly language such as a compute shader or pixel shader in DirectX or OpenGL, or a GPGPU language such as CUDA or OpenCL.

Furthermore, a shader kernel must be launched via a run-time system through a device driver to the GPU, and an execution context is created within the GPU prior to execution. A GPU may also use a dedicated system memory partition where the data must reside, and in some cases the GPU will also provide a dedicated fast-memory unit.

GPGPU programming has both memory data set-up and program set-up overhead through the run-time system, and unless several kernels are executed sequentially in the GPU to hide the overhead, the set-up and tear-down overhead for a single kernel can exceed any benefit gained via the GPU SIMD/SIMT processing.

The decision to use a data parallelism SIMT programming model affects program design and portability. The use of SIMT is not necessary, and in any case a standard programming language like C++ must be used to control the SIMT run-time environment, as well as the entire vision pipeline. However, the performance advantages of a data-parallel SIMT model are in some cases dramatically compelling and the best choice. Note, however, that GPGPU SIMT programming may actually be slower than using multiple CPU cores with SIMD instructions, coarse-grained threading, and data tiling, especially in cases where the GPU does not support enough parallel threads in hardware, which is the case for smaller GPUs.

Shader Kernel Languages and GPGPU

As shown in Table 8-8, there are several alternatives for creating SIMD SIMT data-parallel code, sometimes referred to as GPGPU or stream processing. As mentioned above, the actual GPGPU programs are known as *shaders* or *kernels*. Historically, pixel shaders and vertex shaders were developed as data-parallel languages for graphics standards like OpenGL and DirectX. However, with the advent of CUDA built exclusively for NVIDIA GPUs, the idea of a standard, general-purpose compute capability within the GPU emerged. The concept was received in the industry, although no killer apps existed and pixel shaders could also be used to get equivalent results. In the end, each GPGPU programming language translates into machine language anyway, so the choice of high-level GPGPU language may not be significant in many cases.

However, the choice of GPGPU language is sometimes limited for a vendor operating system. For example, major vendors such as Google, Microsoft, and Apple do not agree on the same approach for GPGPU and they provide different languages, which means that industry-wide standardization is still a work in progress and portability of shader code is elusive. Perhaps the closest to a portable standard solution is OpenCL, but compute shaders for DirectX and OpenGL are viable alternatives.

Advanced Instruction Sets and Accelerators

Each processor has a set of advanced instructions for accelerating specific operations. The vendor processor and compiler documentation should be consulted for the latest information. A summary of advanced instructions is shown in Table 8-9.

Table 8-9. *Advanced Instruction Set Items*

Instruction Type	Description
Trancendentals	GPU's have special assembler instructions to compute common transcendental math functions for graphics rendering math operations, such as dot product, square root, cosine, and logarithms. In some cases, CPUs also have transcendental functions.
Fused instructions	Common operations such as multiply and add are often implemented in single fused MADD instruction, where both multiply and add are performed in a single clock cycle; the instruction may have three or more operands.
SIMD instructions	CPUs have SIMD instruction sets, such as the Intel SSE and Intel AVX instructions, similar SIMD for AMD processors, and NEON for ARM processors.
Advanced data types	Some instruction sets, such as for GPU's, provide odd data types not supported by common language compilers, such as half-byte integers, 8-bit floating point numbers, and fixed-point numbers. Special data types may be supported by portions of the instruction set, but not all.
Memory access modifiers	Some processors provide strided memory access capability to support scatter-gather operations, bit-swizzling operations to allow for register contents to be moved and copied in programmable bit patterns, and permuted memory access patterns to support cross-lane patterns. Intel processors also provide MPX memory protection instructions for pointer checking.

(continued)

Table 8-9. (*continued*)

Instruction Type	Description
Security	Cryptographic accelerators and special instructions may be provided for common ciphers such as SHA or AES ciphers; for example, INTEL AES-NI. In addition, Intel offers the INTEL SGX extensions to provide curtained memory regions to execute secure software; the curtained regions cannot be accessed by malware.
Hardware accelerators	Common accelerators include GPU texture samplers for image warping and sub-sampling, and DMA units for fast memory copies. Operating systems provide APIs to access the DMA unit [494]. Graphics programming languages such as OpenGL and DirectX provide access to the texture sampler, and GPGPU languages such as OpenCL and CUDA also provide texture sampler APIs.

APIs provided by operating system vendors may or may not use the special instructions. Compilers from each processor vendor will optimize all code to take best advantage of the advanced instructions; other compilers may or may not provide optimizations. However, each compiler will provide different flags to control optimizations, so code tuning and profiling are required. Using assembler language is the best way to get all the performance available from the advanced instruction sets.

Vision Algorithm Optimizations and Tuning

Optimizations can be based on intuition or on performance profiling, usually a combination of both. Assuming that the hot spots are identified, a variety of optimization methods can be applied as discussed in this section. Performance hotspots can be addressed from the data perspective, the algorithm perspective, or both. Most of the time memory access is a hidden cost, and not understood by the developer (the algorithms are hard enough). However memory optimizations alone can be the key to increasing performance. Table 8-11 summarizes various approaches for optimizations, which are discussed next.

Data access patterns for each algorithm can be described using the Zinner, Kubinger, and Isaac taxonomy [494] shown in Table 8-10. Note that usually the preferred data access pattern is in-place (IP) computations, which involve reading the data once into fast registers, processing and storing the results in the registers, and writing the final results back on top of the original image. This approach takes maximal advantage of the cache lines and the registers, avoiding slower memory until the data is processed.

Table 8-10. *Image Processing Data Access Pattern Taxonomy (from Zinner et al.[494])*

Type	Description	Source Images	Destination Images	READ	WRITE
(1S)	1 source, 0 destination	1	0	Source image	no
(2S)	2 source, 0 destination	2	0	Source images	no
(IP)	*In-place**	*1*	*0*	*Source image*	*Source image*
(1S1D)	1 source, 1 destination	1	1	Source image	Destination image
(2S1D)	2 source, 1 destination	2	1	Source images	Destination image

*IP processing is usually the simplest way to reduce memory read/write bandwidth and memory footprint.

Compiler And Manual Optimizations

Usually a good compiler can automatically perform many of the optimizations listed in Table 8-11; however, check the compiler flags to understand the options. The goal of the optimizations is to keep the CPU instruction execution pipelines full, or to reduce memory traffic. However, many of the optimizations in Table 8-11 require hand coding to boil down the algorithm into tighter loops with more data sharing in fast registers and less data copying.

Table 8-11. *Common Optimization Techniques, Manual And Compiler Methods*

Name	Description
Sub-function inlining	Eliminating function calls by copying the function code in-line
Task chaining	Feeding the output of a function into a waiting function piece by piece
Branch elimination	Re-coding to eliminate conditional branches, or reduce branches by combining multiple branch conditions together
Loop coalescing	Combining inner and outer loops into fewer loops using more straight line code
Packing data	Rearranging data alignment within structures and adding padding to certain data items for better data alignment to larger data word or page boundaries to allow for more efficient memory read and write

(continued)

Table 8-11. (*continued*)

Name	Description
Loop unrolling	Reducing the loop iteration count by replicating code inside the loop; may be accomplished using straight line code replication or by packing multiple iterations into a VLIW
Function coalescing*	Rewriting serial functions into a single function, with a single outer loop to read and write data to system memory; passing small data items in fast registers between coalesced functions instead of passing large images buffers
ROS-DMA*	Double-buffering DMA overlapped with processing; DMA and processing occur in parallel, DMA the new data in during processing, DMA the results out

* Function coalescing and ROS-DMA are not compiler methods, and may be performed at the source code level.

Note: See references[498,499] for more information on compiler optimizations, and see each vendor's compiler documentation for information on available optimization controls.

Tuning

After optimizing, tuning a working vision pipeline can be accomplished from several perspectives. The goal is to provide run-time *controls*. Table 8-12 provides some examples of tuning controls that may be implemented to allow for run-time or compile-time tuning.

Table 8-12. *Run-Time Tuning Controls for a Vision Pipeline*

Image Resolution	Allowing variable resolution over an octave scale or other scale to reduce workload
Frames per second	Skipping frames to reduce the workload
Feature database size and accuracy	Finding ways to reduce the size of the database, for example have one data base with higher accuracy, and another database with lower accuracy, each built using a different classier
Feature database organization and speed	Improving performance through better organization and searching, perhaps have more than one database, each using a different organization strategy and classifier

Feature Descriptor Retrofit, Detectors, Distance Functions

As discussed in Chapter 6, many feature descriptor methods such as SIFT can be retro-fitted to use other representations and feature descriptions. For example, the LBP-SIFT retrofit discussed in Chapter 6 uses a local binary pattern in place of the gradient methods used by SIFT for impressive speedup, while preserving the other aspects of the SIFT pipeline.

The ROOT-SIFT method is another SIFT acceleration alternative discussed in Chapter 6. Detectors and descriptors can be mixed and matched to achieve different combinations of invariance and performance, see the REIN framework [397].

In addition to the descriptor extractor itself, the distance functions often consume considerable time in the feature matching stage. For example, local binary descriptors such as FREAK and ORB use fast Hamming distance, while SIFT uses the Euclidean distance, which is slower. Retro-fitting the vision pipeline to use a local binary descriptor is an example of how the distance function can have a significant performance impact.

It should be pointed out that the descriptors reviewed in Chapter 6 are often based on academic research, not on extensive engineering field trials and optimizations. Each method is just a starting point for further development and customization. We can be sure that military weapon systems have been using similar, but far more optimal feature description methods for decades within vision pipelines in deployed systems. See Figure 8-13.

Boxlets and Convolution Acceleration

Convolution is one of the most common operations in feature description and image pre-processing, so convolution is a key target for optimizations and hardware acceleration. The boxlet method [392] approximates convolution and provides a speed vs. accuracy tradeoff. Boxlets can be used to optimize any system that relies heavily on convolutions, such as the convolutional network approach used by LeCun and others [85,336,339]. The basic approach is to approximate a pair of 2D signals, the kernel and the image, as low-degree polynomials, which quantizes each signal and reduces the data size; and then differentiating the two signals to obtain the impulse functions and convolution approximation. The full convolution can be recovered by integrating the result of the differentiation.

Another convolution and general area processing acceleration method is to reuse as much overlapping data as possible while it exists in fast registers, instead of reading the entire region of data items for each operation. When performing area operations, it is possible to program to use sliding windows and pointers in an attempt to reuse data items from adjacent rectangles that are already in the register files, rather than copying complete new rectangles into registers for each area operation. This is another area suited for silicon acceleration.

Also, scatter-gather instructions can be used to gather the convolution data into memory for accelerated processing in some cases, and GPUs often optimize the memory architecture for fast area operations.

Data-Type Optimizations, Integer vs. Float

Software engineers usually use integers as the default data type, with little thought about memory and performance. Often, there is low-hanging fruit in most code in the area of data types. For example, conversion of data from int32 to int16, and conversion from double to float, are obvious space-savings items to consider when the extra bit precision is not needed.

In some cases, floating-point data types are used when an integer will do equally well. Floating-point computations in general require nearly four times more silicon area, which consumes correspondingly more power. The data types consume more memory and may require more clock cycles to compute. As an alternative to floating point, some processors provide fixed-point data types and instructions, which can be very efficient.

Optimization Resources

Several resources in the form of software libraries and tools are available for computer vision and image processing optimizations. Some are listed in Table 8-13.

Table 8-13. *Vision Optimization Resources*

Method	Acceleration Strategy	Examples
Threading libraries	Coarse-grained parallelism	Intel TBB, pthreads
Pipeline building tools	Connect functions into pipelines	PfeLib Vision Pipeline Library [495] Halide [543]*
Primitive acceleration libraries	Functions are pre-optimized	Intel IPP, NVIDIA NPP, Qualcomm FastCV
GPGPU languages	Develop SIMT SIMD code	CUDA, OpenCL, C++ AMP, INTEL CILK++, GLSL, HLSL, Compute Shaders for OpenGL and Direct3D, RenderScript
Compiler flags	Compiler optimizes for each processor; see Table 8-10	Vendor-specific
SIMD instructions	Directly code in assembler, or use compiler flags for standard languages, or use GPGPU languages.	Vendor-specific
Hardware accelerators	Silicon accelerators for complex functions	Texture Samplers; others provided selectively by vendors
Advanced instruction sets	Accelerate complex low-level operations, or fuse multiple instructions; see Table 8-9	INTEL AVX, ARM NEON, GPU instruction sets

Open source available.

Summary

This chapter ties together the discussions from previous chapters into complete vision systems by developing four purely hypothetical high-level application designs. Design details such as compute resource assignments and optimization alternatives are discussed for each pipeline, intended to generate a discussion about how to design efficient systems (the examples are sketchy at times). The applications explored include automobile recognition using shape and color features, face and emotion detection using sparse local features, whole image classification using global features, and augmented reality. Each example illustrates the use of different feature descriptor families from the Vision Metrics Taxonomy presented in Chapter 5, such as polygon shape methods, color descriptors, sparse local features, global features, and depth information. A wide range of feature description methods were used in the examples to illustrate the challenges in the pre-processing stage.

In addition, a general discussion of design concepts for optimizations and load balancing across the compute resources in the SOC fabric (CPU, GPU, and memory) was provided to explore HW/SW system challenges, such as power reductions. Finally, an overview of SW optimization resources and specific optimization techniques was presented.

APPENDIX A

■ ■ ■

Synthetic Feature Analysis

This appendix provides analysis of several common detectors against the synthetic feature alphabets described in Chapter 7. The complete source code, shell scripts, and the alphabet image sets are available from Springer Apress at:
http://www.apress.com/source-code/ComputerVisionMetrics

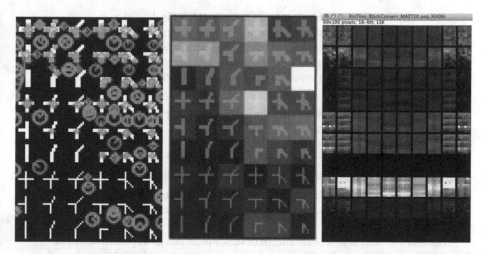

Figure A-1. *Example analysis results from Test #4 below, (left) annotated image showing detector locations, (center) count of each alphabet feature detected, shown as a 2D shaded histogram, (right) set of 2D shaded histograms for rotated image sets showing all 10 detectors*

This appendix contains:

- Background on the analysis, methodology, goals, and expectations.

- Synthetic alphabet ground truth image summary.

- List of detector parameters used for standard OpenCV methods: SIFT, SURF, BRISK, FAST, HARRIS, GFFT, MSER, ORB, STAR, SIMPLEBLOB. Note: No feature descriptors are computed or used, only the detector portions of BRISK, SURF, SIFT, ORB, and STAR are used in the analysis.

- Test 1: Interest point alphabets.

- Test 2: Corner point alphabets.

- Test 3: Synthetic alphabet overlays onto real images.

- Test 4: Rotational invariance of detectors against synthetic alphabets.

Background Goals and Expectations

The main goals for the analysis are:

- To develop some simple intuition about human vs. machine detection of interest point and corner detectors, to observe detector behavior on the synthetic alphabets, and to develop some understanding of the problems involved in designing and tuning feature detectors.

- To measure detector anomalies among white, black, and gray versions of the alphabets. A human would recognize the same pattern easily whether or not the background and foreground are changed; however, detector design and parameter settings influence detector invariance to background and foreground polarity.

- To measure detector sensitivity to slight pixel interpolation artifacts under rotation.

■ **Note**   Experienced practitioners with well-developed intuition regarding capabilities of interest point and corner detector methods may not find any surprises in this analysis.

The analysis uses several well-known detector methods as implemented in the OpenCV library; see Table A-1. The analysis provides detector information only, with no intention to compare detector goodness against any criteria. Details on which features from the synthetic alphabets are recognized by the various detectors is shown in summary tables, counting the number of times a feature is detected with each grid cell. For some applications, the synthetic interest point alphabet approach could be useful, assuming that an application-specific alphabet is designed, and detectors are designed and tuned for the application, such as a factory inspection application to identify manufactured objects or parts.

Table A-1. *Tuning Parameters for Detectors*

Detector	Tuning Parameters
BRISK	octaves = 3 threshold = 30
FAST	threshold = 10 nonMaximalSuppression = TRUE
HARRIS	maxCorners = 60000 (to capture all detections) qualityLevel = 1.0 minDistance = 1 blockSize = 3 useHarrisDetecror = TRUE k = .04
GFFT	maxCorners = 60000 (to capture all detections) qualityLevel = .01 minDistance = 1.0 blockSize = 3 useHarrisDetector = FALSE k = .04
MSER	Delta = 5 minArea = 60 maxArea 14400 maxvariation = .25 minDiversity = .2 maxEvolution = 200 areaThreshold = 1.01 minMargin = .003 edgeBlurSize = 5
ORB	WTA_K = 2 edgeThreshold = 31 firstLevel = 0 nFeatures = 60000 (to capture all detections) nLevels = 8 patchSize = 31 scaleFactor = 1.2 scoreType = 0
SIFT	contrastThreshold = 4.0 edgeThreshhold = 10.0 nFeatures = 0 nOctaveLayers = 3 sigma = 1.0

(continued)

Table A-1. (*continued*)

Detector	Tuning Parameters
STAR	maxSize = 45 responseThreshold = 30 lineThresholdProjected = 10 lineThresholdBinarized = 8
SURF	Extended = 0 hessianThreshold = 100.0 nOctaveLayers = 3 nOctaves = 4 upright = 0
SIMPLEBLOB	thresholdStep = 10 minThreshold = 50 maxThreshold = 220 minRepeatability = 2 minDistBetweenBlobs = 10 filterByColor = **true** blobColor = 0 filterByArea = **true** minArea = 25 maxArea = 5000 filterByCircularity = **false** minCircularity = 0.8f maxCircularity = std::numeric_limits<**float**>::*max*() filterByInertia = **true** minInertiaRatio = 0.1f maxInertiaRatio = std::numeric_limits<**float**>::*max*() filterByConvexity = **true** minConvexity = 0.95f maxConvexity = std::numeric_limits<**float**>::*max*()

Test Methodology and Results

The images in the ground truth data set are used as input for a few modified OpenCV tests:

- opencv_test_features2d

  (BRISK, FAST, HARRIS, GFFT, MSER, ORB, STAR, SIMPLEBLOB)

- opencv_test_nonfree

  (SURF, SIFT)

The tuning parameters used for each detector are shown in Table A-1; see the OpenCV documentation for more information. Note: no attempt is made to tune the detector parameters for the synthetic alphabets. Parameter settings are reasonable defaults; however, the maximum keypoint feature count is bumped up in some cases to allow all the detected features to be recorded.

Each test produces a variety of results, including:

1. Annotated images showing location and orientation (if provided) for detected features.

2. Summary count of each detected synthetic feature across the grid in text files, including interest point coordinates, detector response strength, orientation if provided by the detector, and the number of total detected synthetic features found.

3. 2D histograms showing bin count for each feature in the alphabet.

Detector Parameters Are Not Tuned for the Synthetic Alphabets

No feature detector tuning is attempted here. Why? In summary, feature detector tuning has very limited value in the absence of (1) a specific feature descriptor to use the keypoints, and (2) an intended application and use-cases. Some objections may be raised to this approach, since detectors are designed to be tuned and must be tuned to get best results for real applications. However, the test results herein are only a starting point, intended to allow for simple observations of detector behavior compared to human expectations.

In some cases, a keypoint is not suitable for producing a useful feature descriptor, even if the keypoint has a high score and high response. If the feature descriptor computed at the keypoint produces a descriptor that is too weak, the keypoint and corresponding descriptor should both be rejected. Each detector is designed to be useful for a different class of interest points, and tuned accordingly to filter the results down to a useful set of good candidates for a specific feature extractor.

Since we are not dealing with any specific feature descriptor methods here, tuning the keypoint detectors has limited value, since detector parameter tuning in the absence of a specific feature description is ambiguous. Furthermore, detector tuning will be different for each detector-descriptor pair, different for each application, and potentially different for each image.

Tuning detectors is not simple. Each detector has different parameters to tune for best results on a given image, and each image presents different challenges for lighting, contrast, and image pre-processing. For typical applications, detected keypoints are culled and discarded based on some filtering criteria. OpenCV provides several novel methods for tuning detectors, however none are used here. The OpenCV tuning methods include:

- **DynamicAdaptedFeatureDetector** class will tune supported detectors using an *adjusterAdapter()* to only keep a limited number of features, and to iterate the detector parameters several times and re-detect features in order to try and find the best parameters, keeping only the requested number of best features. Several OpenCV detectors have an *adjusterAdapter()* provided while some do not, and the API allows for adjusters to be created.

- **AdjusterAdapter** class implements the criteria for culling and keeping interest points. Criteria may include KNN nearest matching, detector response or strength, radius distance to nearest other detected points, removing keypoints for which a descriptor cannot be computed, or other.

- **PyramidAdaptedFeatureDetector** class is can be used to adapt detectors that do not use a scale-space pyramid, and this adapter will create a Gaussian pyramid and detect features over the pyramid.

- **GridAdaptedFeatureDetector** class divides an image into grids, and adapts the detector to find the best features within each grid cell.

Expectations for Test Results

The reader should treat these tests as information only to develop intuition about feature detection. The test results do not prove the merits of any detector. Interpretation of the test results should be done with the following information in mind:

1. One set of detector tuning parameters is used for all images, and detector results will vary widely based on tuning parameters. In fact, the parameters are deliberately set to over-sensitive values for ORB, SURF, and other detectors to generate the maximum number of possible keypoints that can be found.

2. Sometimes an alphabet feature generates multiple detections; for example, a single corner alphabet feature may actually contain several corner features.

3. The detection results may not be repeatable over the distribution of replicated features in the image feature grid. In other words, identical patterns, which look about the same to a human, are sometimes not recognized at different locations. Without looking in detail at each algorithm, it is hard to say what is happening.

4. Detectors that use an image pyramid such as SIFT, SURF, ORB, STAR, and BRISK may identify keypoints in a scale space that are offset or in between the actual alphabet features. This is expected, since the detector is using features from multiple scales.

Summary of Synthetic Alphabet Ground Truth Images

The ground truth dataset is summarized here. Note that rotated versions of each image file in the set are provided from 0 to 90 degrees at 10-degree intervals. The 0-degree image in each set is 1024x1024 pixels, and the rotated images in each set are slightly larger to contain the entire rotated 1024x1024 pixel grid.

Synthetic Interest Point Alphabet

The synthetic interest point alphabet contains multiples of the 83 unique patterns, as shown in Figure A-2. A total of 7 x 7 sets of the 83 features fit within the 1024 x 1024 image. Total unique feature count for the image is 7 x 7 x 83 = 4116, with 7 x 7 = 49 instances of each feature. The features are laid out on a 14x14 pixel grid composed of 10 rows and 10 columns, including several empty grid locations. Gray image pixel values are 0x40 and 0xc0, black and white pixel values are 0x0 and 0xff.

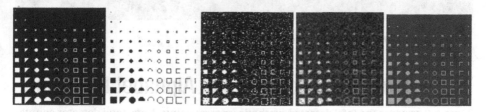

Figure A-2. Synthetic interest points

Synthetic Corner Point Alphabet

The synthetic corner point alphabet contains multiples of the 63 unique patterns, as shown in Figure A-3. A total of 8 x 12 sets of the 63 features fit within the 1024x1024 image. Total unique feature count is 8 x 12 x 63 = 6048, with 8 x 12 = 96 instances of each feature. Each feature is arranged on a grid of 14 x 14 pixel rectangles, including 9 rows and 6 columns of features. Gray image pixel values are 0x40 and 0xc0, black and white pixel values are 0x0 and 0xff.

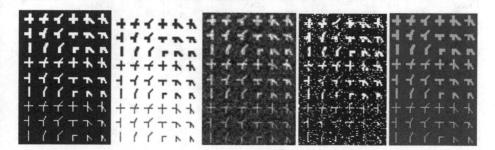

Figure A-3. Synthetic corner point

Synthetic Alphabet Overlays

A set of images with the synthetic alphabets overlaid is provided, including rotated versions of each image, as shown in Figure A-4.

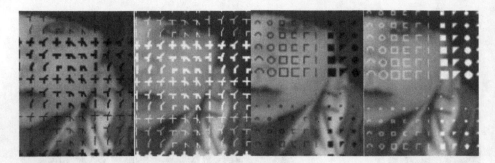

Figure A-4. Synthetic alphabets overlaid on real images

Test 1: Synthetic Interest Point Alphabet Detection

Table A-2 provides the total detected synthetic interest points. Note: total detector counts include features computed at each scale of an image pyramid. For detectors, which report feature detections at each level of an image pyramid, individual pyramid level detections are shown in Table A-3.

Table A-2. Summary Count of Detected Features Found in the Synthetic Interest Point Alphabet, 0 degree Rotation

Detector	Interest Points White On Black	Interest Points Black On White	Interest Points White On Black Salt Pepper Noise	Interest Points White On Black Gaussian Filtered	Interest Points Lt. Gray on Dk. Gray
SURF	18178	19290	33419	22951	13526
SIFT	11672	15208	18323	19054	8519
BRISK	823	4634	25070	9075	550
FAST	343	4971	41265	50711	2112
HARRIS	14833	14217	47025	23473	14854
GFFT	16296	14069	52415	58804	15876
MSER	0	1	2758	2289	0
ORB	32414	42675	56653	55044	27996
STAR	3486	5847	3692	4336	2277
SIMPLEBLOB	441	1201	68	385	441

Table A-3. *Octave Count of Detected Features Found in the Synthetic Interest Point Alphabet, 0 degree Rotation*

Detector	Interest Points White On Black	Interest Points Black On White	Interest Points White On Black Salt Pepper Noise	Interest Points White On Black Gaussian Filtered	Interest Points Lt. Gray on Dk. Gray
SURF total:	18178	19290	33419	22951	13526
Octave 0:	9044	9807	24820	15667	8176
Octave 1:	4392	4505	5199	3936	2801
Octave 2:	4623	4862	3270	3226	2435
Octave 3:	119	116	130	122	114
BRISK total:	823	4634	25070	9075	326
Octave 0:	258	3482	24686	8256	143
Octave 1:	21	170	2	226	0
Octave 2:	402	851	315	555	179
Octave 3:	136	101	54	31	4
ORB total	32414	42675	56653	55044	27996
Octave 0:	330	4924	13030	13030	330
Octave 1:	5507	9467	10859	10859	5126
Octave 2:	7437	8519	9049	9049	7003
Octave 3:	6114	6333	7541	7541	5704
Octave 4:	4575	4625	6284	6284	3922
Octave 5:	3390	3495	4744	3869	2787
Octave 6:	2988	3150	3173	2793	2061
Octave 7:	2073	2162	1973	1619	1063

The total number of features detected in each alphabet cell is provided in summary tables from the annotated images. Note that several features may be detected within each 14x14 cell, and the detectors often provide non-repeatable results, which are discussed at the end of this appendix. The counts show the total number of alphabet features detected across the entire image, as shown in Figure A-5.

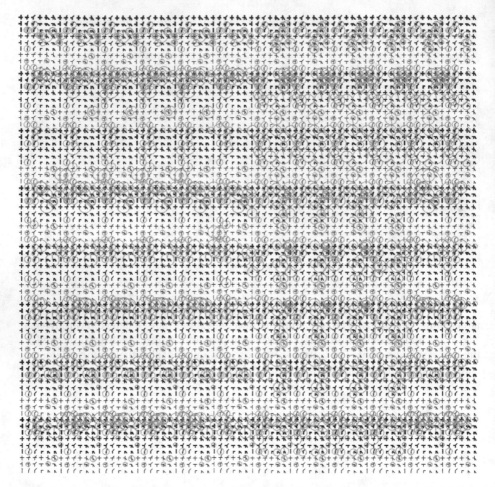

Figure A-5. *Annotated BRISK detector results. NOTE: there are several non-repeatability anomalies*

Annotated Synthetic Interest Point Detector Results

For ORB and SURF detectors, the annotated renderings using the *drawkeypoints()* function are too dense to be useful for visualization, but are included in the online test results.

The diameter of the circle drawn at each detected keypoint corresponds to the "diameter of the meaningful keypoint neighborhood," according to the OpenCV KeyPoint class definition, which varies in size according to the image pyramid level where the feature was detected. Some detectors do not use a pyramid, so the diameter is always the same. The position of the detected features is normalized to the full resolution image, and all detected keypoints are drawn.

Entire Images Available Online

To better understand the detector results for each test, the entire image should be viewed to see the anomalies, such as where detectors fail to recognize identical patterns. Figure A-5 is an entire image showing BRISK detector results, while others are available online. Test results shown in Figures A-6 through A-15 only show a portion of the images.

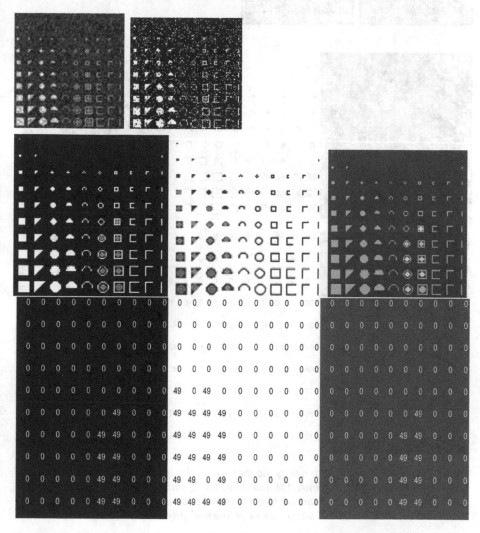

Figure A-6. *SIMPLEBLOB detector, with results shown for a single alphabet grid set. (Top row) Gaussian and salt/pepper response. (Middle row) Black, white, and gray response. (Bottom row) Summary count of individual alphabet feature detections across all the alphabets in the grid, across each 1024x1024 image, black, white and gray images, color-coded tables*

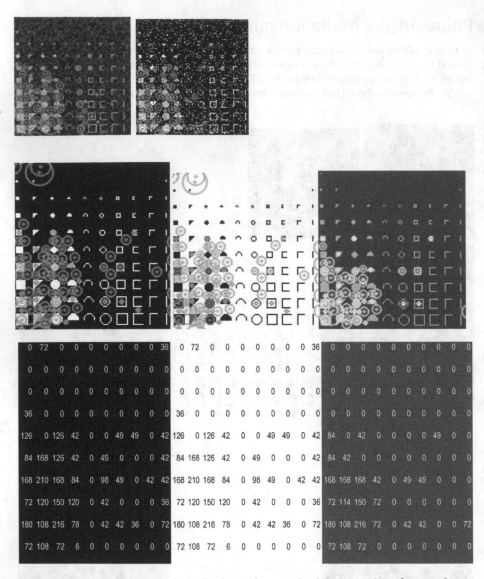

Figure A-7. *STAR detector, with results shown for a single alphabet grid set. (Top row) Gaussian and salt/pepper response. (Middle row) Black, white, and gray response. (Bottom row) Summary count of individual alphabet feature detections across all the alphabets in the grid across each 1024x1024 image, black, white and gray images, color-coded tables*

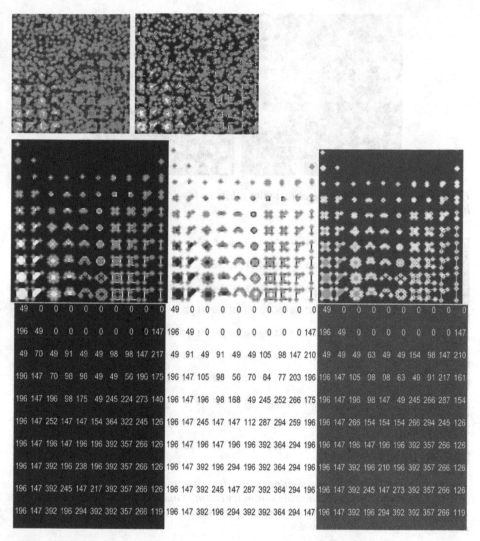

Figure A-8. *GFFT detector, with results shown for a single alphabet grid set. (Top row) Gaussian and salt/pepper response. (Middle row) Black, white, and gray response. (Bottom row) Summary count of individual alphabet feature detections across all the alphabets in the grid, across each 1024x1024 image, black, white, and gray images, color-coded tables*

Figure A-9. *MSER detector (black on white, white on black, and light gray on dark gray have no detected features)*

150	52	0	0	0	0	0	0	7	17
224	195	31	47	37	27	52	27	49	186
193	212	220	228	228	243	244	241	235	158
198	233	223	245	326	316	374	312	278	169
194	209	180	208	283	334	496	340	273	154
317	285	198	235	441	529	671	396	354	150
422	376	320	234	482	634	721	471	426	171
571	448	503	346	483	707	801	567	451	194
613	505	909	384	504	715	751	656	415	221
571	512	558	369	489	760	757	599	427	222

156	54	0	0	0	0	0	0	8	21
223	200	33	46	38	26	52	28	50	189
194	213	220	229	228	247	244	240	233	164
197	236	224	245	331	307	380	311	280	176
201	209	183	210	290	333	509	333	270	156
315	286	202	231	434	518	680	393	355	156
421	377	329	238	477	643	728	461	433	178
572	452	509	348	488	704	821	565	450	194
614	505	912	384	510	717	770	649	417	220
566	511	562	371	492	765	770	587	420	227

93	25	0	0	0	0	0	0	0	3
192	159	15	15	14	6	24	13	27	137
177	195	195	194	183	206	225	220	201	130
197	222	215	232	282	274	343	284	240	140
185	204	177	201	265	297	461	310	245	110
307	276	188	225	396	497	628	359	298	112
403	369	308	221	426	580	653	397	353	130
531	428	469	333	411	566	632	450	389	148
553	433	860	359	412	544	606	444	366	157
543	442	535	358	371	612	564	421	353	174

Figure A-10. *ORB detector (annotations using default parameters not useful, images provided online), with results showing summary count of individual alphabet feature detections across all the alphabets in the grid, across each 1024x1024 image, black, white, and gray images, color-coded tables*

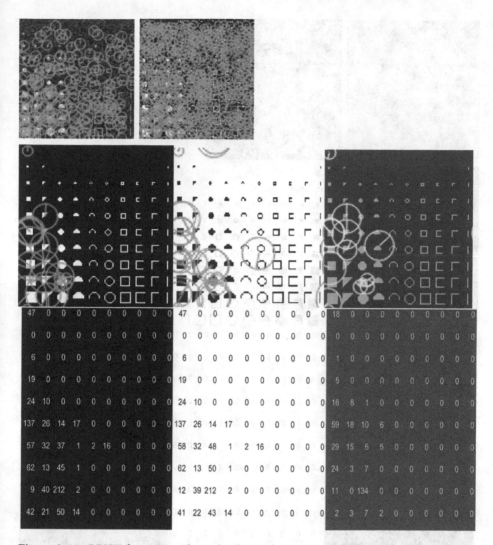

Figure A-11. BRISK detector, with results shown for a single alphabet grid set. (Top row) Gaussian and salt/pepper response. (Middle row) Black, white, and gray response. (Bottom row) Summary count of individual alphabet feature detections across all the alphabets in the grid, across each 1024x1024 image, black, white, and gray images, color-coded tables

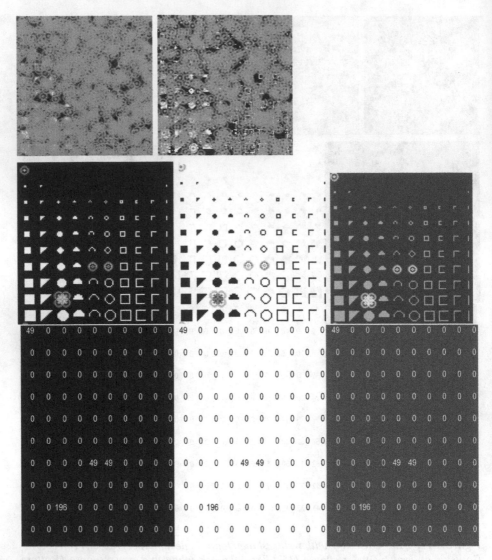

Figure A-12. *FAST detector, with results shown for a single alphabet grid set. (Top row) Gaussian and salt/pepper response. (Middle row) Black, white, and gray response. (Bottom row) Summary count of individual alphabet feature detections across all the alphabets in the grid, across each 1024x1024 image, black, white, and gray images, color-coded tables*

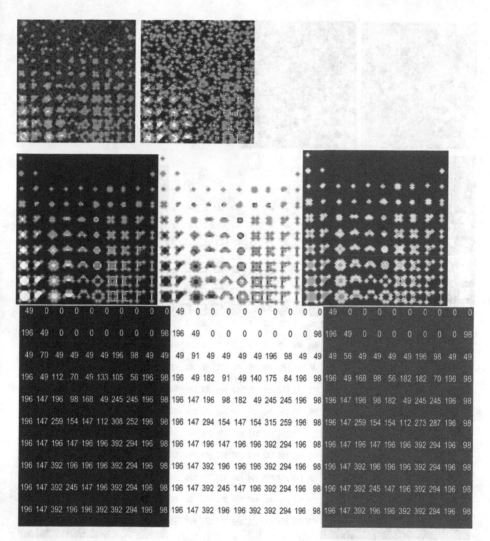

Figure A-13. *HARRIS detector, with results shown for a single alphabet grid set. (Top row) Gaussian and salt/pepper response. (Middle row) Black, white, and gray response. (Bottom row) Summary count of individual alphabet feature detections across all the alphabets in the grid, across each 1024x1024 image, black, white, and gray images, color-coded tables*

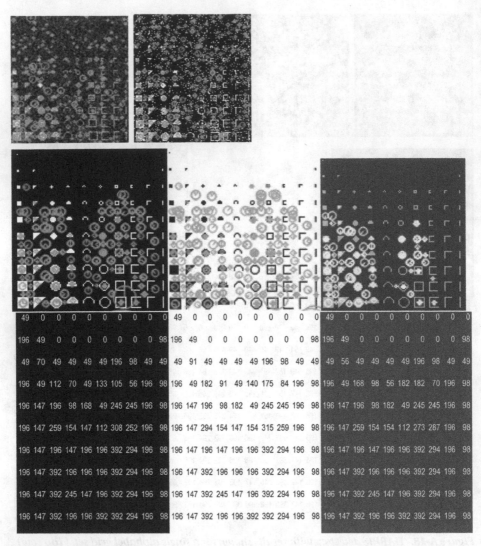

Figure A-14. *SIFT detector, with results shown for a single alphabet grid set. (Top row) Gaussian and salt/pepper response. (Middle row) Black, white, and gray response. (Bottom row) Summary count of individual alphabet feature detections across all the alphabets in the grid, across each 1024x1024 image, black, white, and gray images, color-coded tables*

98	0	126	0	84	49	49	0	91	42	98	0	126	0	84	49	0	0	85	42	42	0	42	0	84	49	0	0	85	0
134	212	133	0	98	156	188	201	162	251	134	212	133	0	98	156	188	201	162	196	0	36	42	0	0	58	6	54	84
140	140	196	183	147	163	165	110	238	126	140	140	196	183	147	163	165	110	238	126	98	98	98	134	49	58	116	110	232	42
182	189	245	183	150	98	98	147	127	126	182	189	245	183	150	98	98	147	127	126	140	147	196	98	98	49	0	49	49	84
140	231	245	189	245	245	196	203	287	168	140	231	245	189	245	245	196	203	287	168	140	231	245	147	196	147	98	147	287	168
133	182	245	189	245	196	98	196	343	210	133	182	245	189	245	196	98	245	343	210	91	182	245	189	196	98	49	98	287	126
224	231	294	196	245	245	238	343	301	168	224	231	294	147	196	245	238	343	301	168	140	231	294	98	245	196	147	147	287	168
140	241	98	165	245	147	245	244	238	84	140	241	98	165	245	147	343	293	238	84	140	241	98	165	196	98	196	55	147	84
140	176	281	147	147	294	441	378	245	84	140	176	281	147	196	245	441	378	245	84	140	176	281	147	196	196	441	336	203	84
98	196	98	0	196	245	287	441	350	6	98	196	98	0	196	245	287	441	350	6	98	196	98	0	196	245	238	294	294	0

Figure A-15. *SURF detector (annotations using default parameters not useful, images provided online), with results showing summary count of individual alphabet feature detections across all the alphabets in the grid, across each 1024x1024 image, black, white, and gray images, color-coded tables*

Test 2: Synthetic Corner Point Alphabet Detection

Table A-4 provides the total detected synthetic corner points at all pyramid levels; some detectors do not use pyramids. Note: for detectors that report features separately over image pyramid levels, individual pyramid-level detections are shown in Table A-5.

Table A-4. *Summary Count of Detected Features Found in the Synthetic Interest Point Alphabet, 0 degree Rotation*

Detector	Corner Points White On Black	Corner Points Black On White	Corner Points White On Black Salt Pepper Noise	Corner Points White On Black Gaussian Filtered	Corner Points Lt. Gray on Dk. Gray
SURF	28579	28821	32637	26806	26406
SIFT	17996	17515	22377	28624	16122
BRISK	1852	2286	22472	12522	550
FAST	2112	2304	37283	51266	2112
HARRIS	28616	29210	45615	30868	29760
GFFT	32720	31578	51969	55069	32597
MSER	0	0	3751	2446	0
ORB	40162	40373	59549	58693	37665
STAR	5932	6178	5589	7473	4251
SIMPLEBLOB	0	96	1	1	0

Table A-5. *Octave Count of Detected Features Found in the Synthetic Corner Point Alphabet, 0 degree Rotation*

Detector	Interest Points White On Black	Interest Points Black On White	Interest Point White On Black Salt Pepper Noise	Interest Points White On Black Gaussian Filtered	Interest Points Lt. Gray on Dk. Gray
SURF total:	28579	28821	32637	26806	26406
Octave 0:	16122	16217	20494	15402	16120
Octave 1:	2327	2315	2925	2008	1692
Octave 2:	9989	10141	9062	9297	8582
Octave 3:	141	148	156	99	12
BRISK total:	1852	2286	22472	12522	550
Octave 0:	1356	1223	21913	11686	426
Octave 1:	172	278	2	183	0
Octave 2:	324	727	535	644	124
Octave 3:	0	57	22	8	0
ORB total	40162	40373	59549	58693	37665
Octave 0:	1932	2105	13030	13030	1932
Octave 1:	6752	6653	10859	10859	6594
Octave 2:	9049	9049	9049	9049	9049
Octave 3:	6870	6920	7541	7541	6664
Octave 4:	4334	4343	6284	6284	4140
Octave 5:	4072	4181	5237	5010	3751
Octave 6:	3909	3919	4364	4080	3316
Octave 7:	3244	3203	3185	2840	2219

Each feature exists within a 14x14 pixel region, and the total number of features detected in each cell is provided in summary tables with the annotated images. Note that several features may be detected within each 14 x 14 cell, and the detectors often provide non-repeatable results, which are discussed at the end of this appendix.

Annotated Synthetic Corner Point Detector Results

Test 2 is exactly like the interest point detector results in Test 1. As such, for ORB and SURF detectors, the annotated renderings using the *drawkeypoints( )* function are too dense to be useful, but are included in the online test results.

The diameter of the circle drawn at each detected keypoint corresponds to the "diameter of the meaningful keypoint neighborhood," according to the OpenCV KeyPoint class definition, which varies in size according to the image pyramid level where the feature was detected. Some detectors do not use a pyramid, so the diameter is always the same. The position of the detected features is normalized to the full resolution image, and all detected keypoints are drawn.

Entire Images Available Online

To better understand the detector results for each test, the entire image should be viewed to see the anomalies, such as where detectors fail to recognize identical patterns. Test results shown in Figures A-16 through A-25 only show a portion of the images.

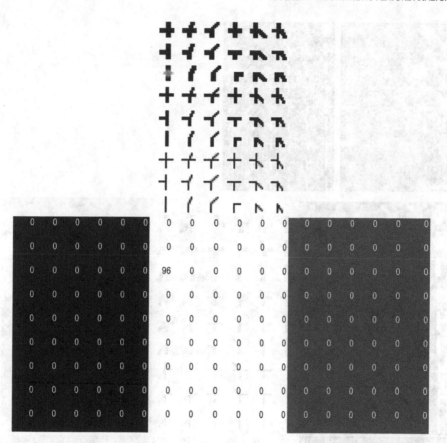

Figure A-16. *SIMPLE BLOB detector (black on white is the only image with detected features), with results showing summary count of individual alphabet feature detections across all the alphabets in the grid, across each 1024x1024 image, black, white, and gray images, color-coded tables*

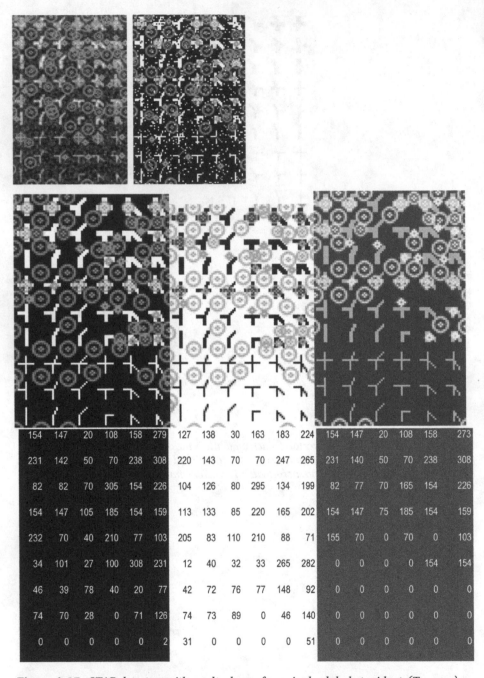

Figure A-17. *STAR detector, with results shown for a single alphabet grid set. (Top row) Gaussian and salt/pepper response. (Middle row) Black, white, and gray response. (Bottom row) Summary count of individual alphabet feature detections across all the alphabets in the grid, across each 1024x1024 image, black, white, and gray images, color-coded tables*

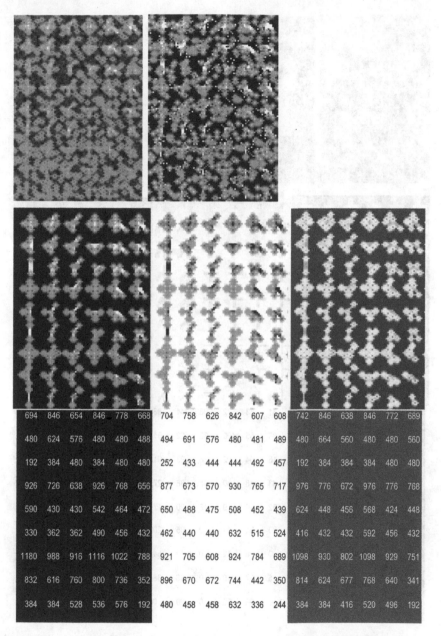

Figure A-18. *GFFT detector, with results shown for a single alphabet grid set. (Top row) Gaussian and salt/pepper response. (Middle row) Black, white, and gray response. (Bottom row) Summary count of individual alphabet feature detections across all the alphabets in the grid, across each 1024x1024 image, black, white, and gray images, color-coded tables*

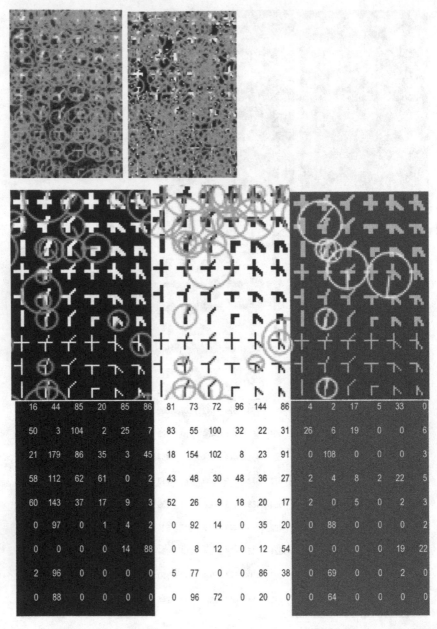

Figure A-19. *BRISK detector, with results shown for a single alphabet grid set. (Top row)*
Gaussian and salt/pepper response. (Middle row) Black, white, and gray response. (Bottom
row) Summary count of individual alphabet feature detections across all the alphabets in
the grid, across each 1024x1024 image, black, white, and gray images, color-coded tables

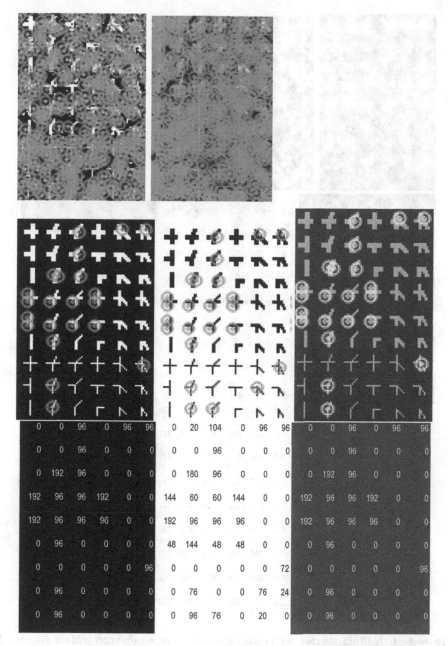

Figure A-20. *FAST detector, with results shown for a single alphabet grid set. (Top row) Gaussian and salt/pepper response. (Middle row) Black, white, and gray response. (Bottom row) Summary count of individual alphabet feature detections across all the alphabets in the grid, across each 1024x1024 image, black, white, and gray images, color-coded tables*

389

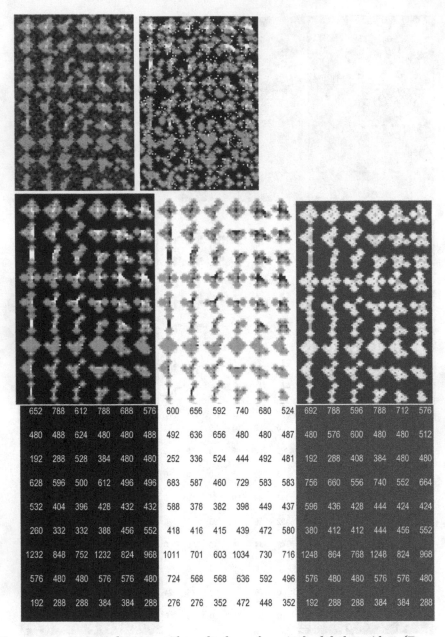

Figure A-21. *HARRIS detector, with results shown for a single alphabet grid set. (Top row) Gaussian and salt/pepper response. (Middle row) Black, white, and gray response. (Bottom row) Summary count of individual alphabet feature detections across all the alphabets in the grid, across each 1024x1024 image, black, white, and gray images, color-coded tables*

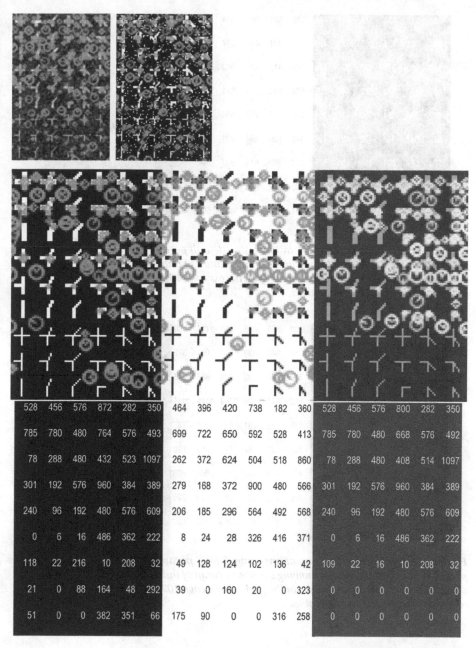

Figure A-22. *SIFT detector, with results shown for a single alphabet grid set. (Top row) Gaussian and salt/pepper response. (Middle row) Black, white, and gray response. (Bottom row) Summary count of individual alphabet feature detections across all the alphabets in the grid, across each 1024x1024 image, black, white, and gray images, color-coded tables*

523	516	433	574	381	468	516	531	502	634	422	458	520	485	384	509	381	463
664	361	428	607	523	484	627	391	486	597	465	444	664	361	427	607	518	401
346	368	375	487	525	388	369	410	426	503	497	451	344	368	371	487	525	385
690	470	622	672	442	505	574	512	558	611	509	578	681	414	526	643	442	505
692	348	654	750	417	351	688	385	601	886	445	344	580	294	512	650	417	351
513	647	436	426	451	434	441	559	466	401	466	515	395	606	333	379	348	377
704	567	501	566	591	577	676	650	619	537	544	548	694	551	461	524	530	418
829	660	738	620	565	492	860	662	643	595	596	523	750	562	651	543	612	346
540	404	697	531	504	522	584	454	653	441	507	461	520	381	677	530	494	509

Figure A-23. *SURF detector (annotations using default parameters not useful, images provided online), with results showing summary count of individual alphabet feature detections across all the alphabets in the grid, across each 1024x1024 image, black, white, and gray images, color-coded tables*

841	887	874	812	1160	1022	868	880	845	821	1114	986	811	833	820	781	1025	939
776	820	876	597	827	941	777	849	899	593	901	879	710	764	838	581	815	831
617	919	925	521	645	753	584	877	899	528	685	746	555	877	880	491	626	646
1012	898	1034	1044	1041	1037	993	943	1006	1064	1179	1014	981	866	1001	1012	987	988
862	851	890	696	889	843	865	792	891	672	768	735	835	830	871	684	885	820
473	856	783	454	633	722	563	923	887	584	802	828	471	834	746	416	622	697
510	683	793	498	608	784	471	714	792	479	603	808	492	642	754	483	588	750
425	673	591	378	606	678	385	608	562	352	663	726	358	604	518	331	565	640
391	686	594	423	466	544	341	616	617	403	465	528	275	566	487	340	399	504

Figure A-24. *ORB detector (annotations using default parameters not useful, images provided online), with results showing summary count of individual alphabet feature detections across all the alphabets in the grid, across each 1024x1024 image, black, white, and gray images, color-coded tables*

Figure A-25. *MSER detector (black on white, white on black, and light gray on dark gray have no detected features)*

Test 3: Synthetic Alphabets Overlaid on Real Images

Table A-6 provides the total detected synthetic features found in the test images of little girls, shown in Figure A-3. Note that only the 0-degree version is used (no rotations), and both the black versions and the white versions of each alphabet are overlaid. In general, the white feature overlays produce more interest points and corner-point detections.

Table A-6. *Summary Count of Detected Features Found in the Synthetic Overlay Images of Little Girls*

Detector	Normal image, no overlays	Black Corners Overlay	White Corners Overlay	Black Interest Points Overlay	White Interest Points Overlay
SURF	3945	16458	20809	10134	14196
SIFT	1672	12417	15347	8017	11551
BRISK	600	7919	10351	5914	8741
FAST	9026	25463	24952	17770	17995
HARRIS	475	9393	22201	4408	11097
GFFT	4474	23009	25120	11632	13872
MSER	1722	174	163	309	209
ORB	7325	53080	57016	41300	50946
STAR	477	3135	5558	2728	4756
SIMPLEBLOB	19	45	10	551	405

Annotated Detector Results on Overlay Images

Annotated images are available online.

Test 4: Rotational Invariance for Each Alphabet

This section provides results showing detector response as *rotational invariance* across the full 0 to 90 degree rotated image sets of black, white, and gray alphabets. Key observations:

- **Black on white, white on black:** Rotational invariance is generally less using black and white images with the current set of detectors and parameters, mainly owing to (1) the maxima and minima values of 0x0 and 0xff used for pixel values, and (2) un-optimized detector tuning parameters. The detectors each seem to operate in a similar manner on images at orientations of 0 degrees and 90 degrees that contain no rotational anti-aliasing artifacts on each alphabet pattern; however, for the other rotations of 10 to 80 degrees, pixel artifacts combine to reduce rotational invariance for these alphabet patterns—each detector behaves differently.

- **Light gray on dark gray:** Rotational invariance is generally better for the detectors using the reduced-range gray scale image alphabet sets using pixel values of 0x40 and 0xc0, rather than the full maxima and minima range used in the black and white image sets. The gray alphabet detector results generally show the most well-recognized alphabet characters under rotation. This may be due to the less pronounced local curvature of closer range gray values in the local region at the interest point or corner.

Methodology for Determining Rotational Invariance

The methodology for determining rotational invariance is illustrated in Figures A-26 through A-30, and illustrated via pseudo-code as follows:

```
For (degree = 0; degree < 100; degree += 10)

        Rotate image (degree)
        For each detector (SURF, SIFT, BRISK, ...):
                Compute interest point locations
                Annotate rotated image showing interest point locations
                Compute bin count (# of times) each alphabet feature is detected
                Create bin count image: pixel value = bin count for each
alphabet character
```

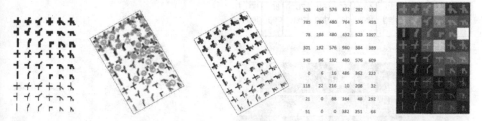

Figure A-26. *Method of computing and binning detected alphabet features across rotated image sets, mocked-up SIFT data for illustration. (Left) Original image. (Center left) Rotated image annotated with detected points. (Center) Count of all detected points across entire image superimposed on alphabet cell regions. (Center right) Summary bin counts of detected alphabet features in grid cells. (Right) 2D histogram rendering of bin counts as an image; each pixel value is the bin count. Brighter pixels in the image have a higher bin count, meaning that the alphabet cell has a higher detection count*

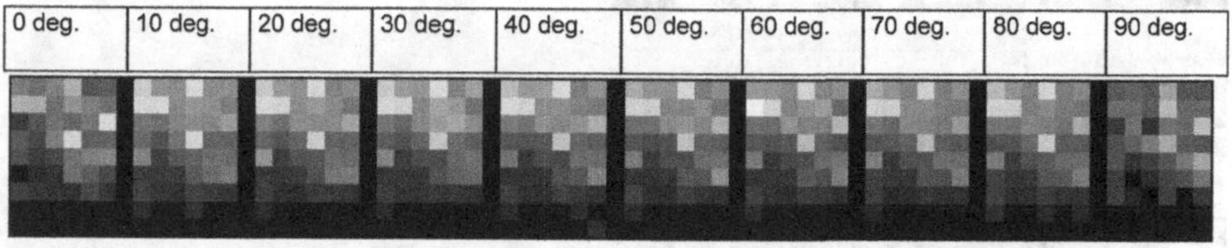

0 deg.	10 deg.	20 deg.	30 deg.	40 deg.	50 deg.	60 deg.	70 deg.	80 deg.	90 deg.

Figure A-27. *Group of 10 SIFT gray scale corner alphabet feature detection results displayed as a 2D histogram image, sephia LUT applied, with pixel values set to the histogram bin values. The histogram for each rotated image is shown here: left image = 0 degree rotation; left-to-right sequence: 0,10,20,30,40,50,60,70,80,90 degree rotations. Note that the histogram bin counts are computed across the entire image, summing all detections of each alphabet feature*

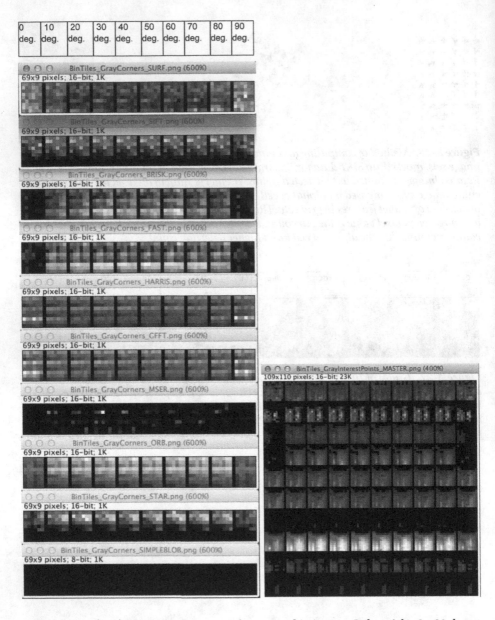

Figure A-28. (Left) Gray corner points 2D histogram bin images. Left to right: 0 - 90 degree rotations, gray scale LUT applied, and light gray on dark gray interest points alphabet 2D histogram binning image, contrast enhanced, sephia LUT applied

Figures A-26 and A-30 show the summary bin counts of synthetic corner point detections across 0 to 90 degree rotations. The ten columns in each image show, left to right, the 0 to 90 degree rotated image final bin counts displayed as images.

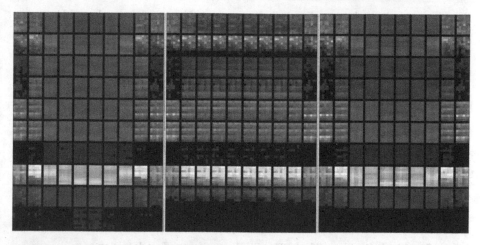

Figure A-29. *Summary bin counts of detected corner alphabet features displayed as a set of 6x9 pixel images, where each pixel value is the bin count. (Left 10 x 10 image group) Black on white corners. (Center 10 x 10 image group) Light gray on dark gray corners. (Right 10 x 10 image group) White on black corners. Note that the gray alphabets are detected with the best rotational invariance. The columns are left to right 0-90 degree rotations, and rows are top to bottom, SURF, SIFT, BRISK, FAST, HARRIS, GFFT, MSER, ORB, STAR, SIMPLEBLOB. Sephia LUT applied*

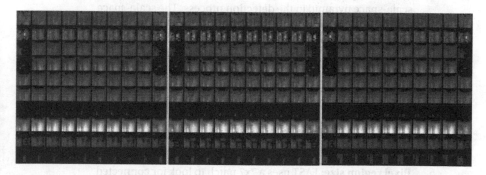

Figure A-30. *Summary bin counts of detected interest point alphabet features displayed as a set of 10x10 pixel images, where each pixel value is the bin count. (Left 10 x 10 image group) Black on white corners. (Center 10 x 10 image group) Light gray on dark gray corners. (Right 10 x 10 image group) White on black corners. Note that the gray alphabets are detected with the best rotational invariance. The columns are left to right 0-90 degree rotations, and rows are top to bottom, SURF, SIFT, BRISK, FAST, HARRIS, GFFT, MSER, ORB, STAR, SIMPLEBLOB. Sephia LUT applied*

Analysis of Results and Non-Repeatability Anomalies

Complete analysis results are online, including annotated images showing detected keypoint locations and text files containing summary information on each detected keypoint.

Caveats

There are deliberate reasons why each interest point detector is designed differently; no detector may be considered superior in all cases by any absolute measure. A few arguments against loosely interpreting these tests results are as follows:

1. **Unpredictability:** Interest point detectors find features that are often unpredictable from the human visual system standpoint, and they are not restricted by design into the narrow boundaries of synthetic interest points and corners points shown here. Often, the interest point detectors find features that a human would not choose.

2. **Pixel aliasing artifacts:** The aliasing artifacts affect detection and are most pronounced for the rotated images using maxima and minima alphabets, such as black on white or white on black, and are less pronounced for light gray on dark gray alphabets.

3. **Scale Space:** Not all the detectors use scale space, and this is a critical point. For example, SIFT, SURF, and ORB use a scale-space pyramid in the detection process. The scale-space approach filters out synthetic alphabet features that are not visible in some levels of a scale-space pyramid.

4. **Binary vs. scalar values:** FAST uses a binary value comparison to build up the descriptor, while other methods use scalar values such as gradients. Binary value methods, such as FAST, will detect the same feature regardless of polarity or gray value range; however, scalar detectors based on gradients are more sensitive to pixel value polarity and pixel value ranges.

5. **Pixel region size:** FAST uses a 7x7 patch to look for connected circle perimeter regions, while other features like SIFT, SURF, and ORB use larger pixel regions that bleed across alphabet grid cells, resulting in interest points being centered between alphabet features, rather than on them.

6. **Region shape:** Features such as MSER and SIMPLEBLOB are designed to detect larger connected regions with no specific shape, rather than smaller local features such as the interest point alphabets. An affine-invariant detector, such as SIFT, may detect features in an oval or oblong region corresponding to affine scale and rotation transformations, while a non-affine detector, such as FAST, may only detect the same feature as a template in a circular or square region with some rotational invariance at scale.

7. **Offset regions from image boundary:** Some detectors, such as ORB, SURF, and SIFT, begin detector computations at an offset from the image boundaries, so features are not computed across the entire image.

8. **Proven value:** Each detector method used here has proved useful and valuable for real applications.

With these caveats in mind, the test results can be allowed to speak for themselves.

Non-Repeatability in Tests 1 and 2

One interesting anomaly visible in Tests 1 and 2 appears in the annotated images, illustrating that detector results are not repeatable on the synthetic interest point and corner alphabets. In some cases, the nonlinearity is striking; see the annotated images for Tests 1 and 2. The expectation of a human is that identical interest points should be equally well recognized. Here are some observations:

1. A human would recognize the same pattern easily whether or not the background and foreground are changed; however, some detectors do not have much invariance to extreme background and foreground polarity. The anomalies between detector behavior across white, black, and gray versions of the alphabets are less expected and harder to explain without looking deeper into each algorithm.

2. Some detectors compute over larger region boundaries than the 14x14 alphabet grid, so detectors virtually ignore the alphabet feature grid and use adjacent pieces of alphabet features.

3. Some detectors use scale space, so individual alphabet features are missed in some cases at higher scale levels, and detectors such as SIFT DoG use multiple scales together.

In summary, interest point detection and parameter tuning are analogous to image processing operators and their parameters: there are endless variations available to achieve the same goals. It is hoped that, by studying the test results here, intuition will be increased and new approaches can be devised.

Other Non-Repeatability in Test 3

We note non-repeatability anomalies with Test 3 using little girl images with synthetic overlays, but there is less expectation of repeatability in this test. Some analysis of the differences between the positive (white) and negative (black) feature overlays can be observed in the annotated synthetic overlay images online.

Test Summary

Take-away analysis for all tests includes the following:

1. **Non-repeatability:** some non-repeatability anomalies detecting nearly identical features, differeing only under rotation by local pixel interpolation artifacts. Some detectors also detect the black, white and gray alphabets differently.

2. **Gray level alphabets (lt. gray on dk.gray)** are detected generally most similar to human expectations. The results show that detectors, with the current tuning parameters, respond more uniformly across rotation with gray level patterns, rather than maxima black and white patterns.

3. **Real images overlaid with synthetic images tests** provide interesting information to develop intuition about detector behavior—for illustration purposes only.

Future Work

Additional analysis should include devising and using alternative alphabets suited for a given type of application, including a larger range of pixel sizes and scales, especially alphabets with closer gray level value polarity, rather than extreme maxima and minima pixel values. Detector tuning should also be explored across the alphabets.

APPENDIX B

■ ■ ■

Survey of Ground Truth Datasets

Table B-1 is a brief survey of public domain datasets in various categories, in no particular order. Note that many of the public domain datasets are freely available from universities and government agencies.

Table B-1. *Public domain datasets*

Name	Labelme
Description	Annotated scenes and objects
Categories	Over 30,000 images; comprehensive; hundreds of categories, including car, person, building, road, sidewalk, sky, tree
Contributions	Open to contributions
Tools and apps	Labelme app for iPhone to contribute to database
Key papers	[67][68]
Owner	MTI CSAIL
Link	http://new-labelme.csail.mit.edu/Release3.0/

Name	SUN
Description	Annotated scenes and objects
Categories	908 scene categories, 3,819 object categories,13,1072 objects, and growing
Contributions	Open to contributions
Tools and apps	Image classifier source code + API, iOS app, Android app
Key papers	[70]
Owner	MTI CSAIL
Link	http://groups.csail.mit.edu/vision/SUN/

Name	UC Irvine Machine Learning Repository
Description	Very useful; huge repository of many categories of images
Categories	Too many to list; very wide range of categories, many attributes of the data are specifically searchable and designed into the ground truth datasets
Contributions	Ongoing
Tools and apps	Online assistant to search for specific ground truth datasets
Key papers	[550]
Link	http://archive.ics.uci.edu/ml/datasets.html

Name	Stanford 3D Scanning Repository
Description	High-resolution 3D scanned images with sub-millimeter accuracy, including XYZ and RGB datasets
Categories	Several scanned 3D objects with 3D point clouds, resolution ranging from 3,400,000 scanned point to 750,000 triangles and upwards
Link	http://graphics.stanford.edu/data/3Dscanrep/

Name	KITTI Benchmark Suite, Karlsruhe Institute of Technology
Description	Stereo datasets for various city driving scenes
Categories	KITTI benchmark suite covers optical flow, odometry, object detection, object orientation estimation; Karlsruhe sequences cover gray scale stereo sequences taken from a moving platform driving through a city; Karlsruhe objects cover gray scale stereo sequences taken from a moving platform driving through a city
Link	http://www.cvlibs.net/datasets/index.html

Name	Caltech Object Recognition Datasets
Description	Old but still useful; objects in hundreds of categories, some annotated with outlines
Categories	Over 256 categories, animals,plants, people, common objects, common food items, tools, furniture, more.
Key papers	[71]
Link	http://www.vision.caltech.edu/Image_Datasets/Caltech101/ http://www.vision.caltech.edu/Image_Datasets/Caltech256/ http://authors.library.caltech.edu/7694/ (latest versions of 101 and 256)

Name	Imagenet + Wordnet
Description	Labeled, annotated, bounding-boxed, and feature-descriptor marked images; over 14,197,122 images indexed into 21,841 sets of similar images, or synsets, created using sister app Wordnet
Categories	Categories include almost anything
Contributions	Images taken from Internet searches
Tools and apps	Online controls: http://www.image-net.org/download-API Source Code: ImageNet Large Scale Visual Recognition Challenge (ILSVRC2010) http://www.image-net.org/challenges/LSVRC/2010/index
Key papers	[72]; several see http://www.image-net.org/about-publication
Owner	Images have individual owners; website is © Stanford and Princeton
Link	http://www.image-net.org/ http://www.image-net.org/challenges/LSVRC/2012/

Name	**Middlebury Computer Vision Datasets**
Description	Scholarly and comprehensive datasets, and algorithm comparisons over most of the datasets
Categories	Stereo vision (excellent), multi-view stereo (excellent), MRF, Optical Flow (excellent), Color processing
Contributions	Algorithm benchmarks over the datasets can be submitted
Key papers	Several; see website
Owner	Middlebury College
Link	http://vision.middlebury.edu/

Name	**ADL Activity Recognition Dataset**
Description	Annotated scenes for activity recognition of common living scenes
Categories	Daily life
Tools and apps	Activity recognition code available (see link below)
Key papers	[73]
Link	http://deepthought.ics.uci.edu/ADLdataset/adl.html

Name	**MIT Indoor Scenes 67, Scene Classification**
Description	Annotated dataset specifically containing diverse indoor scenes
Categories	15,620 images organized into 67 indoor categories, some annotations in Labelme format
Key papers	[74]
Link	http://web.mit.edu/torralba/www/indoor.html

Name	**RGB-D Object Recognition Dataset, U of W**
Description	Dataset contains RGB and corresponding depth images
Categories	300 common household objects, 51 categories using Wordnet similar to Imagenet style (Imagenet dataset reviewed above), each object recorded in RGB and Kinect depth at various rotational angles and viewpoints
Key papers	[75]
Link	http://www.cs.washington.edu/rgbd-dataset/

Name	**NYU Depth Datasets**
Description	Annotated dataset of indoor scenes using RGB-D datasets + accelerometer data
Categories	Over 500,000 frames, many different indoor scenes and scene types, thousands of classes, accelerometer data, inpainted and raw depth information
Tools and apps	Matlab toolbox + g++ code
Key papers	[76]
Link	http://cs.nyu.edu/~silberman/datasets/nyu_depth_v2.html

Name	**Intel Labs Seattle - Egocentric Recognition of Handled Objects**
Description	Annotated dataset for egocentric handled objects using a wearable camera
Categories	Over 42 everyday objects under varied lighting, occlusion, perspectives; over 6GB total video sequence data
Key papers	[77] [78]
Link	http://seattle.intel-research.net/~xren/egovision09/

Name	**Georgia Tech GTEA Egocentric Activities - Gaze(+)**
Description	Annotated dataset for egocentric handled objects using a wearable camera
Categories	Many everyday objects under varied lighting, occlusion, perspectives
Tools and apps	Code library of vision functions and mathematical functions
Key papers	[79]
Link	http://www.cc.gatech.edu/~afathi3/GTEA_Gaze_Website/

Name	**CUReT: Columbia-Utrecht Reflectance and Texture Database**
Description	Extensive texture sample and illumination datasets directions
Categories	Over 60 different samples with over 200 viewing and illumination combinations, BRDF measurement database, more
Key papers	[80]
Link	http://www.cs.columbia.edu/CAVE/software/curet/

Name	**MIT Flickr Material Surface Category Dataset**
Description	Dataset for identifying material categories including fabric, glass, metal, plastic, water, foliage, leather, paper, stone, wood
Categories	Contains images of materials for surface property analysis, in contrast to object or texture analysis; 10 categories of materials + 100 images in each category
Key papers	[81]
Link	http://people.csail.mit.edu/celiu/CVPR2010/index.html

Name	**Faces in the Wilds**
Description	Collection of over 13,000 images of faces annotated with names of people
Categories	Faces
Key papers	[82]
Link	http://vis-www.cs.umass.edu/lfw/

Name	**The CMU Multi-PIE Face Database**
Description	Annotated face and emotion database with multiple pose angles
Categories	750,000 face images are taken over a period of several months for each of 337 subjects over 15 viewpoints and 19 illuminations, annotated facial expressions
Key papers	[83]
Link	http://www.multipie.org/

Name	**Stanford 40 Actions**
Description	People actions image database
Categories	People performing 40 actions, bounding-box annotations, 9,532 images, 180-300 images per action class
Key papers	[84]
Link	http://vision.stanford.edu/Datasets/40actions.html

Name	**NORB 3D Object Recognition from Shape**
Description	NYU object recognition benchmark
Categories	Stereo image pairs; 194,400 total images of 50 toys under 36 azimuths, 9 elevations, and 6 lighting conditions
Tools and apps	EBLEARN C++ learning and vision library, LUSH programming language, VisionGRader object detection tool http://www.cs.nyu.edu/~yann/software/index.html
Key papers	[85]
Link	http://www.cs.nyu.edu/~yann/research/norb/

Name	**Optical Flow Algorithm Evaluation**
Description	Tools and data for optical flow evaluation purposes
Categories	Many optical flow sequence ground truth datasets
Tools and apps	Tool for generating optical flow data, some optical flow code algorithms
Key papers	[86]
Link	http://of-eval.sourceforge.net/

Name	**PETS Crowd Sensing Dataset Challenge**
Description	Multi-sensor camera views composed into a dataset containing sequences of crowd activities
Categories	Challenge goals include crowd estimation, density, tracking of specific people, flow of crowd
Key papers	[94]
Link	http://www.cvg.rdg.ac.uk/PETS2009/a.html

Name	I-LIDS
Description	Security-oriented challenge ground truth dataset to enable competitive benchmarking including scenes for locating parked vehicles, abandoned baggage, secure perimeters, and doorway surveillance
Categories	Various categories in the security domain
Contributions	No, funded by UK government
Tools and apps	n.a.
Key papers	n.a.
Link	http://computervision.wikia.com/wiki/I-LIDS

Name	TRECVID, NIST, US Government
Description	NIST-sponsored public project spanning 2001-2013 for research in automatic segmentation, indexing, and content-based video retrieval
Categories	1. Semantic indexing (SIN) 2. Known-item search (KIS) 3. Instance search (INS) 4. Multimedia event detection (MED) 5. Multimedia event recounting (MER) 6. Surveillance event detection (SER), natural scenes, humans, vegetation, pets, office objects, more
Contributions	Annually by U.S. Government
Tools and apps	The Framework For Detection Evaluations (F4DE) tool, story evaluation tool, and others
Key papers	[95]
Link	http://www-nlpir.nist.gov/projects/trecvid/

Name	Microsoft Research Cambridge
Description	Pixel-wise labeled or segmented objects
Categories	Several hundred objects
Link	http://research.microsoft.com/en-us/projects/objectclassrecognition/

Name	Optical Flow Algorithm Evaluation
Description	Volume-rendered video scenes for optical flow algorithm benchmarking
Categories	Various scenes for optical flow; mainly synthetic sequences generated via ray tracing
Contributions	n.a.
Tools and apps	Yes, Tcl/Tk
Key papers	[96]
Link	http://of-eval.sourceforge.net/

Name	Pascal Object Recognition VOC Challenge Dataset
Description	Standardized ground truth data for a research challenge spanning 2005-2013 in the area of object recognition; competitions include classification, detection, segmentation, and actions over each of 20 classes of data
Categories	Consists of over 20 classes of objects in scenes including persons, animals, vehicles, indoor objects
Contributions	Via the Pascal conference
Tools and apps	Includes a developer kit and other useful software for labeling data and database access, and tools for reporting benchmarks results
Key papers	[97]
Link	http://pascallin.ecs.soton.ac.uk/challenges/VOC/

Name	CRCV
Description	Very extensive; University of Central Florida's Center for Research in Computer Vision hosts a large collection of research data covering several domains
Categories	Comprehensive set of categories (aerial views, ground views) including dynamic textures, multi-modal iPhone sensor ground truth data (video, accelerometer, gyro), several categories of human actions, crowd segmentation, parking lots, human actions, much more
Contributions	n.a.
Tools and apps	n.a.
Key papers	[98]
Link	http://vision.eecs.ucf.edu/datasetsActions.html

Name	**UCB Contour Detection and Image Segmentation**
Description	U.C. Berkeley Computer Vision group provides a complete set of ground truth data, algorithms, and performance evaluations for contour detection, image segmentation, and some interest point methods
Categories	500 ground truth images on natural scenes containing a wide range of subjects and labeled ground truth data
Contributions	n.a.
Tools and apps	Benchmarking code (*globalPB* for CPU and GPU)
Key papers	[99]
Link	http://www.eecs.berkeley.edu/Research/Projects/CS/vision/ grouping/resources.html#bench

Name	**CAVIAR Ground Truth Videos for Context-Aware Vision**
Description	Project site containing labeled and annotated ground truth data of humans in cities and shopping centers, including 52 videos with 90K frames total including people in indoor office scenes and shopping centers
Categories	Both scripted and real-life activities in shopping centers and offices, including walking, browsing, meeting, fighting, window shopping, entering/exiting stores
Contributions	n.a.
Tools and apps	n.a.
Key papers	[100]
Link	http://homepages.inf.ed.ac.uk/rbf/CAVIAR/caviar.htm

Name	**Boston University Computer Science Department**
Description	Image and video database covering a wide range of subject categories
Categories	Video sequences for head tracking and sign language; some datasets are labeled; still images for hand tracking, multi-face tracking, vehicle tracking, more
Contributions	Anonymous FTP
Tools and apps	n.a.
Key papers	[101]
Link	http://www.cs.bu.edu/groups/ivc/data.php

Imaging and Computer Vision Resources

This appendix contains a list of some resources for computer vision and imaging, including commercial products, open-source projects, organizations, and standards bodies.

Commercial Products

Name	Matlab
Description	Industry standard math package with many scientific package options for various fields including imaging and computer vision. Includes a decent software development environment, providing add-on libraries for computer vision, image processing, visualization, more. Suited well for code development.
Library API	Extensive API libraries Internal to the SDE.
SDE	Includes software development environment for coding.
Open Source	Not for the product, but possibly for some code developed by users.
Link	http://www.mathworks.com/products/matlab/
Name	Mathematica
Description	Industry standard math package with many scientific package options for various fields, including image processing and computer vision. Excellent for creation of publication-ready visualizations and math notebooks. Add-on libraries for computer vision, image processing, visualization, more.
Library API	Extensive API libraries Internal to the SDE.
SDE	Includes a default function-based script development environment, and some code development add-ons.
Open Source	Not for the product, but possibly for code developed by users.
Link	http://www.wolfram.com/mathematica/

Name	Intel TBB, Intel IPP, Intel CILK++
Description	Intel provides libraries, languages, and compilers optimized for the IA instruction set. Intel TBB is a multi-threading library for single and multi-core processors, Intel IPP provides imaging and computer vision performance primitives optimized for IA and SIMD instructions and in some cases GPGPU, and Intel CILK++ is a language for writing SIMD/SIMT parallel code.
Library API	Extensive API libraries.
SDE	No, but Intel CILK++ is a programming language.
Open Source	No.
Link	http://software.intel.com/en-us/intel-tbb
	http://software.intel.com/en-us/intel-ipp

Open Source

Name	OpenCV
Description	Industry standard computer vision and image processing library, used worldwide by major corporations and others.
Library API	Extensive API library.
SDE	No.
Open Source	BSD license.
Link	http://opencv.org/
Name	ImageJ - FIJI
Description	Application for image processing, visualization, and computer vision. Developed by the USG National Institutes of Health[502], available for public use. Extensive. FIJI is a distribution of ImageJ with many plug-ins submitted by the user community.
Library API	No.
SDE	No.
Open Source	Public domain use.
Link	http://rsbweb.nih.gov/ij/index.html
	http://rsb.info.nih.gov/ij/plugins/
	http://fiji.sc/Fiji

Name	**VLFEAT**
Description	C library containing a range of common computer vision algorithms for feature description, pattern matching, and image processing.
Library API	Extensive API library.
SDE	No.
Open Source	BSD license.
Link	http://vlfeat.org

Name	**VTK**
Description	C++ library containing a range of common image processing, graphics, and data visualization functions. Includes GUI widgets. VTL also provides consulting.
Library API	Extensive API library.
SDE	No.
Open Source	BSD license.
Link	http://vtk.org/

Name	**Meshlab**
Description	Application for visualizing, rendering, annotating, and converting 3D data meshes such as point clouds and CAD designs. Extensive. Uses the VCG library from ISTI – CNR.
Library API	No.
SDE	No.
Open Source	BSD license.
Link	http://meshlab.sourceforge.net/

Name	**PfeLIb**
Description	Library for image processing and computer vision acceleration.
Library API	Yes.
SDE	No.
Open Source	No.
Link	See reference[495].

413

Name	Point Cloud Library (PCL)
Description	Extensive open-source library for dealing primarily with 3D point clouds, including implementations of many cutting-edge 3D descriptors from the latest academic research and visualization methods.
Library API	Yes.
SDE	No.
Open Source	Yes.
Link	`http://pointclouds.org/downloads/`
	`http://pointclouds.org/documentation/`
	`http://docs.pointclouds.org/trunk/a02944.html`

Name	Shogun Machine Learning Toolbox
Description	Library for machine learning and pattern matching. Extensive.
Library API	Yes.
SDE	No.
Open Source	GPL.
Link	`http://shogun-toolbox.org/page/features/`

Name	Halide High-Performance Image Processing Language
Description	C++ language classes optimized for SIMD, SIMT, and GPGPU.
Library API	Yes.
SDE	No.
Open Source	Open-source MIT license.
Link	`http://halide-lang.org/`

Name	REIN (Recognition INfrastructure) Vision Algorithm Framework
Description	Framework for computer vision in robotics; uses ROS operating system. See references[397,503].
Library API	Yes.
SDE	No.
Open Source	Open-source MIT license.
Link	`http://wiki.ros.org/rein`

Name	ECTO –Graph Network Construction for Computer Vision
Description	Library for creating directed acyclic graphs of functions for computer vision pipelines, supports threading. Written in a C++/Python framework. Can integrate with OpenCV, PCL and ROS.
Library API	Yes.
SDE	No.
Open Source	Apparently.
Link	http://plasmodic.github.io/ecto/

Organizations, Institutions, and Standards

Microsoft Research
http://academic.research.microsoft.com/

Microsoft Research has one of the largest staff of computer vision experts in the world, and actively promotes conferences and research. Provides several good resources online.

CIE
http://www.cie.co.at/

International Commission on Illumination, abbreviated CIE after the French name, provides standard illuminant data for a range of light sources as it pertains to color science, as well as standards for the well-known color spaces CIE XYZ, CIE Lab and CIE Luv.

ICC
http://www.color.org/index.xalter

International Color Consortium provides the ICC standard color profiles for imaging devices, as well as many other industry standards, including the sRGB color space for color displays.

CAVE Computer Vision Laboratory
http://www.cs.columbia.edu/CAVE/

Computer Vision Laboratory at Columbia University, directed by Dr. Shree Nayar, provides world-class imaging and vision research.

RIT Munsel Color Science Laboratory
http://www.rit.edu/cos/colorscience/

Rochester Institute of Technology Munsel Color Science Laboratory is among the leading research institutions in the area or color science and imaging, provides a wide range of resources, and has with strong ties to industry imaging giants such as Kodak, Xerox, and others.

(continued)

OPENVX KHRONOS

http://www.khronos.org/openvx

OPENVX is a proposed standard for low-level vision primitive acceleration, operated with the KHRONOS standards group.

SPIE

Society for Optics and Photonics

Journal of Medical Imaging

Journal of Electronic Imaging

Journal of Applied Remote Sensing

http://spie.org/

Interdisciplinary approach to the science of light, including photonics, sensors, and imaging; promotes conferences, publishes journals.

IEEE

CVPR, Computer Vision and Pattern Recognition

PAMI, Pattern Analysis and Machine Intelligence

ICCV, International Conference on Computer Vision

IP, Trans. Image Processing

http://ieee.org

Society for publication of journals and conferences, including various computer vision and imaging topics.

CVF

Computer Vision Foundation

http://www.cv-foundation.org/

Promotes computer vision, provides dissemination of papers.

NIST – Image Group (USG)

National Institute Of Standards

http://www.nist.gov/itl/iad/ig/

Promotes computer vision and imaging grand challenges; covers biometrics standards, fingerprint testing, face, iris, multimodal testing, next generation test bed.

I20 - Darpa information innovation office (USG)

http://www.darpa.mil/
Our_Work/I20/Programs/

http://www.darpa.mil/
OpenCatalog/index.html

Extensive array of computer vision and related program research for military applications.

Some work is released to the public via the *OpenCatalog*.

Journals and Their Abbreviations

CVGIP Graphical Models /graphical Models and Image Processing /computer Vision, Graphics, and Image Processing

CVIU Computer Vision and Image Understanding

IJCV International Journal of Computer Vision

IVC Image and Vision Computing

JMIV Journal of Mathematical Imaging and Vision

MVA Machine Vision and Applications

TMI - IEEE Transactions on Medical Imaging

Conferences and Their Abbreviations

3DIM International Conference on 3-D Imaging and Modeling

3DPVT 3D Data Processing Visualization and Transmission

ACCV Asian Conference on Computer Vision

AMFG Analysis and Modeling of Faces and Gestures

BMCV Biologically Motivated Computer Vision

BMVC British Machine Vision Conference

CRV Canadian Conference on Computer and Robot Vision

CVPR Computer Vision and Pattern Recognition

CVRMed Computer Vision, Virtual Reality and Robotics in Medicine

DGCI Discrete Geometry for Computer Imagery

ECCV European Conference on Computer Vision

EMMCVPR Energy Minimization Methods in Computer Vision and Pattern Recognition

FGR IEEE International Conference on Automatic Face and Gesture Recognition

ICARCV International Conference on Control, Automation, Robotics and Vision

ICCV International Conference on Computer Vision

ICCV Workshops

ICVS International Conference on Computer Vision Systems

ICWSM International Conference on Weblogs and Social Media

ISVC International Symposium on Visual Computing

NIPS Neural Information Processing Systems

Scale-Space Scale-Space Theories in Computer Vision

VLSM Variational, Geometric, and Level Set Methods in Computer Vision

WACV Workshop on Applications of Computer Vision

Online Resources

Name	CVONLINE
Description	Huge list of computer vision software and projects, indexed to Wikipedia
Link	http://homepages.inf.ed.ac.uk/rbf/CVonline/environ.htm
Name	**Annotated Computer Vision Bibliography**
Description	Huge index of links to computer vision topics, references, software, more
Link	http://www.visionbib.com/bibliography/contents.html
Name	**NIST Online Engineering Statistics Handbook (USG)**
Description	Handbook for statistics, includes examples and software
Link	http://www.itl.nist.gov/div898/handbook/
Name	**The Computer Industry (David Lowe)**
Description	Includes links to major computer vision and imaging product companies
Link	http://www.cs.ubc.ca/~lowe/vision.html

APPENDIX D

■ ■ ■

Extended SDM Metrics

Figure D-1 provides a visualization of image texture using SDM's.

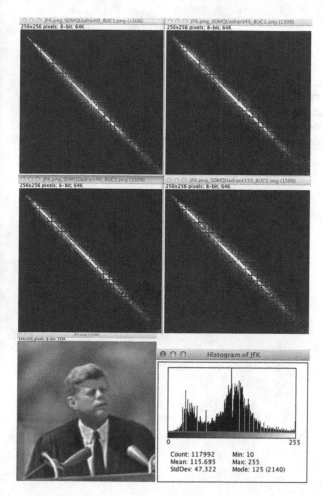

Figure D-1. *SDM extended metrics*

Listing D-1 illustrates the extended SDM metrics from Chapter 3. The code is available online at

http://www.apress.com/source-code/ComputerVisionMetrics

Listing D-1. Extended SDM Metrics from Chapter 3

```
/*
**        CREATED 1991 (C) KRIG RESEARCH, SCOTT KRIG - UNPUBLISHED SOFTWARE
**        PORTED TO MAC 2014
**
**                        ALL RIGHTS RESERVED
**
**        THIS SOFTWARE MAY BE USED FREELY FOR ACADEMIC AND RESEARCH PURPOSES.
**        REFERENCE THIS BOOK AND PROVIDE THIS NOTICE WHEN USING THE SOFTWARE.
*/


using namespace std;

#include <math.h>
#include <stdio.h>
#include <opencv2/opencv.hpp>
#include "/usr/local/include/opencv/cv.h"
#include "/usr/local/include/opencv2/core/core.hpp"
#include "/usr/local/include/opencv2/highgui/highgui.hpp"
#include <iostream>

using namespace cv;

#define TINY        0.0000000001
#define F6U         "%6f.3"
#define F6F         "%.6f"
#define F3F         "%.3f"
#define FXF         "%.0f"
#define FALSE 0
#define TRUE 1

typedef struct area {
        int x;
        int y;
        int dx;
        int dy;
} area_t;

typedef struct {
        double        t0;
        double        t90;
        double        t135;
        double        t45;
```

```
        double          tave;
        } ctab;

typedef struct {
        double          median;
        double          ave;
        double          adev;
        double          sdev;
        double          svar;
        double          skew;
        double          curt;
        int             min;
        int             max;
        ctab            xcentroid;
        ctab            ycentroid;
        ctab            _asm;
        ctab            low_frequency_coverage;
        ctab            total_coverage;
        ctab            corrected_coverage;
        ctab            total_power;
        ctab            relative_power;
        ctab            locus_length;
        ctab            locus_mean_density;
        ctab            bin_mean_density;
        ctab            containment;
        ctab            linearity;
        ctab            linearity_strength;
        ctab            autocorrelation;
        ctab            covariance;
        ctab            inertia; /* haralick contrast */
        ctab            absolute_value;
        ctab            inverse_difference; /* haralick */
        ctab            entropy; /* haralick */
        ctab            correlation; /* haralick */
        } glob_t;

glob_t          gt;

/* FUNCTIONS */

int i_sort(
int             *x,
int             n,
int             parm)
{
        int             k,i,ii;
        int             y,found;
```

```c
        int        xi;
        int        n2, n2p;

        x--;
        for (k=1; k<n+1; k++) {
                y = x[k];
                for (i=k-1, found = FALSE; i>=0 && !found; ) {
                        xi = x[i];
                        ii = i+1;
                        if (y < xi) {
                                x[ii] = xi;
                                i--;
                        } else {
                                found = TRUE;
                        }
                }
                x[ii] = y;
        }
        if (parm == 0) return 0;
        n2p = (n2=(n>>1))+1;
        return ( n % 2 ? x[n2p] : (x[n2] + x[n2p]) >>1 );
}


int lmoment(
int        *data,
int        n,
double     *median,
double     *ave,
double     *adev,
double     *sdev,
double     *svar,
double     *skew,
double     *curt)
{
        int        j;
        double     s,p,ep=0.0;

        if (n <= 1) return 0;

        s=0.0;
        for (j=1; j<=n;j++) s += (double)data[j];
        *ave=s/n;
        *adev=(*svar)=(*skew)=(*curt)=0.0;
        for (j=1;j<=n;j++) {
                *adev += abs(s=(double)data[j]-(*ave));
                *svar += (p=s*s);
                *skew += (p *= s);
                *curt += (p *= s);
        }
```

```
        *adev /=n;
        *svar = (*svar - ep*ep / n) / (n-1);
        *sdev=sqrt(*svar);
        if (*svar) {
                s = (n*(*svar)*(*sdev));
                if (s != 0) *skew /=s;
                else *skew = 0;
                s = (n*(*svar)*(*svar))-3.0;
                if (s != 0) *curt = (*curt) / s;
                else *curt = 0;
        } else {
                *skew = *curt = 0.0;
        }
        *median = 0;
        if (n > 20000) return 0;

        *median = (double)i_sort(data, n, 1);

        return 0;

}


int         mean_sdev(
int         xp,
int         yp,
int         *xdata,
double      *xmean,
double      *xsdev,
double      *ymean,
double      *ysdev)
{
        double    u_x1, a_x1;
        int       mx, my,v,t,x,y,z, offset;
        int       dif[256];

        /* first calculate mean */
        offset = 256 * yp;
        x = y = 0;
        for (z=0; z < 256; x += xdata[offset+z], z++);
        for (z=0; z < 256; y += xdata[xp + (z*256)], z++);

        mx = x / 256.;
        *xmean = (double)mx;
        my = y / 256.;
        *ymean = (double)my;
```

```c
        /* now calculate standard deviation */
        x = y = 0;
        z=0;
        while (z < 256) {
                v = mx - xdata[offset+z];
                x += v*v;
                v = my - xdata[xp + (z*256)];
                y += v*v;
                z++;
        }
        *xsdev = x / 256;
        *ysdev = y / 256;

        return 0;
}


int lohi(
int     n,
int     *cv,
int     *lo,
int     *hi)
{
        int     x;
        int     lv, hv;

        lv = 0x1fffff;
        hv =0;
        x=0;
        while (x < n) {
                if (cv[x] < lv) lv = cv[x];
                if (cv[x] > hv) hv = cv[x];
                x++;
        }

        *lo = lv;
        *hi = hv;

        return 0;
}

int        savegt(
ctab       *ctp,
double     dv1,
double dv2,
```

```c
double    dv3,
double    dv4)
{
        ctp->t0 = dv1;
        ctp->t90 = dv2;
        ctp->t135 = dv3;
        ctp->t45 = dv4;
        ctp->tave = (dv1 + dv2 + dv3 + dv4) / 4;

        return 0;
}

int     gtput(
char    *prompt,
char    *fs,
ctab    *ctp,
FILE    *fstream)
{
        char        str[256];
        char        form[256];

        fputs(prompt, fstream);
        sprintf(form, "%s      %s      %s      %s      %s \n", fs, fs, fs, fs, fs);
        sprintf(str, form, ctp->t0, ctp->t90, ctp->t135, ctp->t45, ctp->tave);
        fputs(str, fstream);

        return 0;

}

int     put_txfile(
FILE    *fstream)
{
        char        str[256];

        sprintf(str, "gray value moments: min:%u max:%u mean:%u\n",
                gt.min,gt.max, (int)gt.ave);
        fputs(str, fstream);
        sprintf(str, "moments:  adev:%.4f sdev:%.4f svar:%.4f  skew:%.6f
                curt:%.6f \n",gt.adev, gt.sdev, gt.svar, gt.skew, gt.curt);
        fputs(str, fstream);
```

```
        fputs("\n", fstream);
        fputs("            --------------------------------------\n", fstream);
        fputs("            0deg   90deg   135deg   45deg   ave\n", fstream);
        fputs("            --------------------------------------\n", fstream);
        gtput("xcentroid                   ", FXF, &gt.xcentroid, fstream);
        gtput("ycentroid                   ", FXF, &gt.ycentroid, fstream);
        gtput("low_frequency_coverage      ", F3F, &gt.low_frequency_coverage,
                                fstream);
        gtput("total_coverage              ", F3F, &gt.total_coverage, fstream);
        gtput("corrected_coverage          ", F3F, &gt.corrected_coverage, fstream);
        gtput("total_power                 ", F3F, &gt.total_power, fstream);
        gtput("relative_power              ", F3F, &gt.relative_power, fstream);
        gtput("locus_length                ", FXF, &gt.locus_length, fstream);
        gtput("locus_mean_density          ", FXF, &gt.locus_mean_density, fstream);
        gtput("bin_mean_density            ", FXF, &gt.bin_mean_density, fstream);
        gtput("containment                 ", F3F, &gt.containment, fstream);
        gtput("linearity                   ", F3F, &gt.linearity, fstream);
        gtput("linearity_strength          ", F3F, &gt.linearity_strength, fstream);

        return 0;

}

int     texture(
char    *filename)
{
        char        str[256];
        int         pmx[256], pmy[256];
        int         x,y,z,dx,dy,dz,sz,bpp;
        int         accum, tmin, tmax;
        int         tmin2, tmax2, yc;
        int         *data;
        int         mval0, mval90, mval135, mval45;
        double  median, ave, adev, sdev, svar, skew, curt;
        double  median2, ave2, adev2, sdev2, svar2, skew2, curt2;
        int         *dm0, *dm90, *dm135, *dm45;
        FILE    *fstream;
        int         i0, i90, i135, i45, iave, n;
        int         c0, c90, c135, c45, cave;
        int         p0, p90, p135, p45, pave;
        double  d0, d90, d135, d45, dave;
        double  f0, f90, f135, f45;
```

```
/*************************************************************/
/* READ THE INPUT IMAGE, EXPECT IT TO BE 8-bit UNSIGNED INT  */
/* Mat type conversion is simple in openCV, try it later     */

Mat imageIn = cv::imread(filename);
dx = imageIn.rows;
dy = imageIn.cols;
unsigned char *pixels = imageIn.data;

cout << "dx " << dx << " dy " << dy << " elemSize() " <<
        imageIn.elemSize() << endl;
data = (int *)malloc(dx * dy * 4);
if (data == 0)
{
        cout << "malloc error in texture()" << endl;
}
for (y=0; y < dy; y++) {
        for (x=0; x < dx; x++) {
                int pixel = (int)*(imageIn.ptr(x,y));
                if (pixel > 255) { pixel = 255; }
                data[(y * dx) + x] = pixel;
        }
}


/*************************************************************/
/* PART 1 - get normal types of statistics from pixel data */

lmoment(data, sz, &median, &ave, &adev, &sdev, &svar, &skew, &curt);
lohi(sz, data, &tmin, &tmax);

gt.median = median;
gt.ave = ave;
gt.adev = adev;
gt.sdev = sdev;
gt.svar = svar;
gt.skew = skew;
gt.curt = curt;
gt.min = tmin;
gt.max = tmax;

fstream = fopen("SDMExtended.txt", "w");
if (fstream <= 0) {
        cout << "#cannot create file" << endl;
        return 0;
}
```

```
      sprintf(str, "texture for object:      %s\n", filename);
      fputs(str, fstream);
      sprintf(str, "area:                    %u, %u \n", dx, dy);
      fputs(str, fstream);


      /**********************************************************/
      /* PART 2 - calculate the 4 spatial dependency matricies */

      dm0   = (int *)malloc( 256*256*4 );
      dm90  = (int *)malloc( 256*256*4 );
      dm135 = (int *)malloc( 256*256*4 );
      dm45  = (int *)malloc( 256*256*4 );
      if ((dm0==0) || (dm90==0) || (dm135==0) || (dm45==0)) {
              cout << "malloc error in texture2" << endl;
              return 0;
      }


      x=0;
      while (x < 256*256) {
              dm0[x] = dm90[x] = dm135[x] = dm45[x] = 0;
              x++;
      }


      y=0;
      while (y < dy-1) {
              yc = dx * y;

              x=0;
              while (x < dx-1) {

                  dm0[ (data[yc + x]&0xff) + ((( data[yc + x + 1]  )<<
                      8)&0xff00) ]++;
                  dm0[ (data[yc + x + 1]&0xff) + ((( data[yc + x]  )<<
                      8)&0xff00) ]++;
                  dm90[ (data[yc + x]&0xff) + ((( data[yc + x + dx]  )<<
                      8)&0xff00) ]++;
                  dm90[ (data[yc + x + dx]&0xff) + ((( data[yc + x]  )<<
                      8)&0xff00) ]++;
                  dm135[ (data[yc + x]&0xff) + ((( data[yc + x + dx + 1]
                      )<< 8)&0xff00) ]++;
                  dm135[ (data[yc + x + dx + 1]&0xff) + ((( data[yc + x]
                      )<< 8)&0xff00) ]++;
                  dm45[ (data[yc + x + 1]&0xff) + ((( data[yc + x + dx]  )<<
                      8)&0xff00) ]++;
                  dm45[ (data[yc + x + dx]&0xff) + ((( data[yc + x + 1]  )<<
                      8)&0xff00) ]++;
```

```
                x++;
        }
        y++;
}


/***************** CALCULATE TEXTURE METRICS *****************/

/* centroid */
pmx[0] = pmx[1] = pmx[2] = pmx[3] = 0;
pmy[0] = pmy[1] = pmy[2] = pmy[3] = 0;
i0 = i90 = i135 = i45 = 0;
y=0;
while (y < 256) {
        x=0;
        while (x < 256) {
                z = x + (256 * y);
                pmx[0] += (x * dm0[z]);
                pmy[0] += (y * dm0[z]); i0 += dm0[z];
                pmx[1] += (x * dm90[z]);
                pmy[1] += (y * dm90[z]); i90 += dm90[z];
                pmx[2] += (x * dm135[z]);
                pmy[2] += (y * dm135[z]); i135 += dm135[z];
                pmx[3] += (x * dm45[z]);
                pmy[3] += (y * dm45[z]); i45 += dm45[z];
                x++;
        }
        y++;
}
pmx[0] = pmx[0] / i0;
pmy[0] = pmy[0] / i0;
pmx[1] = pmx[1] / i90;
pmy[1] = pmy[1] / i90;
pmx[2] = pmx[2] / i135;
pmy[2] = pmy[2] / i135;
pmx[3] = pmx[3] / i45;
pmy[3] = pmy[3] / i45;
x = (pmx[0] + pmx[1] + pmx[2] + pmx[3]) / 4;
y = (pmy[0] + pmy[1] + pmy[2] + pmy[3]) / 4;

gt.xcentroid.t0 = pmx[0];
gt.ycentroid.t0 = pmy[0];
gt.xcentroid.t90 = pmx[1];
gt.ycentroid.t90 = pmy[1];
gt.xcentroid.t135 = pmx[2];
gt.ycentroid.t135 = pmy[2];
gt.xcentroid.t45 = pmx[3];
```

429

```
gt.ycentroid.t45 = pmy[3];
gt.xcentroid.tave = x;
gt.ycentroid.tave = y;

/* low frequency coverage */
i0 = i90 = i135 = i45 = 0;
c0 = c90 = c135 = c45 = 0;
x=0;
while (x < 256*256) {
        if ((dm0[x] != 0) && (dm0[x] < 3)) i0++;
        if ((dm90[x] != 0) && (dm90[x] < 3)) i90++;
        if ((dm135[x] != 0) && (dm135[x] < 3)) i135++;
        if ((dm45[x] != 0) && (dm45[x] < 3)) i45++;
        if (!dm0[x]) c0++;
        if (!dm90[x]) c90++;
        if (!dm135[x]) c135++;
        if (!dm45[x]) c45++;
        x++;
}
d0 = (double)i0 / 0x10000;
d90 = (double)i90 / 0x10000;
d135 = (double)i135 / 0x10000;
d45 = (double)i45 / 0x10000;

savegt(&gt.low_frequency_coverage, d0, d90, d135, d45);

d0 = (double)c0 / 0x10000;
d90 = (double)c90 / 0x10000;
d135 = (double)c135 / 0x10000;
d45 = (double)c45 / 0x10000;

savegt(&gt.total_coverage, d0, d90, d135, d45);

d0 = (c0-i0) / (double)0x10000;
d90 = (c90-i90) / (double)0x10000;
d135 = (c135-i135) / (double)0x10000;
d45 = (c45-i45) / (double)0x10000;

savegt(&gt.corrected_coverage, d0, d90, d135, d45);

/* power */
i0 = i90 = i135 = i45 = 0;
c0 = c90 = c135 = c45 = 0;
p0 = p90 = p135 = p45 = 0;
y=0;
```

```
while (y < 256) {
        z = y * 256;
        x=0;
        while (x < 256) {
                n = x-y;
                if (n < 0) n = -n;
                if (dm0[x+z] != 0) { i0 += n; c0++;  }
                if (dm90[x+z] != 0) { i90 += n; c90++; }
                if (dm135[x+z] != 0) { i135 += n; c135++; }
                if (dm45[x+z] != 0) { i45 += n; c45++; }
                x++;
        }
        y++;
}
d0 =  (i0 / 0x10000);
d90 = (i90 / 0x10000);
d135 = (i135 / 0x10000);
d45 = (i45 / 0x10000);

savegt(&gt.total_power, d0, d90, d135, d45);

d0 =  (i0 / c0);
d90 = (i90 / c90);
d135 = (i135 / c135);
d45 = (i45 / c45);

savegt(&gt.relative_power, d0, d90, d135, d45);

/* locus density */
d0 = d90 = d135 = d45 = 0.0;
c0 = c90 = c135 = c45 = 0;
p0 = p90 = p135 = p45 = 0;
y=0;
while (y < 256) {
        z = y * 256;
        i0 = i90 = i135 = i45 = 0;
        x=0;
        while (x < 256) {
                n = x-y;
                if (n < 0) n = -n;
                if ((dm0[x+z] != 0) && (n < 7)) { c0++; p0 += dm0[x+z]; }
                if ((dm90[x+z] != 0) && (n < 7)) { c90++; p90 += dm90[x+z]; }
                if ((dm135[x+z] != 0) && (n < 7)) { c135++; p135 +=
                        dm135[x+z]; }
                if ((dm45[x+z] != 0) && (n < 7)) { c45++; p45 += dm45[x+z]; }
```

431

```
                if ((dm0[x+z] == 0) && (n < 7)) { i0++; }
                if ((dm90[x+z] == 0) && (n < 7)) { i90++; }
                if ((dm135[x+z] == 0) && (n < 7)) { i135++; }
                if ((dm45[x+z] == 0) && (n < 7)) { i45++; }

                x++;
            }
            if (!i0) d0 += 1;
            if (!i90) d90 += 1;
            if (!i135) d135 += 1;
            if (!i45) d45 += 1;
            y++;
    }

    savegt(&gt.locus_length, d0, d90, d135, d45);

    d0 = (p0/c0);
    d90 = (p90/c90);
    d135 = (p135/c135);
    d45 = (p45/c45);

    savegt(&gt.locus_mean_density, d0, d90, d135, d45);

    /* density */
    c0 = c90 = c135 = c45 = 0;
    p0 = p90 = p135 = p45 = 0;
    x=0;
    while ( x < 256*256) {
            if (dm0[x] != 0) { c0 += dm0[x]; p0++; }
            if (dm90[x] != 0) { c90 += dm90[x]; p90++; }
            if (dm135[x] != 0) { c135 += dm135[x]; p135++; }
            if (dm45[x] != 0) { c45 += dm45[x]; p45++; }
            x++;
    }
    d0 = c0 / p0;
    d90 = c90 / p90;
    d135 = c135 / p135;
    d45 = c45 / p45;

    savegt(&gt.bin_mean_density, d0, d90, d135, d45);

    /* containment */
    i0 = i90 = i135 = i45 = 0;
    x=0;
    while (x < 256) {
            if (dm0[x]) i0++; if (dm0[256*256 - x - 1]) i0++;
            if (dm90[x]) i90++; if (dm90[256*256 - x - 1]) i90++;
```

```
        if (dm135[x]) i135++; if (dm135[256*256 - x - 1]) i135++;
        if (dm45[x]) i45++; if (dm45[256*256 - x - 1]) i45++;

        if (dm0[x*256]) i0++; if (dm0[(x*256)+255]) i0++;
        if (dm90[x*256]) i90++; if (dm90[(x*256)+255]) i90++;
        if (dm135[x*256]) i135++; if (dm135[(x*256)+255]) i135++;
        if (dm45[x*256]) i45++; if (dm45[(x*256)+255]) i45++;

  x++;
}


d0 = 1.0 - ((double)i0 / 1024.0);
d90 = 1.0 - ((double)i90 / 1024.0);
d135 = 1.0 - ((double)i135 / 1024.0);
d45 = 1.0 - ((double)i45 / 1024.0);

savegt(&gt.containment, d0, d90, d135, d45);

/* linearity */
i0 = i90 = i135 = i45 = 0;
c0 = c90 = c135 = c45 = 0;
y=0;
while (y < 256) {
        z = y * 256;
        if (dm0[z + y] > 1) { i0++; c0 += dm0[z+y]; }
        if (dm90[z + y] > 1) { i90++; c90 += dm90[z+y]; }
        if (dm135[z + y] > 1) { i135++; c135 += dm135[z+y]; }
        if (dm45[z + y] > 1) { i45++; c45 += dm45[z+y]; }
        y++;
}
d0 = (double)i0 / 256.;
d90 = (double)i90 / 256.;
d135 = (double)i135 / 256.;
d45 = (double)i45 / 256.;

savegt(&gt.linearity, d0, d90, d135, d45);

/* linearity strength */
d0 = (c0/(i0+.00001)) / 256.;
d90 = (c90/(i90+.00001)) / 256.;
d135 = (c135/(i135+.00001)) / 256.;
d45 = (c45/(i45+.00001)) / 256.;

savegt(&gt.linearity_strength, d0, d90, d135, d45);

/* WRITE ALL STATISTICS IN gt. STRUCTURE TO OUTPUT FILE */
put_txfile(fstream);
```

433

```
/*  clip to max value 255 */
mval0 = mval90 = mval135 = mval45 = 0;
x=0;
while (x < 256*256) {
        if (dm0[x] > 255)  dm0[x] = 255;
        if (dm90[x] > 255)  dm90[x] = 255;
        if (dm135[x] > 255)  dm135[x] = 255;
        if (dm45[x] > 255)  dm45[x] = 255;
        x++;
}

/*****************************************************/
/* Convert data to unsigned char to write into png */

unsigned char *dm0b   = (unsigned char *)malloc( 256*256);
unsigned char *dm90b  = (unsigned char *)malloc( 256*256);
unsigned char *dm135b = (unsigned char *)malloc( 256*256);
unsigned char *dm45b  = (unsigned char *)malloc( 256*256);
if ((dm0b==0) || (dm90b==0) || (dm135b==0) || (dm45b==0)) {
        cout << "malloc error in texture3" << endl;
        return 0;
}

x=0;
while (x < 256*256) {
        dm0b[x] = (unsigned char) (dm0[x] & 0xff);
        dm90b[x] = (unsigned char) (dm90[x] & 0xff);
        dm135b[x] = (unsigned char) (dm135[x] & 0xff);
        dm45b[x] = (unsigned char) (dm45[x] & 0xff);
        x++;
}

/*
 * write output to 4 quadrants:        0=0, 1=90, 2=135, 3=145
 */

char outfile[256];

sprintf(outfile, "%s_SDMQUadrant_0deg_8UC1.png", filename);
Mat SDMQuadrant0(256, 256, CV_8UC1, dm0b);
imwrite(outfile, SDMQuadrant0);
sprintf(outfile, "%s_SDMQUadrant_90deg_8UC1.png", filename);
Mat SDMQuadrant90(256, 256, CV_8UC1, dm90b);
imwrite(outfile, SDMQuadrant90);
sprintf(outfile, "%s_SDMQUadrant_135deg_8UC1.png", filename);
Mat SDMQuadrant135(256, 256, CV_8UC1, dm135b);
imwrite(outfile, SDMQuadrant135);
```

```
        sprintf(outfile, "%s_SDMQUadrant_45deg_8UC1.png", filename);
        Mat SDMQuadrant45(256, 256, CV_8UC1, dm45b);
        imwrite(outfile, SDMQuadrant45);

        free(dm0);
        free(dm90);
        free(dm135);
        free(dm45);
        free(data);
        free(dm0b);
        free(dm90b);
        free(dm135b);
        free(dm45b);
        fclose(fstream);

        return 0;

}

int main (int argc, char **argv)
{
        cout << "8-bit unsigned image expected as input" << endl;
        texture (argv[1]);
        return 0;
}
```

Bibliography

> **Note** Entries do not appear in alphabetical order.

1. Bajcsy, R. "Computer Description of Textured Surfaces." International Conference on Artificial Intelligence, 1973.
2. Bajcsy, R., and L. Lieberman. "Texture Gradient as a Depth Cue." *Computer Graphics and Image Processing* 5, no. 1 (1976).
3. Cross, G. R., and A. K. Jain. "Markov Random Field Texture Models." *PAMI* 54, no. 1 (1983).
4. Gonzalez R., and R. Woods. *Digital Image Processing*, 3rd ed. Englewood Cliffs, NJ: Prentice-Hall, 2007.
5. Haralick, R. M. "Statistical and Structural Approaches to Texture." *Proceedings of the International Joint Conference on Pattern Recognition,* 1979.
6. Haralick, R. M., R. Shanmugan, and I. Dinstein. "Textural Features for Image Classification." *IEEE Transactions on. Systems, Man Cybernetics.* SMC-3, no. 6 (1973).
7. Hu, M. K. "Visual Pattern Recognition by Moment Invariants." *IRE Transactions on Information Theory, Volume: 8, Issue: 2,* (1962)
8. Lu, H. E., and K. S. Fu. "A Syntactic Approach to Texture Analysis." *Computer Graphics Image Processing* 7, no. 3 (1978).
9. Pratt, W. K. *Digital Image Processing,* 3rd ed. Hoboken, NJ: John Wiley, 2002.
10. Rosenfeld A., and A. C. Kak. *Digital Picture Processing,* 2nd ed. New York: Academic Press, 1982.
11. Tomita, F., Y. Shirai, and S. Tsuji. "Description of Texture by a Structural Analysis." *Pattern Analysis and Machine Intelligence* 4, no. 2 (1982).
12. Wong, R. Y., and E. L. Hall. "Scene Matching with Invariant Moments." *Computer Graphics Image Processing* 8 (1978).
13. Guoying Zhao and Matti Pietikainen. "Dynamic Texture Recognition Using Local Binary Patterns with an Application to Facial Expressions." *Transactions of Pattern Analysis and Machine Intelligence* (2007).
14. Kellokumpu, Vili, Guoying Zhao, and Matti Pietikäinen. "Human Activity Recognition Using a Dynamic Texture Based Method."

15. Guoying Zhao and Matti Pietikäinen. Dynamic Texture Recognition Using Local Binary Patterns with an Application to Facial Expressions." *Pattern Analysis and Machine Intelligence* 2007.

16. Eichmann, G., and T. Kasparis. "Topologically Invariant Texture Descriptors." *Computer Vision, Graphics and Image Processing* 41, no. 3 (March 1988).

17. Lam, S. W. C., and H. H. S. Ip. "Structural Texture Segmentation Using Irregular Pyramid." *Pattern Recognition Letters* 15, no. 7 (July 1994).

18. Pietikäinen, Matti, Guoying Zhao, and Ahonen Hadid. *Computer Vision Using Local Binary Patterns.* New York: Springer, 2011.

19. Ojala, T., M. Pietikäinen, and D. Hardwood. "Performance Evaluation of Texture Measures with Classification Based on Kullback Discrimination of Distributions." *Proceedings of the International Conference on Pattern Recognition,* 1994.

20. Ojala T., M. Pietikäinen, and D. Hardwood. "A Comparative Study of Texture Measures with Classification Based on Feature Distributions." *Pattern Recognition* 29 (1996).

21. Van Ginneken, Bram, and Jan J. Koenderink. "Texture Histograms as a Function of Irradiation and Viewing Direction," *International Journal of Computer Vision 31(2/3), 169–184 (1999).*

25. Aioanei, Stelu, Arati Kurani, and Dong-Hui Xu. Texture Analysis for Computed Tomography Studies. *Visual Computing Workshop DePaul University (2004).*

26. Krig, Scott A. "Image Texture Analysis Using Spatial Dependency Matrices." *Krig Research White Paper Series,* October 1994.

27-31. Not used.

32. Laws, K. I. "Rapid Texture Identification." *SPIE* 238 (1980).

33. Bajcsy, R. K. "Computer Identification of Visual Surfaces." *Computer Graphics and Image Processing* Volume 2, Issue 2, Pages 118–130 (October 1973).

34. Kaizer, H. *A Quantification of Textures on Aerial Photographs.* MS thesis, Boston University, 1955.

35. Laws, K. I. "Texture Energy Measures." *Proceedings of the Image Understanding Workshop,* November 1979.

36. Laws, K. I. "Rapid Texture Identification." *SPIE* 238 (1980).

37. Laws, K. I. *Textured Image Segmentation.* PhD thesis, University of Southern California, 1980.

38. Ade, F. "Characterization of Textures by 'Eigenfilters.'" *Signal Processing* 5 (1983).

39. Davis, L. S. "Computing the Spatial Structures of Cellular Texture." *Computer Graphics and Image Processing* 11, no. 2 (October 1979).

40. Eichmann, G., and T. Kasparis. "Topologically Invariant Texture Descriptors." *Computer Vision Graphics and Image Processing* 41, no. 3 (March 1988).

41. Lam, S. W. C., and H. H. S. Ip. "Structural Texture Segmentation Using Irregular Pyramid." *Pattern Recognition Letters* 15, no. 7 (July 1994).

42. Pietikäinen, Matti, Guoying Zhao, and Hadid, Ahonen, *Computer Vision Using Local Binary Patterns.* New York: Springer, 2011.

43. Ojala, T., M. Pietikäinen, and D. Hardwood. "Performance Evaluation of Texture Measures with Classification Based on Kullback Discrimination of Distributions." *Proceedings of the International Conference on Pattern Recognition,* 1994.

44. Ojala T., M. Pietikäinen, and D. Hardwood. "A Comparative Study of Texture Measures with Classification Based on Feature Distributions." *Pattern Recognition* 29 (1996).

45. Pun, C. M., and M. C. Lee. "Log-polar Wavelet Energy Signatures for Rotation and Scale Invariant Texture Classification." *Transactions of.Pattern Analysis and Machine Intelligence* 25, no. 5 (May 2003).

46. Spence, A., M. Robb, M. Timmins, and M. Chantler. "Real-time per-pixel Rendering of Textiles for Virtual Textile Catalogues." *Proceedings of INTEDEC, Edinburgh,* September, 2003.

47. Lam, Steven W. C., and Horace H. S. Ip. *Adaptive Pyramid Approach to Texture Segmentation,* Computer Analysis of Images and Patterns Lecture Notes in Computer Science Volume 719, 1993, pp. 267–274.

48. Dana, K. J., B. van Ginneken, S. K. Nayar, and J. J. Koenderink. "Reflectance and Texture of Real World Surfaces." Technical report CUCS-048-96, Columbia University, 1996.

49. Dana, K. J., B. van Ginneken, S. K. Nayar, and J. J. Koenderink. "Reflectance and Texture of Real World Surfaces." Conference on Computer Vision and Pattern Recognition, 1997.

50. Dana, K. J., B. van Ginneken, S. K. Nayar, and J. J. Koenderink. "Reflectance and Texture of Real World Surfaces." *ACM Transactions on Graphics* (1999).

51. Suzuki, M. T., and Yoshitomo Yaginuma. "A Solid Texture Analysis Based on Three Dimensional Convolution Kernels." *Proceedings of the SPIE, Volume 6491,* (2007).

52. Suzuki, M. T., Yoshitomo Yaginuma, Tsuneo Yamada, and Yasutaka Shimizu. "A Shape Feature Extraction Method Based on 3D Convolution Masks. *Eighth IEEE International Symposium on Multimedia, ISM'06.* (2006)

53. Guoying Zhao and Matti Pietikainen. "Dynamic Texture Recognition Using Local Binary Patterns with an Application to Facial Expressions." *Transations on Pattern Analysis and Machine Intelligence* Volume 29 (2007).

54. Hadjidemetriou, E., M. D. Grossberg, and S. K. Nayar. "Multiresolution Histograms and Their Use for Texture Classification." *IEEE PAMI Volume 26.*

55. Hadjidemetriou, E., M. D. Grossberg, and S. K. Nayar. "Multiresolution Histograms and Their Use for Recognition." *IEEE PAMI* (vol. 26 no. 7) (2004).

56. Lee and Chen, "A New Method for Coarse Classification of Textures and Class Weight Estimation for Texture Retrieval, *Pattern Recognition and Image Analysis.* Vol. 12, no. 4 (2002).

57. Van Ginneken, Bram, and Jan J. Koenderink. "Texture Histograms as a Function of Irradiation and Viewing Direction." *International Journal of Computer Vision 31(2/3), 169–184 (1999).*

58. Shu Liao and Albert C. S. Chung. *Texture Classification by Using Advanced Local Binary Patterns and Spatial Distribution of Dominant Patterns.* ICASSP 2007. IEEE International Conference on Acoustics, Speech and Signal Processing, 2007.

59. Aioanei, Stelu, Arati Kurani, and Dong-Hui Xu. *Texture Analysis for Computed Tomography Studies,.* Visual Computing Workshop DePaul University (2004).

60. Ade, F. "Characterization of Textures by 'Eigenfilters.'" *Signal Processing* 5 (1983).

61. Rosin, Paul L. "Measuring Corner Properties." *Computer Vision & Image Understanding, Vol.73, No. 2.*

62. Russel, Bryan, Jianxiong Xiao, and Antonio Torralba. "Localizing 3D Cuboids in Single-view Images." *Conference on Neural Information Processing Systems, 2012.*

63. Snavely, Noah, Steven M. Seitz, and Richard Szeliski. "Photo Tourism: Exploring Photo Collections in 3D." *ACM Transactions on Graphics* (SIGGRAPH Proceedings) (2006).

64. Snavely, Noah, Steven M. Seitz, and Richard Szeliski. "Modeling the World from Internet Photo Collections." *International Journal of Computer Vision* (TBP).

65. Furukawa, Yasutaka, Brian Curless, Steven M. Seitz, and Richard Szeliski. "Towards Internet-Scale Multi-View Stereo." *Conference on Computer Vision and Pattern Recognition, 2010.*

66. Yunpeng Li, Noah Snavely, Dan Huttenlocher, and Pascal Fua. "Worldwide Pose Estimation using 3D Point Clouds." European Conference on Computer Vision, 2012.

67. Russell, B., A. Torralba, K. Murphy, and W. T. Freeman. "LabelMe: A Database and Web-based Tool for Image Annotation." *International Journal of Computer Vision* Volume 77 (2007).

68. Oliva, A., and A. Torralba. "Modeling the Shape of the Scene: A Holistic Representation of the Spatial Envelope." *International Journal of Computer Vision Volume 42 (2001).*

69. Lai, Kevin, Liefeng Bo, Xiaofeng Ren, and Dieter Fox. "A Large-Scale Hierarchical Multi-View RGB-D Object Dataset." International Conference on Robotics and Automation, 2011.

70. Xiao, J., J. Hays, K. Ehinger, A. Oliva, and A. Torralba. "SUN Database: Large-scale Scene Recognition from Abbey to Zoo." Conference on Computer Vision and Pattern Recognition, 2010.

71. Fei-Fei, L., R. Fergus, and P. Perona. "Learning Generative Visual Models from Few Training Examples: An Incremental Bayesian Approach Tested on 101 Object Categories." Conference on Computer Vision and Pattern Recognition, 2004.

72. Fei-Fei, L. "ImageNet: Crowdsourcing, Benchmarking & Other Cool Things." *CMU VASC Seminar, March 2010.*

73. Pirsiavash, Hamed, and Deva Ramanan. "Detecting Activities of Daily Living in First-person Camera Views." Conference on Computer Vision and Pattern Recognition, 2012.

74. Quattoni, A., and A. Torralba. "Recognizing Indoor Scenes." Conference on Computer Vision and Pattern Recognition, 2009.

75. Lai, Kevin, Liefeng Bo, Xiaofeng Ren, and Dieter Fox. "A Large-Scale Hierarchical Multi-View RGB-D Object Dataset." *International Conference on Robotics and Automation, May 2011.*

76. Silberman, Nathan, Derek Hoiem, Pushmeet Kohli, and Rob Fergus. "Indoor Segmentation and Support Inference from RGBD Images." *European Conference on Compuper Vision, 2012.*

77. Xiaofeng Ren and Matthai Philipose. "Egocentric Recognition of Handled Objects: Benchmark and Analysis." *CVPR Workshops 2009.*

78. Xiaofeng Ren and Chunhui Gu. "Figure-Ground Segmentation Improves Handled Object Recognition in Egocentric Video." Conference on Computer Vision and Pattern Recognition, 2009.

79. Fathi, Alireza, Yin Li, and James M. Rehg, "Learning to Recognize Daily Actions Using Gaze." European Conference on Computer Vision, 2012.

80. Dana, K. J., B. van Ginneken, S. K. Nayar, and J. J. Koenderink. "Reflectance and Texture of Real World Surfaces." *Transactions on Graphics* (TOG)18, no.1 (January 1999).

81. Ce Liu, Lavanya Sharan, Edward H. Adelson, and Ruth Rosenholtz. "Exploring Features in a Bayesian Framework for Material Recognition." *Conference on Computer Vision and Pattern Recognition, 2010.*

82. Huang, Gary B., Manu Ramesh, Tamara Berg, and Erik Learned-Miller. "Labeled Faces in the Wild: A Database for Studying Face Recognition in Unconstrained Environments." *Technical report 07-49, University of Massachusetts, Amherst, October 2007.*

83. Gross, R., I. Matthews, J. F. Cohn, T. Kanade, and S. Baker. "Multi-PIE." *Proceedings of the Eighth IEEE International Conference on Automatic Face and Gesture Recognition, 2008.*

84. Yao, B., X. Jiang, A. Khosla, A. L. Lin, L. J. Guibas, and L. Fei-Fei. "Human Action Recognition by Learning Bases of Action Attributes and Parts." *International Conference on Computer Vision, 2011.*

85. Y LeCun, F J Huang, L Bottou, "Learning Methods for Generic Object Recognition with Invariance to Pose and Lighting." *Proceedings of the Conference on Computer Vision and Pattern Recognition, 2004.*

86. McCane, B., K. Novins, D. Crannitch, and B. Galvin. "On Benchmarking Optical Flow." *Computer Vision and Image Understanding* 84, no. 1 2001.

87. Pirsiavash, Hamed, and Deva Ramanan. "Detecting Activities of Daily Living in First-person Camera Views." Conference on Computer Vision and Pattern Recognition, Providence, Rhode Island, June 2012.

88. Hamarneh, Ghassan, Preet Jassi, and Lisa Tang. "Simulation of Ground-Truth Validation Data via Physically- and Statistically-Based Warps." *MICCAI 2008, the 11th International Conference on Medical Image Computing and Computer Assisted Intervention.*

89. Prastawa, Marcel, Elizabeth Bullitt, and Guido Gerig. "Synthetic Ground Truth for Validation of Brain Tumor MRI Segmentation." *MICCAI 2005, the 8th International Conference on Medical Image Computing and Computer Assisted Intervention.*

90. Vedaldi, Andrea, Haibin Ling, and Stefano Soatto. "Knowing a Good Feature When You See It: Ground Truth and Methodology to Evaluate Local Features for Recognition." *Computer Vision Studies in Computational Intelligence Volume 285, 2010, pp. 27–49.*

91. Dutagaci, Helin, Chun Pan Cheung, and Afzal Godil. "Evaluation of 3D Interest Point Detection Techniques via Human-generated Ground Truth." *The Visual Computer September 2012, Volume 28* (2012).

92. Rosin, Paul L. "Augmenting Corner Descriptors." *Graphical Models and Image Processing, Volume 58, Issue 3, May 1996.*

93. Rockett, P. I. "Performance Assessment of Feature Detection Algorithms: A Methodology and Case Study on Corner Detectors." *Transaction on Image Processing* 12, no. 12 (2003).

94. Shahrokni, A., A. Ellis, and J. Ferryman. "Overall Evaluation of the PETS2009 Results." *IEEE PETS* (2009).

95. Over, P, Awad, G, Sanders G, Shaw B, Martial M, Fiscus, J, Kraaij, W, Smeaton, AF "TRECVID 2013: An Overview of the Goals, Tasks, Data, Evaluation Mechanisms, and Metrics, *NIST USA, March 7, 2013*.

96. Horn, B. K. P., and B. G. Schunck. "Determining Optical Flow." AI memo 572, Massachusetts Institute of Technology, 1980.

97. Everingham, M., L. Van Gool, C. K. I. Williams, J. Winn, and A. Zisserman. "The PASCAL Visual Object Classes (VOC) Challenge." *International Journal of Computer Vision* 88, no. 2 (2010).

98. Liu, Jingen, Jiebo Luo, and Mubarak Shah. "Recognizing Realistic Actions from Videos 'in the Wild.'" Conference on Computer Vision and Pattern Recognition, 2009.

99. Arbelaez, P., M. Maire, C. Fowlkes, and J. Malik. "Contour Detection and Hierarchical Image Segmentation". *Transactions on Pattern Analysis and Machine Intelligence*, (Volume: 33, Issue: 5) May 2011.

100. Fisher, R. B. "PETS04 Surveillance Ground Truth Data Set." *Proceedings of IEEE PETS*, 2004.

101. Quan Yuan, Ashwin Thangali, Vitaly Ablavsky, and Stan Sclaroff. "Learning a Family of Detectors via Multiplicative Kernels." *Pattern Analysis and Machine Intelligence* (Volume: 33, Issue: 3) (2011).

102. Ericsson, Anders, and Johan Karlsson. "Measures for Benchmarking of Automatic Correspondence Algorithms." *JMIV* (2007).

103. Takhar, Dharmpal, et al. "A New Compressive Imaging Camera Architecture using Optical-Domain Compression. *In Proc. IS&T/SPIE Symposium on Electronic Imaging (2006).*

104. Marco F. Duarte, Richard G. Baraniuk, Kronecker Compressive Sensing, *IEEE Transactions on Image Processing (Volume: 21, Issue: 2) 2012.*

105. Weinzaepfel, Philippe, Herv'e Jegou, and Patrick Perez. "Reconstructing an Image from Its Local Descriptors." Conference on Computor Vision and Pattern Recognition, 2011.

106. Dalal, Navneet, and Bill Triggs. "Histograms of Oriented Gradients for Human Detection." Conference on Computer Vision and Pattern Recognition, 2005.

107. Tuytelaars1, Tinne, and Krystian Mikolajczyk. *Local Invariant Feature Detectors: A Survey*. Foundations and Trends□ in Computer Graphics and Vision (Vol 3, Issue 3, 2007, pp. 177–280).

108. Hartigan, J. A. *Clustering Algorithms*. New York: John Wiley, 1975.

109. Fischler, Martin A., and Robert C. Bolles. "Random Sample Consensus: A Paradigm for Model Fitting with Applications to Image Analysis and Automated Cartography." *Communications of the ACM Volume* 24, no. 6 (June 1981).

110. Sunglok Choi, Taemin Kim, and Wonpil Yu. "Performance Evaluation of RANSAC Family." British Machine Vision Association, (2009).

111. Hartigan, J. A., and M. A. Wong. "Algorithm AS 136: A K-Means Clustering Algorithm." *Journal of the Royal Statistical Society, Series C (Applied Statistics)* Vol. 28, No. 1 (1979, pp. 100–108).

112. Voronoi, Georgy. "Nouvelles applications des paramètres continus à la théorie des formes quadratiques." *Journal für die Reine und Angewandte Mathematik* 133 (1908).

113. Capel, David. "Random Forests and Ferns." Penn. State University Compter Vision Labatory, seminar lecture notes online:. ForestsAndFernsTalk.pdf.

114. Xiaofeng Ren and Jitendra Malik. "Learning a Classification Model for Segmentation."

115. Lai, Kevin, Liefeng Bo, Xiaofeng Ren, and Dieter Fox. "Sparse Distance Learning for Object Recognition Combining RGB and Depth Information."

116. Xiaofeng Ren and Deva Ramanan. "Histograms of Sparse Codes for Object Detection." Conference on Computer Vision and Pattern Recognition, 2013.

117. Liefeng Bo, Xiaofeng Ren, and Dieter Fox. "Multipath Sparse Coding Using Hierarchical Matching Pursuit." *Conference on Computer Vision and Pattern Recognition, 2013.*

118. Herbst, Evan, Xiaofeng Ren, and Dieter Fox. "RGB-D Flow: Dense 3-D Motion Estimation Using Color and Depth." *IEEE International Conference on Robotics and Automation (ICRA) 2013.*

119. Xiaofeng Ren and Liefeng Bo. "Discriminatively Trained Sparse Code Gradients for Contour Detection." *Conference on Neural Information processing Systems, 2012.*

120. Rublee, Ethan, Vincent Rabaud, Kurt Konolige, and Gary Bradski. "ORB: An Efficient Alternative to SIFT or SURF." *ICCV '11 Proceedings of the 2011 International Conference on Computer Vision.*

121. Rosenfeld, A., and J. L Pfaltz. "Distance Functions on Digital Images." *Pattern Recognition, Pergamon Press 1968 Vol. 1 pp. 33–61.*

122. Richardson, Andrew, and Edwin Olson. "Learning Convolutional Filters For Interest Point Detection." *IEEE International Conference on Robotics and Automation ICRA'13, pages 631–637. IEEE, (2013).*

123. Moon, Todd K., and Wynn C. Stirling. *Mathematical Methods and Algorithms for Signal Processing.* Englewood Cliffs, NJ: Prentice-Hall, 1999.

124. Liefeng Bo, Xiaofeng Ren, and Dieter Fox. "Multipath Sparse Coding Using Hierarchical Matching Pursuit." *Conference on Computer Vision and Pattern Recognition, 2013.*

125. Xiaofeng Ren and Deva Ramanan. "Histograms of Sparse Codes for Object Detection." *Conference on Computer Vision and Pattern Recognition, 2013.*

126. Olshausen, B., and D. Field. "Emergence of Simple-cell Receptive Field Properties by Learning a Sparse Code for Natural Images." *Nature. 1996 Jun 13; 381(6583): 607-9.*

127. d'Angelo, Emmanuel, Alexandre Alehi, and Pierre Vandergheynst. "Beyond Bits: Reconstructing Images from Local Binary Descriptors." Swiss Federal Institute of Technology, 21st International Conference on Pattern Recognition (ICPR), 2012.

128. Dengsheng Zhang and Guojun Lu. "Review of Shape Representation and Description Techniques." Journal ofthe Pattern Recognition SOciety, No. 37 (2004) 1–19.

129. Yang Mingqiang, Kpalma Kidiyo, and Ronsin Joseph. "A Survey of Shape Feature Extraction Techniques." *Pattern Recognition (November 2008), pp. 43–90.*

130. Alehi, Alexandre, Raphael Ortiz, and Pierre Vandergheynst. "Freak: Fast Retina Keypoint." Conference on Computer Vision and Pattern Recognition, 2012.

131. Leutenegger, Stefan, Margarita Chli, and Roland Y. Siegwart. "BRISK: Binary Robust Invariant Scalable Keypoints." International Conference on Computer Vision, 2011.

132. Calonder, Michael, Vincent Lepetit, Christoph Strecha, and Pascal Fua. "BRIEF: Binary Robust Independent Elementary Features." ECCV'10 Proceedings of the 11th European conference on Computer vision: Part IV 2010.

133. Calonder, Michael et al. "BRIEF: Computing a Local Binary Descriptor Very Fast." *Pattern Analysis and Machine Intelligence,* Vol. 34 (2012).

134. Rublee, Ethan, Vincent Rabaud, Kurt Konolige, and Gary Bradski. "ORB: An Efficient Alternative to SIFT or SURF." *ICCV '11 Proceedings of the 2011 International Conference on Computer Vision* 2011.

135. von Hundelshausen, Felix, and Rahul Sukthankar. "D-Nets: Beyond Patch-Based Image Descriptors." Conference on Computer Vision and Pattern Recognition, 2012.

136. Krig, Scott. "RFAN Radial Fan Descriptors." Picture Center Imaging and Visualization System, White Paper Series, 1992.

137. Krig, Scott. "Picture Center Imaging and Visualization System." Krig Research White Paper Series, 1994.

138. Rosten, Edward, and Tom Drummond. "FAST Machine learning for High-speed Corner Detection." European Conference on Computer Vision, 2006.

139. Rosten, Edward, and Tom Drummond, "Fusing Points and Lines for High Performance Tracking." International Conference on Ccomputer Vision, 2005.

140. Liefeng Bo, Xiaofeng Ren, and Dieter Fox. "Hierarchical Matching Pursuit for Image Classification: Architecture and Fast Algorithms." Conference on Neural Information Processing Systems, 2011.

141. Miksik, Ondrej, and Krystian Mikolajczyk. "Evaluation of Local Detectors and Descriptors for Fast Feature Matching." International Conference on Pattern Recognition, 2012.

142. Yoav Freund, Robert E Schapire, "A Decision-theoretic Generalization of On-line Learning and an Application to Boosting." *Journal of Computer and System Sciences Volume 55, Issue 1, August 1997, Pages 119–139.*

143. Gleason, Josh, BRISK (Presentation by Josh Gleason) at International Conference on Computer Vision, 2011.

144. Mikolajczyk, K., and C. Schmid. "A Performance Evaluation of Local Descriptors." *Pattern Analysis and Machine Intelligence, IEEE Transactions on (Volume: 27, Issue: 10)* (2005).

145. Gauglitz, Steffen, Tobias Höllerer, and Matthew Turk. "Evaluation of Interest Point Detectors and Feature Descriptors for Visual Tracking." *International Journal of Computer Vision* Volume 94 Issue 3, September 2011.

146. Viola and Jones. "Robust Real Time Face Detection." *International Journal of Computer Vision* Volume 57 Issue 2, May 2004.

147. Thevenaz, P., Urs E. Ruttimann, and M. Unser. "A Pyramid Approach to Subpixel Registration Based on Intensity." *IEEE Transactions on* Image Processing Volume 7 Issue 1 (1998).

148. Qi Tian and Michael N. Huhns. "Algorithms for Subpixel Registration." *Computer Vision, Graphics, and Image Processing* Vol. 35 (August 1986).

149. Jie Zhu and Lei Yang. "Subpixel Eye Gaze Tracking." Automatic Face and Gesture Recognition Conference, 2002.

150. Cheezum, Michael K., William F. Walker, and William H. Guilford. "Quantitative Comparison of Algorithms for Tracking Single Fluorescent Particles." *Biophysical Journal* Oct 2001; 81(4): 2378–2388.

151. Guizar-Sicairos, Manuel, Samuel T. Thurman, and James R. Fienup. "Efficient Subpixel Image Registration Algorithms." *Optics Letters, Vol. 33, Issue 2, pp. 156–158 (2008).*

152. Hadjidemetriou, E., M. D. Grossberg, and S. K. Nayar. "Multiresolution Histograms and their Use for Texture Classification." *International Workshop on Texture Analysis and Synthesis,* Volume 26 Issue 7 *2003.*

153. Mikolajczyk, K., et al. "A Comparison of Affine Region Detectors." Conference on Computer Vision and Pattern Recognition, 2006.

154. Canny, A. "Computational Approach to Edge Detection. *Transactions on Pattern Analysis and Machine Intelligence* 8, no. 6 (November 1986).

155. Gunn, Steve R. "Edge Detection Error in the Discrete Laplacian of Gaussian." *International Conference on Image Processing, ICIP 98. Proceedings. 1998 (Volume: 2).*

156. Harris, C., and M. Stephens. "A Combined Corner and Edge Detector." *Proceedings of the 4th Alvey Vision Conference,* 1988.

157. Shi, J., and C. Tomasi. "Good Features to Track." Conference on Computer Vision and Pattern Recognition, 1994.

158. Turk, Matthew, and Alex Pentland. "Eigenfaces for Recognition." Journal of Cognitive Neuroscience, Vol. 3 No. 1, 1991 © MIT Media Lab, 1991.

159. "Haja, Andreas, Bernd Jahne, and Steffen Abraham. "Localization Accuracy of Region Detectors." IEEE CVPR 2008.

160. Bay, Herbert, Andreas Ess, Tinne Tuytelaars, and Luc Van Gool. "Speeded-Up Robust Features (SURF)." *Computer Vision and Image Understanding Volume 110, Issue 3, June 2008, Pages 346–359.*

161. Lowe, David G. "SIFT Distinctive Image Features from Scale-Invariant Keypoints." *International Journal of Computer Vision, Volume 60 Issue 2, November 2004 Pages 91–110* (2004).

162. Kadir, Timor, Andrew Zisserman, and Michael Brady. "An Affine Invariant Salient Region Detector." European Conference on Computer Vision, 2004.

163. Kadir, T., and J. M. Brady. "Scale, Saliency and Image Description." *International Journal of Computer Vision, Volume 45 Issue 2, November 2001 Pages 83–105.*

164. Smith, Stephen M. and J. Michael Brady. "SUSAN—A New Approach to Low Level Image Processing", Technical report TR95SMS1c (patended), Crown Copyright (1995), 1995, Defence Research Agency, UK.

165. Smith, Stephen M. and J. Michael Brady. "SUSAN—A New Approach to Low Level Image Processing, *International Journal of Computer Vision archive Volume 23 Issue 1, May 1997 Pages 45–78.*

166. Baohua Yuan, Honggen Cao, and Jiuliang Chu, "Combining Local Binary Pattern and Local Phase Quantization for Face Recognition." International Symposium on Biometrics and Security Technologies, 2012.

167. Ojansivu, Ville, and Janne Heikkil. "Blur Insensitive Texture Classification Using Local Phase Quantization." *Proceedings of Image and Signal Processing,* 2008.

168. Chan, C. H, M. A. Tahir, J. Kittler, and M. Pietikäinen. "Multiscale Local Phase Quantization for Robust Component-based Face Recognition Using Kernel Fusion of Multiple Descriptors. *PAMI* (2012).

169. Ojala, T., M. Pietikäinen, and D. Hardwood. "Performance Evaluation of Texture Measures with Classification Based on Kullback Discrimination of Distributions." *Proceedings of the International Conference on Pattern Recognition,* 1994.

170. Ojala, T., M. Pietikäinen, and D. Hardwood. "A Comparative Study of Texture Measures with Classification Based on Feature Distributions." *Pattern Recognition* 29 (1996).

171. Pietikäinen, Matti, and Janne Heikkilä. "Tutorial on Image and Video Description with Local Binary Pattern Variants." Conference on Computer Vision and Pattern Recognition, 2011.

172. Shu Liao and Albert C. S. Chung. *Texture Classification by Using Advanced Local Binary Patterns and Spacial Distribution of Dominant Patterns*, IEEE International Conference on Acoustics, Speech and Signal Processing, 2007. ICASSP.

173. Pietikäinen, M., A. Hadid, G. Zhao, and T. Ahonen. *Computer Vision Using Binary Patterns,* Computational Imaging and Vision Series, vol. 40. New York: Springer, 2011.

174. Arandjelovi, Arandjelović, and Andrew Zisserman. "Three Things Everyone Should Know to Improve Object Retrieval." Conference on Computer Vision and Pattern Recognition, 2011.

175. Guoying Zhao, and Matti Pietikainen. "*Dynamic Texture Recognition Using Local Binary Patterns with an Application to Facial Expressions.*" Pattern Analysis and Machine Intelligence, IEEE Transactions on (Volume: 29, Issue: 6) (2007).

176. Kellokumpu, Vili, Guoying Zhao, and Matti Pietikäinen. "*Human Activity Recognition Using a Dynamic Texture Based Method.*" British machine Vision Conference 2008.

177. Zabih, Ramin, and John Woodfill. "*Nonparametric Local Transforms for Computing Visual Correspondence.*" European Conference on Computer Vision, 1994.

178. Lowe, David G. "*Object Recognition from Local Scale-Invariant Features.*" The Proceedings of the Seventh IEEE International Conference on Computer Vision, 1999.

179. Abdel-Hakim, Alaa E., and Aly A. Farag. "CSIFT: A SIFT Descriptor with Color Invariant Characteristics." Conference on Computer Vision and Pattern Recognition, 2006.

180. Vinukonda, Phaneendra. *A Study of the Scale-Invariant Feature Transform on a Parallel Pipeline.* Thesis project.

181. Alcantarilla, Pablo F., Luis M. Bergasa, and Andrew Davison. *Gauge-SURF Descriptors*: Elsevier, 2011.

182. Christopher Evans, "Notes on the OpenSURF Library", University of Bristol Technical Paper, January 18, 2009."

183. Yan Ke and Rahul Sukthankar. "PCA-SIFT: A More Distinctive Representation for Local Image Descriptors." Conference on Computer Vision and Pattern Recognition, 2004.

184. Gauglitz, Steffen, Tobias Höllerer, and Matthew Turka. "Evaluation of Interest Point Detectors and Feature Descriptors for Visual Tracking." *International Journal of Computer Vision*, Volume 94 2011.

185. Agrawal, Motilal, Kurt Konolige, and Morten Rufus Blas. "CenSurE: Center Surround Extremas for Realtime Feature Detection and Matching." European Conference on Computer Vision, 2008.

186. Viola, Paul, and Michael Jones. "Robust Real-time Object Detection." *International Journal of Computer Vision 57(2):137–154 (2002).*

187. Grigorescu, S. E., N. Petkov, and P. Kruizinga. "Comparison of Texture Features Based on Gabor Filters." *IEEE Transactions on Image Processing, (Volume: 11, Issue: 10) 2002.*

188. Alcantarilla, Pablo, Luis M. Bergasa, and Andrew Davison. *Gauge-SURF Descriptors.* IVC(31), No. 1, January 2013, pp. 103–116. Elsevier via DOI 1302.

189. Agrawal, M., K. Konolige, and M. R. Blas. "CenSurE: Center Surround Ex-tremas for Realtime Feature Detection and Matching." European Conference on Computer Vision, 2008.

190. Morse, Bryan S. Lecture 11: Differential Geometry. Brigham Young University, 1998–2000. http://morse.cs.byu.edu/650/lectures/lect10/diffgeom.pdf.

191. Bosch, Anna, Andrew Zisserman, and Xavier Munoz. "Representing Shape with a Spatial Pyramid Kernel.", CIVR '07 Proceedings of the 6th ACM international conference on Image and video retrieval.

192. Rubner, Yossi, Carlo Tomasi, and Leonidas J. Guibas. "The Earth Mover's Distance as a Metric for Image Retrieval." International Journal of Computer Vision Volume 40 Issue 2, Nov. 2000 Pages 99–121.

193. Oliva, Aude, and Antonio Torralba. "Modeling the Shape of the Scene: A Holistic Representation of the Spatial Envelope." International Journal of Computer Vision (2001).

194. Matas, J., O. Chum, M. Urba, and T. Pajdla. "Robust Wide Baseline Stereo from Maximally Stable Extremal Regions." Proceedings of British Machine Vision Conference, 2002.

195. Scovanner, P., S. Ali, and M. Shah. "A 3-dimensional SIFT Descriptor and its Application to Action Recognition." ACM Proceedings of the 15th International Conference on Multimedia, pages 357–360. (2007).

196. Klaser, A., M. Marszalek, and C. Schmid. "A Spatio-temporal Descriptor Based on 3d-gradients." British Machine Vision Conference, 2008.

197. Laptev, I. "On Space-time Interest Points.: Intenational Journal of Computer Vision 64 (2005).

198. Oreifej, Omar, and Zicheng Liu. "HON4D: Histogram of Oriented 4D Normals for Activity Recognition from Depth Sequences." Conference on Computer Vision and Pattern Recognition, 2013.

199. Ke, Y., et al. "Efficient Visual Event Detection using Volumetric Features." International Conference on Computer Vision, 2005.

200. Zhang, Lisha, Manuel João da Fonseca, and Alfredo Ferreira. "Survey on 3D Shape Descriptors." União Europeia - Fundos Estruturais Governo da República Portuguesa Referência: POSC/EIA/59938/2004.

201. Tangelder, Johan W. H., and Remco C. Veltkamp. A Survey of Content-based 3D Shape Retrieval Methods. New York: Springer, 2007.

202. Heikkila, Marko, Matti Pietikäinen, and Cordelia Schmid. Description of Interest Regions with Center-Symmetric Local Binary Patterns. Computer Vision, Graphics and Image Processing Lecture Notes in Computer Science Volume 4338, 2006, pp. 58–69.

203. Schmidt, Adam, Marek Kraft, Michał Fularz, and Zuzanna Domagała. "The Comparison of Point Feature Detectors and Descriptors in the Context of Robot Navigation." Workshop on Perception for Mobile Robots Autonomy, 2012.

204. Bongjin Jun and Daijin Kim. "Robust Face Detection Using Local Gradient Patterns and Evidence Accumulation." Pattern Recognition Volume 45, Issue 9, September 2012, Pages 3304–3316.

205. Froba, Bernhard, and Andreas Ernst. "Face Detection with the Modified Census Transform." International Conference on Automatic Face and Gesture Recognition, 2004.

206. Freeman, H. "On the Encoding of Arbitrary Geometric Configurations." IRE Transactions on Electronic Computers (1961).

207. Salem, Abdel-Badeeh M., Adel A. Sewisy, and Usama A. Elyan. "A Vertex Chain Code Approach for Image Recognition." International Journal on Graphics, Vision and Image Processing ICGST-GVIP, 2005.

208. Kitchen, L., and A. Rosenfeld. "Gray-level Corner Detection." *Pattern Recognition Letters* Volume 1 (1992).

209. Koenderink, J., and W. Richards. "Two-dimensional Curvature Operators." *Journal of the Optical Society of America* JOSA A, Vol. 5, Issue 7, pp. 1136–1141 (1988).

210. Bretzner, L., and T. Lindeberg. "Feature Tracking with Automatic Selection of Spatial Scales." *Computer Vision and Image Understanding Volume 71, Issue 3, September 1998, Pages 385–392.*

211. Lindeberg, T. "Junction Detection with Automatic Selection of Detection Scales and Localization Scales." *Proceedings of First International Conference on Image Processing, 1994.*

212. Lindeberg, Tony. "Feature Detection with Automatic Scale Selection." *International Journal of Computer Vision November 1998, Volume 30, Issue 2, pp. 79–116.*

213. Wang, H., and M. Brady. "Real-time Corner Detection Algorithm for Motion Estimation." *Image and Vision Computing Volume 13, Issue 9, November 1995, pp. 695–703.*

214. Trajkovic, M., and M. Hedley. "Fast Corner Detection." *Image and Vision Computing Volume 16, Issue 2, 20 February 1998, Pages 75–87.*

215. Tola, E., V. Lepetit, and P. Fua. "DAISY: An Efficient Dense Descriptor Applied to Wide Baseline Stereo." *PAMI (Volume: 32, Issue: 5) 2010.*

216. Arbeiter, Georg, et al. "Evaluation of 3D Feature Descriptors for Classification of Surface Geometries in Point Clouds." *International Conference on Intelligent Robots and Systems (IROS), 2012 IEEE/RSJ.*

217. Rupell, A., F. Weisshardt, and A. Verl. "A Rotation Invariant Feature Descriptor O-DAISY and its FPGA Implementation." IROS, 2011.

218. Ambai, Mitsuru, and Yuichi Yoshida. "CARD: Compact and Real-time Descriptors." International Conference on Computer Vision, 2011.

219. Takacs, Gabriel, et al. "Unified Real-Time Tracking and Recognition with Rotation-Invariant Fast Features. Conference on Computer Vision and Pattern Recognition, 2010.

220. Taylor, Simon, Edward Rosten, and Tom Drummond. "Robust Feature Matching in 2.3μs." Conference on Computer Vision and Pattern Recognition, 2009.

221. Grauman, Kristen, and Trevor Darrell. "The Pyramid Match Kernel: Discriminative Classification with Sets of Image Features." *IEEE International Conference on Computer Vision, 2005. ICCV 2005. Tenth (Volume: 2).*

222. Takacs, Gabriel, et al. "Unified Real-Time Tracking and Recognition with Rotation-Invariant Fast Features. Conference on Computer Vision and Pattern Recognition, 2010.

223. Chandrasekhar, Vijay, et al. "CHoG: Com- pressed Histogram of Gradients, a Low Bitrate Descriptor. Conference on Computer Vision and Pattern Recognition, 2009.

224. Mainali, Gauthier Lafruit, et al. "SIFER: Scale-Invariant Feature Detector with Error Resilience." *International Journal on Computer Vision* (2013).

225. Fowers, Spencer G., D. J. Lee, Dan Ventura, and Doran K. Wilde. "A Novel, Efficient, Tree-Based Descriptor and Matching Algorithm (BASIS)." Conference on Computer Vision and Pattern Recognition, 2012.

226. Fowers, S. G., D. J. Lee, D.A. Ventura, and J. K. Archibald. "Nature Inspired BASIS Feature Descriptor and its Hardware Implementation." *IEEE Transactions on Circuits and Systems for Video Technology, 2012.*

227. Bracewell, Ronald. *The Fourier Transform & Its Applications,* McGraw-Hill Science/ Engineering/Math; 3 edition (June 8, 1999).

228. Duda, R. O., and P. E. Hart. "Use of the Hough Transformation to Detect Lines and Curves in Pictures." *Communicaations of the. ACM* January 1972.

229. Ballard, D. H. "Generalizing the Hough Transform to Detect Arbitrary Shapes." *Pattern Recognition* 13, no. 2 (1981).

230. Illingsworth, J., and K. Kitter. "A Survey of the Hough Transform." *Computer Vision, Graphics and Image Processing* (1988).

231. Slaton, Gerard, and Michael J. MacGill. *Introduction to Modern Information Retrieval.* New York: McGraw-Hill, 1983.

232. Niebles, Juan Carlos, Hongcheng Wang, and Li Fei-Fei. "Unsupervised Learning of Human Action Categories Using Spatial-Temporal Words." *International Journal of Computer Vision* (2008).

233. Bosch, Anna, Andrew Zisserman, and Xavier Muñoz. "Scene Classification via pLSA." European Conference on Computer Vision, 2006.

234. Csurka, G., C. Bray, C. Dance, and L. Fan. "Visual Categorization with Bags of Key-points." SLCV workshop, European Conference on Computer Vision, 2004.

235. Dean, Thomas, Rich Washington, and Greg Corrado, "Sparse Spatiotemporal Coding for Activity Recognition." Brown University Tech. Report, 2010.

236. Quoc V. Le, Will Y. Zou, Serena Y. Yeung, and Andrew Y. Ng, "Learning Hierarchical Invariant Spatio-temporal Features for Action Recognition with Independent Subspace Analysis." Conference on Computer Vision and Pattern Recognition, 2011.

237. Olshausen, B., and D. Field. "Emergence of Simple-cell Receptive Field Properties by Learning a Sparse Code for Natural Images." *Nature 381, 607–609 (13 June 1996).*

238. Belongie, Serge, Jitendra Malik, and Jan Puzicha. "Matching with Shape Context." *CBAIVL '00 Proceedings of the IEEE Workshop on Content-based Access of Image and Video Libraries.*

239. Belongie, Serge, Jitendra Malik, and Jan Puzicha. "Shape Context: A New Descriptor for Shape Matching and Object Recognition." Conference on Neural Information processing Systems, 2000.

240. Belongie, Serge, Jitendra Malik, and Jan Puzicha. "Shape Matching and Object Recognition Using Shape Contexts." *PAMI (Volume: 24, Issue: 4)* (2002).

241. Belongie, Serge, Jitendra Malik, and Jan Puzich. "Matching Shapes with Shape Context." *CBAIVL '00 Proceedings of the IEEE Workshop on Content-based Access of Image and Video Libraries.*

242. Liefeng Bo, Xiaofeng Ren, and Dieter Fox. "Unsupervised Feature Learning for RGB-D Based Object Recognition." *ISER, volume 88 of Springer Tracts in Advanced Robotics, pages 387–402. Springer, (2012).*

243. Loy, Gareth, and Alexander Zelinsky. "A Fast Radial Symmetry Transform for Detecting Points of Interest." European Conference on Computer Vision, 2002.

244. Wolf, Lior, Tal Hassner, and Yaniv Taigman. "Descriptor Based Methods in the Wild." European Conference on Computer Vision, 2008.

245. Kurz, Daniel, and Selim Ben Himane. "Inertial Sensor-aligned Visual Feature Descriptors." Conference on Computer Vision and Pattern Recognition, 2011.

246. Kingsbury, Nick. "Rotation-Invariant Local Feature Matching with Complex Wavelets." *Proc. European Conf. Signal Processing (EUSIPCO), 2006.*

247. Dinggang Shen, and Horace H. S. Ip. "Discriminative Wavelet Shape Descriptors for Recognition of 2-D Patterns." *Pattern Recognition Volume 32, Issue 2, February 1999, Pages 151–165.*

248. Edelman, S., N. Intrator, and T. Poggio. "Complex Cells and Object Recognition." Conference on Neural Information Processing Systems, 1997.

249. Hunt, R. W. G., and M. R. Pointer. *Measuring Colour.* Hoboken, NJ: John Wiley, 2011.

250. Hunt, R. W. G. *The Reproduction of Color, Wiley; 6 edition (October 29, 2004).*

251. Berns, Roy S. *Billmeyer and Saltzman's Principles of Color Technology.* Hoboken, NJ: John Wiley, 2000.

252. Morovic, Jan. *Color Gamut Mapping.* Hoboken, NJ: John Wiley, 2008.

253. Fairchild, Mark. *Color Appearance Models.* Addison Wesley Longman; 1st edition (January 1998).

254. Ito, Masayasu, Masayoshi Tsubai, and Akira Nomura. "Morphological Operations by Locally Variable Structuring Elements and Their Applications to Region Extraction in Ultrasound Images." *Systems and Computers in Japan Volume 34, Issue 3, pages 33–43, March 2003.*

255. Tsubai, Masayoshi, and Masayasu Ito. "Control of Variable Structure Elements in Adaptive Mathematical Morphology for Boundary Enhancement of Ultrasound Images." *ELECTRONICS AND COMMUNICATIONS IN JAPAN PART 3 FUNDAMENTAL ELECTRONIC SCIENCE; 87, 11; 20–33.*

256. Mazille, J. E. "Mathematical Morphology and Convolutions." *Journal of Microscopy* Vol. 156, (1989).

257. Achanta, Radhakrishna, et al. "SLIC Superpixels Compared to State-of-the-art Superpixel Methods." *PAMI (vol. 34 no. 11)* (2012).

258. Achanta, Radhakrishna, et al. "SLIC Superpixels." EPFL technical report no. 149300, June 2010.

259. Felzenszwalb, P., and D. Huttenlocher. "Efficient Graph-based Image Segmentation." *International Journal of Computer Vision* (2004).

260. Levinshtein, A., et al. "Turbopixels: Fast Superpixels Using Geometric Flows." *PAMI* (2009).

261. Lucchi, A., et al. "A Fully Automated Approach to Segmentation of Irregularly Shaped Cellular Structures in EM Images." MICCAI, 2010.

262. Shi, J., and J. Malik. "Normalized Cuts and Image Segmentation." *PAMI* (2000).

263. Vedaldi, A., and S. Soatto. "Quick Shift and Kernel Methods for Mode Seeking." European Conference on Computer Vision, 2008.

264. Felzenszwalb, Pedro F., and Daniel P. Huttenlocher. "Efficient Graph-Based Image Segmentation." *International Journal of Computer Vision September 2004, Volume 59, Issue 2, pp. 167–181.*

265. Felzenszwalb, P., and D. Huttenlocher. "Efficient Graph-based Image Segmentation." *International Journal of Computer Vision* Volume 59 (2004).

266. Comaniciu, D., and P. Meer. "Mean Shift: A Robust Approach Toward Feature Space Analysis." *PAMI* (Volume: 24, Issue: 5) (2002).

267. Vedaldi, A., and S. Soatto. "Quick Shift and Kernel Methods for Mode Seeking." European Conference on Computer Vision, 2008.

268. Vincent, L., and P. Soille. "Watersheds in Digital Spaces: An Efficient Algorithm Based on Immersion Simulations." *PAMI Volume 13 Issue 6, June 1991.*

269. Levinshtein, A., et al. "Turbopixels: Fast Superpixels Using Geometric Flows." *PAMI December 2009 (vol. 31 no. 12)*.

270. Scharstein, D., and C. Pal. "Learning Conditional Random Fields for Stereo." Conference on Computer Vision and Pattern Recognition, 2007.

271. Hirschmüller, H., and D. Scharstein. "Evaluation of Cost Functions for Stereo Matching." Conference on Computer Vision and Pattern Recognition, 2007.

272. Goodman, J. W. *Introduction to Fourier Optics*. new York: McGraw-Hill, 1968.

273. Gaskill, J. D. *Linear Systems, Fourier Transforms, Optics*. Hoboken, NJ: John Wiley, 1978.

274. Thibos, L., R. A. Applegate, J. T. Schweigerling, and R. Webb. "Standards for Reporting the Optical Aberrations of Eyes." In *OSA Trends in Optics and Photonics, Vision Science and its Applications*, ed. V. Lakshminarayanan. Washington, DC: Optical Society of America, 2000.

275. Sun-Kyoo Hwang and Whoi-Yul Kim. "A Novel Approach to the Fast Computation of Zernike Moments." *Pattern Recognition* Vol. 39 (2006).

276. Khotanzad, Alireza and Yaw Hua Hong. "Invariant Image Recognition by Zernike Moments." *PAMI Vol. 12* (1990).

277. Chao Kan, Mandyam, and D. Srinath. "Invariant Character Recognition with Zernike and Orthogonal Fourier-Mellin Moments." *Pattern Recognition Volume 35, January 2002,*

278. Hyung Shin Kim, and Heung-Kyu Lee. "Invariant Image Watermark Using Zernike Moments." *IEEE TRANSACTIONS ON CIRCUITS AND SYSTEMS FOR VIDEO TECHNOLOGY, VOL. 13, NO. 8, AUGUST 200* (2003).

279. Papakostas, G. A, D. A. Karras, and B. G. Mertzios. "Image Coding Using a Wavelet Based Zernike Moments Compression Technique." In proceeding of: Digital Signal Processing, 2002. Volume: 2 *DSP* (2002).

280. Mukundan, R. and K. R. Ramakrishnan. "Fast Computation of Legendre and Zernike Moments." *Volume 28, Issue 9, September 1995, Pages 1433–1442*

281. Yongqing Xin, Miroslaw Pawlak, and Simon Liao. "Image Reconstruction with Polar Zernike Moments." *ICAPR'05 Proceedings of the Third international conference on Pattern Recognition and Image Analysis - Volume Part II 2005.*

282. Singh, Chandan, and Rahul Upneja. "Fast and Accurate Method for High Order Zernike Moments Computation." *Applied Mathematics and Computation Volume 218, Issue 15, 1 April 2012, Pages 7759–7773.*

283. Pratt, W., Wen-Hsiung Chen, and L. Welch. "Slant Transform Image Coding." *IEEE Transactions On Communications (Volume: 22, Issue: 8)* 1974.

284. Enomoto, H., and K. Shibata. "Orthogonal Transform Coding System for Television Signals." *IEEE Trans. on Electromagnetic Compatibility, (Volume: EMC-13, Issue: 3)* 1974.

285. Dutra da Silva, Ricardo, William Robson, and Helio Pedrini Schwartz. "Image Segmentation Based on Wavelet Feature Descriptor and Dimensionality Reduction Applied to Remote Sensing." *Chilean Journal of Statistics Vol. 2* (2011).

286. Arun, Nerella, Mani Kumar, and P. S. Sathidevi. "Wavelet SIFT Feature Descriptors for Robust Face Recognition." *Springer Advances in Intelligent Systems and Computing* Vol. 177 (2013).

287. Dinggang Shen, and Horace H. S. Ip, "Discriminative Wavelet Shape Descriptors for Recognition of 2-D Patterns." *Pattern Recognition* Vol. 32 (1999).

288. Kingsbury, Nick. "Rotation-Invariant Local Feature Matching with Complex Wavelets." Proc. European Conf. Signal Processing EUSIPCO, 2006.

289. Wolfram Research Mathematica Wavelet Analysis Libraries.

290. Strang, Gilbert. "Wavelets." *American Scientist* 82, no. 3 (May-June 1994).

291. Mallat, Stephane. *A Wavelet Tour of Signal Processing: The Sparse Way*, 3rd ed.: Elsevier, 2008.

292. Percival, Donald B., and Andrew T. Walden. *Wavelet Methods for Time Series Analysis.* Cambridge: Cambridge University Press, 2006.

293. Gabor, D."Theory of Communication." *Journal of the IEE* 93 (1946).

294. Minor, L. G., and J. Sklansky. "Detection and segmentation of Blobs in Infrared Images." *IEEE Tranactions on Systems Man and Cyberneteics (Vol. 11 Issue 3)* (1981).

295. van Ginkel, M., C. K. Luengo Hendriks, and L. J. van Vliet. "A Short Introduction to the Radon and Hough Transforms and How They Relate to Each Other." *Number QI-2004-01 in the Quantitative Imageing Group Technical Report Series 2004.*

296. Toft, P. A. "Using the Generalized Radon Transform for Detection of Curves in Noisy Images." *1996 IEEE International Conference on Acoustics, Speech, and Signal Processing, 1996. ICASSP-96. Conference Proceedings., (Volume: 4).*

297. J. Radon. "Über die Bestimmung von Funktionen durch ihre Integralwerte längs gewisser Mannigfaltigkeiten." Berichte Sächsische Akademie der Wissenschaften, Leipzig, Mathematisch-Physikalische Klasse 69 (1917).

298. Fung, James, Steve Mann, and Chris Aimone. "OpenVIDIA: Parallel GPU Computer Vision." *Proceedings of the ACM Multimedia, 2005.*

299. Bazin, M. J., and J. W. Benoit. "Off-line Global Approach to Pattern Recognition for Bubble Chamber Pictures." *Transactions on Nuclear Science* 12 (August 1965).

300. Deans, S. R. "Hough Transform from the Radon Transform." *Transactions on Pattern Analysis and Machine Intelligence* 3, no. 2 (March 1981).

301. Rosenfeld, A. *Digial Picture Processing by Computer.* New York: Academic Press, 1982.

302. Tomasi, C., and R. Manduchi. "Bilateral Filtering for Gray and Color Images." *ICCV '98 Proceedings of the Sixth International Conference on Computer Vision* (1998).

303. See the documentation for the Imagej, Imagej2 or Fiji software package for complete references to each method, [global] Auto Threshold command and Auto Local Threshold command. http://fiji.sc/ImageJ2.

304. Garg, Rajesh, Bhawna Mittal, and Sheetal Garg. "Histogram Equalization Techniques for Image Enhancement." IJECT, *International Journal of Electronics And Communications Technology* Vol. 2 (2011).

305. Sung, A. Pearce, and C. Wang. "Spatial-temporal Antialiasing." *Transactions on Visualization and Computer Graphics* Vol. 8 (2002).

306. Mikolajczyk, Krystian, and Cordelia Schmid. "Scale & Affine Invariant Interest Point Detectors." *International Journal of Computer Vision Vol. 60* (2004).

307. Ozuysal, Mustafa, Michael Calonder, Vincent Lepetit, and Pascal Fua. "Fast Keypoint Recognition Using Random Ferns." *PAMI* Volume 32 (2010).

308. Schaffalitzky, F., and A. Zisserman. "Automated Scene Matching in Movies." *CIVR 2004, In Proceedings of the Challenge of Image and Video Retrieval, London, LNCS 2383.*

309. Tola, E., V. Lepetit, and P. Fua. "A Fast Local Descriptor for Dense Matching." Conference on Computer Vision and Pattern Recognition, 2008.

310. Davis, L. S. "Computing the Spatial Structures of Cellular Texture." *Computer Graphics and Image Processing* 11, no. 2 (October 1979).

311. Pun, C. M., and M. C. Lee. "Log-polar Wavelet Energy Signatures for Rotation and Scale Invariant Texture Classification." *Transactions of Pattern Analysis and Machine Intelligence* 25, no. 5 (May 2003).

312. Spence, A., M. Robb, M. Timmins, and M. Chantler. "Real-time Per-Pixel Rendering of Textiles for Virtual Textile Catalogues." *Proceedings of INTEDEC*, 2003.

313. Lam, Stephen W. C., and Horace H. S. Ip. *Adaptive Pyramid Approach to Texture Segmentation*. Computer Analysis of Images and Patterns Lecture Notes in Computer Science Volume 719, 1993, pp. 267–274.

314. Yinpeng Jin, Laura Fayad, and Andrew Laine. "Contrast Enhancement by Multi-scale Adaptive Histogram Equalization." Proceedings of SPIE, vol. 4478 2001.

315. Jianguo Zhang and Tieniu Tan. "Brief Review of Invariant Texture Analysis Methods." *Pattern Recognition Vol. 35* (2002).

316. Tomita, Fumiaki, Yoshiaki Shirai, and Saburo Tsuji. "Description of Textures by a Structural Analysis." IEEE Transactions on Pattern Analysis and Machine Intelligence archive Volume 4 *PAMI* (1982).

317. Tomita, Fumiaki, and Saburo Tsuji. *Computer Analysis of Visual Textures.* New York: Springer, 1990.

318. Burt, Peter J., and Edward H. Adelson. "The Laplacian Pyramid as a Compact Image Code." IEEE Transactions on Communications (1983).

319. Otsu, Nobuyukk. "A Threshold Selection Method from Gray-level Histograms." IEEE Transactions on Systems, Man and Cybernetics 9(1):62–66 *TSMC* (1979).

320. Sezgin, M., and B. Sankur. "Survey over Image Thresholding Techniques and Quantitative Performance Evaluation." *SPIE Journal of Electronic Imaging* (2004).

321. Haralick, Robert M., and Linda G. Shapiro. "Image Segmentation Techniques." *Computer Vision, Graphics, and Image Processing Volume 29, 1985, Pages 100–132.*

322. Raja, Yogesh, and Shaogang Gong. "Sparse Multiscale Local Binary Patterns", *British Machine Vision Conference 2006*

323. Fleuret, F. "Fast Binary Feature Selection with Conditional Mutual Information." *Journal of Machine Learning Research* Volume 5, 12/1/2004 (2004).

324. Szelinski, Richard. *Computer Vision, Algorithms and Applications.* New York: Springer, 2011.

325. Pratt, William K. Digital Image Processing: PIKS Scientific Inside., *Wiley-Interscience; 4 edition (February 9, 2007).*

326. Russ, John C. *The Image Processing Handbook*, CRC Press; 5 edition (December 19, 2006).

327. Klein, Georg, and David Murray. "Parallel Tracking and Mapping for Small AR Workspaces." IMAR, 2007.

328. Newcombe, Richard A., et al. "KinectFusion: Real-Time Dense Surface Mapping and Tracking." *ISMAR '11 Proceedings of the 2011 10th IEEE International Symposium on Mixed and Augmented Reality* (October 2011).

329. Izadi, Shahram, et al. "KinectFusion: Real-time 3D Reconstruction and Interaction Using a Moving Depth Camera." ACM Symposium on User Interface Software and Technology, October 2011.

330. Moravec, H. "Obstacle Avoidance and Navigation in the Real World by a Seeing Robot Rover." Tech Report CMU-RI-TR-3, Robotics Institute, Carnegie-Mellon University, 1980.

331. Mikolajczyk, K., and C. Schmid. "Indexing Based on Scale Invariant Interest Points. International Conference on Computer Vision, 2001.

332. Turcot, Panu, and David G. Lowe. "Better Matching with Fewer Features: The Selection of Useful Features in Large Database Recognition Problems." International Conference on Computer Vision, 2009.

333. Feichtinger, Hans G., and Thomas Strohmer. *Gabor Analysis and Algorithms*. Birkhäuser; 1997 edition (December 18, 1997).

334. Ricker, Norman. "Wavelet Contraction, Wavelet Expansion, and the Control of Seismic Resolution." *Geophysics, v. 18, pp. 769–792*, (1953).

335. Goshtasby, Ardesby. "Description and Discrimination of Planar Shapes Using Shape Matrices." *PAMI Volume 7 Issue 6, June 1985*.

336. Vapnik, V. N., E. Levin, and Y. LeCun, "Measuring the Dimension of a Learning Machine." Neural Computation September 1994, Vol. 6, No. 5, Pages 851–876.

337. Cowan, J. D., G. Tesauro, and J. Alspector. "Learning Curves: Asymptotic Values and Rate of Convergence." *Advances in Neural Information Processing Vol. 6* (1994).

338. Vapnik, V. N. *The Nature of Statistical Learning Theory*. New York: Springer, 1995.

339. LeCun, Y., L. Bottou, Y. Bengio, and P. Haffner. *Gradient-Based Learning Applied to Document Recognition: Intelligent Signal Processing,* Proceedings of the IEEE, 86(11): 2278-2324, November 1998.

340. Krizhevsky, Alex, Ilya Sutskever, and E. Hinton. "ImageNet Classification with Deep Convolutional Neural Networks." Conference on Neural Information Processing Systems, 2012.

341. Boser, Bernhard E. Isabelle M. Guyon, and Vladimir N. Vapnik. "A Training Algorithm for Optimal Margin Classifiers." COLT '92 Proceedings of the fifth annual workshop on Computational learning theory, 1992.

342. Cortes, Corinna, and Vladimir N. Vapnik. "Support-Vector Networks." *Machine Learning* 20 (1995).

343. Burges, Christopher J. C. "A Tutorial on Support Vector Machines for Pattern Recognition." *Kluwer Data Mining and Discovery* Vol. 2 (1998).

344. Weinzaepfel, P., J. Revaud, Z. Harchaoui, and C. Schmid. "DeepFlow: Large Displacement Optical Flow with Deep Matching." International Conference on Computer Vision, 2013.

345. Keysers, T., C. Deselaers, Gollan, and H. Ney. "Deformation Models for Image Recognition." *Transactions of PAMI* Vol. 20 (2007).

346. Kim, J., C. Liu, F. Sha, and K. Grauman. "Deformable Spatial Pyramid Matching for Fast Dense Correspondences." *Conference on Computer Vision and Pattern Recognition, 2013*.

347. Boureau, Y-Lan, Jean Ponce, and Yann LeCu. "A Theoretical Analysis of Feature Pooling in Visual Recognition." *IML, 2010. 27TH INTERNATIONAL CONFERENCE ON MACHINE LEARNING, HAIFA, ISRAEL*.

348. Schmid, Cordelia, and Roger Mohr. "Object Recognition Using Local Characterization and Semi-local Constraints." PAMI Volume 19, Number 3 1997.

349. Ferrari, Vittorio, Tinne Tuytelaars, and Luc Van Gool. "Simultaneous Object Recognition and Segmentation from Single or Multiple Model Views." *International Journal of Computer Vision* Vol. 67 (2005).

350. Schaffalitzky, Frederik, and Andrew Zisserman. "Automated Scene Matching in Movies." CIVR, 2002.

351. Estivill-Castro, Vladimir. "Why So Many Clustering Algorithms—A Position Paper." ACM SIGKDD Explorations Newsletter Vol. 4 Issue 1, June 2002.

352. Kriegel, Hans-Peter, Peer Kröger, Jörg Sander, and Arthur Zimek. "Density-based Clustering." *Wiley Interdisciplinary Reviews: Data Mining and Knowledge Discovery Volume 1, Issue 3, pages 231–240, May/June 2011.*

353. Hartigan, J. A. *Clustering Algorithms.* Hoboken, NJ: John Wiley, 1975.

354. Hartigan, J. A., and M. A.Wong. "Algorithm AS 136: A K-Means Clustering Algorithm." *Journal of the Royal Statistical Society* Vol. 28, No. 1 (1979).

355. Hastie, Trevor, Robert Tibshirani, and Jerome Friedman. *Hierarchical Clustering: The Elements of Statistical Learning,* 2nd ed. New York: Springer, 2009.

356. Dempster, A.P., N. M. Laird, and D. B. Rubin. "Maximum Likelihood from Incomplete Data via the EM Algorithm." *Journal of the Royal Statistical Society Series B 39(1): 1–38 (1977).*

357. Pearson, K. "On Lines and Planes of Closest Fit to Systems of Points in Space." *Philosophical Magazine* (1901).

358. Hotelling, H. "Relations between Two Sets of Variates." *Biometrika (1936) 28 (3-4): 321–377.*

359. Cortes, Corinna, and Vladimir N. Vapnik. "Support-Vector Networks." *Machine Learning September 1995, Volume 20, Issue 3, pp. 273–297.*

360. Haykin, S. *Neural Networks: A Comprehensive Foundation,* 2nd ed. Englewood Cliffs, NJ: Prentice-Hall, 1999.

361. Vapnik, V. *Statistical Learning Theory.* Hoboken, NJ: John Wiley, 1998.

362. Hofmann, Thomas, Bernhard Scholkopf, and Alexander J. Smola. "Kernel Methods in Machine Learning." *The Annals of Statisics Volume 36, Number 3 (2008), 1031 (2008).*

363. Raguram, Rahul, Jan-Michael Frahm, and Marc Pollefeys. "A Comparative Analysis of RANSAC Techniques Leading to Adaptive Real-Time Random Sample Consensus." European Conference on Computer Vision, 2008.

364. Weinberger, Kilian Q., John Blitzer, and Lawrence K. Saul. "Distance Metric Learning for Large Margin Nearest Neighbor Classification." Conference on Neural Information Processing Systems, 2004.

365. Schmid, Cordelia, and Roger Mohr. "Local Gray Value Invariants for Image Retrieval." *PAMI* Vol. 19, No. 5. (1997).

366. Dork, Gyuri, and Cordelia Schmid. "Object Class Recognition Using Discriminative Local Features." *Technical Report RR-5497, INRIA - Rhone-Alpes - February 2005.*

367-376. Not used.

377. Schlkopf, Bernhard, and Alexander J. Smola. *Learning with Kernels: Support Vector Machines, Regularization, Optimization, and Beyond.* Cambridge, MA: MIT Press, 2001.

378. Ferrari, Vittorio, Tinne Tuytelaars, and Luc Van Gool. "Simultaneous Object Recognition and Segmentation from Single or Multiple Model Views." *International Journal of Computer Vision* Vol. 67, No. 2 (2006).

379. Cinbis, Ramaqzan Gokberk, Jakob Verbeek, and Cordelia Schmid. "Segmentation Driven Object Detection with Fisher Vectors." International Conference on Ccomputer Vision, 2013.

380. Fischler, M., and R. Bolles. "Random Sample Consensus: A Paradigm for Model Fitting with Applications to Image Analysis and Automated Cartography." *Communications of the ACM* Volume 24 Issue 6, June 1981 (1981).

381. Freund, Yoav, and Robert E. Schapire. "A Short Introduction to Boosting." Japanese Society for Artificial Intelligence, Vol. 14, No. 5. (1999).

382. Freund, Yoav, and and Robert E. Schapire. "A Decision-theoretic Generalization of On-line Learning and an Application to Boosting." *Journal of Computer and System Sciences Volume 55, Issue 1, August 1997, Pages 119–139.*

383. Heckerman, David. "A Tutorial on Learning with Bayesian Networks." Microsoft Research technical report, 1996.

384. Amit, Y., and D. Geman. "Shape Quantization and Recognition with Randomized Trees." *Neural Computation* Volume 9 Issue 7, Oct. 1, (1997).

385. Rabiner, L. R., and B. H. Juang. "An Introduction to Hidden Markov Models." *IEEE Acoustics, Speech, and Signal Processing magazine (ASSP 1986).*

386. Krogh A, B. Larsson, G. von Heijne, and E. L. Sonnhammer. "Predicting Transmembrane Protein Topology with a Hidden Markov Model: Application to Complete Genomes." *Journal of Molecular Biology* (2001).

387. Nister, David, and Henrik Stewenius. "Scalable Recognition with a Vocabulary Tree." Conference on Computer Vision and Pattern Recognition, 2006.

388. Freeman, William T., and Edward H. Adelson. "The Design and Use of Steerable Filters." *PAMI* Volume 13 Issue 9 (1991).

389. Leung, T., and J. Malik. "Representing and Recognizing the Visual Appearance of Materials Using Three-dimensional Textons." *International Journal of Computer Vision* Volume 43 Issue 1 (2001).

390. Schmid, C. "Constructing Models for Content-based Image Retrieval." Conference on Computer Vision and Pattern Recognition, 2001.

391. Alahi, Alexandre, Pierre Vandergheynst, Michel Bierlaire, and Murat Kunt. "Cascade of Descriptors to Detect and Track Objects Across Any Network of Cameras." *Computer Vision and Image Understanding Volume 114, Issue 6, June 2010, Pages 624–640* (2010).

392. Simard, Patrice, Léon Bottou, Patrick Haffner, and Yann LeCun. "Boxlets: A Fast Convolution Algorithm for Signal Processing and Neural Networks." Conference on Neural Information Processing Systems, 1999.

393. Vedaldi, Andrea, and Andrew Zisseman. "Efficient Additive Kernels via Explicit Feature Maps." *PAMI* Volume 34 Issue 3 (2012).

394. Brox, Thomas, and Jitendra Malik. "Large Displacement Optical Flow: Descriptor Matching in Variational Motion Estimation." *PAMI* (Vol. 33 No. 3) (2010).

395. Martin Ester, Hans-Peter Kriegel, Jörg Sander, Xiaowei Xu. "A Density-Based Algorithm for Discovering Clusters in Large Spatial Databases with Noise." *In Second International Conference on Knowledge Discovery and Data Mining (1996), pp. 226–231.*

396. Mihael Ankerst, Markus M. Breunig, Hans-Peter Kriegel, Jorg Sander "OPTICS: Ordering Points to Identify the Clustering Structure." SIGMOD '99 Proceedings of the 1999 ACM SIGMOD international conference on Management of data.

397. Muja, Marius, Radu Bogdan Rusu, Gary Bradski, and David G. Lowe. "REIN - A Fast, Robust, Scalable Recognition Infrastructure." International Conference on Robotics and Automation, 2011.

398. Rusu, R. B., G. Bradski, R. Thibaux, and J. Hsu. "Fast 3D Recognition and Pose Using the Viewpoint Feature Histogram." *Intelligent Robots and Systems (IROS), 2010.*

399. Alvaro Collet, Manuel Martinez, and Siddhartha S. Srinivasa. "MOPED: A Scalable and Low Latency Object Recognition and Pose Estimation System." International Conference on Robotics and Automation, 2010.

400. Jacob, M., and M. Unser. "Design of Steerable Filters for Feature Detection Using Canny-Like Criteria." *PAMI* vol. 26, no. 8 (2004).

401. Moré, Jorge J. "The Levenberg-Marquardt Algorithm Implementation and Theory." *Numerical Analysis Lecture Notes in Mathematics Volume 630, 1978, pp. 105–116.*

402. *Lecun, Yann. "Learning Invariant Feature Hierarchies." European Conference on Computer Vision, 2012.*

403. Ranzato, Marc'Aurelio, Fu-Jie Huang, Y-Lan Boreau, and Yann Le Cun. "Unsupervised Learning of Invariant Feature Hierarchies with Applications to Object Recognition." Conference on Computer Vision and Pattern Recognition, 2007.

404. Boureau, Y-Lan, Jean Ponce, and Yann LeCun. "A Theoretical Analysis of Feature Pooling in Vision Algorithms." International Confeence on Machine Learning, 2010.

405. Kingma, Diederik, and Yann LeCun. "Regularized Estimation of Image Statistics by Score Matching." Conference on Neural Information Processing systems, 2010.

406. Losson, O., L. Macaire, and Y. Yang. "Comparison of Color Demosaicing Methods." *Advances in Imaging and Electron Physics Volume 162, 2010, Pages 173–265.*

407. Xin Li, Bahadir Gunturk, and Lei Zhang. "Image Demosaicing: A Systematic Survey." *Proc. SPIE 6822, Visual Communications and Image Processing 2008, 68221J (2008).*

408. Tanbakuchi, Anthony A. et al. "Adaptive Pixel Defect Correction." *Proc. SPIE 5017, Sensors and Camera Systems for Scientific, Industrial, and Digital Photography Applications IV, (16 May 2003).*

409. Ibenthal, Achim. "Image Sensor Noise Estimation and Reduction." ITG Fachausschuss 3.2 "Digitale Bildcodierung" (2007).

410. An Objective Look at FSI and BSI, Aptina White Paper.

411. Cossairt, O., D. Miau, and S. K. Nayar. "Gigapixel Computational Imaging." ICCP, IEEE International Conference on Computational Photography (2011).

412. Eastman Kodak Company, "E-58 Technical Data / Color Negative Film." Kodak 160NC Technical Data Manual July 2000.

413. Kuthirummal, S., and S. K. Nayar. "Multiview Radial Catadioptric Imaging for Scene Capture." *ACM Trans. on Graphics (also Proc. of ACM SIGGRAPH), Jul, 2006.*

414. Zhou, C., and S. K. Nayar. "Computational Cameras: Convergence of Optics and Processing." IEEE Transactions on Image Processing, Vol. 20, No. 12, Dec, 2011.

415. Krishnan, G., and S. K. Nayar. "Towards A True Spherical Camera." *Proc. SPIE 7240, Human Vision and Electronic Imaging XIV, 724002 (28 January 2009).*

416. Reinhard, Heidrich, Pattanaik Debevec, Myszkowski Ward, and Morgan Kaufmann. "High Dynamic Range Imaging, 2nd Edition Acquisition, Display, and Image-Based Lighting." *Morgan Kaufmann; 2 edition (June 8, 2010).*

417. Gallo, Orazio, et al. "Artifact-free High Dynamic Range Imaging." IEEE International Conference on Computational Photography (ICCP) 2009.

418. Grossberg, M. D., and S. K. Nayar. "High Dynamic Range from Multiple Images: Which Exposures to Combine?" International Conference on Computer Vision, 2003.

419. Nayar, S. K., G. Krishnan, M. D. Grossberg, and R. Raskar. "Fast Separation of Direct and Global Components of a Scene using High Frequency Illumination." *Proceedings of SIGGRAPH, 2006.*

420. Wilson, T., R. Juskaitis, M. Neil, and M. Kozubek. "Confocal Microscopy by Aperture Correlation." *Optics Letters, Vol. 21, Issue 23, pp. 1879–1881 (1996).*

421. Corle, T. R., and G. S. Kino. *Confocal Scanning Optical Microscopy and Related Imaging Systems.* New York: Academic Press, 1996.

422. Fitch, J. Patrick. *Synthetic Aperture Radar.* New York: Springer-Verlag, 1988.

423. Ng, Ren, et al. "Light Field Photography with a Hand-held Plenoptic Camera." Stanford Tech Report CTSR 2005-02.

424. Ragan-Kelley, Jonathan, et al. "Decoupling Algorithms from Schedules for Easy Optimization of Image Processing Pipelines." *ACM Transactions on Graphics Vol. 31(4)* (2012).

425. Levoy, Marc. "Experimental Platforms for Computational Photography." *Computer Graphics and Applications Vol. 30* (2010).

426. Adams, Andrew, et al. "The Frankencamera: An Experimental Platform for Computational Photography." *Proceedings of SIGGRAPH,* 2010.

427. Salsman, Kenneth. "3D Vision for Computer Based Applications." Technical Report, Aptina, Inc., October 2010.

428. Cossairt, Oliver, and Shree Nayar. "Spectral Focal Sweep: Extended Depth of Field from Chromatic Aberrations. *IEEE International Conference on Computational Photography (ICCP), Mar, 2010.* (see also US Patent EP2664153A1).

429. Fife, Keith, Abbas El Gamal, and H.-S. Philip Wong. "A 3D Multi-Aperture Image Sensor Architecture." *Proceedings of the IEEE Custom Integrated Circuits Conference, pp. 281–284, September 2006.*

430. Wang, Albert, Patrick Gill, and Alyosha Molnar. "Light Field Image Sensors Based on the Talbot Effect." *Applied Optics, Vol. 48, Issue 31, pp. 5897–5905 (2009).*

431. Shankar, Mohan, et al. "Thin Infrared Imaging Systems Through Multichannel Sampling." *Applied Optics, Vol. 47, Issue 10, pp. B1–B10 (2008).*

432. Barbara Zitová Jan Flusser, "Image registration methods: a survey", *Image and Vision Computing Volume 21, Issue 11, October 2003, Pages 977–1000.*

433. Hirschmûller, H. "Accurate and Efficient Stereo Processing by Semi-Global Matching and Mutual Information." Conference on Computer Vision and Pattern Recognition, 2005.

434. Tuytelaars, Tinne, and Luc Van Gool. "Wide Baseline Stereo Matching based on Local, Affinely Invariant Regions." British Machine Vision Conference, 2000.

435. Faugeras, Olivier. *Three Dimensional Computer Vision.* Cambridge, MA: MIT Press, 1993.

436. Stephen J. Maybank, Olivier D. Faugeras "A Theory of Self-calibration of a Moving Camera." *International Journal of Computer Vision Volume 8, Issue 2* (1992).

437. Richard Hartley and Andrew Zisserman. *Multiple View Geometry in Computer Vision.* Cambridge: Cambridge University Press, 2004.

438. Luong, Q.-T., and O. D. Faugeras. "The Fundamental Matrix: Theory, Algorithms, and Stability Analysis." *International Journal of Computer Vision Vol. 17* (1995).

439. Hartley, R. I. "Theory and Practice of Projective Rectification." *International Journal of Computer Vision Vol. 35* (1999).

440. Scharstein, Daniel, and Richard Szeliski. "A Taxonomy and Evaluation of Dense Two-Frame Stereo Correspondence Algorithms." *International Journal of Computer Vision Vol. 47* (2002).

441. Lazaros, Nalpantides, Georgios Christou Sirakoulis, and Antonios Gasteratos. Review of Stereo Vision Algorithms: From Software to Hardware." *IVO International Journal of Optomechatronics, Vol. 2, No. 4, 01.01.2008, pp. 435–462, 2008.*

442. Clark, Daniel E., and Spela Ivekovic. "The Cramer-Rao Lower Bound for 3-D State Estimation from Rectified Stereo Cameras." IEEE *Fusion* (2010).

443. Nayar, S. K., and M. Gupta. "Diffuse Structured Light." International Conference on Computational Photography, 2012.

444. Cattermole, F. *Principles of Pulse Code Modulation.* American Elsevier Pub. Co; 1st edition (1969).

445. Pagès, J., and J. Salvi. "Coded Light Projection Techniques for 3D Reconstruction." *J3eA, Journal sur l'enseignement des sciences et technologies de l'information et des systèmes, Volume 4, Hors-Série 3, 1 (2005).*

446. Gu, J., et al. "Compressive Structured Light for Recovering Inhomogeneous Participating Media." European Conference on Computer Vision, 2008.

447. Nayar, Shree K. "Computational Cameras: Approaches, Benefits and Limits." Technical Report, Computer Science Department, Columbia University, 2011.

448. Lehmann, M., et al. "CCD/CMOS Lock-in Pixel for Range Imaging: Challenges, Limitations and State-of-the-art." *CSEM, Swiss Center for Electronics and Microtechnology, 2004.*

449. Andersen, J. F., J Busck, and H Heiselberg. "Submillimeter 3-D Laser Radar for Space Shuttle Tile Inspection." *Danisch Defense Reasearch Establishment, Copenhagen, Denmark 2013.*

450. Grzegorzek, M., Theobalt, C., Koch, R., Kolb, A. (Eds.), Time-of-Flight and Depth Imaging. Sensors, Algorithms, and Applications Lecture Notes in Computer Science, Springer 2013.

451. Levoy, Marc, and Pat Hanrahan. "Light Field Rendering." *SIGGRAPH '96 Proceedings of the 23rd annual conference on Computer graphics and interactive techniques* (1996).

452. Curless, Brian, and Marc Levoy. "A Volumetric Method for Building Complex Models from Range Images." *SIGGRAPH '96 Proceedings of the 23rd annual conference on Computer graphics and interactive techniques* (1996).

453. Drebin, Robert A., Loren Carpenter, and Pat Hanrahan, "Volume Rendering." *SIGGRAPH* (1988).

454. Levoy, Marc. "Display of Surfaces from Volume Data." *CG&A* (1988).

455. Levoy, Marc. "Volume Rendering using the Fourier Projection Slice Theorum." Technical report CSL-TR-92–521, Stanford University, April 1992.

456. Klein, Georg, and David Murray. "Parallel Tracking and Mapping on a Camera Phone." *ISMAR '09 Proceedings of the 2009 8th IEEE International Symposium on Mixed and Augmented Reality* (2009).

457. Klein, Georg and David Murray. "Parallel Tracking and Mapping for Small AR Workspaces." *In Proc. International Symposium on Mixed and Augmented Reality (ISMAR'07, Nara).*

458. Lucas, B. D., and T. Kanade. "An Image Registration Technique with an Application to Stereo Vision." *Proceedings of Image Understanding Workshop, 1981.*

459. Beauchemin, S., and J. D. Barron. "The Computation of Optical Flow." *ACM Computing Surveys* Volume 27 Issue 3, Sept. 1995 (1995).

460. Barron, J., D. Fleet, and S. Beauchemin. "Performance of Optical Flow Techniques. *International Journal of Computer Vision February 1994, Volume 12, Issue 1, pp. 43–77.*

461. Baker, Simon, et al. "A Database and Evaluation Methodology for Optical Flow." *International Journal of Computer Vision* Volume 92, Issue 1, pp. 1–31, (2009).

462. Quénot, G. M., J. Pakleza, and T. A. Kowalewski. "Particle Image Velocimetry with Optical Flow." In *Experiments in Fluids August 1998, Volume 25, Issue 3, pp. 177–189.*

463. Trulls, Eduard, Alberto Sanfeliu, and Francesc Moreno-Noguer, "Spatiotemporal Descriptor for Wide-Baseline Stereo Reconstruction of Non-Rigid and Ambiguous Scenes." European Conference on Computer Vision, 2012.

464. Steinman, Scott B., Barbara A. Steinman, and Ralph Philip Garzia. *Foundations of Binocular Vision: A Clinical Perspective.* New York: McGraw-Hill, 2000.

465. Roy, S., J. Meunier, and I. J. Cox. "Cylindrical Rectification to Minimize Epipolar Distortion." Conference on Computer Vision and Pattern Recognition, 1997.

466. Oram, Daniel. "Rectification for Any Epipolar Geometry." British Machine Vision Conference 2001, BMVC 2001.

467. Takita, Kenji, et al. "High-Accuracy Subpixel Image Registration Based on Phase-Only Correlation." Institute of Electronics, Information and Communication Engineers(IEICE), 2003.

468. Huhns, Tian. "Algorithms for Sub Pixel Registration." CGIP Computer Graphics and Image Processing, 1986.

469. Foroosh (Shekarforoush), Hassan, Josiane B. Zerubia, and Marc Berthod. "Extension of Phase Correlation to Subpixel Registration." IEEE Transactions on Image Processing 2002.

470. Zitnick, Lawrence, and Takeo Kanade. "A Cooperative Algorithm for Stereo Matching and Occlusion Detection." Carnegie Mellon University, Technical report CMU-RI-TR-99-35.

471. Jian Sun, Yin Li, Sing Bing Kang, and Heung-Yeung Shum. "Symmetric Stereo Matching for Occlusion Handling." *CVPR '05 Proceedings of the 2005 IEEE Computer Society Conference on Computer Vision and Pattern Recognition (CVPR'05) - Volume 2.*

472. Sing Bing Kang, Richard Szeliski, Jinxiang Chai "Handling Occlusions in Dense Multi-view Stereo." Conference on Computer Vision and Pattern Recognition, 2001.

473. Curless, Brian, and Marc Levoy. "A Volumetric Method for Building Complex Models from Range Images." *SIGGRAPH Proceedings* (1996).

474. Izadi, Shahram, et al. "KinectFusion: Real-time 3D Reconstruction and Interaction Using a Moving Depth Camera." UIST '11 Proceedings of the 24th annual ACM symposium on User interface software and technology 2011.

475. Newcombe, Richard A., et al. "KinectFusion: Real-Time Dense Surface Mapping and Tracking." ISMAR '11 Proceedings of the 2011 10th IEEE International Symposium on Mixed and Augmented Reality.

476. Durrant-Whyte, Hugh, and Tim Bailey. "Simultaneous Localisation and Mapping (SLAM): Part I The Essential Algorithms." IEEE ROBOTICS AND AUTOMATION MAGAZINE 2006.

477. Bailey, Tim, and Hugh Durrant-Whyte. "Simultaneous Localisation and Mapping (SLAM): Part II State of the Art." IEEE ROBOTICS AND AUTOMATION MAGAZINE 2006.

478. Seitz, Steven, et al. "A Comparison and Evaluation of Multi-View Stereo Reconstruction Algorithms.", CVPR 2006, vol. 1, pages 519–526.

479. Scharstein, D., and R. Szeliski. "A Taxonomy and Evaluation of Dense Two-Frame Stereo Correspondence Algorithms." *International Journal of Computer Vision Vol. 47* (2002).

480. Baker, Simon, and Ian Matthews. "Lucas-Kanade 20 Years On: A Unifying Framework." *International Journal of Computer Vision* Vol. 56 (2004).

481. Gallup, D., M. Pollefeys, and J. M. Frahm. "3D Reconstruction Using an n-layer Heightmap." Pattern Recognition Lecture Notes in Computer Science Volume 6376, 2010.

482. Newcombe, Richard A., Steven J. Lovegrove, and Andrew J. Davison. "DTAM: Dense Tracking and Mapping in Real-Time." International Conference On Computer Vision (ICCV), pages 2320–2327. IEEE, (2011).

483. Hwangbo, Myung, Jun-Sik Kim, and Takeo Kanade. "Inertial-aided KLT Feature Tracking for a Moving Camera." Intelligent Robots and Systems (IROS) - IEEE 2009.

484. Lovegrove, S. J., and A. J. Davison. "Real-time Spherical Mosaicing Using Whole Image Alignment. European Conference on Computer Vision, 2010.

485. Malis, E. "Improving Vision-based Control Using Efficient Second-order Minimization Techniques." *International Conference on Robotics and Automation, 2004.*

486. Kaiming He, J. Sun, and X. Tang. "Guided Image Filtering." European Conference on Computer Vision, 2010.

487. Rhemann, Christoph, et al. "Fast Cost-Volume Filtering for Visual Correspondence and Beyond." *CVPR, pages 3017–3024. IEEE, (2011).*

488. Fattal, R."Edge-Avoiding Wavelets and Their Applications." *SIGGRAPH* (2009).

489. Gastal, E. S. L., and M. M. Oliveira. "Domain Transform for Edge- Aware Image and Video Processing." *ACM SIGGRAPH 2011 papers Article No. 69.*

490. Wolberg, George. *Digital Image Warping.* Hoboken, NJ: John Wiley, 1990.

491. Baxes, Gregory. *Digital Image Processing: Principles and Applications.* Hoboken, NJ: John Wiley, 1994.

492. Fergus, Rob, et al. "Removing Camera Shake from a Single Photograph." *ACM Transactions on Graphics (TOG) - Volume 25 Issue 3, July 2006.*

493. Rohr, K. *Landmark-Based Image Analysis using Geometric and Intensity Models.* Dordrecht: Kluwer Academic Publishers, 2001.

494. Corbet Jonathan, Alessandro Rubini, and Greg Kroah-Hartman. *Linux Device Drivers,* 3rd ed. O'Reilly Media; 3 edition (February 14, 2005).

495. Zinner, Christian, Wilfried Kubinger, and Richard Isaacs. "PfeLib—A Performance Primitives Library for Embedded Vision." EURASIP, 2007.

496. Houston, Mike. "OpenCL Overview." *SIGGRAPH OpenCL BOF* (2011), also on KHRONOS website.

497. Zinner, C., and W. Kubinger. "ROS-DMA: A DMA Double Buffering Method for Embedded Image Processing with Resource Optimized Slicing." *IEEE RTAS 2006, Real-Time and Embedded Technology and Applications Symposium* (2006).

498. Kreahling, William C., et al. "Branch Elimination by Condition Merging." *Euro-Par 2003 Parallel Processing Lecture Notes in Computer Science Volume 2790, 2003.*

499. Ullman, Jeffrey D., and Alfred V. Aho. *Principles of Compiler Design* Addison-Wesley (August 1977).

500. Ragan-Kelley, Jonathan, et al. "Decoupling Algorithms from Schedules for Easy Optimization of Image Processing Pipelines." *ACM Transactions on Graphics (TOG) - SIGGRAPH Volume 31 Issue 4, July 2012.*

501. Alcantarilla, Pablo F., Adrien Bartoli, and Andrew J. Davison. "KAZE Features." European Conference on Computer Vision, 2012.

502. Schneider, C. A., Rasband, W. S., and Eliceiri, K. W. "NIH Image to ImageJ: 25 Years of Image Analysis." *Nature Methods* 9 (2012).

503. Muja, Marius. "Recognition Pipeline and Object Detection Scalability." Summer 2010 Internship Presentation, University of British Columbia.

504. Viola, Paul A., and Michael J. Jones. "Rapid Object Detection Using a Boosted Cascade of Simple Features." Conference on Computer Vision and Pattern Recognition, 2001.

505. Swain, Michael, and Dana H. Ballard. "Color Indexing." *International Journal of Computer Vision Volume 7* (1991).

506. Zhengyou Zhang. "A Flexible New Technique for Camera Calibration." *EEE Transactions on Pattern Analysis and Machine Intelligence, 22(11): 1330–1334, 2000*

507. Viola, Paul A., and Michael J. Jones. "Robust Real Time Object Detection." *International Journal of Computer Vision* (2001).

508. Murase, Hiroshi, and Shree K. Nayar. "Visual Learning and Recognition of 3-D Objects from Appearance." *Intenational Journal of Computer Vision* Volume 14 (1995).

509. Grosse, R., et al. "Ground-truth Dataset and Baseline Evaluations for Intrinsic Image Algorithms." International Conference on Computer Vision, 2009.

510. Haltakov, Vladimir, Christian Unger, and Slobodan Ilic. "Framework for Generation of Synthetic Ground Truth Data for Driver Assistance Applications." *Pattern Recognition Lecture Notes in Computer Science Volume 8142* (2013).

511. Buades, A., B. Coll, and J.-M. Morel. "A Non-local Algorithm for Image Denoising." *Computer Vision and Pattern* Recognition Vol. 2 (2005).

512. Agaian, Sos S., Khaled Tourshan, and Joseph P. Noonan. "Parametric Slant-Hadamard Transforms." *Proceedings of SPIE, 2003.*

513. Sauvola, J., and M. Pietaksinen. "Adaptive Document Image Binarization." *Pattern Recognition* Volume 33, Issue 2, February 2000.

514. Yen, J. C., F. J. Chang, and S. Chang. "A New Criterion for Automatic Multilevel Thresholding." *Transactions on Image Processing* Volume 4 Issue 3 (1995).

515. Sezgin, M., and B. Sankur. "Survey over Image Thresholding Techniques and Quantitative Performance Evaluation." *Journal of Electronic Imaging Volume 13, Issue 1, January 2004.*

516. Gaskill, Jack D. *Linear Systems, Fourier Transforms, and Optics.* Hoboken, NJ: John Wiley, 1978.

517. Shapiro, L. G., and G. C. Stockman. *Computer Vision.* Upper Saddle River, NJ: Prentice-Hall, 2001.

518. Flusser, Jan, Tomas Suk, and Barbara Zitova. *Moments and Moment Invariants in Pattern Recognition.* Hoboken, NJ: John Wiley, 2009.

519. Mikolajcyk, K., and C. Schmid. "An Affine Invariant Interest Point Detector." International Conference on Computer Vision, 2002.

520. Moravec, Hans P. "Obstacle Avoidance and Navigatio n in the Real World by a Seeing Robot Rover." *Tech. report CMU-RI-TR-80-03, Robotics Institute, Carnegie Mellon University & doctoral dissertation, Stanford University, September, 1980.*

521. Sivic, Josef. "Efficient Visual Search of Videos Cast as Text Retrieval." *PAMI Vol. 31* (2009).

522. X Tan and B. Triggs. "Enhanced Local Texture Feature Sets for Face Recognition Under Difficult Lighting Conditions." *AMFG'07 Proceedings of the 3rd international conference on Analysis and modeling of faces and gestures* (2010).

523. "Scale-space." *Encyclopedia of Computer Science and Engineering*, Hoboken, NJ: John Wiley, 2008.

524. Lindeberg, Tony. "Scale-space Theory: A Basic Tool for Analysing Structures at Different Scales." *Journal of Applied Statistics* Vol. 21(2), pp. 224–270, (1994).

525. Bengio, Yoshua. *Learning Deep Architectures for AI, Foundations and Trends in Machine Learning.* Now Publishers Inc USA (October 28, 2009).

526. Hinton, Geoffrey E., and Simon Osindero. "A Fast Learning Algorithm for Deep Belief Nets." *Neural Computation* July 2006, Vol. 18, No. 7, (2006).

527. Olson, Ed. "AprilTag: A Robust and Flexible Visual Fiducial System." Internatinal Conference on Robotics and Automation, 2011.

528. Farabet, Clement, et al. "Hardware Accelerated Convolutional Neural Networks for Synthetic Vision Systems." *ISCAS, pages 257–260. IEEE, (2010).*

529. Tuytelaars, T., and L. Van Gool. "Matching Widely Separated Views Based on Affine Invariant Regions." *International Journal on Computer Vision* Volume 59 (2004).

530. Fischler, M. A., and R. A. Elschlager. "The Representation and Matching of Pictorial Structures." IEE *Transactions on Computers* (1973).

531. Felzenszwalb, Pedro F., Ross B. Girshick, David McAllester, and Deva Ramanan. "Object Detection with Discriminatively Trained Part-Based Models." *PAMI* (vol. 32 no. 9) (2010).

532. Yi Yang, Deva Ramanan. "Articulated Pose Estimation with Flexible Mixtures-of-parts." Conference on Computer Vision and Pattern Recognition, 2011.

533. Amit, Y., and A. Trouve. "POP: Patchwork of Parts Models for Object Recognition." *International Journal of Computer Vision* Volume 75 (2007).

534. Lazebnik, S., C. Schmid, and J. Ponce. "Beyond Bags of Features: Spatial Pyramid Matching for Recognizing Natural Scene Categories." Conference on Computer Vision and Pattern Recognition, 2006.

535. Grauman, K., and T. Darrell, "The Pyramid Match Kernel: Discriminative Classification with Sets of Image Features." International Conference on Computer Vision, 2005.

536. Michal Aharon, Michael Elad, Alfred Bruckstein "KSVD: An Algorithm for Designing Overcomplete Dictionaries for Sparse Representation". *IEEE Transaction on Signal Processing Vol. 64* (2006).

537. Fei-Fei, L., R. Fergus, and A. Torralba. "Recognizing and Learning Object Categories." Conference on Computer Vision and Pattern Recognition, 2007.

538. Johnson, Andrew. *Spin-Images: A Representation for 3-D Surface Matching* Ph.D. dissertation, technical report CMU-RI-TR-97-47, Robotics Institute, Carnegie Mellon University, 1997.

539. Zoltan-Csaba Marton, Dejan Pangercic, Nico Blodow, Michael Beetz "Combined 2D-3D Categorization and Classification for Multimodal Perception Systems." *International Journal of Robotics Research archive Volume 30 Issue 11, September 2011.*

540. Kass, Michael, Andrew Witkin, and Demetri Terzopoulos. "Snakes: Active Contour Models." *International Journal on Computer Vision* (1988).

541. Tombari, F., S. Salti, and L. Di Stefano. "A Combined Texture-Shape Descriptor for Enhanced 3D Feature Matching." International Conference on Image Processing, 2011.

542. Mikolajczyk, K., and C. Schmid. "Indexing Based on Scale Invariant Interest Points." International Conference on Computer Vision, 2001.

543. Ragan-Kelley, Jonathan, et al. "Halide: A Language and Compiler for Optimizing Parallelism, Locality, and Recomputation in Image Processing Pipelines." *PLDI '13 Proceedings of the 34th ACM SIGPLAN conference on Programming language design and implementation 2013.*

544. Kindratenko, Volodymyr V., et al. "GPU Clusters for High- Performance Computing." In Proc. *Workshop on Parallel Programming on Accelerator Clusters - PPAC'09*, 2009.

545. Munshi, Aaftab, et al. *OpenCL Programming Guide. Addison-Wesley Professional; 1 edition (July 23, 2011).*

546. Prince, Simon. *Computer Vision: Models, Learning, and Inference.* Cambridge: Cambridge University Press, 2012.

547. Lindeberg, Tony. *Scale Space Theory in Computer Vision* Springer, 2010.

548. Pele, Ofir. *Distance Functions: Theory, Algorithms and Applications.* Ph.D. Thesis, Hebrew University, 2011.

549. Robert E. Schapire, Yoram Singer, *Improved Boosting Algorithms Using Confidence-rated Predictions*, Machine Learning 1999.

550. Bache, K. & Lichman, M. UCI Machine Learning Repository [http://archive.ics.uci.edu/ml]. Irvine, CA: University of California, School of Information and Computer Science, 2013.

551. Zach, Christopher. "Fast and High Quality Fusion of Depth Maps." 3DPVT Joint 3DIM/3DPVT Conference 3D Imaging, Modeling, Processing, Visualization, Transmission 2008.

Index